BAILLAIRGÉ BY J.E. LIVERNOIS, C.1874

Charles Baillairgé

ARCHITECT & ENGINEER

Christina Cameron

McGILL-QUEEN'S UNIVERSITY PRESS

MONTREAL AND KINGSTON

1989

© McGill-Queen's University Press 1989
ISBN 0-7735-0638-1

Legal deposit first quarter 1989
Bibliothèque nationale du Québec

Design by Robert Tombs

Printed in Canada on acid-free paper

This book has been published with the help
of a grant from the Social Science
Federation of Canada, using funds provided
by the Social Sciences and Humanities
Research Council of Canada, and with the
assistance of the J. Paul Getty Trust and
The Samuel and Saidye Bronfman Family
Foundation.

Canadian Cataloguing in Publication Data

Cameron, Christina
  Charles Baillairgé
  Includes index.
  Bibliography: p.
  ISBN 0-7735-0638-1
  I. Baillairgé, Charles, 1827–1906. 2. Architects—
  Canada—Biography. 3. Architecture, Modern—19th
  century—Canada. I. Title.
  NA749.B34C34 1989   720′.92′4   C88-090170-5

Contents

Illustrations

Preface

MY INTEREST IN CHARLES BAILLAIRGÉ began in 1970 when, as a new resident in Quebec City, I was hired by the Canadian Inventory of Historic Building, at that time part of the National Historic Sites Service of Parks Canada, to work as a research assistant for A.J.H. Richardson, an authority on Quebec City architecture. My assignments included the task of indexing building contracts in the notarial records of the judicial archives and the mission of tracing, if possible, architectural drawings and records that might have survived from the practice of an important nineteenth-century architect, Charles Baillairgé. Work on the building contracts gradually revealed the quantity, quality, and variety of buildings designed by him, while the genealogical research suggested a number of potential sources, all of which proved fruitless. As members of the Baillairgé family explained to me at the time: "The family did not keep old papers." My last resort was Quebec City Hall where Baillairgé had worked for almost a third of a century. Although he had retired in 1898 and ought, at least in theory, to have removed all his private papers from the building, vague rumours from aged civic employees hinted at the existence of two old cardboard boxes filled with architectural drawings. These rumours proved to be well founded, for a persistent search led to the discovery of about five hundred drawings from his private practice, constituting the core of the fonds Charles Baillairgé in the municipal archives.

My appreciation for the superior quality and diversity of Charles Baillairgé's work increased as my work with Mr Richardson on his Quebec City project progressed, especially during the interior survey of over two hundred buildings in the winter of 1972–3. Since that time, I have slowly accumulated information on Charles Baillairgé in libraries and archives in Quebec City and Ottawa. The project lay dormant until early in 1980 when, encouraged by Professor Luc Noppen of Laval University, I resolved to enrol in the doctoral program and undertake at last this biographical study of Charles Baillairgé, architect.

To A.J.H. Richardson, whose enthusiasm for and knowledge of the architecture of Quebec City have stimulated and inspired me over the years, I wish to express sincere appreciation, for he nurtured in me a respect and delight in historic building. For the opportunity to leave aside my usual work, I acknowledge the generous grant of educational leave by Parks Canada (now Canadian Parks Service), Environment Canada, made possible through the efforts of Barbara Humphreys, then chief of the Canadian Inventory of Historic Building, and Henri Têtu, director of the National Historic Parks and Sites Branch.

A work of this scope and detail cannot be produced in isolation. It draws on the research of other historians and depends on the efforts of a host of archivists, librarians, and other individuals. Without exception, the response to my sometimes excessive requests for information has been overwhelmingly supportive and I wish to record here my deep gratitude to all those institutions and persons who have contributed so willingly to this study. Although it is not possible to mention each one individually, I want particularly to thank Ginette Noël, archivist of *Les archives de la ville de Québec*, and her staff for their aid in facilitating the consultation of the fonds Charles Baillairgé and the other municipal records, and Ghislain Malette and Brian Hallett of the Public Archives of Canada (now National Archives of Canada) for their guidance through the complex records systems of the federal Board of Works and the Department of Public Works. I appreciate the special efforts made by the staff of *Les archives nationales du Québec* to accommodate my research requirements within the confines of a cumbersome control system. Abbé Honorius Provost, former archivist, Georges Drouin, archivist, and the staff of the archives of the Seminary of Quebec have shown the utmost patience and courtesy in searching out documents and suggesting other avenues of inquiry. While the public reference service of the National Archives of Canada has been uniformly superior, I wish particularly to acknowledge the help of Joy Williams, Alain Calvet, Brian Carey, and Richard Huyda of the National Photography Collection, and Thomas Nagy and Dorothy Franklyn of the National Map Collection. At the documentation centre of the Ministère des Affaires culturelles, Marie-Thérèse Thibault has been especially cooperative in providing information and arranging other research services. Many archivists of smaller public and private collections contributed fragments to the puzzle by photocopying and transcribing excerpts of documents and by granting access to their collections: Léo Bérubé, priest at *Les archives de l'archevêché de Rimouski*; Soeur Marcelle Boucher of *Les archives des Ursulines de Québec*; Abbé Armand Gagné of *Les archives de l'archidiocèse de Québec*; Père Lucien Gagné of the Pères Rédemptoristes at the Basilique de Sainte-Anne-de-Beaupré; Soeur Huguette Bordeleau of *Les archives des Soeurs de la Charité d'Ottawa*; Soeur Claire Gagnon of *Les archives du monastère de l'Hôtel-Dieu de Québec*; Renée Landry of the Canadian Centre of Folk Culture Studies; Frère Milot of *Les archives de Notre-Dame de Québec*; and the late Soeur Alice Pruneau and Soeur Annette Dionne of the mother house of the Soeurs du Bon-Pasteur de Québec.

The bibliographic challenges of this biography have necessitated the services of several librarians who have provided valuable advice for reference searches and arranged many interlibrary loans. Parks Canada librarians Hélène Lanthier and Mary Kelman have been cheerful and diligent collaborators in locating and securing copies of obscure material. Diane Chiasson of the CISTI library of the National Research Council of Canada has been helpful in identifying nineteenth-century technical literature. The National Library of Canada has, as always, provided outstanding reference services and reading-room facilities. Librarians of specialized libraries who have responded promptly and carefully to my requests seeking scraps of information on sources of acquisition and other obscure fragments include the librarians of the Blackader Library at McGill University, the Rare Books Room of Laval University Library, Abbé Joseph Lépine of the Seminary of Quebec Library, Lucie Robitaille of the University of Montreal Library, Thomas Rooney of the Ottawa Public Library, and Daniel Olivier of the Salle Gagnon of the municipal library in Montreal.

The collaboration and support of my colleagues at Parks Canada have been significant. In particular, I am grateful to Nathalie Clerk for her constructive criticism, Monique Trépanier for her unflagging technical support, Robin Letellier, Jean-Pierre Jérôme, and Jean Audet for their help in obtaining photographic and graphic material, and Carole Trudel and Louise Malette for their secretarial support. Other individuals who took time from their own concerns to advance the progress of this study include Norman Ball, Philippe Dubé, Robert Hill, Marthe Lacombe, Yves Laliberté, Alyne Lebel, Norma Lee, Eileen Marcil, Evelyn McMann, David Mendel, Luc Noppen, Steve Otto, and Douglas Richardson. Murielle Plouffe has demonstrated great patience in producing a typescript of this manuscript.

I am particularly grateful to the family of Charles Baillairgé's grandson, Jean Lafontaine. In addition to providing me with full access to private papers in their possession, they have welcomed me into their home and, in a room that still contains Charles's dining-room table and other memorabilia, recounted family stories as they remember them.

To my adviser at Laval University, Professor Claude Bergeron, I offer my appreciation for his guidance, patience, criticism, and support during the planning and writing of this biography. For their help in clarifying my thoughts and approaches to the subject, I thank Professor Jean Hamelin and my fellow students in the doctoral seminar on research methodology during the autumn and winter of 1981–2.

Finally, for their personal support and encouragement during the long months of writing and revision, I thank my parents, family, and friends who know only too well what they have contributed to this work.

Introduction

THIS BIOGRAPHY OF CHARLES BAILLAIRGÉ (1826–1906) is the study of an architect's life in Quebec City in the nineteenth century. The focus is architecture, but Baillairgé's training in the related fields of land surveying and civil engineering means that these disciplines occasionally find their way into this account of his professional activities. There has been no attempt to weave the threads of his private life into this biography, beyond the factual compilation of genealogies that trace the history of the Baillairgé dynasty from the arrival in Quebec of the patriarch Jean Baillairgé in 1741 down to Charles Baillairgé's two marriages and the birth of his twenty children.[1] While all available evidence suggests that he was a good husband and father according to the accepted mores of the period, Baillairgé's devotion to work and his lifelong habit of labouring eighteen hours a day imposed natural limits on his participation in the daily events of family life. It is therefore appropriate that the central focus of this study should be Baillairgé's professional activities as architect, civil engineer, and land surveyor.

A typical biography of an architect would include an account of the subject's educational background; an examination of buildings in terms of clients' requirements, design features, construction technology, influences, and so forth; and an assessment of the significance of the work. These are the ingredients of the few full-length biographies of nineteenth-century architects practising in Canada that have been published to date.[2] Baillairgé's biography must, of course, consider these factors, especially since his architectural production reached 181 known projects and commissions.[3] But he presents the biographer with more complex issues, for he was an exceptional man of diverse talents, especially in the literary, scientific, and technical fields. In addition, then, to tracing the successes and failures of his architectural commissions and assessing their impact on his career and on the environment, this biograpy has to consider the more general and profound influence that he made on the profession of architecture through his voluminous writings and active participation in professional associations. To compensate for the boredom that Baillairgé experienced during a period of over thirty years as city engineer, he produced at least 253 publications – including books, articles, and pamphlets – on a vast range of subjects: architecture, engineering, language, mathematics, and other miscellaneous topics.[4] Had he remained in private practice or had he succeeded in his sustained ambition to become chief architect in the Department of Public Works, his career might well have been more orthodox and hence more easily evaluated.

Through an examination of Baillairgé's professional life, this biography by extension touches on a number of related but more general subjects. It tabulates and analyses innovations in architectural design and construction technology in Quebec City and elsewhere in the middle of the nineteenth century, the period during which Baillairgé carried on his private architectural practice. It documents the radical change in the role of the architect from the architect/artisan of the previous century to the professional man who, while functioning as the liaison between client and builders by designing the structure, preparing estimates and specifications, and measuring the work, no longer physically executed any of the construction himself. The study also investigates the practices of the single most important employer of architectural services in Canada under the Act of Union (1841–67), the infamous Board of Works or, as it was more often called, the Department of Public Works. Baillairgé's later years as city engineer lead naturally to a consideration of conflicting views on city embellishment and municipal planning in Quebec and elsewhere, in particular in light of the progressive urban renewal schemes in Paris under Napoleon III. Finally, owing to Baillairgé's participation in professional groups, this biography touches on the late nineteenth-century phenomenon of the rise of associations concerned with the establishment of standards, training, and codes of ethics in specialized fields such as surveying, civil engineering, and architecture.

Why should an architecturally oriented biography be written on Charles Baillairgé? It is true that brief outlines of the major events and accomplishments of his life have been published in several standard biographical dictionaries, most written while he was still alive, including *The Canadian Biographical Dictionary and Portrait Gallery of Eminent and Self-Made Men: Quebec and the Maritime Provinces Volume* (1881), *A Cyclopaedia of Canadian Biography being Chiefly Men of the Time* (1888), *The Canadian Album. Men of Canada; or, Success by Example, in Religion, Patriotism, Business, Law, Medicine, Education and Agriculture* (1891), *The Canadian Album: Encyclopedic Canada or the Progress of a Nation* (1896), and *The Canadian Men and Women of the Time: A Handbook of Canadian Biography* (1898). Indeed, an extensive biography by Edgar La Selve was even published in the Parisian *Revue Exotique Illustrée* on 1 October 1889. These all follow the model of Baillairgé's first biography published in Italy in the *Rivista universale* on 10 February 1878 and reprinted in Canada in the *Opinion publique* on 25 April 1878, each one paying tribute to the sheer volume of his productivity by listing his various accomplishments and awards. The one biographical study that might have escaped this dreary cataloguing was the proposed fascicule number eight by his brother George-Frédéric Baillairgé in the series *Notices biographiques* on the Baillairgé family. George-Frédéric unfortunately died before that volume had been written.[5]

Published before Charles Baillairgé's death, all the nineteenth-century biographies are incomplete and fail to give a full examination of his career. They list only the major buildings and ignore the legacy of less important but handsome structures that he designed and superintended, many of which have survived to this day in and around Quebec. They make no attempt to assess his contribution to the practice of architecture, to follow his evolution from the neoclassical tradition of his mentor Thomas Baillairgé to the progressive stylistic and technological theories and methods that were circulating in North America, the United Kingdom, and France in the nineteenth century. Moreover, these standard biographies catalogue his achievements in long lists, without integrating isolated buildings into his conceptual framework and without making the link between his prodigious writings on technical subjects and his architectural practice. Indeed, on first encountering these early biographies, the reader gets the impression that Baillairgé had several distinct and virtually unrelated careers. Only after careful study do the common characteristics underlying the apparent contradictions in his professional life become clear. Although the earlier Baillairgés, Jean, François, and Thomas, have received much critical attention from three generations of architectural historians and have been the subject of major studies,

Charles Baillairgé has been ignored to a large extent with the exception of Robert Caron's monograph on one of his buildings, the Hospice des Soeurs de la Charité, *Un couvent du XIXe siècle: la maison des Soeurs de la Charité de Québec* (1980).[6] With this extensive biography, it is my intention to restore the balance and give to Charles his well-earned place in the Baillairgé dynasty.

METHODOLOGY

In tackling a study of the professional life of Charles Baillairgé, certain basic questions must be addressed before a general assessment of the significance of his career can be attempted. What training, both structured and informal, did he receive in order to become an architect, surveyor, and civil engineer? What buildings did he design? What were his professional activities? Only after a sufficient corpus of documentary evidence has been assembled to respond to these fundamental questions can one begin to evaluate Baillairgé's contribution within the broader context of nineteenth-century architectural history.

Details on Baillairgé's formation as an architect may be pieced together from various printed and manuscript sources. The most precise and accurate indications come from Baillairgé himself, both in his printed works, in particular his *Bilan de M. Baillairgé, comme Architecte, Ingénieur, Arpenteur-Géomètre, durant les 21 ans, avant d'entrer au service de la Cité, ès-qualité d'Ingénieur des Ponts et Chaussées; ou de 1845 à 1866. Puis – entre heures – de 1866 à 1899, mais non compris les Travaux Civiques relatés dans un rapport supplémentaire* (1899), and in a job application to the minister of public works in 1853 in which he described at great length his early training.[7] Less direct but of great value in supplying details of his home life are early accounts of the Baillairgé family, especially the *Notices biographiques* written at the end of the nineteenth century by Charles's elder brother, George-Frédéric Baillairgé, and, to a lesser extent, the first-hand description of the family by a Baillairgé relation, Jean-Jacques Girouard.[8] Other sources that offer clues to the events of his early years include the collection of course outlines from the Seminary of Quebec for precisely those years that Baillairgé attended the school,[9] as well as the research carried out by Luc Noppen on the work of Charles's teacher, Thomas Baillairgé, and his development and propagation of neoclassical theory in collaboration with Seminary professor, the Abbé Jérôme Demers.[10] The surviving descendants of Charles Baillairgé have little new information to add and possess few relevant family papers that might have shed further light on the subject.

Part of a nineteenth-century architect's training involved the study of architectural books, often with large engraved plates illustrating the famous works of earlier masters. Charles Baillairgé is no exception, for he built up an impressive library of architectural books from several countries, ranging in subject matter from standard reference works to modern technological treatises. The contents of this library were recorded in the inventory of his property made in 1878 after the death of his first wife, Euphémie. Thanks in part to this inventory and to the scholarly foresight of one of Canada's early ethnologists, Dr Marius Barbeau, I have been able to reconstitute a preliminary list of Charles Baillairgé's architectural library. Barbeau's interest in the work of the earlier members of the Baillairgé dynasty caused him in the 1920s to seek out Charles Baillairgé's widow, who was at that time still occupying the family home at 72, rue Saint-Louis in Quebec, built by her husband near the end of his life. Barbeau made a list of the architectural books still on the shelves of the family library on the second floor, a list which was later transcribed from his cryptic notes by a typist at the Museum of Man where Barbeau worked. This typescript – though containing many errors and omissions, probably as a result of the transcription – survives in the Barbeau collection of the Canadian Centre for Folk Culture Studies in Ottawa.

A comparison of these two lists with specialized bibliographic reference books, such as the *Catalog of the Avery Memorial Architectural Library, Columbia University*, the *Catalogue of the Royal Institute of British Architects Library*, and the *Index to the British Catalogue of Books Published during the Years 1837 to 1857 Inclusive Compiled by Sampson Low*, yielded accurate bibliographic information in most cases. A search was then undertaken in an effort to locate Baillairgé's own copies of these books, with the expectation (which eventually proved to be well-founded) that the architect might have jotted down some personal notes or sketches on the pages, thereby allowing insight into his use of architectural books as sources for his own work. With the help of the Union Catalogue of Books, housed in the National Library in Ottawa, and tips from two colleagues, architect Robert Hill of Toronto and architectural historian Robert Caron of Quebec, certain libraries became the focus of an intense manual search. Books once belonging to Charles Baillairgé turned up in the main library and Rare Books Room of Laval University, the Blackader Library of McGill University, the library of the Seminary of Quebec, and the library of the municipal archives in Quebec, confirming the statement of one descendant who claimed that the furniture and books belonging to Charles Baillairgé's family were dispersed at auction in 1925 or 1926.[11] Most of these books were signed by the architect on the fly leaf or title page and many were not part of either initial list. This newly reconstituted architectural library provides an important tool for carrying out an accurate and objective examination of the influence of architectural publications on the architect.

The easy way to establish a *catalogue raisonné* or basic list of an architect's work is to refer to his job book, a ledger or journal that architects often maintained to keep track of each commission. In Baillairgé's case, however, no journal has ever been mentioned or located, suggesting that he did not keep one. Thus the catalogue of Baillairgé's architectural works, annexed to this biography as Appendix 2, has had to be compiled through careful research in several disparate record groups. Five major sources provided the bulk of documentation, supplemented on occasion by other less rewarding archival collections and printed works.

Once again Baillairgé's own writings – especially the *Bilan* cited earlier and his complementary *Rapport de l'Ex-Ingénieur de la Cité, des travaux faits sous le Maire, Hon. S.N. Parent et le Conseil-de-Ville actuels et sous leurs prédécesseurs durant le dernier tiers de Siècle: 1866 à 1899* (1899) – provide important information about the authorship of his buildings. The weakness of these books as sources is that they are essentially self-centred and hence do not give much factual information on dates of construction, names of craftsmen, materials, and so forth. The same limited information is available for the early period of Baillairgé's career in the Quebec newspapers, especially in the calls for tenders signed by the architect and in the occasional full-length articles about new construction in the city. To supplement the partial list drawn up from Baillairgé's printed works, additional information has been gathered through a systematic search of *Le Canadien* between the years 1846, when he began his practice, and 1860, when he began work for the government on the new Quebec Jail, and spot searches around precise key dates in other Quebec newspapers.

Although his own writings and the newspapers are important elements in establishing a catalogue of his buildings, the three richest sources for information on particular structures are the architectural drawings conserved in the fonds Baillairgé at Les archives de la ville de Québec, the building contracts located in the notarial files held at Les archives nationales du Québec, and the records of the federal Department of Public Works in the National Archives of Canada. The fonds Baillairgé, recently made more accessible through a detailed finding aid prepared by Annik Faussurier under the direction of city archivist Ginette Noël entitled *Inventaire analytique du fonds Charles-Philippe-Ferdinand Baillairgé* (1982), contains over five hundred plans, elevations, sections, and details for projects and completed buildings from his years in private practice.

The building contracts, known as *marchés de construction*, are legally binding agreements made between clients and contractors for the construction of specific buildings. The architect's name is sometimes mentioned, but only in the body of the text, not as one of the parties to the agreement; on other occasions, detailed specifications or *devis* are appended to the contract. Through the consultation of building contracts in which Baillairgé's name is mentioned, as identified in the finding aids by Geneviève G. Bastien, Doris D. Dubé, and Christina [Cameron] Southam, *Inventaire des marchés de construction des archives civiles de Québec 1800–1870* (1975), and by Danielle Blanchet and Sylvie Thivierge, *Inventaire des marchés de construction des actes notariés de la ville de Québec, 1871–1899* (1982), and through the examination of handwriting on the specifications of contracts which might potentially have involved Baillairgé, the catalogue of his architectural works has been substantially increased.

The other fruitful source, though difficult to consult because of its sheer volume, is the surviving record of public works correspondence ledgers, subject files, and architectural drawings, made accessible through a finding aid by Brian Hallett, *Public Records Division General Inventory Series: No. 8 Records of the Department of Public Works (RG 11)* (1977), and the card catalogue in the National Map Collection of the National Archives of Canada. Instrumental in documenting Baillairgé's proposals and executed buildings for the federal government, public works files also provide insight into the role of the architect in the middle of the nineteenth century in Canada.

Other record groups which have supplied information for this catalogue of architectural works include the Conseil et comités collection at the Quebec municipal archives, which often confirms and adds to Baillairgé's own account of projects undertaken during his tenure as city engineer; parish archives; research files at the Canadian Inventory of Historic Building, especially the dockets prepared under the guidance of architectural historian A.J.H. Richardson; and the Gérard Morisset collection of research data on specific buildings and parishes, now deposited in the documentation centre of the Inventaire des Biens culturels of the Ministère des Affaires culturelles. Finally, printed works, in particular the nineteenth-century biographies of Baillairgé and local histories by writers of the calibre of historian James Macpherson Lemoine, occasionally contain good leads for the identification and documentation of his architectural production.

In compiling a comprehensive list of Baillairgé's printed works, one is guided – and misled – by the first bibliography of his writings, presumably drawn up by Baillairgé himself and published in the *Proceedings and Transactions of the Royal Society of Canada for the Year 1894* (1895). New books and pamphlets were merely added at the end of this list a few years later in the brochure *Bibliographie de M.C. Baillairgé: Extraite du volume des "Transactions" pour 1894, de la Société Royale du Canada. Addenda jusqu'à ce jour, Québec, mai 1899* (1899). There are problems with these bibliographies: first, since they were written by an aging man who probably did not have all his publications immediately at hand, there are errors in titles and dates as well as omissions, especially of articles from magazines and professional journals; second, titles are listed that almost certainly were never published, including the text for his play "Berthuzabel ou le diable devenu cuisinier" and the long report on fire safety; finally, since the bibliography was not updated after 1899, no printed works written after that date are included in the list.

Although searches in standard bibliographic reference books and data bases provide more precise bibliographic information about Baillairgé's books, pamphlets, and articles, even a finding aid of the scope of the National Library of Canada's *Canadiana 1867–1900: Monographs. Canada's National Bibliography* (1980) includes a considerable number of errors, since references have been entered on the basis of the less-than-accurate Royal Society of Canada bibliography. The bibliography of printed works by Charles Baillairgé presented in this study contains only those books, pamphlets, and articles actually located and read by the author, as the result of a voluminous letter campaign to libraries and archives in Canada, the United States, Great Britain, and France, and systematic coverage of the following periodicals for the years indicated: *Canadian Architect and Builder* (1888–1906), *Canadian Engineer* (1893–1906), *Proceedings and Transactions of the Royal Society of Canada* (1882–1906), and *Transactions of the Canadian Society of Civil Engineers* (1887–1906). There may still be other printed works by Baillairgé as yet unseen by the author, but at present the list stands at a formidable 253 titles.

Information about Baillairgé's professional activities – in particular his lectures and participation in associations of architects, engineers, and land surveyors – can be found sporadically in his own writings and his scrapbook, now part of the holdings of the Musée du Québec, in which he pasted lecture invitations, newspaper clippings of speeches, diplomas, and other memorabilia. But the best sources for documenting his professional activities remain the transactions of the Royal Society of Canada and the Canadian Society of Civil Engineers, as well as the verbatim accounts of the annual meetings of the Province of Quebec Association of Architects that were published in the *Canadian Architect and Builder*, official journal for the architectural associations in Ontario and Quebec at the end of the nineteenth century. Through their tabulation of membership and executive officers, and their reports of the papers and ensuing discussions at the annual meetings, these publications provide sufficient information to assess Baillairgé's involvement in the different professional organizations.

Once a solid research base has been established, clarifying the nature of his training and documenting his architectural works, publications, and professional activities, Baillairgé's achievements can be analysed and evaluated within the broader context of Quebec, Canadian, and international developments. For the local context, the author of this study has had the privilege of participating in a major survey of Quebec City architecture in the early 1970s, under the direction of A.J.H. Richardson, at that time employed by Parks Canada in the National Historic Parks and Sites Branch. During four years, over two hundred historic buildings were documented through intense archival research; many of them were visited and recorded. The cumulative knowledge of building activity in Quebec from the seventeenth century to the early twentieth century acquired through this experience has proved invaluable in measuring Baillairgé's importance in the context of Quebec City.[12]

As for published material, although many books and brochures treat Quebec City as a tourist haven, there is a dearth of serious scholarly work in the field of Quebec architectural history, especially dealing with the second half of the nineteenth century, the period during which Baillairgé was active. The pioneering catalogues of churches and manor houses by provincial archivist Pierre-Georges Roy, *Les vieilles églises de la province de Québec 1647–1800* (1925) and *Old Manors, Old Houses* (1927), recently up-dated by Luc Noppen in *Les églises du Québec (1600–1850)* (1977) and Raymonde Gauthier in *Les manoirs du Québec* (1976), concentrate on the French regime and the early part of the nineteenth century, with only an occasional mention of later structures. Architect Ramsay Traquair's important study *The Old Architecture of Quebec* (1947) follows suit, largely ignoring the later period in favour of a close examination and documentation of French regime and early nineteenth-century work. It is only with A.J.H. Richardson's innovative "Guide to the Architecturally and Historically Most Significant Buildings in the Old City of Quebec" (1970), which appeared as an issue of the *Bulletin of the Association for Preservation Technology*, that middle and late nineteenth-century architecture has received proper attention – although the work is seriously hampered by a complete lack of source references. Richardson's lead has been followed by Luc Noppen, Claude Paulette, and Michel Tremblay in their comprehensive overview *Québec: trois siècles d'architecture* (1979) – again, not properly documented – by France Gagnon-Pratte in her careful examination of a particular functional type in *L'architecture et la nature à Québec au dix-neuvième siècle: les villas* (1980), and by Louise Voyer in her catalogue of vanished churches, *Églises disparues* (1981). The most recent contribution to the field of Quebec City's architectural history is the exhibition catalogue by Luc Noppen and Marc Grignon, *L'art de l'architecte* (1983).

Although more historical than architectural in nature, two books are nonetheless important for an evaluation of Baillairgé's work for the Department of Public Works. The meticulous study by political scientist J.E. Hodgetts, *Pioneer Public Service: An Administrative History of the United Canadas, 1841–1867* (1955), was used extensively by Douglas Owram in his *Building for Canadians: A History of the Department of Public Works, 1840–1960* (1979), and David B. Knight provides a fascinating analysis of the selection of Canada's capital city in *Choosing Canada's Capital: Jealousy and Friction in the 19th Century* (1977).

This, then, is a biographical study of an architect, engineer, and land surveyor, and his milieu in Quebec City in the second half of the nineteenth century. Organized chronologically, it touches general themes such as historical styles, construction technology, architectural practice, and professional associations. Drawing as it does on manuscript and printed sources not formerly exploited for this purpose, the biography will perhaps rescue Charles Baillairgé from obscurity – "one of the forgotten figures in French-

Canadian historiography," as one historian called him as recently as 1971[13] – and restore him to his rightful place as a worthy representative of the Baillairgé dynasty and a major contributor to the practice of architecture in nineteenth-century Canada.

Abbreviations

AAQ   Les archives de l'archidiocèse de Québec

AAR   Les archives de l'archdiocèse de Rimouski

ABSAB   Les archives de la Basilique de Sainte-Anne-de-Beaupré

ACM   Les archives civiles de Montmagny

ACQ   Les archives civiles de Québec

ACSC   Les archives du cimetière Saint-Charles

ACSJB   Les archives civiles de Saint-Joseph de Beauce

AMHDQ   Les archives du monastère l'Hôtel-Dieu de Québec

ANDQ   Les archives de Notre-Dame de Québec

ANQ   Les archives nationales du Québec

APT   *Bulletin of the Association for Preservation Technology*

ASBP   Les archives des Soeurs du Bon-Pasteur

ASC   Les archives des Soeurs de la Charité de Québec

ASCO   Les archives des Soeurs de la Charité d'Ottawa

ASQ   Les archives du Séminaire de Québec

AUL   Les archives de l'Université Laval

AUQ   Les archives des Ursulines de Québec

AVQ   Les archives de la ville de Québec

BEQ   Le bureau d'enregistrement de Québec

BRH   *Le bulletin des recherches historiques*

CAB   *The Canadian Architect and Builder*

CCFCS   Canadian Centre for Folk Culture Studies

CE   *The Canadian Engineer*

CIHB   Canadian Inventory of Historic Building

CMC   Canadian Museum of Civilization

IBC   Inventaire des Biens culturels

JCAH   *The Journal of Canadian Art History*

JSAH   *The Journal of the Society of Architectural Historians*

MAC   Ministère des Affaires culturelles du Québec

MQ   Le Musée du Québec

MSQ   Le Musée du Séminaire de Québec

NA   National Archives of Canada

NHPS   National Historic Parks and Sites, Canadian Parks Service

NMC	National Map Collection (now known as Cartographic and Architectural Archives Division)
OMA	Ottawa Municipal Archives
QMM	McGill University Library
QQBS	La bibliothèque du Séminaire de Québec
QQLA	Laval University Library
RHAF	*La revue d'histoire de l'amérique française*
ROM	Royal Ontario Museum
SIQ	La Société immobilière du Québec

Charles Baillairgé

PLATE I   Picturesque manor house at Saint-Roch des Aulnaies. Heritage Recording Services, Environment Canada

PLATE 2   Venner Monument at the cimetière
Saint-Charles. Photograph by François
Leclair

PLATE 3   Private chapel from Saint-Michel
de Bellechasse, now moved to La
Guadeloupe. Heritage Recording Services,
Environment Canada

PLATE 4   Interior of chapel from Saint-
Michel de Bellechasse. Heritage Recording
Services, Environment Canada

PLATE 5 Iron fence at Notre-Dame de
Québec. Photograph by François Leclair

PLATE 6   Chapelle du Bon-Pasteur,
Quebec. Photograph by François Leclair

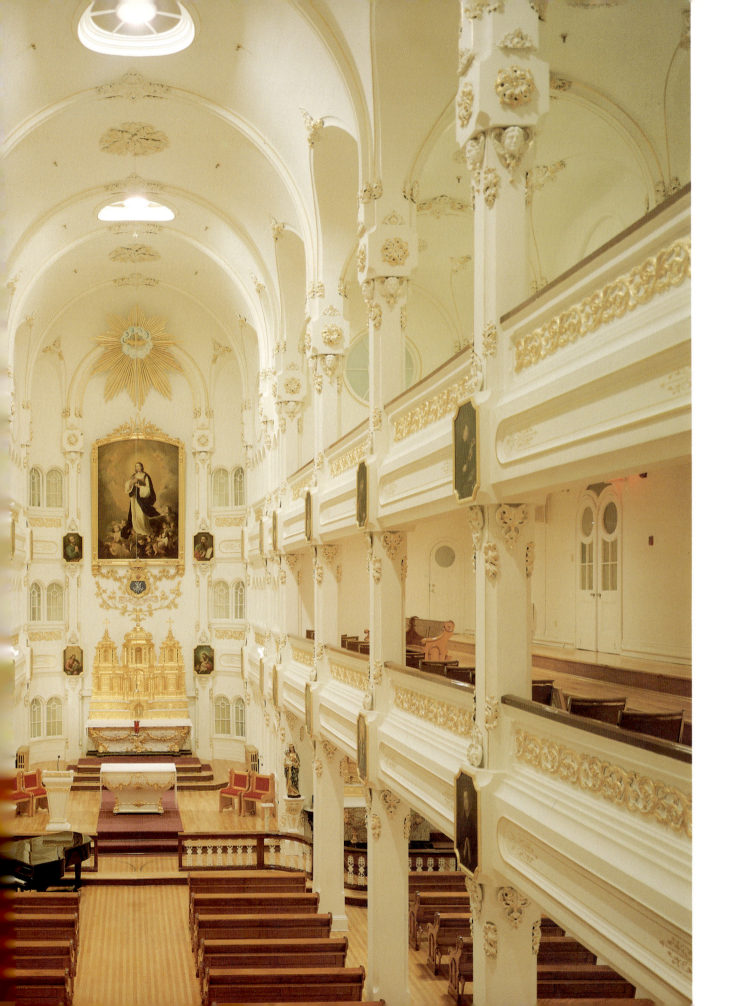

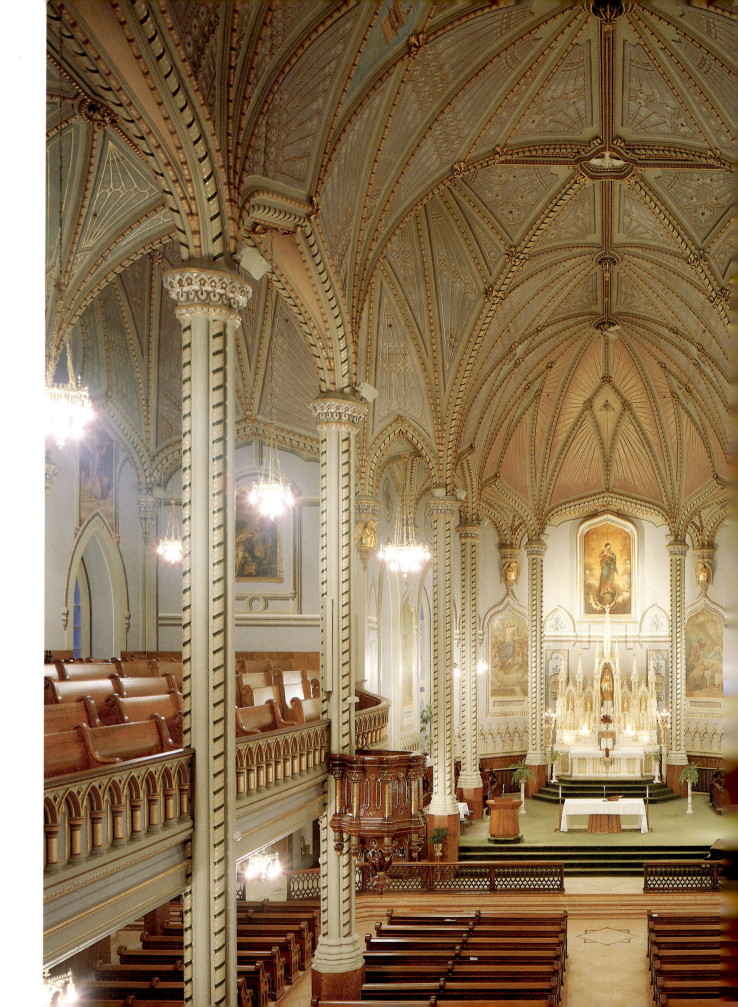

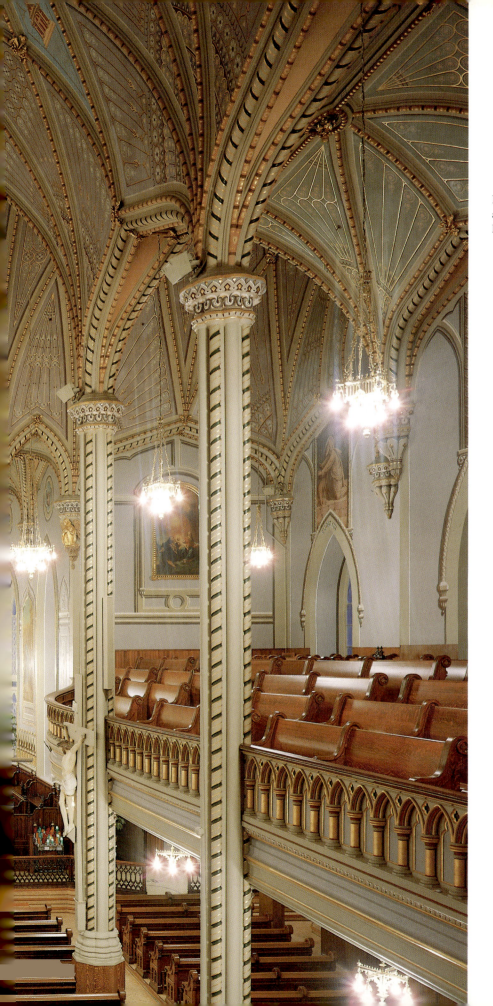

PLATE 7   Gothic Revival interior of church at Sainte-Marie de Beauce. Photograph by François Leclair

PLATE 8   Pulpit from church at Sainte-
Marie de Beauce. Photograph by François
Leclair

1 The Making of an Architect, Engineer, and Surveyor

SECOND SON IN AN ARTISTIC and culturally diverse family, Charles Baillairgé was born in Quebec City at a time of political and social upheaval. His innate curiosity about technical and mechanical subjects manifested itself early in his life and blossomed under the tutelage of his father's cousin, Thomas Baillairgé, at that time Quebec's best native architect and sculptor. At the age of seventeen, Charles abandoned his formal education at the Seminary of Quebec, impatient to get on with his chosen profession. With the successful completion of two apprenticeships with Thomas Baillairgé – one in architecture, the other in surveying – and an informal preparation in civil engineering, a youthful and enthusiastic Charles Baillairgé was ready to begin his career.

Charles-Philippe-Ferdinand-Baillairgé was born on 29 September 1826, son of a bookbinder living on the rue Saint-Jean, Théophile Baillairgé, and his wife Charlotte, London-educated daughter of Lieutenant Richard Howard Horsley (an officer of the Royal Navy who had fought with Nelson at the Battle of Trafalgar).[1] In the period of political unrest leading up to the 1837 rebellion, one can only guess at the divided loyalties that young Charles must have felt in a household shared by a French-Canadian father and an English-bred unilingual mother.

Since their arrival in Canada four generations earlier, the Baillairgé's had demonstrated more than once their support for the French cause in Canada. The patriarch Jean had fought with Montcalm's army on the Plains of Abraham and was, in later years, a friend of Louis-Joseph Papineau's father.[2] Jean's son, Pierre-Florent, was one of the collaborators of the nationalist newspaper *Le Canadien*; the printing press which British soldiers smashed in 1810 was housed in the Baillairgé home and workshop on the rue Saint-François, now rue Ferland. Jean's daughter Marie-Anne was the mother of Jean-Jacques Girouard, a patriot in the 1837 rebellion.[3] Théophile himself was a defender of his language and religion, and, according to his elder son, "always fought against the adversaries of his nationality."[4] Yet, in apparent contradiction, his wife could speak only English and was a member of the Anglican communion.[5] Their two sons, nurtured in two cultures and languages and schooled at the foremost Catholic institutions in the city of Quebec, were thus unwittingly prepared to play a role in the broad context of Canadian and even international affairs.

Well-established in the French-Canadian milieu in Quebec, the Baillairgés were a family of sculptors, painters, and architects. Jean Baillairgé, a young craftsman from Saint-Antoine de Villaret in the Poitou region of France, had been brought to New France in 1741 by Monseigneur de Pontbriand, leader of the Roman Catholic church in New France who sought out French artisans to improve church construction in the colony. Jean established himself in Quebec City as a *maître charpentier* or master carpenter, working on a variety of religious and secular projects. In later years he even called himself an "*architecte*," in the sense of designer, and a few drawings in his hand have survived.[6]

Jean's son, François, continued in the building tradition of his father but his work reached a new level of refinement. Recognizing early his talents in painting and sculpture, his father and the Seminary of Quebec arranged to send François to the mother country for three years to attend the Académie royale de peinture et de sculpture in Paris from 1778 to 1781. While in France, François purchased important treatises that later became part of Charles's architectural library. On his return to Quebec, François excelled as a sculptor and painter, carving many altars and retables for parish churches, handsome figure-heads for ships, and painting large religious canvases and more fanciful decorative works, including the coat of arms on the Duke of Kent's carriage when the latter was stationed at Quebec.[7] Although he was not formally trained in architecture at the separate Parisian institution called the Académie royale d'architecture, he did at least experiment with architectural perspective while in France, as drawings of staircases from his French period indicate.[8] While François's major contribution was in sculpture and, to a lesser extent, painting – indeed, he gave formal classes in these disciplines – he did design several important buildings, most notably the Quebec Prison (1808–14); 44, rue Saint-Stanislas, Quebec, inspired most probably by that French interpreter of Italian Renaissance taste, Philibert de l'Orme; and later the interior of the church at Saint-Joachim, Montmorency (1816–29).[9]

François's son, Thomas, though apprenticed to the Montreal area sculptor René Saint-James, eventually developed his skills in architecture under his father's guidance to become first and foremost an architect. Thomas Baillairgé's collaboration with the Abbé Jérôme Demers, professor of philosophy at the Seminary of Quebec, has been thoroughly documented and examined by Luc Noppen.[10] With Baillairgé's help, Demers attempted to set down the rules and guidelines for architectural design, particularly as articulated by two major proponents of European neoclassicism, Vignola and Blondel, in his *Précis d'architecture* (1828), a course outline for the class on architecture introduced by Demers at the Seminary. Thomas carved models of the classical orders to help illustrate the teachings. He also designed a series of handsome and richly decorated churches in the Quebec City area which, through their symmetry, harmony, and rational integration of forms, illustrate the tenets set forth in the *Précis d'architecture*.[11] Finally, Thomas Baillairgé contributed to the improvement of the practice of architecture and sculpture in Quebec City through active instruction. In the tradition of the European guild system, he accepted apprentices into his workshop, training them for three years before issuing them certificates of professional competency.[12]

Charles's artistic legacy did not come from his paternal ancestry alone. His mother, Charlotte Horsley, possessed some training and talent as an artist in her own right, as a surviving pencil sketch of a stylized horse's head proves. It was signed "C.J. Horsley, 1826," the year that Charles was born, and was obviously cherished by her son who kept it in his scrapbook.

This, then, is the context into which Charles Baillairgé was born. His father, who had been educated in commerce, worked as a clerk and bookbinder at the printing shop and bookstore of the *Quebec Gazette* at the foot of the côte de la Montagne. It was in this shop that he first encountered his future wife, the young daughter of Lieutenant Horsley. According to his elder son, Théophile grew restless in this job and readily accepted the municipality's offer to become assistant engineer of public works in 1828, a position he held (under a variety of titles as the municipal organization evolved) for thirty-seven years until his death in 1865. What qualifications he held to secure this position is not clear. Possibly Théophile's uncle, François, who was city road treasurer, helped him to get the job and initiated him in the work. His duties included responsibility for the maintenance of roads, sewers, and waterfront facilities belonging to the city as well as the design and construction, when needed, of market halls.[13] Théophile was reputed to be a gifted administrator and devoted to work, a model not lost on either of his sons. During Charles's youth, the family moved from the congested and commercial location on the rue Saint-Jean to the residential avenue Sainte-Geneviève on the Governor's garden. In the 1830s the latter street bore little resemblance to its present aristocratic appearance, being, as Quebec historian and writer, James Macpherson Lemoine described the area in 1830, "occupied by carters, old French market gardeners and descendants of French artisans."[14]

Whether Charles Baillairgé had any formal education before the age of ten is not known. In order to avoid the cholera epidemic, his mother had sent his older brother to an English school called "Woodland" at Lake Beauport, from 1832 to 1834, and it is possible that Charles attended as well. In 1836, following his brother, Charles was enrolled as a day boy at the Seminary of Quebec, along with his classmate Hector Langevin who was to play a significant role in his later career. During the next seven years, Charles followed the regular curriculum of the Seminary, which leaned heavily towards French, English, Latin, Greek, history, and geography – a "classical and technical" education, as he later called it.[15] Given his fluency in the English language, he probably excelled in this subject, a part of the Seminary program enthusiastically encouraged in 1839 by the editor of *Le Canadien*.[16] In later years, he attributed his love of theatre to his experiences at the Seminary. He allowed a rare glimpse into school life in his description of a holiday excursion to the country retreat belonging to the Seminary at Saint-Joachim, where, at the close of the day's activities, "we all used to say our evening prayers – the rosary – while walking along ... in the dusk."[17]

Impatient with the slow pace of formal learning, Charles withdrew from the Seminary in 1843 at the age of seventeen, before completing the last three years of the program (rhetoric, philosophy 1 and 2). As he explained ten years later in a letter to the chief commissioner of public works for the Province of Canada: "I received my education at the Seminary of Quebec. I left after the year of Rhetoric. I yearned so much to increase my knowledge of philosophy and mathematics that I grew impatient with the slow pace of that institution. So I studied by myself day and night to learn in one year what I would have learned in three years at the Seminary."[18] By leaving at this time he missed the opportunity to follow – in a formal way, at any rate – Demers's architecture course, which was only offered in the philosophy year. It is possible that Jérôme Demers's decision to abandon his teaching career at the Seminary in 1842 had some influence on Baillairgé's decision. Having failed to complete his formal studies, Charles quite naturally asserted in later years that uneducated persons had a greater chance of success in life and that schools encouraged narrow-mindedness.[19]

After leaving the Seminary, Charles followed family tradition by beginning an apprenticeship with his father's cousin, Thomas Baillairgé. In the latter's workshop on the rue Saint-François, Charles worked during the day on Thomas's current projects, along with the other apprentices, and in the evenings attended formal classes in mathematics, sculpture, statuary, and architecture, the latter presumably similar in content to the *Précis d'architecture*. In addition, Charles immersed himself in his cousin's wonderful library of professional books. While studying the theory and practice of architecture in Thomas's workshop, Charles apparently found time to work occasionally as a draughtsman for his father, then road inspector for the city and as such responsible for market halls. Drawings have survived for work at Saint Paul Market signed:

Del. C. Baillairgé A.D. 1843
Thé. Baillairgé.[20]

Although he began simultaneously his preparation for careers in architecture, surveying, and civil engineering, he concentrated first on architecture and, at a time when no other form of licensing existed, received from Thomas Baillairgé a certificate of proficiency in architecture in 1846 after three years' study. His earliest surviving plans with the title "architect" are dated March 1846.[21] Without pausing, he pushed on with his second program, this one in surveying, and, as he explained, "while studying surveying I practised as an architect after office hours."[22] After another three years of study, he attained his certificate in this discipline and in 1848 received his commission as provincial land surveyor for Lower Canada.[23]

By 1848 Charles Baillairgé could rightly claim to be an architect and provincial land surveyor. Just how he assumed the professional title of civil engineer is less clear. Unlike the two formal apprenticeships that he served, he apparently studied civil engineering on his own. He claimed that he began his studies in civil engineering at the same time as those in architecture. To train himself, he read voraciously on the subject, ordering as many scientific books as he could, and, by his own account, assiduously copied the plans and details of numerous bridges, wharves, and locks. By March 1849 he advertised himself as a practitioner and teacher of architecture, surveying, and civil engineering.[24] That his training in this last discipline was independent rather than formal is confirmed by his statement in 1853 to the chief commissioner of public works: "I am as perfect a civil engineer as it is possible to be from study alone. In other words, I am like anyone who has completed his training.[25]

At the completion of his apprenticeship with Thomas Baillairgé, Charles supplemented his formal training with reading, travel, and observation of other architects' work. Throughout his life he was a copious writer and a voracious reader. His exposure to architectural literature probably began at Thomas Baillairgé's home, where Thomas had an extensive library inherited in part from his father, François, and augmented by his own purchases.[26] That Thomas was a cultivated literary man is evident from a letter written during his retirement in which he explained that "I keep busy with my organ, my books and journals," and from his will in which he made specific provisions for his various books.[27] Charles Baillairgé's library contained a number of these books, either signed by Thomas himself or inscribed by Charles with the date "1858," the year prior to Thomas's death. Charles also made numerous purchases, in spite of his small budget, in order to keep abreast of current developments in the field. His 1853 letter to the chief commissioner of public works reveals the quantity and scope of his acquisitions:

I have brought in from Europe and from the United States at great expense for my reduced means all the best treatises on surveying, architecture and civil engineering along with many volumes on the arts, sciences and manufacturing. I have read, reread and studied them again and again. I am not only acquainted with all the important works that have existed or still exist in Europe and in other parts of the world, but I also understand their construction techniques. I subscribe to publications which keep me abreast of all the developments in the scientific world.[28]

If one suspects him of exaggeration, the list of his own books – so many of them from the 1840s and 1850s – supports his claims.[29]

The books in Baillairgé's library clearly indicate that this was a studious man, a designer, not a builder, a thinker rather than a doer. The books are not compact portable pattern books to be carried easily to the construction site; instead, they are large folio volumes, handsomely bound in leather, sometimes with gold-leaf lettering, containing magnificent engraved plates on thick handmade paper. In content, they included the expected traditional texts of Palladian and neoclassical theory and example, found in such authors as Vignola, Blondel, Philibert de l'Orme, Félibien, Ferrerio, Gibbs, Letarouilly, Domenico de Rossi, Wood, and even the English neoclassicist Soane. Other titles by authors such as Buchotte, Dupain de Montesson, Jeaurat, Johnson, Sanderson, Taylor, Weale, and Worthen deal with the techniques of preparing architectural drawings and calculating quantities of materials for estimates and specifications. But the library goes beyond these basic tools to include books on the most up-to-date manifestation of neoclassicism, Greek Revival, books which were certainly purchased by Charles, and included Foulston, Jackson, Lafever, and Knight. Other titles which broke away entirely from neoclassicism, and showed the early nineteenth-century interest in Northern European architecture (in particular, the history and manifestations of the Gothic style), included works by Arnot, Brandon, Gwilt, Hope, Parker, Pugin and Willson, and Sanderson. Yet another group dealt with details of construction and engineering, with a bias towards geometry and mathematical calculation of forms: Borgnis, Cresy, Fairbairn, Hoppus (which has been used like a notebook with numerous annotations in François's or Thomas's handwriting), Fergusson, Leeds, Nicholson, Rondelet, and Telford. Finally, there is a heterogeneous collection of books on specific functional types such as schools (Barnard), prisons (Foulke and Jebb), churches (Brandon), rural houses (Duval, Parker, Pattisson, Sanderson, and Sloan), urban houses (Normand, Vitry), tombstones (Normand), and gates (Weale and Wickersham). Charles Baillairgé's library reflects an inquisitive mind, a sort of Renaissance man who made all knowledge his province, a man who wanted to become acquainted – in the minutest detail and the broadest overview – with all that existed in his chosen profession.

Books were no substitute for firsthand experience, so Charles travelled to different parts of the country to observe just how buildings were being erected at that time. Information is scanty about his travel in this formative period. While it remains in the realm of speculation, he may well have accompanied Thomas Baillairgé in 1846 on his only trip to visit Montreal and his relatives at Saint-Benoit. Charles's brother George-Frédéric, by that time employed as a draughtsman for the Department of Public Works in Montreal, met Thomas at the steamboat and reported that they spent two or three days roaming around Montreal, making a careful examination of the

FIG. 1. The main façade of 9, rue Haldimand, Quebec (1831–2), possibly designed by Irish architect George Browne. CIHB

FIG. 2. The town house at 43, rue d'Auteuil, Quebec (1834–6), designed by Frederick Hacker. CIHB

Gothic Revival church of Notre-Dame de Montréal, the commercial streets near the port, and the Lachine Canal, on which George-Frédéric was working. What most surprised Thomas was the regular cut-stone work of so many of the large buildings.[30]

While it is unclear whether Charles accompanied his mentor to Montreal, it is certain that he visited the principal towns in the eastern United States, Ontario, and Quebec in September 1850. He described this experience a few years later, explaining how he took every occasion to learn about the practical aspect of building: "I have visited all the major cities and towns in the United States and have spent entire days at those sites where I saw a bridge or a lock under construction to consider all the practical means to use in building these works."[31]

In addition to books and travel, Charles Baillairgé could study close at hand in his own city the buildings designed by British architects up-to-date with the latest architectural fashions in Britain. There were, of course, two or three good examples of the earlier Palladian influence – notably the Anglican Cathedral (1799–1804) and the Court House (1799–1802). Baillairgé's curiosity was surely aroused by the various renditions of the more fashionable Greek Revival mode, including Henry Musgrave Blaiklock's Custom House (1830–3) and Marine Hospital (1834), as well as a series of smooth ashlar town houses, some with recessed arcading, such as 9, rue Haldimand (1831–2) (fig. 1), 56, rue Saint-Louis (1830–1), 73, rue Sainte-Ursule (1830), and 29, rue Desjardins (1841–2), and at least one with a complete classical doorway in the Doric order – 43, rue d'Auteuil (1834–6) (fig. 2).[32] These were the work of a few British-trained architects who had come to Quebec in the 1830s: George Blaiklock, Henry Musgrave Blaiklock, George Browne, and Frederick Hacker. Hacker's experience included employment in the offices of one of Britain's most fashionable architects, John Nash. These buildings and the presence of their architects in Quebec City offered a young man like Charles Baillairgé an opportunity to become acquainted with current British neoclassical theory and practice.

Most influential in the early stages of his career was the practical training he acquired while working as an apprentice for Thomas Baillairgé. From 1842 to 1846 Charles helped to prepare detailed plans for the major commissions in Thomas's workshop – the façade of Notre-Dame de Québec (1843–4) (figs. 3, 24), the Episcopal Palace (1844–7), and the parish church in the suburb of Saint-Roch (1845–7). These three buildings are, in the opinion of architectural historian Luc Noppen, mature examples of Thomas Baillairgé's neoclassicism.[33] They shared common characteristics such as symmetrical composition and classically inspired vocabulary, and strove for unity and monumentality, in part through austerity of design, in part through the use of smoothly dressed and evenly coursed stone walls. Not surprisingly, these features influenced Charles Baillairgé's early work.

An early example of Charles Baillairgé's working method at this time is provided by one of these commissions, the church at Saint-Roch (figs. 4–5). Noppen has establish the proper chronology for the construction of the church, in particular the new extension and façade which were designed by Thomas Baillairgé in 1841. After its destruction in the 1845 fire, the parish decided to rebuild following the earlier plan, with the exception of the steeples which were to be redesigned by Charles Baillairgé, then aged twenty.[34] It is significant that the young architect turned for inspiration to

Fig. 3. The façade elevation for the church of Notre-Dame de Québec was drawn by architect Thomas Baillairgé in 1843. ANDQ, photograph courtesy of Les services audio-visuels Laval

Fig. 4. The parish church of Saint-Roch (1841), designed by Thomas Baillairgé with steeples by Charles Baillairgé (1846). ANQ, photothèque, GH-871-19

one of the buildings in Quebec as well as to his library. The steeples were modelled on those of the Anglican Cathedral in Quebec City, but, to be absolutely certain of his design, Baillairgé worked from the source of their inspiration, the steeple of James Gibbs's St Martin-in-the-Fields in London, England, reproduced in Gibbs's *A Book of Architecture* (1728). Like Gibbs's engraving, but unlike the plainer Anglican Cathedral steeple, the steeples at Saint-Roch have urns at the corners of the square base. Proof positive of Baillairgé's use of Gibbs as a model exists in the pages of his personal copy of *A Book of Architecture* (the second edition of 1739), now preserved in the Blackader Library of McGill University. Here, on the plate illustrating St Martin, Baillairgé has jotted down numbers around that part of the steeple he copied, with the date "1846" on the left and, in the upper right corner in his handwriting, "pour la hauteur Echelle No. 2. Largeur do. No. 3."[35]

Thomas Baillairgé excelled in church designs, and Notre-Dame de Québec clearly follows the neoclassical precepts of Jérôme Demers and Blon-

FIG. 5. Charles Baillairgé based his design for the steeples at the church of Saint-Roch on an illustration of London's St Martin-in-the-Fields in James Gibbs, *A Book of Architecture* (1728). Baillairgé had the 2nd edition of this book in his library

FIG. 6. Shown in a sketch in Alfred Hamel's *Topographical and Pictorial Map of the City of Québec* (1858), the Episcopal Palace is a rare example of Thomas Baillairgé's domestic architecure, albeit on a large scale. NA, NMC-C-118207

del. But the Episcopal Palace, being a domestic building type, deserves special examination as a potential model for Charles's commercial, residential, and governmental structures (figs. 6–7). It is somewhat old-fashioned, summing up design criteria of the early nineteenth century rather than breaking new ground. Like the Court House in Quebec, built over forty years earlier, it has many features that are often called Palladian: gradation of the three storeys into rusticated base (clearly marked by the string course and segmentally arched windows), *piano nobile* with tall windows and bedroom level with shorter windows; central projecting frontispiece crowned with a pediment; and quoins (not pilasters) that delineate the major vertical divisions. While the composition is derived from Palladian prototypes – hence out-of-date by 1844 – the treatment of the wall surface as a smooth uninterrupted plane and the Greek vocabulary of the portico are manifestations of the new current of neoclassicism. The dormer windows have nothing to do with either mode, being vestiges of traditional French-Canadian building.

Charles Baillairgé's early work quite naturally reflected Thomas's brand of interwoven Palladian and neoclassical themes. When the Saint Paul market was destroyed by fire in 1845, Charles perhaps hoped that his family connections with the city (his father was by then road inspector) would help him win the commission for the new market. He prepared three different proposals, dated 1845, 1846, and 1847,[36] before another recently arrived British architect, Edward Staveley, was chosen for the job.[37] Although never erected, these designs for market halls reveal Charles Baillairgé's early architectural tendencies. Conspicuous borrowings from Thomas's work show how greatly he was indebted to his master. The 1845 project drew heavily on the Episcopal Palace for its composition, with pedimented frontispiece, rusticated base with string course, quoins, and window treatment of the lower storey. The roofs of the second project adopted in one version the small lantern from the Episcopal Palace and in the other the raised clerestory of Frederick Hacker's 1833 proposal, but the rhythmic false arcades of the wall surface recalled more directly his father Théophile's Upper Town Market Hall, built in 1844.[38] In the 1847 proposal (fig. 8), Charles tried to create a more unified and monumental design. He crowned the roof with a substantial dome similar to that on Thomas's Legislative Building of 1831, but more likely inspired by two recent domed market halls he had probably visited, Bonsecours Market, Montreal (1842), by architect William Footner, and Kingston Town Hall and Market House (1842–4) (fig. 9) by George Browne.[39] Baillairgé's 1847 proposal is especially close to the Kingston example, confirming the hypothesis that Charles did travel to Montreal in 1846 with Thomas Baillairgé and perhaps continued on to Kingston. This would explain the radical difference in conception between the 1846 and 1847 proposals.

These three proposals also reveal Charles's inherent weakness in drawing technique, a difficult he acknowledged more than once during his practice. In the 1845 and 1846 proposals he tried, not very successfully, to create the illusion of light and shadow through the rudimentary application of light and heavy vertical lines; in the 1847 proposal he failed to achieve a sense of depth in the portico. The designs themselves were in some ways awkward first efforts. The first two lacked focus and had a dull repetition of motifs, while the third blatantly erred against the classical rules of proportion in the irregular spaces between the portico columns and the eight to one (instead of four to one) ratio of the pediment.

These years of preparation also had their lighter moments. Charles would certainly have shared in the social evenings so charmingly sketched by his brother George-Frédéric. On Saturday nights a circle of friends – a sort of gentleman's club – assembled at Thomas Baillairgé's home. The group included his cousins Louis-de-Gonzague Baillairgé, a lawyer, and Théophile (Charles's father), Archange Parent and Edouard Glackemeyer, both notaries, the historian and city clerk François-Xavier Garneau, Louis Fiset, the protonotary, and architect Louis-Thomas Berlinguet. George-Frédéric described how the discussion ranged from the latest political news to science and history. From time to time, some of them played chess while others smoked the calumet pipe, symbol of peace and friendship. He added that no hard liquor was served.[40] One can easily imagine young Charles, his intellectual curiosity aroused, following closely the convivial debates of his elders.

Two incidents from this period – curiously and tragically interrelated – foreshadow aspects of his professional career: the manufacturing of his "automobile" and the fire of 1846. His mechanical bent of mind led to experiments with steam engines. At the age of seventeen, Charles and his friend Francis Molt built a vehicle propelled by a two-cylinder steam engine, which Baillairgé later claimed was the first automobile in North America. He recounted with obvious delight how the two youngsters used to drive from Montmorency Falls to Cap-Rouge, until they were finally removed from the public roads by the police after numerous complaints that the steam from the boilers was frightening the horses. This was not the only hazard. One of these experiments apparently ended in near disaster when the engine exploded in the Baillairgé's back yard. Charles vividly recalled this incident years later in a description that illustrates his powers of observation and bent for scientific matters:

We had returned from one of these outings, and intending to go out again, did not draw the fire, but laid up during dinner time at my father's then residence, No. 17 Genevieve street, Cape, when hearing an uproar in the yard, I got my head out just in time to see the valve returning almost vertically downwards from the height to which it had been blown by the increasing force of the vapor from within. This vapor continued to escape from the valve in a solid cylindrical form of some ten feet at least in height, before it was sufficiently cooled down and disintegrated by the resistance of the atmosphere to become visible as condensed steam, showing the super-heating it had attained to under confinement, and in fact the whole contents of the boiler, water and all, were in some 20 seconds thoroughly cleaned out.[41]

The two-cylinder engine was eventually dismantled from the car and sold to the owner of a river boat near Trois-Rivières.

The second incident, the fire at the theatre, a former riding school building on the Place d'Armes, affected Baillairgé in another way. The upper floor was being used for an exhibition of illuminated paintings on 12 June 1846 when a lamp fell from the ceiling and set the theatre curtain on fire. The single exit and the weakness of the staircase, which collapsed under the weight of the crowd, blocked egress from the building and caused the death of forty-six persons, including Baillairgé's close friend and co-inventor Francis Molt, aged nineteen.[42] This tragic loss may explain Baillairgé's concern with fire-safety standards in public buildings.

FIG. 7. The Episcopal Palace by Thomas Baillairgé, shown here in a more recent photograph with modifications to the roof and south façade to the right. CIHB

FIG. 8. This 1847 façade elevation was Charles Baillairgé's third proposal for the Saint Paul Market in Quebec. AVQ, fonds Charles Baillairgé, no. 6-40

FIG. 9. Architect George Browne's Kingston Town Hall and Market House (1842–4) probably served as a model for Charles Baillairgé's final proposal for the Saint Paul Market in Quebec. CIHB

Through this period of learning and preparation Baillairgé exhibited the determination of an ambitious young man who set out to train himself in a thorough and systematic way for his chosen profession. He had mastered the principles of architecture, surveying, and civil engineering. At twenty he was already practising as an architect, and by twenty-two he had added surveying to his accomplishments. His assertion to the chief commissioner of public works in 1853 was surely correct, "for me studying has always been and will always be my only pleasure; I prefer it to all other amusement."[43]

2   Baillairgé the Professional Man

ON BECOMING AN ARCHITECT IN 1846, Charles Baillairgé immediately took steps to consolidate and expand his knowledge in the disciplines of architecture, surveying, and civil engineering by setting up his own library and by acquainting himself firsthand with the work of other architects, both at home and abroad. In his own practice he discarded the traditional "artisan-architect" role that Thomas Baillairgé and his forefathers had followed; instead, Charles adopted the role of the architect as a professional man.

From the outset of his career, Baillairgé imposed his perception of the professional architect as creator of plans and specifications, liaison between client and craftsman, and as controller of all aspects of the construction process. This attitude reflected current European practice and, indeed, found its roots in the architectural practice of the Italian Renaissance. Baillairgé was familiar with this approach through his reading. Among the books in his library was a copy of John Soane's *Plans, Elevations and Sections of Buildings*(1788). He probably purchased the volume himself, since only his name appears inside with the price paid. In the introductory pages Soane summarized his thoughts on the role of the architect by quoting from the Italian Renaissance architect Alberti: "I will not rank the mechanic with the architect; but I shall call him an architect, who, from his earliest youth, by long and extensive study, has acquired abilities to design, and judgment to execute great and useful works, only to be effected by men of science."[1]

How this statement must have struck a sympathetic chord in Baillairgé! Soane went on to outline the professional responsibilities of the architect in a paragraph which is worth citing in its entirety, given the relevance to Baillairgé's difficulties in later years:

The business of the architect is to make the designs and estimates, to direct the works and to measure and value the different parts; he is the intermediate agent between the employer, whose honour and interest he is to study and the mechanic, whose rights he is to defend. His situation implies great trust; he is responsible for the mistakes, negligences, and ignorances of those he employs; and above all, he is to take care that the workmen's bills do not exceed his own estimates. If these are the duties of an architect, with what propriety can his situation and that of the builder, or the contractor be united?[2]

In his own practice, Charles Baillairgé exercised to the full extent the various aspects of his professional calling: preparation of general plans, working drawings and specifications, calling of tenders, estimation of quantities, supervision of works, and measurement of completed works. For the Laval University project, for example, he drew up a set of general plans, composed of twenty-three sheets which, by his own account, "kept me busy for a month and a half of constant work."[3] To accompany these general plans he produced detailed specifications for the various building contracts. The identifiable characteristics of Baillairgé's specifications (and those of architects trained by him) are, first, that the specifications are separate documents appended to the *marchés* or building contracts; second, that they are laid out on the page with a large left-hand margin on which is recorded a sort of

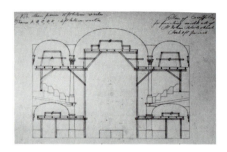

FIG. 10. Working drawings for the scaffolding to finish the vaults of the church of Saint-Jean-Baptiste in Quebec. AVQ, fonds Charles Baillairgé, no. 4–17

running index of subject headings; and, finally, that they contain an extraordinary amount of detail. Only British-trained architects in Quebec such as George Browne and Edward Staveley were producing specifications of similar quality.[4]

Once the contracts were signed, Baillairgé had to furnish working drawings for each detail of the plan. In the case of Laval University, he or his apprentices had sometimes to produce duplicate copies for plans lost or damaged on the work site. With his characteristic attention to detail, Baillairgé informed the Seminary in 1858 that he had made precisely 315 working plans on 161 sheets of paper for the two buildings.[5] Through these working drawings the architect controlled every aspect of the design: the location of each stone on the façade, the depth of the cut-stone garland at the entrance, the size and disposition of the tables in the reading rooms, the position of the lamps, and so forth.[6] In the case of the Saint-Jean-Baptiste church, the detailed specifications were supplemented by numerous working drawings, even down to the design of scaffolding needed to reach the vaulted ceiling (fig. 10). This fascination with the detail of construction – in marked contrast to Thomas Baillairgé who rarely prepared working drawings and showed little interest in the construction site – is characteristic of Charles who, it will be remembered, prepared himself simultaneously for a career in civil engineering. One of his reminiscences in later years about the Saint-Jean-Baptiste church illustrates his concern for proper construction:

When the writer built the St. Jean Baptiste church in 1854 – the two piers between the three front doors some 2 1/2 x 3 ft. only, were put in of solid cutstone layers as well inside as out to insure equality of settlement.

When the same church was rebuilt after its destruction by fire in 1882, under another architect, the same piers were rebuilt with outside cut stone facings and inside rubble ... the settlement of the inner facing being greater than that of the outer, where thinner and less numerous horizontal joints prevailed, the effect was that the inner and outer faces parted companionship, so I could thrust my arm in between the two. The thing was left unattended to in time and the settlement extending to the upper portions of the portal of the church, the whole central portion of the superincumbent masonry between the flanking towers had to be taken down and rebuilt at a cost of not less than $35,000.00.[7]

Baillairgé explained his motivation in preparing such careful plans and specifications when he discussed in later life an incident that occurred at the Beauport church. In 1849 he produced his usual voluminous plans and specifications for this church, including instructions that each tower was to have four walls in order to bear evenly the weight of the steeples which soared to a height of over 200 feet. To cut costs, the church wardens decided to omit the two inner walls, substituting a single timber post to support the inner corner. When the two towers eventually settled and leaned towards each other, Baillairgé's professional method stood him in good stead, for he was able to exonerate himself from accusations of poor design by referring to his original plans and specifications.[8] Recalling this incident, Baillairgé articulated his views on the architect's job: "Design the thing as it should be, and so specify the work; and let the paper writing there remain, as well the plans and sections, to show and prove that you proposed what you considered right and essential; and then leave it to the proprietor, if so he should elect, to cut and curtail as he may please."[9]

Another aspect of the architect's role was the estimation and measurement of quantities of material. In the Laval University project the architect's estimates of quantities were important, for workmen submitted their tenders on the basis of these figures. The calculations demonstrated Baillairgé's interest and ability in mathematics, pointing to his future involvement in this discipline. For instance, the quantities of cut stone for the dormitory were estimated at 6233 linear feet of dressed cut stone and 1484 linear feet of rougher stone for the side and rear elevations.[10] But even at this time Baillairgé understood the pitfalls of such estimates. When he calculated the weight of iron fire doors, based on Templeton's tables for weight per square foot of iron, he added that in iron work the actual product often exceeded the calculations because the craftsmen, being paid by weight, were interested in making the product as thick as possible. He noted that such behaviour was difficult to prevent.[11]

The discrepancy between an architect's *estimate* of quantities before the work was performed and *measurement* of quantities of actual work done was a frequent bone of contention between architect and craftsman. At issue, of course, were payments for "extras" versus the architect's responsibility to guarantee the cost estimates to his client. The debate was more intense when a project was funded from public monies, as Baillairgé was to discover so painfully in Ottawa. During construction of the university buildings, he dealt with one such dispute over the plasterwork. Thomas Murphy, the master plasterer who would later be a key player in orchestrating Baillairgé's dismissal in Ottawa, challenged his measurement of the plasterwork at Laval University and demanded extra payment. Interpreting the council's hesitation as a vote of non-confidence, Baillairgé resolved the issue by calling for outside architects as arbiters.[12]

As supervising architect, Baillairgé also had to coordinate the craftsmen and control the quality of their production. In those pre-telephone days, he appears to have spent many hours visiting the workshops of Pye, Whitty, Murphy, Peebles & Andrews, and others to ensure that the work met his standard and was proceeding on schedule.[13] Having stipulated in the building specifications that the architect reserved the right to reject any materials of unacceptable quality, Baillairgé apparently exercised this right in the case of the cut stone, causing a delay in the construction of the residence.[14] This may explain a curious newspaper notice in 1856 in which Pierre Châteauvert, the master mason responsible for the façade of this building, offered for sale "a large quantity of CUT STONES from Deschambault."[15]

Baillairgé, then, saw his role as the controller of all aspects of a project: preparation of plans, specifications, and estimates, measurement of works, liaison between client and craftsmen, coordination of schedules, and quality control of materials and workmanship. By playing this role, he was an unwitting participant in the destruction of the era of traditional craftsmanship. During the French regime and up to the middle of the nineteenth century in Quebec, specialized artisans such as master masons, master joiners, master plasterers, and master painters had been responsible for the product in their area of expertise. The architect, when there was one, drew up general plans and elevations but left the detailed execution to the craftsman, often enough himself. Thomas Baillairgé, for instance, worked simultaneously as architect, woodcarver, and painter. What is new in Charles Baillairgé's approach is that he did not physically execute his plans himself;

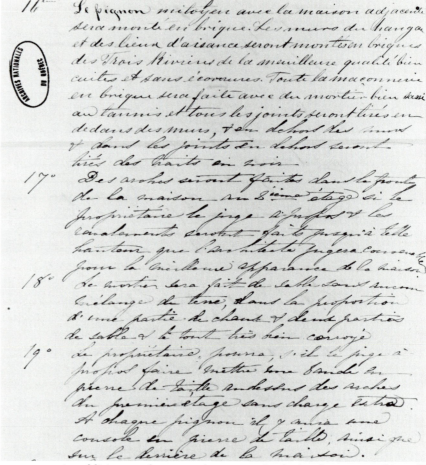

Fig. 11. In these detailed specifications for work on an 1850 town house in Quebec, an apprentice has drafted the routine sections and Baillairgé has described his proposed treatment of the façade arcades. ANQ, gr. Joseph Petitclerc, no. 5612, marché, François-Xavier Méthot–Isaac Dorion, Quebec, 27 Feb. 1850

moreover, in addition to the general concept, he insisted on controlling all aspects of design and construction. This encroachment on the creative role of artisans, added to the influx of factory-produced components as the industrial revolution advanced, hastened the demise of the specialized artisan, not only in Quebec but throughout the industrialized world.[16]

The volume of work that Baillairgé undertook during these years in private practice meant that he could not do it all himself. Like Thomas and François before him, Charles formally accepted apprentices who worked in his office.[17] While occupied with the on-going supervision of the Beauport church, the Hospice de la Charité, the Music Hall, and about ten houses, he had at least five apprentices in training, some in architecture, some in surveying.[18] The apprentice system in the 1850s worked much as it had a generation earlier in Thomas Baillairgé's time. When a prospective apprentice reached his late teens, his father made a formal contract with an architect or surveyor, usually signed in the presence of a notary. The document was called a *brevet*, *brevet de cléricature* or indenture. It was agreed that, in return for instruction and practical training in the profession, the apprentice was bound for a period – three years for surveying, four for architecture – to obey his master in all respects, to protect scrupulously the business secrets of the office, to work the hours assigned to him, never absenting himself from the office without permission from his master, and to carry out his duties in a faithful and honest way "as a student should do, in order to merit the esteem and favour of his master."[19] As part of their training, they carried out routine tasks, such as the preparation of specifications and the copying of architectural plans for the notarial contracts. Baillairgé only intervened when unusual or complicated features were involved. A clear example is found in the specifications for the Méthot house (fig. 11). The handwriting changes abruptly where an apprentice obviously left a space for Baillairgé to draft the clauses concerning the arcading of the façade. The surviving drawings for the Trudelle house show the same pattern. The general plans are prepared by an apprentice but the detailed drawings for attaching tin to the roof are in Baillairgé's hand. The apprentice looked after his own food and lodging. The master received on the average approximately £25 a year for each apprentice. Baillairgé began to accept students as early as 1849 and continued to do so well into the 1870s.[20]

Baillairgé also undertook other professional activities. Together with a former apprentice, he formed the firm of Baillairgé & Fortin, surveyors, and undertook many surveying jobs.[21] By his own account, he was considered the best theoretician and practitioner of surveying in Quebec. It is typical of his intellectual curiosity and love of hard work that he studied even those aspects of the discipline that were not required by law: "I have taken care to learn all that one usually neglects. Not only am I capable of carrying out the usual tasks of the surveyor such as the subdivision or measurement of a piece of land; but I also can execute the most complex and difficult geodesic operations, such as the surveys required for a geographic map, where one must take into consideration the curve of the globe's surface."[22]

Given Baillairgé's study of civil engineering, one should not be surprised to find him active in the pioneer era of railway construction. He began in 1852 by developing a scheme for building a railway bridge between Quebec and Levis, the narrowest and deepest part of the Saint Lawrence River, in order to provide an uninterrupted link between the Halifax/Quebec intercolonial line on the south shore and the Quebec/Montreal line on the north shore. His plan, involving construction of massive stone piers in the river, a feat that most experts claimed could not succeed, was published in the *New York Mechanic's Magazine*. Although the letter has not been found, Baillairgé reported that the magazine editor informed him that it was "an article of much merit, showing much brilliance and genius on my part."[23] Baillairgé never gave up this idea, and continued to promote it for the next fifty years by producing among other things a thirty-foot long watercolour elevation that was displayed at City Hall, and, near the end of his life, by preparing a broadsheet of his proposal for the Paris exhibition of 1900.[24] Baillairgé could not hide his disappointment when the decision was finally taken at the end of the century to build the first Quebec bridge at Sainte-Foy.[25]

Baillairgé may have been in New York City in the spring of 1853 to attend the Industrial World's Fair, which opened at the end of May. Enticed by the active recruiting campaign of James Whitman, who visited Quebec at least twice in 1852 to round up participants, and the lure of the new crystal palace built for the occasion, Baillairgé entered a plan of his invention for "Baillairgé's marine revolving steam express," a type of steam boat propelled by a large wheel which gathered velocity by the constant displacement of its centre of gravity. He wrote years later that his work was ignored because there was a similar proposal submitted by an American clergyman, so that Baillairgé's invention "attracted the less attention on account of its coming from such an end-of-the-world sort of place as Quebec."[26] Charles's participation explains the tantalizing comment in one of Thomas Baillairgé's letters to Madame Girouard in April 1853: "I want to visit the New York exhibition. If this comes to pass, I will visit you on my return passage."[27]

It was during this period that Baillairgé began his lifelong campaign to vulgarize technical knowledge in order to make it accessible to the general public. His first book – or rather pamphlet, being twenty-three pages in length – was about his own invention, a central heating system that he had the tinsmith Zéphirin Chartré install in some of his houses. In *Description et plan d'un nouveau calorifèr [sic] à air chaud, sur le système tubulaire, pour chauffer less édifices privés et publics* (1853), Baillairgé explained in layman's terms how and why his system would be more efficient than other hot air furnaces. In a review of the booklet, *Le Journal de Québec* invited the public to see the system in operation at "the beautiful cut stone residence that Mr. C. Têtu has built on the Cape." The system's merits were itemized as "economy of combustion, an even, gentle heat and perfect ventilation."[28] The book clearly showed Baillairgé's awareness of current experiments and inventions. In his pursuit of the most up-to-date technology, he even went so far as to visit several private houses in New York City in order to inspect their central heating systems.[29]

Baillairgé also discovered that he had a talent for giving public lectures, a useful outlet for the diffusion and discussion of technical subjects. Since 1848 he had received invitations to speak before two of the important sponsoring groups at that time, the *Institut canadien* and the *Association de la chambre de lecture de Saint-Roch*, the latter organization dedicated to the education of the working classes. In 1853 he delivered a series of lectures at Saint-Roch on steam and steam engines, balloons and aerial navigation, and railways.[30] According to a newspaper account, Baillairgé not only knew his subject matter thoroughly, but he was a "a first-rate talent as a *speaker*" because he had a good voice, clear diction, and a distinct and assured delivery.[31] This, incidentally, is the earliest public description of Baillairgé's personality and physical characteristics. So interesting did one reporter find these lectures that he suggested to the directors of the *Institut canadien* that they sponsor a repeat performance of these "scientific and instructive evenings" at their more central location.[32]

Thus, from the beginning of his career, Charles Baillairgé advanced the practice of architecture in his native city by discarding the traditional "artisan-architect" role in favour of the professional architect. As a member of the professional middle class, rather than the working class of the artisans, Baillairgé extended his activities to include the creation of mechanical inventions and the dissemination of technical knowledge through publications and lectures. In the context of Quebec City, he was in the vanguard of professional practice and joined a small and exclusive group of recently arrived British architects.

3 First Commissions: Experiments in Neoclassicism and the Gothic Revival

IN 1847 CHARLES BAILLAIRGÉ BEGAN his own practice with the help of Thomas Baillairgé, the Roman Catholic clergy, and French-Canadian merchants. The buildings from this initial period – mainly religious structures, large retail stores, and private residences – reveal Charles's debt to the neoclassical training of Thomas Baillairgé. But they also demonstrate Charles's experimental approach to architectural design through the use of the Gothic Revival style for the Beauport church and the chapel of the Soeurs de la Charité, and the daring scale and spatial organization of dry goods stores for the DeBlois heirs and the merchant Louis Bilodeau. By the end of this early phase, with over £175,000 of building under his supervision, Charles Baillairgé had established himself as a responsible and innovative architect capable of designing unconventional buildings.[1]

Baillairgé was fortunate to be starting his practice on the threshold of an economic boom arising from Quebec's location as the trans-shipping point for squared timber from the Ottawa region, the expansion of naval construction in the shipyards around Quebec, the growth of the railways, and the import/export trade. Admittedly there was not much building activity in Quebec City in the early 1840s, but there was a slight upsurge in 1848, only to be dampened by the cholera epidemic of 1849.[2] But the signs augured well for future prosperity. Statistics reveal that exportation from Britain to the port of Quebec reached a record volume in 1854 and naval construction peaked in the middle of the decade, confirming the observation of Narcisse Rosa, a contemporary participant in Quebec shipbuilding, that the 1850s represented the golden age for Quebec and Levis.[3] With this prosperity came the phenomenon of a rejuvenated French-Canadian mercantile class, ready to engage the services of compatriot architects for its handsome stores and residences. But before the economic boom really took hold, Charles Baillairgé's major client was the Roman Catholic religious establishment.

EGLISE SAINT-JEAN-BAPTISTE

Through Thomas Baillairgé's influence, Charles obtained his first important commission, the Saint-Jean-Baptiste church, at the age of nineteen or twenty. If the date in Charles Baillairgé's handwriting on a surviving drawing for the Saint-Jean-Baptiste church can be trusted, he may have been working on proposals for this parish church as early as May 1846, although 1847 seems the more probable date.[4] It is surprising that such a young man would be entrusted to design and supervise construction of this important building, which measured 180 feet by 80 feet and was to seat 2000 people. It is for this reason, as Luc Noppen has pointed out, that early attributions – including his own – credited Thomas Baillairgé with the church until documentary research proved beyond a doubt that Charles was the architect.[5] For many years Thomas Baillairgé had been in fact if not in title the diocesan architect. With Charles's assumption of the commission for the Saint-Jean-Baptiste church, the family ritual of handing over the reins of power was being played out. The smooth transition of authority from older to younger generation was being effected, just as Thomas had taken over from his father

FIG. 12. Perched on a height of land over-looking the valley of the Saint Charles River, Baillairgé's 1847 parish church of Saint-Jean-Baptiste towers above the neighbouring houses. The west façade is visible in this c. 1860 photograph by Samuel McLaughlin. NA, PA-118083

FIG. 13. In this sketch of the Saint-Jean-Baptiste church by J.F. Peachy, the tight grid of horizontal and vertical elements and minimal ornamentation are evident. Private collection

François, and François from his father Jean before him. Charles continued to work out of Thomas's workshop on the rue Saint-François. The advantages of this paternal benediction are clear; through the contacts of the experienced master, the first difficult commissions could be secured. In the case of the Saint-Jean-Baptiste church, the clients were Thomas's frequent patrons, the church wardens of Notre-Dame de Québec.

Charles Baillairgé made two proposals for the Saint-Jean-Baptiste church, one to be built entirely of cut stone, the other to be of rough masonry except for the façade. The church wardens chose the simpler version.[6] Since the church was destroyed by fire in 1881, analysis is based on incomplete

sources, including photographs and sketches of the exterior and a set of plans for the more elaborate proposal which was not built (figs. 12–14). No visual record has survived of the interior as built. To assess the importance of this project in Charles Baillairgé's work, it is useful to examine the church as built as well as the drawings of the elaborate proposal, which reflected his intentions in terms of design.

In some ways, the Saint-Jean-Baptiste church clearly issued from Thomas Baillairgé's workshop. It belonged to Thomas's twin-towered church type documented by Luc Noppen, of which Notre-Dame de Québec, the Saint-Roch church, and the Sainte-Geneviève church at Pierrefonds were the most complete expression. This type evolved under Thomas Baillairgé's and Jérôme Demers's rigorous logic until the exterior design reflected the interior disposition of space: the pedimented frontispiece corresponded to the nave, the twin towers indicated the existence of side aisles, and the rows of windows hinted at ground and gallery levels. In Thomas's churches, one observes lingering irregularity in the alignment of doors and windows, as well as vestiges of sculptural ornamentation and curved forms.

Charles's design for Saint-Jean-Baptiste church differed from this prototype in important respects. The young architect responded to the functional aspect of neoclassical theory then gaining popularity but first articulated one hundred years earlier by the French apologist, Jesuit priest M.-A. Laugier. In his book *Essai sur l'architecture*, published in Paris in 1753, Laugier called for a return to logical and rational architecture, which he saw as being strictly functional. Using as his frontispiece for the second edition of 1755 the image of the primitive hut with its simple structure, Laugier sought to reduce design to an honest statement of supporting and supported elements. He urged architects to eschew curves and arches which were viewed as illogical and to adopt instead horizontal and vertical members – illustrated by

FIG. 14. As seen from the Saint-Roch ward, with Baillairgé's steeples for the parish church in the foreground, the Saint-Jean-Baptiste church reveals itself as a plain building with a simple rectangular plan. ANQ, photothèque, N-475-23

FIG. 15. Charles Baillairgé's more elaborate proposal for the Saint-Jean-Baptiste church, which was not accepted. AVQ, fonds Charles Baillairgé, no. 4–7

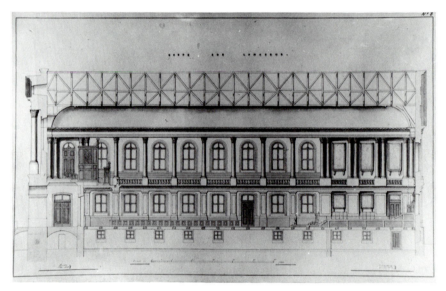

FIG. 16. This longitudinal cross-section for the more elaborate proposal for the church of Saint-Jean-Baptiste reveals Charles Baillairgé's rigorous approach to composition. AVQ, fonds Charles Baillairgé, no. 4–10

the column, entablature, and frontispiece of the primitive hut – in pursuit of perfect beauty.[7] Baillairgé's exposure to these theories probably came from such authors as Durand and Rondelet, both proponents of French structural rationalism, and both represented in his architectural library.[8]

When the Saint-Jean-Baptiste church is considered in the context of rationalist theories of neoclassicism, the avant-garde aspect is more apparent. Charles has pushed the logic of Thomas Baillairgé and Demers even farther. Doors and windows are lined up in perfect rows, like soldiers on parade. The façade has become a tight grid of horizontal and vertical projections. Even the triangular outline of the pediment is blurred by a parapet which leaves an overall impression of horizontality. The façade of the elaborate proposal (figs. 15–16), which featured a stronger central projection with free-standing columns on the upper level, would have placed greater emphasis on the grid effect though giving it at the same time more three-dimensionality. In this proposal, the side elevation created an even more insistent grid through the superimposed pilasters, the string course, and cornice.

The interior displayed the same rigour and followed Laugier's precepts. The supporting members of the galleries, usually a series of arches or arcading in Thomas's church interiors, were transformed into a double-order solution with piers which logically supported the horizontal entablature on which the Corinthian columns were placed, directly above the piers. Laugier had criticized the use of arcades in Parisian church interiors and recommended the use of superimposed orders crowned by a curved vault, a solution that he considered logical.[9] The details on Baillairgé's drawing appear to have been executed more or less as planned, if James Macpherson Lemoine's description is accurate: "The ceiling is well finished, the nave divided from the aisles by fine Corinthian columns and all the interior neat and elegant."[10]

That the church wardens did not build the church exactly as proposed was a disappointment to the architect who was concerned for his reputation. The ornamentation was eliminated and the height of the vault was scaled down in an effort to reduce costs. The soaring effect sought by the architect was ruined. The general public found the design wanting, *Le Journal de Québec* thought the vault crushed the observer, and Lemoine called it "a large but not very elegant temple" and regretted that it had been erected "unfortunately not according to the design of the architect, which accounts for some discrepancy in its proportions."[11] Had the original proposal been accepted, perhaps a monumental effect would have been achieved.

As his first major commission produced in Thomas Baillairgé's workshop, presumably under the master's watchful eye, Saint-Jean-Baptiste church revealed Baillairgé as an innovator and experimenter. The stripped-down version that was built can hardly be considered an aesthetic success, though academically sound. What the Saint-Jean-Baptiste church illustrated was Charles Baillairgé's ability to consult disparate sources – in this case Thomas's twin-towered church tradition and rationalist theories of neoclassicism – and synthesize them into an original conception. Although Charles Baillairgé predictably chose Thomas Baillairgé's idiom for his first major commission, he affirmed his independent spirit and revealed his own experimental approach by synthesizing this tradition with European rationalist theories.

EGLISE DE BEAUPORT

In 1849, in the midst of the cholera epidemic, Charles Baillairgé secured a second important contract from the Roman Catholic establishment, this time the parish church at Beauport (figs. 17–18). This commission illustrated the power of his family connections, for Thomas Baillairgé had designed a new façade for these parishioners in 1831.[12] Charles again adopted Thomas's twin-tower formula, but there the resemblance with his master's work ended, for the decorative vocabulary of the Beauport church was Gothic.

To appreciate how radical this choice was in the context of conservative Quebec City, one would do well to recall the controversy over the style for Notre-Dame de Montréal in 1824. Without recounting all the events which have been explained elsewhere,[13] Thomas Baillairgé's statement to the Montreal parish is worth examining: "Having only studied Greek and Roman architecture, believing this to be sufficient for this country, I have only a superficial knowledge of the gothic style."[14] In this rejection of the Gothic Revival style, he was following the edicts of Demers and Blondel who had both condemned it as being heavy and in poor taste.[15] Thomas Baillairgé,

FIG. 17. As this magazine illustration shows, Charles Baillairgé's twin-tower Beauport church fell within the conventions of Quebec church architecture at the time, though the use of the Gothic Revival repertoire was unusual. George Monro Grant, *Picturesque Canada*, vol. 1 (Toronto: Belden Bros. 1882), 55

faithful to his classical training, never did work in the Gothic idiom throughout his long career. What, then, led Charles to flout tradition and choose Gothic for the Beauport church? It may have been the result of his reading, for several books in his library contained material on the Gothic style, including authors David Henry Arnot, Raphael and J. Arthur Brandon, James Fergusson, Joseph Gwilt, Thomas Hope, John Henry Parker, Augustus C. Pugin, and E.J. Willson. He may also have been influenced by the Wesleyan church being built at that time in Quebec, the city's first Gothic Revival church, designed by architect Edward Staveley.[16] But the key element is Baillairgé's character. He liked to experiment and hated to repeat himself. An inveterate innovator, Baillairgé gave proof of his disdain for dull repetition when he complained some years later to Monseigneur Baillargeon about the traditional approach to rural church design: "As for our country churches, it is the parishes' business, if they want to perpetuate all over the province the same boring plan that one finds everywhere."[17]

The church at Beauport was emphatically not like those of other parishes. Yet, in spite of his attempt to be different, the design was still under the influence of the classical tradition. The Gothic features – pointed windows, buttresses, and turrets – appeared as adornments applied to a symmetrical and classically proportioned building. This superficial interpretation of the Gothic idiom is exactly like Staveley's Wesleyan church.[18] Neither architect had mastered the rational integration of Gothic forms advocated by the Ecclesiologists in the early nineteenth century in England. Moreover, the classical proportion of one to two (width of tower to width of portal) used at Beauport had been a key element of Thomas Baillairgé's twin tower designs. Charles acknowledged his debt in his comments on the proposed rebuilding of the Beauport church following the 1890 fire:

The old Beauport church ... is a case in point, its towers ... bore to the total width of frontage the due proportion and hence more pleasing to the eye; but the effect will now be destroyed in the restored structure by ... increasing the width between the

FIG. 18. Baillairgé's 1850 church at Beauport was severely damaged by fire in 1890. The vestiges that survived at the time of this photograph reveal a superficial application of Gothic details such as buttresses and pointed windows to a symmetrical and classically proportioned façade. ANQ, photothèque, N-376-133

towers without at the same time adding to their width and thus returning to the hybrid type of our Canadian church fronts with towers or imitation ones only one-quarter, one-fifth or less of the breadth of portal, instead of the majestic strength and beauty of the prototypes of ages.[19]

As this statement shows, despite his experimentation Baillairgé always returned to his spiritual base, neoclassicism.

HOSPICE DES SOEURS DE LA CHARITÉ

Baillairgé's third major commission from the Roman Catholic clergy was the Hospice des Soeurs de la Charité. This project came through the archbishop, Monseigneur Turgeon, who arranged to bring to Quebec some of the Grey Nuns from the mother house in Montreal to provide care for orphans, the elderly, and the sick, and to give free instruction to poor children.[20] Thomas Baillairgé had, as usual, already worked on the project, having prepared plans for the 1845 orphanage (fig. 19).[21] Charles's first involvement was in 1849 in his capacity of surveyor, for he drew up a site plan for the future institution. The same year, Monseigneur Turgeon sent him to Montreal to study the mother house, the Hôpital-Général, which was to serve as a model for the Quebec building.

When the property, bounded by four streets, Saint-Olivier, des Glacis, Richelieu, and Saint-Eustache, was assembled in 1850, Charles Baillairgé drew up the final plans. Robert Caron, in his history of the asylum, has shown that the present building is the result of several reconstructions after major fires, making it difficult to read Baillairgé's original intentions. Caron has established that the 1850 plans in the municipal archives, though not the actual ones used in construction, are close enough to the final version to provide a basis for analysis of Baillairgé's conception (figs. 20–23).[22]

The asylum for the Soeurs de la Charité provided a considerable challenge for the architect. It required not simply a chapel and living quarters for the nuns, but classrooms, hospital facilities, dormitories for each different group, and so forth. Moreover, the site was not an easy one, dropping off as it did towards the valley of the Saint Charles River. Some idea of the scale of the project may be grasped from the fact that after five years of construction the building had not yet been completed and the estimated final cost was £21,012, or approximately $84,048 (in 1854 dollars).[23]

In his analysis, Caron quite properly emphasizes the curious mingling of two architectural traditions, neoclassicism for the Saint-Olivier façade and Gothic Revival for the chapel on Richelieu. Baillairgé's inspiration for such a combination was certainly not the Hôpital-Général in Montreal, although it is feasible that the mother house provided the model for the open E-type plan with the chapel integrated into the centre of the complex. Caron considers that this juxtaposition of two seemingly incompatible modes is an example of eclecticism which ranks Charles Baillairgé with the so-called Victorian architects. Without denying the novelty of Baillairgé's choice, one should perhaps consider the parameters of the project. The design for the asylum was in large measure dictated by the 1845 orphanage by Thomas Baillairgé, which was situated at the corner of Saint-Olivier and des Glacis in such a way that it would automatically become one wing of the larger structure. It had, moreover, been stipulated that this almost new orphanage was to be incorporated into the complex. With its plain masonry walls and elliptically arched doorway, it controlled the character of the

FIG. 19. Thomas Baillairgé designed this orphanage for the Soeurs de la Charité in 1845. As sketched by one of the sisters, it was a plain stone building with French casement windows and an elliptical fanlight over the door. ASC, photo courtesy of Les services audio-visuels Laval

FIG. 20. When Charles Baillairgé designed
the façade for the asylum of the Soeurs de
la Charité in 1850, he had to incorporate
Thomas Baillairgé's recent orphanage into
the overall scheme. AVQ, fonds Charles
Baillairgé, no. 3–3

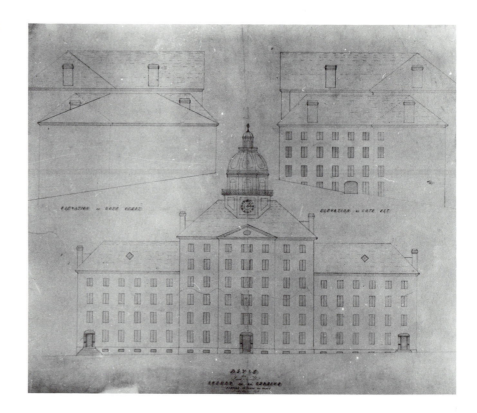

FIG. 21. Charles Baillairgé's 1850 design for
the chapel for the Soeurs de la Charité, situated on a higher parcel of land adjoining
the asylum, adopted the Gothic Revival
idiom, thereby placing a Gothic steeple
beside a Roman dome. AVQ, fonds Charles
Baillairgé, no. 3–1

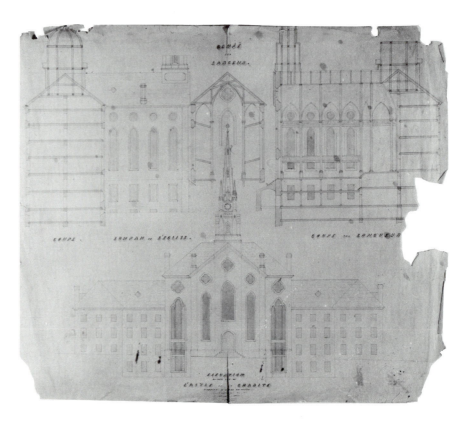

entire façade, a plain symmetrical composition with a central projecting frontispiece and pediment. As for the Gothic idiom for the chapel, it will be remembered that the Beauport church brought to light Baillairgé's boredom with traditional church designs. When he was designing the asylum for the Soeurs de la Charité, he was still involved in the supervision of the Beauport church. It would seem natural for him to choose Gothic Revival for this chapel as well.

The juxtaposition of the two styles is, nonetheless, odd. It appears to be Baillairgé's own invention, for no model has been found to explain it. Even he seems to have had second thoughts about the design. In a letter in 1853 addressed to the archbishop, who was clearly appalled at the prospect of placing a Gothic steeple beside a Roman dome, Baillairgé admitted to some extent his failure: "I sincerely believe that there is no defect in the placement of a steeple beside a dome, although no examples of this exist elsewhere. There could be more appropriate combinations than that of a gothic chapel beside a building which is not gothic, but I believe that it would be worse to have a church without a steeple than to have a steeple side by side with a dome."[24]

In terms of sheer building, the asylum for the Soeurs de la Charité provided a clear demonstration of Baillairgé's competence at interior spatial organization and his technical knowledge of construction. The central section of the building on Saint-Olivier was, after all, six storeys high, not counting the dome, making it the tallest in Quebec at that time. This height was achieved using traditional materials and methods for solid masonry walls, demonstrating his grasp of civil engineering and the calculation of weights, pressures, and forces. In the chapel he combined this technical skill with spatial innovation to create the first triple-balcony church interior in the province.[25] This design responded to the functional requirements of the institution, for persons inhabiting each floor of the asylum, many of them sick or elderly, needed to gain access to the chapel at their own level without having to negotiate stairs. An unsigned newspaper article in 1856 described the completed interior and praised the "genius" of the architect for his "audacious yet gracious" handling of space. Referring to the chapel, the writer admired: "The ingenious idea of superimposed balconies on either side of the sanctuary. With their elegant columns, gracious ornaments and this bright obscurity in which they appear, as in an infinite distance, the artist has succeeded in creating a character of originality and in capturing within this small jewel of a church the sense of the immensity of a cathedral."[26]

Baillairgé's difficulties with the church wardens over the stripping down of his proposal for Saint-Jean-Baptiste church probably seemed minor in comparison to his wrangling with the archbishop, Monseigneur Turgeon, and with Monseigneur Baillargeon over the implementation of his design for the asylum. The problem of the client versus the architect was to plague Baillairgé – as well as most architects then and now – throughout his career. His fantastic and grandiose conceptions all too often faltered in the face of economic reality. First it was the dome, then the steeple that the archbishop tried to suppress for lack of funds. Conscious that the outcome could seriously affect his reputation as an architect, Baillairgé entreated him to build the dome as planned: "The building's design is such that it absolutely requires a dome to complete it. I have a reputation to protect, Monseigneur. It has already suffered considerably, when I had to conform to the bizarre

THE GREY SISTERS ASYLUM.

FIG. 22. This 1858 sketch from Alfred Hamel's *Topographical and Pictorial Map of the City of Quebec*, shows the chapel of the Soeurs de la Charité as rebuilt after the 1854 fire. NA, NMC-C-118207

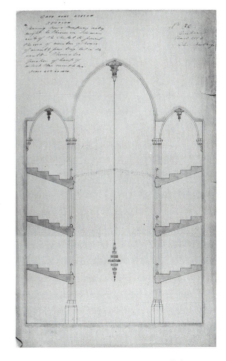

FIG. 23. In this 1854 cross-section of the sanctuary, the architect proposes to adapt the interior for an emergency session of parliament by adding a false ceiling to contain the orators' voices. AVQ, fonds Charles Baillairgé, no. 3–36

ideas of the wardens responsible for the construction of the church in the suburbs [Saint-Jean-Baptiste church]. It will certainly be subjected to further assault if your asylum is absolutely hideous to look at (as it will no doubt be) if it is not crowned by a suitable dome."[27] Baillairgé won his point and the dome was built, but his triumph was short-lived. The dome was eliminated in the reconstruction after the 1854 fire.

These three important commissions for the Roman Catholic church revealed Baillairgé's natural dependence on the neoclassical training he had received from Thomas Baillairgé. Yet the strict interpretation of neoclassical theories at the Saint-Jean-Baptiste church and the daring introduction of the Gothic Revival style for the parish church at Beauport and the chapel of the Soeurs de la Charité set him apart from his more conservative contemporaries and emphasized his experimental approach to architectural design. It is hardly surprising that this innovative attitude influenced Baillairgé's other buildings from this period.

EMPORIA

Although the Roman Catholic clergy were Baillairgé's first sponsors, French-Canadian merchant soon followed suit, perhaps on the strength of his work at the Saint-Jean-Baptiste church. Needing new retail stores and warehouses, these merchants, more than the clergy, provided the young architect with an opportunity to create a new class of building not seen until then in Quebec City.

The revitalization of the commercial centre began coincidentally at almost the same time as Baillairgé's practice. The two suburbs of Saint-Roch and Saint-Jean had been consumed by fire in 1845 and immediately rebuilt in a substantial manner, leading one journalist to remark in 1850 that the suburbs were then better built than the walled city.[28] At about the same time, the main commercial streets of the Upper Town began to show signs of renewal. The first of these tall cut-stone buildings appeared at the corner of rue Saint-Jean and cote du Palais in 1847, designed by architect Michel Patry.[29] This was a three-storey building of dressed stone with large shop windows set between pilasters. On a grander scale were the stores of merchants Henderson and Scott, standing side by side on the rue Buade, probably both designed in 1849 by Edward Staveley (fig. 24). These buildings, which have survived in an altered state, were remarkable for their four-storey height and vast interior spaces.[30]

Charles Baillairgé participated in this renewal as early as 1847 with the Drolet building, 1039–45, rue Saint-Jean, an unexceptional building similar to those of other local architects. Its design was based on an oversimplification of the neoclassical grid, composed of string courses and vertical strip pilasters, reminiscent of the stiff approach that Baillairgé had adopted for the Saint-Jean-Baptiste church of the same date. Like all beginners, he got his share of renovations, rear wings, and small shops, but he was also fortunate in these early years to attract influential clients with major works in mind – men such as the merchant Abraham Hamel (one of the wardens for Saint-Jean-Baptiste church and a client for whom Baillairgé had already designed a house), Dr Pierre Baillargeon, a dentist, the heirs De Blois (one of whom was René-Edouard Caron, his uncle Louis-de-Gonzague Baillairgé's law partner), merchant François DeFoy, and Louis Bilodeau, the most extravagant of them all. The satisfaction of these clients is demonstrated by the fact that they each

subsequently engaged Baillairgé for other projects. The opportunity provided by their early sponsorship allowed Baillairgé to establish himself as a daring and innovative architect, a designer of imposing and magnificent buildings.

His work for Hamel & Frère and Dr Baillargeon revealed him as a thorough and meticulous man. The Hamel & Frère store has been demolished and visual evidence is scanty. Formerly situated at the upper end of rue Sous-le-Fort near the Champlain stairs, the building is lost in street views by nineteenth-century photographers. By 1873 three additional storeys had been built, but the woodcut from the newspaper announcement of this date is still the best surviving image (fig. 25). The original shop front with entablature, pilasters, and large windows is visible in the woodcut. Dr Baillargeon's building, which was part office and part shop, has survived, although the cut-stone pilasters and entablature of the shop fronts, described in detail in the specifications, have disappeared and the gable roof has been transformed (fig. 26).

It is Baillairgé's specifications that reveal the determination of the architect to erect solid and graceful buildings. A close look at them indicates not only the particular quality of these two buildings, but offers a general

FIG. 24. Heralding the renewal of the Upper Town, the pair of tall cut-stone stores to the right on Buade Street were built for Henderson and Scott in 1849, probably from designs by architect Edward Staveley. This nineteenth-century photograph shows the impact of the Baillairgé family on the city, with Thomas's cupola atop the Episcopal Palace (left) and his façade for Notre-Dame de Québec, as well as Charles's iron fence in front of the cathedral. Université de Montréal, fonds Baby

FIG. 25. The Hamel & Frère building on the rue Sous-le-Fort in 1850, initially three storeys high. *Le Courrier du Canada*, 23 May 1873, 3

FIG. 26. This pair of Upper Town stores with offices and living quarters above were designed by Baillairgé in 1847 and 1850 for Dr Baillargeon (on the left) and Mr Drolet, though the shop fronts have only partially survived. CIHB

notion of his working method. As with most important jobs, he wrote the specifications himself. Details are very explicit. For example, the directives for both façades include the use of Deschambault cut stone, to be finished in fine bush-hammered work, without cracks, bad veins, or other defects. This phrase "sans une seule écornure, mauvaise veine ou autre défaut" is a hallmark of Baillairgé's specifications, repeated again and again for important buildings. Precise dimensions for individual pieces of stone guarantee the strength and aesthetic quality of the building: pilasters to be single blocks of stone fifteen inches wide by two feet deep; capitals and bases to be made from single blocks; cornices of the shop-front entablatures to be composed of pieces of stone five or six feet long. These blocks of stone are still visible on the Baillargeon façade.

Perhaps because Dr Baillargeon intended to live in half of his building, the living quarters in that part were more elegantly finished. Baillairgé's control of all aspects of the project is well illustrated in his instructions for the decorative plasterwork, to be "au goût de l'architecte." He called for cornices of varying widths (twenty-six inches, twenty-two inches, etc.) and rosettes two and three feet in diameter for the shop and drawing rooms. His personal touch is felt in the small flowers to be attached every fifteen to eighteen inches onto the cornice moulding of the drawing rooms. With his characteristic attention to detail, he created special models for the flowers and even gave instructions to the plasterers on how to prepare the plaster paste for the moulds.

The other stores of this group were located in the fashionable commercial centre of the Upper Town. The De Blois heirs obviously wanted an outstanding building for their tenant, dry goods merchant Henry Benjamin, and were ready to pay for it. Baillairgé met the challenge by designing a building that was unusually tall for Quebec – four storeys, just like Staveley's pair of stores on the rue Buade – with a gentle roof slope and no dormer windows, and a discreet façade of smooth-dressed Deschambault stone (fig. 27). The shop front repeated the neoclassical format used by Baillairgé at Hamel & Frère, with stone pilasters and entablature and large shop windows. The scaling down of windows on the upper level, a vestige of Palladianism, reflected the function of the building, in that the first two levels served as public shops and the upper storeys were reserved for lodgings.

The interior space was vast, twenty-six feet across by ninety feet in depth, and a height of fifteen feet, with Doric columns punctuating the space while bearing the weight of the upper storeys. At the far end a formal staircase rose and branched to either side, inviting the customer to mount to the second floor. Finishing touches included plaster ceiling rosettes and 125 drawers. In a somewhat patriotic newspaper article in the spring of 1850, this store was considered superior to Patry's and Staveley's work and the best in Quebec, Montreal, or the United States. The author summed up his impressions by writing: "All the decoration is in perfect harmony with the architecture of the ensemble which makes it incontestably the most beautiful shop that we have ever seen, whether in Montreal or the United States. When the gas lamps light up this vast room and these gigantic windows, it will be a magnificent sight, capable of attracting customers and obliging them to enter. Mr. Benjamin cannot ask for more."[31] All that remains today of Benjamin's store is the exterior shell, much altered by the removal of a storey and the infilling of windows.

FIG. 27. The De Blois building on rue de la Fabrique, seen in this 1895 photograph at the time of the construction of the City Hall, was one of Baillairgé's best commercial buildings at mid-century. ANQ, photothèque, N-80-1-102

But the most grandiose of Baillairgé's early commercial projects was undoubtedly Louis Bilodeau's store (figs. 28–30). Visual evidence is not complete, for its situation on the street meant that nineteenth-century photographers caught it from a side angle, cutting off the upper storeys. Those early photographers who dared to climb the tower of Notre-Dame de Québec inadvertently recorded the store's roof and lantern. The woodcut of the premises that Bilodeau used on his letterhead and in newspaper advertisements is inaccurate because the artist has added a fifth column.[32] Documentary evidence is scant as well, since no building contracts have been located for this £5000 project.

Louis Bilodeau epitomized a new breed of French-Canadian entrepreneur whose energy and individual spirit of enterprise led him to operate on a grand scale. For the land alone he paid the princely sum of £3500.[33] Having made his arrangements with Baillairgé, he set off for Europe on a three-month buying spree to stock his new store. Something of the drama created in Quebec by his daring venture is recorded in a newspaper article in October 1850: "How many have said, as they watched the slow progress of the long stone columns crowned by a massive masonry wall: 'Mr. Bilodeau will never complete this store; it is a foolish undertaking, beyond his capacity.' And if bad weather momentarily stopped the workers, there were plenty of voices crying in unison: 'the work has ceased!'"[34]

Quebec City had never seen a store of this scale. It was admittedly only four storeys high, like the De Blois store and Staveley's stores for Henderson and Scott, but the Doric columns of the ground level were a staggering twenty-seven feet high, the equivalent of three storeys in ordinary buildings as the photograph showing the neighbouring store indicates. The total height was an impressive sixty-five feet. The roof slope, like the De Blois building, had a gentler pitch and no dormers, unlike most Quebec structures. Bilodeau's roof had an added feature which Baillairgé often used, a dome or lantern from which one had a clear view of the Saint Lawrence River. Unusual too was the iron balcony at the third-floor level of the façade. It was decorated with scroll motifs interwoven with maple leaves, signifying

FIG. 28. Baillairgé outdid himself in the 1849–50 Bilodeau store on the rue de la Fabrique. ANQ, photothèque, N-78-18-18

FIG. 29. Woodcut of Bilodeau's store. *Le Canadien*, 29 Sept. 1851, 3

the Canadian origins of the proprietor. But what most impressed contemporary observers were the gigantic shop windows, seven feet by six feet, illuminated by gas jets and protected by shutters of iron slats that rolled up on winches.

Inside, Baillairgé's skills at spatial organization and dramatic effects were apparent. The enormous interior, thirty-seven feet by ninety feet, rising to a height of thirty feet, was fitted with a floating mezzanine supported by two superimposed levels of Egyptian columns, similar except for the choice of order to the arrangement at the Saint-Jean-Baptiste church. This was the first commercial building in the city to open up the display area through the use of a mezzanine, an idea probably borrowed by Baillairgé from church designs. A regal staircase at the far end, a large ceiling lamp, and sixty-six gas jets completed the fittings, which must have given the impression of a glittering fairyland.[35] A plan from the municipal archives records the spatial arrangement at a conceptual stage. Unfortunately, no visual record has been found illustrating the interior. Bilodeau himself did not long enjoy the fruits of his energy and vision, for he died in 1855. The building was renovated for use by the *Institut canadien* before it was demolished in 1898 to widen the street.

With these large stores, Baillairgé had a chance to display his originality as an architect. In his work with Thomas Baillairgé, he had not encountered this type of project. He responded by adapting a neoclassical vocabulary to the requirements of the client, thus producing a series of

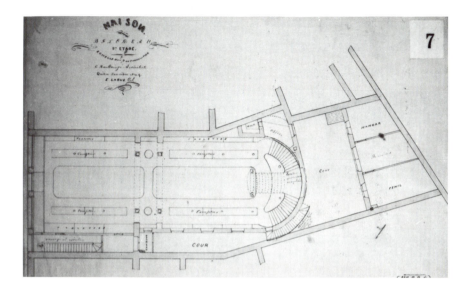

FIG. 30. Baillairgé's conceptual plan for the interior of the Bilodeau store shows the mezzanine and double staircase. AVQ, fonds Charles Baillairgé, no. 1–12

original and magnificent stores. His inspiration may have come from books in his own library, from George Browne's commercial blocks in Kingston which he had likely seen, or from Montreal buildings such as architect John Well's Bank of Montreal building (1846–8) on the Place d'Armes, with its monumental portico of Corinthian columns that Baillairgé so admired.[36] But the achievement was his own. From that moment, his reputation was established as a creative and innovative architect capable of producing sound and beautiful buildings.

TOWN HOUSES AND VILLAS

Designing private homes has never been a profitable part of an architect's practice. Clients are difficult, work is time consuming, and the architect's fee is low, being a percentage of the total cost. The average cost of a house built during these early years by Baillairgé is well below that of his religious or commercial projects. But housing provided a steady income – and a chance to build up a satisfied clientele – which a young architect could not afford to neglect.

The town houses produced by Baillairgé in these early years are plain well-built structures, remarkable for their careful disposition of space (figs. 31–8). They adopted the plan and characteristics of Quebec City row houses of British inspiration, erected in the 1820s and 1830s by architects from the United Kingdom such as George Browne, Henry Musgrave Blaiklock, and Frederick Hacker, and prolific builders such as John Phillips and Robert Jellard. They were usually three bays wide, with off-centre entrance and stair hall, and second-storey drawing room across the breadth of the house overlooking the street.[37] Substantial houses of two and three storeys, they were built to an imposing scale, with the lower floors ranging from twelve to fourteen feet in height. They were usually made of stone, with the notable exception of the Trudelle house which was also meant to be of stone, according to the contract, but ended up brick. None was of wood. Baillairgé's preferences for type of stone depended on the finish: Deschambault or Pointe-aux-Trembles stone for fine bush-hammered façades, Beauport or Château-Richer stone for less refined dressing. The most expensive houses, such as the Hamel and Douglas houses on avenue Sainte-Geneviève and the

FIG. 31. The Trudelle house, designed by Baillairgé in 1848, drew heavily on the Quebec City row houses that had been erected in the 1820s and 1830s by British architects. Among the characteristic features are the scaling of window heights, the recessed arcading beneath the belt or string course, and the second-storey drawing room. CIHB

FIG. 32. The row houses on rue Laporte that Baillairgé designed for Messrs Parent, Têtu, and Méthot in 1849 were meant to have rows of recessed arcades at both levels. CIHB

FIG. 33. The row of residences for the Hôtel-Dieu Sisters on rue Collins, while on a larger scale than most of Baillairgé's domestic buildings in 1849, still follows the British town house mode with off-centre entrances, recessed arcading, scaled window sizes, and drawing rooms at the second level. The Hôtel-Dieu houses were originally three storeys high. CIHB

Hôtel-Dieu houses, had façades of smooth, light-grey Deschambault stone.

The organization of the façades still clung to the Palladian habit of scaling down the size of the windows on the upper storey. In most examples the ground floor received different treatment from the upper levels, set apart by a string course which emphasized the sense of a supporting base common to Palladian design. Recessed arcades were Baillairgé's preferred motif in this period, probably borrowed from Quebec's best town houses of the 1830s and 1840s by British-trained architects.[38] In the case of the Méthot house, he tried to convince the client to put two rows of recessed arcading on the façade, an idea that probably was directly inspired by a house recently erected at the corner of rue Saint-Louis and rue Sainte-Ursule.[39] Seen in this context, the stark façades of the Hamel and Douglas houses were more clearly allied to the functional logic of neoclassical ideals and heralded the direction that Baillairgé would take in later residential work when he eliminated most surface decoration. For doorway and carriageway openings, he often adopted the elliptical arch, a common neoclassical adornment that had been made popular in Britain through the works of Robert Adam. The Hamel and Corriveau houses both have this feature. The exterior door and window trim was painted in imitation of dark woods, such as oak and black walnut, and the shutters were invariably painted green. Although the roofs retained the common Quebec dormers, they differed from traditional forms by the reduced slope of the pitch to approximately forty-five degrees, and by the roof covering of imported tin plates, laid diagonally. One of Baillairgé's specialties, found originally on the Corriveau and Trudelle houses, was the flattened roof ridge crowned with a lantern or cupola.

The interiors of the houses were quietly elegant, although not equipped with such conveniences as gas lighting, central heating, or indoor plumbing. They were neatly finished, with well-proportioned mouldings around doors and windows, folding inner shutters with copper knobs and hooks, built-in shelves, cupboards, and lead-lined sinks. The door trim was usually more elaborate for the first two floors, where the public rooms were situated, and in some cases mouldings were used to make a sort of hybrid pilaster with entablature.[40] The doors in Abraham Hamel's house, with their two narrow panels (fig. 36), are the first of their kind in Quebec City and are likely borrowed from one of Baillairgé's books, *The Modern Builder's Guide* (1833) by Minard Lafever.[41]

Baillairgé's concern for quality is revealed in his choice of materials and construction methods. For the windows he called for the best imported glass, usually from England, "Smethwick" glass in particular. He refused to leave the exact method of plastering to the discretion of the craftsmen whose trade it was, but invariably specified three coats of plaster, the first and second to be mixed with cow's hair, the third to be a whitewash composed of lime and sand (*blanc de chaux et sable*) applied without spots or bubbles. For the woodwork he called for two coats of paint with a base of double-boiled linseed oil, and a final coat with turpentine base.

Staircases received special attention in Baillairgé's work, possibly because they were highly visible and also because they could adopt the elegant curved forms that he admired. He usually chose winding staircases for private homes, setting them into curved stairhalls. The maple-leaf motif on the stringers of the Trudelle house stairway is an unusual feature, probably executed at the request of the owner.[42] But the scroll or s-shaped newel

FIG. 34. Baillairgé's 1849 façade elevation for the Corriveau house on rue Couillard has the elliptical fanlights and scaled windows typical of this period in his work. To the left is the large double door which masks the carriageway to the rear courtyard, a characteristic feature of the streetscape in Quebec's crowded Upper Town. AVQ, fonds Charles Baillairgé, no. 1–10

FIG. 35. The stark façade of the Hamel house on avenue Sainte-Geneviève, built in 1848–50, was a precursor to Baillairgé's residential work in the mid-1850s. The elliptical arches are borrowed from British prototypes, specifically the neoclassical repertoire of Robert Adam. CIHB

with decorative reeding found in almost every one of his houses of this period was Baillairgé's own contribution (fig. 38).

What must have satisfied clients most about these houses was their harmonious articulation of space. Some examples have survived more or less intact, including the rear room on the ground floor of the Corriveau house,

FIG. 36. The interior trim of the Hamel house was classical in inspiration, especially the pilasters and entablatures that framed the doorways of the lower levels. Of particular interest is the door with its two vertical panels, a first for Quebec City and probably borrowed directly from one of Baillairgé's pattern books. CIHB

which has a pilaster mantelpiece framed by original four-panel doors on one wall, and, on another wall, two tall cupboards with matching trim that are linked by an elliptical arch. This arch frames the front hall and the matching curve of its doorway. At Abraham Hamel's house, the arch with flanking cupboards that has survived in the former dining room on the ground floor has a recessed niche that was probably meant for the sideboard. The moulding bands of the cornice and rosette, and the suggestion of classical orders in the graceful woodwork, contribute to the effect of elegance and harmony.

Baillairgé's success in town-house design was not matched by his early attempts at villas. "Clermont" and "Ravenswood," his two country houses from this period, show him to be more faithful to neoclassical tenets than to values of the picturesque. "Clermont" was built for lawyer René-Edouard Caron; "Ravenswood" for merchant William Herring. If historian James Macpherson Lemoine raved about the picturesque qualities of these two estates, it was certainly due to their gardens and vistas and not to the houses themselves, which gave little sign of belonging to the environment.[43]

The format for "Clermont" and "Ravenswood" is identical, except that the former was more ornate. "Clermont" (fig. 39) had a pronounced projection to its frontispiece, deep enough to add windows on the sides, and cut-stone neoclassical trim above its windows; the Greek Revival doorway, in the architectural drawing at least, is a direct borrowing from Lafever's *Modern Builder's Guide* (figs. 40–1), as architectural historian France Gagnon-Pratte has shown.[44] The neoclassical features of both villas hardly need to be catalogued: frontispiece, pediment, oeil-de-boeuf, balustrade, Doric columns. What these villas lacked were the features that would soften the rigid mass and integrate the buildings into their rural surroundings. There were no French windows to act as a transition between the interior and the exterior; "Clermont" had a porch that was more suited to a formal town house than a relaxed country home, while the gallery at "Ravenswood," potentially a light and fanciful element, remained stiff and unyielding (figs. 42–3.). The exact model has not been identified, but the two villas are similar in conception and feeling to a monumental free-standing building that Baillairgé knew well, the Episcopal Palace he had worked on as an apprentice in Thomas

FIG. 37. The elliptical arch which frames the mantelpiece, echoing the exterior doorways, and the flanking pilastered bookcases at the Hamel house lend an air of demure elegance to this mid-century town house. CIHB

Baillairgé's workshop. Whatever their source, "Clermont" and "Ravens-wood," though undoubtedly well-built and comfortable, lacked the fanciful qualities called for by the settings and which Baillairgé himself was soon to demonstrate in other villas.

At the end of this early period of his practice, Baillairgé was well-established, thanks in large measure to Thomas's influence with the Roman Catholic clergy and in part to the francophone community which had rallied behind him. He had scored public successes with the Saint-Jean-Baptiste and Beauport churches and the asylum for the Soeurs de la Charité, and had shown himself to be an imaginative designer at the De Blois and Bilodeau stores on the rue de la Fabrique. With the notable exception of his flirtation with Gothic Revival at the Beauport church and the chapel of the Soeurs de la Charité, his work had tended towards a rigid and academic interpretation of neoclassicism. In carrying out the design and supervision of these early commissions, Baillairgé adopted a distinctly professional role from which he never wavered throughout his career. He was the architect, an academically trained man who controlled all aspects of the work and acted as intermediary between client and contractors. In a letter to the secretary of public works in December 1849, Baillairgé at the age of twenty-three could proudly claim, "I am one of the architects in Quebec who have the greatest practise and have already, thoug [sic] only practising since 6 or 7 years done buildings to the amount of upward of £175,000 that is to say made plans for the same and conducted the works."[45] With this experience behind him, Baillairgé was ready to produce some of his most gracious and refined buildings, including his next major project, the Quebec Music Hall.

FIG. 38. The scroll or s-shaped newel with decorative reeding, found in almost every Baillairgé house of the late 1840s and early 1850s, appears to be the architect's own contribution to interior finish. This example is from the Hamel house. CIHB

FIG. 39. "Clermont," the country villa at Sillery that Baillairgé designed in 1848–9, as shown in a painting by Joseph Légaré of about 1850. This neoclassical villa, though stately and elegant, is not well integrated into its magnificent setting overlooking the Saint Lawrence River. MSQ

FIG. 40. Baillairgé's elevation for the entrance doorway at "Clermont" shows his admiration of the Greek Revival style in general and the pattern books of the American architect Minard Lafever in particular. AVQ, fonds Charles Baillairgé, no. 1–7

FIG. 42 (below). "Ravenswood," the 1849 villa that Baillairgé designed at Cap-Rouge. AVQ, fonds Charles Baillairgé, no. 1–9

FIG. 41 (above). Lafever published this doorway elevation in one of his pattern books in 1833. Baillairgé borrowed it directly for his entrance at "Clermont." Minard Lafever, *The Modern Builder's Guide* (1833), plate 80

FIG. 43. As seen in this 1865 photograph, "Ravenswood" was set in a picturesque landscape. The villa, however, appears aloof and poorly integrated into its surroundings. NA, C-11341

4 Discovering Greek Revival: Quebec Music Hall

THE QUEBEC MUSIC HALL ERA witnessed a significant evolution in Baillairgé's work, highlighted by his discovery of the Greek Revival style, popular at that time in Britain and the United States. His major projects, including the City Hall proposal, the Music Hall, the DeFoy store, and residential commissions such as the Têtu, Légaré, and Dorion houses and the manoir de Saint-Roch-des-Aulnaies, featured the smooth wall surfaces and decorative vocabulary associated with the Greek Revival style, specifically as it was represented in the pattern books of New York architect Minard Lafever. Although his projects during these years continued to adhere to traditional construction methods, they were marked by an increased use of glass and iron for non-structural purposes and especially by the introduction of modern conveniences including gas lighting, indoor plumbing, and central heating. Praised for the beauty and utility of his buildings, the Quebec Music Hall period proved to be a successful and rewarding stage in Baillairgé's career.

QUEBEC CITY HALL

Before Baillairgé won the contract for the Music Hall, he made a proposal for an important project in the city – the Quebec City Hall. His design for the City Hall revealed his early attraction to Lafever's version of the Greek Revival style. The municipal government, after occupying a former private residence for ten years, resolved to renovate its building, probably in anticipation of the arrival of the government of the Province of Canada, which intended to rotate the seat of government between Toronto and Quebec after the Montreal Parliament House was burned by an angry mob in 1849. Baillairgé's proposal for the 1850 renovation of City Hall has survived (fig. 44).[1] By its grand scale and sophisticated design it reveals the ambitions that the twenty-four-year-old architect had for himself and his native city. In his proposal, he maintained the width of the principal façade on the rue Saint-Louis (limited as he was by the existing building and the width of the lot), but enlarged the secondary façade to a monumental twelve bays in width by using all the available land behind the house on the rue Sainte-Ursule. Neoclassical in style, both façades were to be of smooth ashlar. They overcame the fussiness of the grid system seen in earlier Baillairgé designs by the strength of the giant pilasters which rose a full two storeys to unify the composition. The Greek Revival details – in particular the eared trim, the *in antis* Doric columns of the entrances, and the delicate scroll motifs – are drawn from Minard Lafever's books and substantiate the hypothesis that Baillairgé was familiar with this architect's work from the beginning of his career.[2]

But Charles Baillairgé was not the only architect competing for this contract. In Quebec City in 1850 there were the artisan-architects, treated with disdain by Baillairgé, craftsmen who had followed the Quebec custom of coming up through the building trades and eventually proclaiming themselves "architect." This group included Pierre Gauvreau and Narcisse Larue, former master masons, and Michel Patry, a master joiner.[3] At the same time, there were academically trained architects who, like Baillairgé, had com-

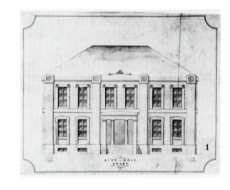

FIG. 44. Baillairgé's unsuccessful proposal in 1850 for the conversion of an old residence into a new Quebec City Hall. AVQ, fonds Charles Baillairgé, no. 6A-58

FIG. 45. The winning entry for the 1850 Quebec City Hall by the firm of Browne & Lecourt. ANQ, photothèque, GH-270–187

pleted a professional apprenticeship in architecture. They included Edward Staveley, who had been trained in England,[4] Joseph-Pierre-Michel Lecourt, who had recently completed his apprenticeship in Quebec with British-trained architect Frederick Hacker,[5] and Goodlatte Richardson Browne, brother of George Browne, the eminent Irish architect who had come from Belfast to Canada in 1830. Both Browne brothers were clever enough to follow the government in its peregrinations from Quebec to Kingston to Montreal, presumably to win the lucrative contracts for government buildings in each new location. Indeed, George Browne was, at least during his years in Kingston, considered to be the government architect.[6] G.R. Browne returned from Montreal to Quebec at the same time as the government in 1849, entering into partnership with Lecourt. It was the firm of Browne & Lecourt which won the Quebec City Hall contract.[7] The new cut-stone façade that they designed in a restrained version of neoclassicism, in particular the variety of window surrounds and the Greek porch with Doric columns and decorative wreaths, constituted one of Baillairgé's first exposures to Greek Revival work (fig. 45).

QUEBEC MUSIC HALL

Baillairgé's opportunity to adopt this new fashion for his own projects came when he was chosen to design and supervise construction of the Quebec Music Hall. This undertaking was sponsored by a group of private citizens led by Archibald Campbell, a notary well known for his devotion to music and the fine arts. Frustrated by the lack of facilities for the performing arts in Quebec, especially after the 1846 fire had destroyed the make-shift theatre in the former riding stable on the Place d'Armes, Campbell created the Quebec Music Hall Association, a non-profit corporation whose first directors included Archibald Campbell, W.H. Anderson, Charles Levey, William

Rhodes, Henry Lemesurier, Charles Alleyn, and Siméon Lelièvre. In order to raise money for the new concert hall, the association sold shares, the return on investment to result from the future profitable operation of the theatre. When the fund-raising campaign faltered, Campbell demonstrated his resolve and generosity by donating over £2500 of his own money.[8]

Just how Charles Baillairgé was selected as architect remains a mystery. The association's records have not survived and the building contracts have curiously not been located. Since the Baillairgé family was active in musical circles in Quebec and since Charles appears briefly as secretary of the Quebec Music Hall Association, it may simply be that these connections gained him the contract.[9] It was also natural that a group of local businessmen and professionals would choose a native son for the job. Indeed, their parochial spirit was made explicit at the association's annual meeting in 1853 when members congratulated themselves on having encouraged indigenous talent.[10]

This project demonstrated Baillairgé's comprehensive approach to the practice of architecture. He began in May 1851 by advertising for a

FIG. 46. The Quebec Music Hall, designed in 1851–3, represents Baillairgé's major achievement in the Greek Revival mode. NA, PA-24091

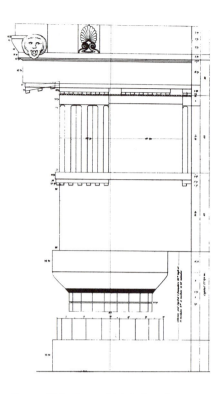

FIG. 47. This plate, which Lafever borrowed from one of the books by British architects Stuart and Revett, shows classical details from the Parthenon in Athens, features that Baillairgé adapted for the façade of the Quebec Music Hall. Lafever, *The Beauties of Modern Architecture* (1835), plate 41

FIG. 48. Lafever's influence on the decoration of the Quebec Music Hall is underscored by this plate from *Beauties*, plate 14

building site suitable for a theatre, not less than 65 feet by 100 feet. Once the land had been purchased and the design completed, Baillairgé called for tenders from contractors for the various works. There seems to have been a problem securing the craftsmen in some trades (plasterer, joiner, tinsmith), for the advertisements continued long after the initial closing date of July 1851.[11] In his role as architect, Baillairgé controlled every aspect of the design, preparing reams of full-scale working drawings and even wooden models to serve as a guide for the contractor for the stone sculpture on the exterior. This control apparently extended to the furnishings, as surviving drawings for the movable seats attest.[12]

For the façade design of the Quebec Music Hall (fig. 46), Baillairgé transformed the familiar five-bay composition with projecting central frontispiece and pediment into an encyclopedia of Greek Revival motifs, some of which had never been seen before in Quebec. The smooth stonework of the underlying wall was, as usual in Baillairgé's work, of excellent quality, as the stone contract makes clear: "All ashlaring to be finished with fine *boucharde*, and all projecting bands, cornices and frames to openings to be, wherever required by the architect, channelled tooled … All the stone to be cut flush in every part without any cavities in the surface or breakings at the corners."[13] The decorative features of the façade – scrolls, rosettes, eared trim, lion's heads, and Doric columns – belong to the Greek repertoire and could have been found individually in a number of the architectural books owned by Baillairgé.[14] Their combination and juxtaposition, however, suggest a blatant dependence on the Greek models presented in the books of New York architect and writer Minard Lafever.

Lafever has five builders' guides to his credit, three of which are highly significant in any assessment of Charles Baillairgé's architecture: *The Young Builder's General Instructor* (1829), *The Modern Builder's Guide* (1833), and *The Beauties of Modern Architecture* (1835).[15] Baillairgé's personal copies of these volumes have not yet been located, but almost exact borrowings from them prove that he owned or had access to these books early in his career.[16] Although Lafever himself worked in a variety of architectural styles, these books contained almost exclusively neoclassical models, a reworking of the five architectural orders drawn from prototypes of ancient Greece. As was customary at that time, Lafever borrowed freely from similar books published in England, crediting Peter Nicholson with the sections on practical carpentry, and Stuart and Revett for the Greek parts.[17] But Lafever went beyond mere reiteration of Greek prototypes. Those architectural historians who have studied his career all agree that Lafever captured the essential delicacy and restraint of the Greek mode and went on to create his own original models – especially in the domestic field for which the Greeks had no counterpart. Lafever himself insisted on the creative and "modern" aspect of his interpretation of the Greek spirit, a feature that undoubtedly appealed to the curious and inventive Charles Baillairgé. In an assessment of Lafever, architectural historian Denys Peter Myers praised his creativity and good taste: "Of all the American handbooks of the time, probably the most influential were those by Minard Lafever (1798–1854). This was fortunate, for Lafever stood well above most of his carpenter-author contemporaries in imaginative invention and refined taste, and among American architects, no designer was more creative in deriving new ornamental detail from Greek precedents."[18] It was especially in *The Beauties of Modern Architecture* that

FIG. 49. The interior of the Quebec Music Hall provides the backdrop for a regimental ball in this lithograph from *Canadian Illustrated News* of 25 Nov. 1871. NA, C-56604

Lafever perfected his architectural ornaments and it was this volume that most influenced Baillairgé, as later comparisons will show. Although Lafever's own buildings had a limited impact, his guides circulated widely among architects and builders, providing an influential source of Greek details in North America in the second quarter of the nineteenth century.

One would search in vain for any plate in Lafever's books that exactly matched the façade of the Quebec Music Hall. Baillairgé's dependence is more subtle. Having absorbed Lafever's models through a sort of creative osmosis, he reworked them selectively to fit the requirements of his own project. In this sense, Baillairgé was a kindred spirit with Lafever, sharing with him a desire to break out from the strait-jacket of the traditional five orders of architecture. Steeped as he was in the classics, Baillairgé was no doubt predisposed to receive this influence. The ground storey of the Music Hall harks back to Lafever's plates illustrating the Grecian Doric order from the temple of Minerva, better known as the Parthenon, in Athens (fig. 47), the building Lafever considered to be "the most beautiful piece of antiquity remaining ... built by Pericles, who employed Ichtimus and Callicrates for his architects."[19] From this model, which Lafever had borrowed from Stuart and Revett,[20] Baillairgé adapted the lion's head and channelled Doric column with narrow incised band near the top for his own purposes, eliminating most of the costly frieze of the original model and pairing the columns and lions' heads in order to achieve a more focused design. The recessed entrance, used earlier in his unsuccessful proposal for the City Hall, is another Lafever device.[21] The source of ornamentation for the windows of the Quebec Music Hall was again Lafever. Several of his models showed eared trim with Greek rosettes, others his graceful interpretation of Greek anthemia or scrolls (fig. 48).[22] Baillairgé's combination was, however, original, and demonstrated his ability to make a creative synthesis of his architectural influences.

Since the Quebec Music Hall was destroyed by fire in 1900, the opulent interior is known to us only through engravings of special events and surviving architectural drawings (figs. 49–52). Arranged like a church inte-

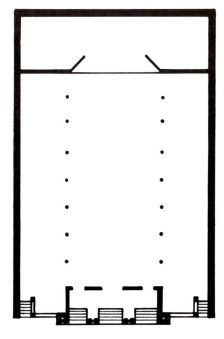

FIG. 50. The plan of the Quebec Music Hall, as reconstituted from iconographic and written evidence, is similar to traditional Quebec church designs. Canadian Parks Service, Heritage Recording Services

FIGS. 51–2. These door elevations for the Quebec Music Hall, with cast-iron rosettes, anthemion scrolls, and Greek meander motifs, reveal once more Baillairgé's reliance on Lafever's pattern books. AVQ, fonds Charles Baillairgé, nos. 6–11, 6–12

rior with slightly arched ceiling, side galleries supported by Doric columns, and a raised stage at the end in place of the choir or apse, this vaulted hall was painted in the habitual Quebec church colours of white and gold, enlivened in this instance by crimson theatre curtain and seats and touches of blue. The balcony tracery of interwoven national emblems was, in the opinion of one newspaper, "worthy of having emanated from the best schools of design, in even France or Belgium."[23] The stone-paved foyer was flanked by comfortably furnished reception rooms and, above the stage, was a series of dressing rooms.[24] Baillairgé's continuing dependence on Lafever as a source of inspiration is apparent in the detailed drawings for doors to the boxes. He has reworked in a new synthesis the Greek key and meander motifs in combination with rosettes and the characteristic Lafever capital (fig. 53).

In this important work, Baillairgé could indulge his love of gadgets and mechanical devices by incorporating the latest conveniences into the structure. In addition to a drop curtain and sliding scenery, the hall had such modern features as gas illumination, affixed to the galleries by brackets with the inevitable Greek-inspired scrolls. Gas lighting was new in Quebec, having been introduced in 1847 in a store on the rue Saint-Jean. Baillairgé went a step farther here by adapting it for the stage footlights.[25] Central heating, another recent improvement in construction technology, was also used for the Music Hall, although the system proved faulty – emitting little heat and much smoke – and had to be replaced almost immediately.[26] It was perhaps this failure that inspired Baillairgé to delve into the question of furnaces and to produce, in the year that the Music Hall opened, a book and patent on a new tubular central heating system.[27] He also experimented with new materials such as coloured glass, used in the circular skylights in the ceiling, and cast iron, specified for some of the ornamental door and gallery trim.

In view of Baillairgé's concern for fire safety, impressed upon him early by the death of his boyhood friend in the Quebec Theatre fire of 1846, it is not surprising that the new Music Hall was carefully designed with alternate exits in case of fire. Baillairgé described his fire safety measures in 1873 when he accused the building's operators of failing to maintain them in working order:

The police should be instructed to see ... that both the outer doors in the rotunda wall of the Music Hall be entirely open to their full and utmost extent on all occasions when the hall is used ... The doors I allude to were to slide entirely into or behind the wall, but have since been so covered with bars and bolts and padlocks and staples, etc., that they cannot be moved in any direction ... There is a door opening from the left side of the hall in Russel's dining room, and another on the opposite side into a lane leading ... to Mount Carmel street ... It should be the duty of the police to see that these doors remain unbolted and that they be arranged if not already so, to open *from* the hall as planned and intended by myself when the hall was built, not *into* it.[28]

But his practical if fantastic fire curtain was never built. It was to be an iron cut-fire curtain faced on the auditorium side with vertical strips of mirror, three feet wide, with silver-edged bars to keep the glass in position. What an effect this shimmering surface would have created, reflecting the richly decorated interior![29]

After almost eighteen months of construction, the Music Hall opened in February 1853 with a gala concert sponsored by the *Société harmonique de Québec*. The local papers raved about the building – its fine acoustics, its convenient seating, its distinguished design. *Le Journal de Québec* called it "an ornament to rival anything on the continent."[30] *Le Canadien* claimed that it was "the most beautiful temple to the arts that existed perhaps in America."[31] In a special review of the inauguration, *Le Canadien* lauded the magnificence of the tasteful classical decoration and the pleasing proportions which let all the audience hear and see properly.[32] But the review which probably pleased Baillairgé most appeared in the *Quebec Mercury* following the Bachelor's Ball in 1853. It praised the Music Hall's design, its quality of construction, and its adaptability to the purposes for which it had been designed.

But to our mind in no way have the admirable and diverse qualities of the establishment been so highly and satisfactorily exhibited as in the use it has of late been put to as a *Salon de danse*. The New Music Hall may challenge any city on this continent, we fairly believe, to shew another like it, possessing similar points of excellence and capable of being put to so many purposes; and we are not aware that a single fault has yet been found with any portion of the structure.

The architect appears to have been eminently successful; notwithstanding the many jets of flame around the Hall, the hundreds of pairs of lamps playing at the same time and within the same space, the violent exercise of polka, waltz and galop, it was remarked by ourselves and many others ... that there was no oppressive heat during any part of the evening. The ventilation was complete.[33]

All united in their praise for the young architect, Charles Baillairgé.

The Quebec Music Hall was used for concerts, banquets, plays, and fancy balls, such as the one for the inauguration of the Grand Trunk Railway when the floor was painted with the company's emblems and supper was served in a tent on stage.[34] After a brief interlude as the temporary quarters for the Legislative Assembly, it resumed its original function. In later years, when Baillairgé turned his hand to literary pursuits, his own play "Berthuzabel ou le diable devenu cuisinier," a comedy set in mid-nineteenth-century Italy at the time of Garibaldi, was performed there in 1873 by a French company under the direction of M. Maugard. Although the text of the play has not been located, it was apparently "charming" and "very warmly applauded."[35]

The Quebec Music Hall demonstrated Baillairgé's most comprehensive use to date of Lafever's Greek Revival models as well as his ability to synthesize this source with his previous neoclassical training to create an entirely original design. The mezzanine plan and interior colour scheme reflected the influence of his early work in church architecture. Though still dependent on traditional solid masonry and wooden roof framing methods, the Music Hall signalled the beginning of Baillairgé's adoption of current technology, in the installation of gas lighting and central heating, and the incorporation of coloured glass and cast iron into the decorative scheme. With the successful completion of the Quebec Music Hall, Charles Baillairgé had established his reputation among the general public as a tasteful and versatile architect. The quality of design and degree of technical innovation displayed in this commission were to permeate his other works from this period and, indeed, throughout the decade.

FIG. 53. This plate from Lafever's *Beauties* (plate 48) contains several of the decorative motifs that Baillairgé synthesized for the interior of the Quebec Music Hall, including the scrolls, Greek key and meander motifs, as well as the characteristic Lafeveresque capital.

FIG. 54. In 1851 Baillairgé renovated this retail store, located at 30–2, rue de la Fabrique in the Upper Town, for the merchant François DeFoy. CIHB

FIG. 55. Behind this crowd of revellers attending Quebec's winter carnival in the 1890s, the DeFoy store front's attractive carved decoration is clearly visible. ANQ, photothèque, N-775-47

STORES AND WAREHOUSES

At the same time that he was involved with the Quebec Music Hall, Baillairgé produced several important commercial buildings. Some were retail stores, similar in design and scale to his earlier structures; others were substantial fireproof warehouses incorporating the new building materials and mechanical devices with which the architect had experimented at the Music Hall. Outstanding among these conservative shop fronts was the renovation that the merchant François DeFoy undertook at his retail establishment on the rue de la Fabrique (figs. 54–6). Probably spurred on by the magnificence of the new stores of his nearby competitors, Louis Bilodeau and Henry Benjamin, both designed by Baillairgé, DeFoy engaged the same architect to refurbish his building. The cut-stone façade, one of the few from this period to survive intact, has sculptured entablatures and shelves for the windows of the three upper storeys, reminiscent of Baillairgé's earlier designs for Dr Baillargeon's building on the rue Saint-Jean. The standard pilastered store front with large windows here became a sophisticated display of Greek Revival motifs, familiar to Baillairgé through his books and, in the case of the wreaths, Browne & Lecourt's newly constructed Quebec City Hall. It is possible that the architect had before him his copy of John Foulston's *Public Buildings Erected in the West of England* (1838), for the plate depicting the Public Library in Plymouth has wreaths on the frieze of the library and pilasters on the neighbouring grocery store with exactly the same Greek key detail as that used by Baillairgé for DeFoy's store (fig. 57). Such a synthesis of sources to produce this outstanding commercial façade would have been typical of Baillairgé's method at this period.

If his retail shops remind us of the Greek repertoire of the Quebec Music Hall, his three Lower Town warehouses from this period recall its scale and innovative use of materials. Baillairgé designed and supervised two enormous warehouses in the commercial centre of Quebec's waterfront. One, measuring 160 feet by 32 feet, was for merchant James Gibb (fig. 58), erected on his new deepwater wharf behind the Estèbe-Fargues house which he had developed as the "Commercial Chambers";[36] the other, measuring 145 feet by 36 feet and facing Gibb's wharf, was for the dry goods firm of L. & C. Têtu, which closed its retail shop on the rue Saint-Jean to concentrate on wholesale distribution.[37] Almost devoid of ornament, the façades of these two buildings had the stark, uninterrupted wall surface and belt courses associated with the neoclassical and Greek Revival styles. The most important feature of these rather plain warehouses, however, was their fireproof construction. Using traditional solid masonry construction techniques, they had walls built of ashlar or fire brick, three rows deep, roofs clad in tin, and doors and windows of all storeys protected by iron shutters. In other words, these warehouses were as safe from fire as current technology would permit. While many drawings have survived for the custom-designed iron shutters of the Têtu building,[38] the actual shutters on Gibb's warehouse – at that time the last surviving example on the Quebec waterfront – were recorded in the early 1970s before the building was demolished. Gibb's warehouse was fitted with pulleys set in special dormer windows to be used for hoisting goods; Têtu's building was illuminated throughout by gas fittings and had three large wheels in the attic for lifting stock from the wharves,[39] probably similar to the fourteen-foot diameter wooden wheel that survived until recently in another Quebec City warehouse of the period (fig. 59).

FIGS. 56–7. The combination of wreaths and Greek key pilasters on the DeFoy building may reveal the way in which Baillairgé synthesized his sources. The inspiration may have come from John Foulston's *The Public Buildings Erected in the West of England* (1838), plate 57. CIHB

FIG. 58. Built in 1853 on the deepwater wharf belonging to merchant James Gibb, this warehouse was as fireproof as current technology could make it. Christina Cameron

FIG. 59. This fourteen-foot diameter wooden hoist found in the Massue warehouse, place Marché Champlain, resembles those that were installed by Baillairgé in the L. & C. Têtu warehouse of 1853–4. Few vestiges of the nineteenth-century waterfront of Lower Town have escaped the massive urban renewal of recent years. CIHB

FIG. 60. The Dorion houses on the avenue Sainte-Geneviève. Canadian Parks Service, Heritage Recording Services

FIG. 61. An elegant hall doorway in the Dorion houses. Canadian Parks Service, Heritage Recording Services

The Têtu building, evidently of first-class quality if the cost is any indication (£3686), attracted the attention of the local press, always quick to emphasize economic growth. A laudatory article that first appeared in the *Canadian Colonist* was cited by *Le Canadien* shortly after the opening of the new building in 1854. It praised "the magnificent warehouse surpassing by far in solidity, capacity and convenience all others of its type in this city and equal to any in the province or in the United States."[40] The owners, architect, and builders were all francophones, a fact that the nationalistic *Le Canadien* could not let pass unnoticed.

These commercial projects, undertaken during the Quebec Music Hall era, reiterated Baillairgé's new orientation towards the Greek Revival style, especially as demonstrated by the ornate façade for DeFoy's retail store, and his experimentation with materials and technical devices to improve the quality and durability of his structures.

TÊTU AND OTHER HOUSES

For those who wanted to build first-class housing, Baillairgé developed the town house into a solid, convenient, and elegant residence suitable for gentlemen of good standing. The most elaborate ones adopted the stylistic vocabulary of the Greek Revival that he had used to such good effect on his most important building from this period, the Quebec Music Hall. In some cases, the influence of Greek Revival theories affected the plan, for the more familiar side hall arrangement was occasionally replaced during this period by the balanced symmetry of the centre hall plan. In all cases, the architect made provision for the introduction of modern conveniences to improve the comfort of these residences.

Baillairgé's basic house type, already seen in his earlier dwellings, did not change in this period. It was a standard row house with off-centre doorway, two or three storeys high, with smooth ashlar façade accented by a string course above the ground level and gable roof, sometimes with dormer windows and often with a cupola on the flattened roof ridge. The dining room, library, and/or office were situated on the ground level; the drawing room occupied the entire width of the second storey overlooking the street. Into this general category fall the Dorion, Jackson, Bilodeau, and Drolet houses (figs. 60–2). "Similar to this format in most respects, the Têtu and Légaré houses (figs. 63, 65–7) were remarkable for their symmetrical plan, reflecting perhaps the architect's desire to integrate neoclassical theories more fully into his housing designs, or perhaps the influence of the palatial residence with centre hall plan just finished on nearby rue Saint-Denis, designed by rival architects Browne & Lecourt (fig. 64).[41] The off-centre doorway of British derivation so frequently found in Quebec City row housing in the 1830s and 1840s was replaced at the Têtu and Légaré houses by a central door with the principal ground-storey rooms arranged to either side of the central hall and staircase.

Like Baillairgé's earlier residences, even the plain ones were well-finished inside with moulded architraves, plaster cornices and rosettes, carved staircases, dividing arches in the double salons, and mantelpieces in the latest style. But what distinguishes this group is the increase in modern conveniences – central heating, gas lighting, and indoor plumbing.[42] Some even had built-in bath tubs similar to one found *in situ* at the manoir de Saint-Roch-des-Aulnaies.[43]

In addition to such conveniences, the Drolet house also featured a communications system made with gutta-percha pipes; each room was equipped with a bell pull linked to a central board in the kitchen on which were mounted bells and the names of each room.[44]

The more ornate houses in this group confirm Baillairgé's attraction to the Greek idiom in general and Minard Lafever's interpretation of Greek prototypes in particular. The Légaré house (at least as it was designed) and the Têtu house both adopted the recessed entrance with Doric columns *in antis* that Baillairgé had first proposed for the City Hall and used in the Music Hall. Inside the Dorion double house, built for Isaac Dorion, the master joiner and general contractor of the Têtu house next door, the ground storey door frames have scrolled anthemia and rosettes applied to a surround of eared trim (fig. 61), an almost perfect match for plate 14 in Lafever's *Beauties of Modern Architecture* (fig. 48). Yet in spite of these obvious borrowings, the Légaré and Dorion houses may be considered plain in comparison with Baillairgé's masterpiece in this period, the Têtu house.

The dwelling that he designed for Cirice Têtu, a wealthy merchant and partner in the importation firm of L. & C. Têtu, was the most thoroughly Greek Revival house erected in Quebec (figs. 65–7). The doorway with its paired baseless Doric columns *in antis* and pilasters is clearly inspired by Lafever's plate for a "Grecian Front Door" (fig. 67). "This elevation," wrote Lafever, "although plain and massy in its parts, will present a beautiful entrance to almost any edifice either private or public. The deep recess of the door and lights, together with the contrast between the columns and pilasters, renders it one of the most beautiful designs in Architecture." He cautioned architects to "give it its proper effect" by observing a similarity to the entire façade.[45] Baillairgé followed this directive by insisting on a smooth cut-stone wall of massive blocks of Deschambault stone dressed with a fine bush-hammer or *bouchardé fin* – the best that money could buy. The building contract specified that the stones were to be of uniform colour and care was to be taken to arrange the shades of blue and white as inconspicuously as possible.[46] Tastefully applied to this plain surface were scrolled anthemia, wreaths, consoles, and baseless Doric columns and pilasters, already used by Baillairgé at the Music Hall and DeFoy's store. Although the decoration was perhaps inspired by a Greek Revival house in Montreal, completed in 1844 by architect John Wells and which Baillairgé most certainly had seen, and ultimately by Lafever, the surprising variation in the motifs grew out of Baillairgé's fertile and creative mind. The exceptional nature of this design is underlined by the use of the flanked windows, a Greek Revival device used sparingly in Quebec since the 1830s but almost never found in Baillairgé's work.[47]

As one would expect, the Têtu house was fitted with gas lighting, indoor plumbing, and the new central heating system that Baillairgé and Chartré had just invented. The hot air system was operated by a series of tubes built into the walls of the house. The tubes could be opened or closed in each room by wooden keys or valves, one of which survives in the attic (fig. 68).

The glory of the Têtu house, however, is its lavish interior. The architect's flair for spatial organization sets the tone. The main hall, for example, is framed by the sculptured inner door and, at the other end, by the carved winding staircase; the vast double drawing room on the second storey

FIG. 62. Like the nearby Dorion residences, the Bilodeau house designed in 1853–4 follows Baillairgé's usual approach to townhouse design. Christina Cameron

FIG. 63. This town house that Baillairgé created in 1851 for the celebrated Quebec painter Joseph Légaré has a centre hall plan, unusual in the architect's repertoire. AVQ, fonds Charles Baillairgé, no. 1–33

FIG. 64. Among the buildings that may have influenced Baillairgé's introduction of the centre hall plan into his town houses is the Gowen house, situated at 16, rue Saint-Denis, designed by Browne & Lecourt in 1850–1. CIHB

is unified by the decorative motifs, matching white marble mantelpieces and crystal chandeliers (fig. 69). Lafever's influence is clearly felt. The ground storey doorways, their eared trim enriched with applied anthemia scrolls, are almost a direct copy of a plate from *The Modern Builder's Guide* (figs. 70–1). The dividing arches of the drawing room, with their extended scroll tendrils, unusual capitals, and sliding doors encrusted with egg-and-dart panels, also draw on Lafever for inspiration. The translation is far from literal, for Baillairgé's designs are a synthesis of several models, filtered through his imagination to become new and original forms (figs. 72–4).[48] There is another difference. One can hardly imagine the tasteful and refined Lafever piling up so much heavy detail in such a confined space or interjecting the semi-circular panels from the Italianate mode into a Greek Revival decorative scheme. For the plasterwork, Baillairgé probably turned to his specialized books by George Jackson and Frederick Knight for well-illustrated details of acanthus leaves, rosettes, wreaths, scrolls, and egg-and-dart moulding.[49] The architect controlled such details by providing the plasterers with wooden models of the ornamental plasterwork.

The Têtu house took two years to build and cost £1575, a significant sum at the time. Such was its quality that its owner did not hesitate to offer it a few years later as the temporary residence for the governor general. Some sense of the graciousness of this house is given in Cirice Têtu's description in 1860 when he offered it to the government: "I have the honor to offer to rent my house ... including all gass [sic] fixtures, glass chandeliers and others, large mirrors in Dining room, parlour and library, including also the Drawing Room furniture and mirrors, chandeliers, curtains with cornices."[50] The two large family portraits, *Cirice Têtu and his daughter Caroline* and *Madame Têtu and her son Amable*, were commissioned from the painter Théophile Hamel in 1852, the very year that construction began.[51] No doubt they added an aristocratic touch to the decoration of the drawing room of this merchant prince's palatial dwelling.

Baillairgé's residential designs remained virtually unchanged for the rest of the decade. Most of them, including the Petitclerc, DeFoy, Morin/Hamel, Leaycraft, Lemoine, and Scott houses (figs. 75–9), shared common characteristics that were already well-established in the architect's repertoire: façades of fine bush-hammered Deschambault stone, doorways "à la vénitienne" often with pilasters and scrolled lintels copied from the flanking doors of the Laval University building, tin-covered roofs with flattened ridges featuring enclosed walkways or skylights, and folding shutters with mobile slats, painted Paris green. Inside, they usually followed the standard side hall plan with second-storey drawing room, and featured basic eared trim often dressed up by flowing tendrils and scrolls inspired by Lafever's books, richly carved staircases, and ornate plasterwork with cornices up to four feet wide and rosettes up to four feet in diameter. The less pretentious ones, such as the Johnston, Morrin, Chartré, and Moisan houses, were built of brick and trimmed with cut stone.

The hallmark of Baillairgé's house designs was the inclusion of sophisticated conveniences. As a rule, they were fitted with one of Baillairgé's and Chartré's tubular hot-air furnaces, sixty-gallon cisterns for hot and cold running water, indoor bathtubs and water closets, gas lighting in every room, and bell systems linked to central switchboards in the kitchen. Though most of these features have long since disappeared, vestiges of the

FIG. 65. The Têtu house, built on Quebec's prestigious avenue Sainte-Geneviève in 1852–4, represents the high point of Baillairgé's dwellings from this period. Christina Cameron

FIG. 66. As the façade elevation for the Têtu house reveals, Baillairgé softened the plain façade by adding the richly carved wreaths, anthemion scrolls and consoles as well as Doric columns and pilasters. AVQ, fonds Charles Baillairgé, no. 1–43

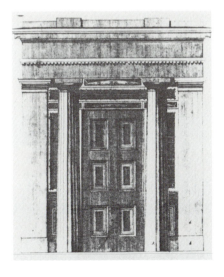

FIG. 67. Lafever's design for a "Grecian front door" published in *The Young Builder's General Instructor* (1829), plate 15

heating system sometimes survive in the form of small circular grills encased in the walls. In a move that indicated his personal success, Baillairgé equipped his own house on the rue Saint-Louis, built in the early 1830s by builders Robert Jellard and John Phillips, with these same modern conveniences.[52]

That Baillairgé was satisfied with the house type that he had slowly developed in the early 1850s is proven by the specifications which frequently refer back to his earlier dwellings. For example, the window trim of the DeFoy house was to be like that of the Dorion houses, but without the sculpture. The leafy rosettes and fluted tapered balusters of the staircase of the DeFoy house were to be modelled on those of the Têtu house. The

FIG. 68. A sliding wooden key to control hot air in the Têtu house. CIHB

FIG. 69. The lavish double drawing room of the Têtu house spans the entire width of the house on the second storey. Baillairgé's elaborate designs for doorways and plastered cornice are matched in ostentation by the pair of crystal chandeliers and white marble mantelpieces purchased by the owner, merchant Cirice Têtu, on a visit to France. Christina Cameron

mantelpieces of the Morrin houses were to be copied from the one in Baillairgé's office. The windows and plasterwork for Lemoine's houses were to be like those at Judge Morin's dwelling, and so forth. This internal reference system, which helps to identify Baillairgé's specifications when they are unsigned, worked well because the same craftsmen often participated in his projects.

Outstanding among this group of first-class residences from the latter part of the decade was the Leaycraft house (fig. 75). It was set back three feet from the street alignment – unusual in the old city – which meant that it had exterior steps and iron balconies on the second and third storeys of the façade. Another remarkable feature was the use of Baillairgé's characteristic lintels with scrolled tendrils, not just for the doorway, which was common enough, but for all the windows as well. Both these ideas – the balconies and the ornamental lintels – had already appeared in his 1853 elevation for Louis Bilodeau's house.[53] Bilodeau for some unknown reason did not adopt the plan. For the Leaycraft house, Baillairgé specified the same curious process that he called for in the Caisse d'économie of the same year, namely that "the whole front of the house including the iron galleries, spouts and the gable wall to the north east to be painted also in 3 coats of a light bluish grey colour."[54] Although some interior details have survived (fig. 80), the Leaycraft house no longer has its original fancy fixtures mentioned in the specification: showers, bell pulls of silver plate, white basins with gilt rim, and silver-plated hot and cold water plugs with silver wire chains.

The example from among these elegant late 1850s town houses that has survived in the best condition is the DeFoy house (figs. 81–3). Seven rosettes and most of its trim are intact. As in Baillairgé's houses from the

FIGS. 70–1. The close influence of Lafever's pattern books for the Greek details is underlined by the ground storey doorways of the Têtu house. CIHB; Lafever, *Modern Builder's Guide*, plate 82

FIGS. 72–4. The elevation for the dividing arches of the drawing room of the Têtu house, alive with flowing tendrils and egg-and-dart carving, reveals the way that Baillairgé absorbs his influences to create a new and original form. Among the models that contributed to his design are two plates from Lafever, one for a sliding door, the other for a modern capital. AVQ, fonds Charles Baillairgé, no. 1–52; Lafever, *Beauties*, plates 11 and 25

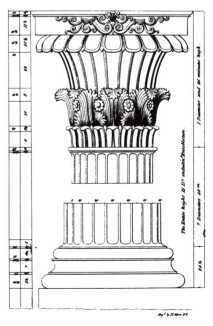

Pl. 11.

FIG. 75. Erected in 1857–8, the Leaycraft house at 3, avenue Sainte-Geneviève is more elaborate than most of the architect's designs from this period. Canadian Parks Service, Heritage Recording Services

FIG. 76. The Petitclerc houses at 83–5, rue Saint-Louis, built in 1855–6, are attributed to Baillairgé on the basis of style and business connections. They possess all the attributes of the architect's residential designs from the period including the façades of fine bush-hammered Deschambault stone and Venetian doorways. CIHB

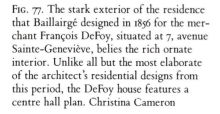

FIG. 77. The stark exterior of the residence that Baillairgé designed in 1856 for the merchant François DeFoy, situated at 7, avenue Sainte-Geneviève, belies the rich ornate interior. Unlike all but the most elaborate of the architect's residential designs from this period, the DeFoy house features a centre hall plan. Christina Cameron

FIG. 78. This pair of houses erected for two merchants, Joseph Hamel and Augustin Morin, are part of Baillairgé's many residential designs from the mid-1850s. Facing the Esplanade at 73–5, rue d'Auteuil, the dwellings have plain ashlar façades alleviated by belt courses and the characteristic Baillairgé scroll lintels. CIHB

early 1850s, the woodwork is copied from models in Lafever's books. For example, the drawing-room arch has capitals directly derived from plate 11 of *The Beauties of Modern Architecture* (fig. 74) and the doors resemble plate 14 of the same book as well as plates 69 and 82 of *The Modern Builder's Guide* (figs. 48, 71). As these examples make clear, Baillairgé refined his town-house type to its most perfect state in the latter part of the decade. He produced well-built residences which offered their owners fashionable Greek design and modern mechanical conveniences.

Although the majority of Baillairgé's residences in this period were town houses, he did undertake two in the country: the Chinic house on the outskirts of Quebec City and the manor house at Saint-Roch-des-Aulnaies. They differ from their city counterparts by being single detached structures set in picturesque environments. Influenced by his own books or perhaps by other villas being built in Quebec at the time, Baillairgé now succeeded, where he earlier had failed, in creating designs which truly reflected the qualities of the picturesque.

The villa for hardware merchant Eugène Chinic was situated near the toll-gate on the road leading to Sainte-Foy, on a rise of land known as Mount Pleasant (fig. 84). Baillairgé's concern for picturesque effects found expression in the two-storey balcony, unusual for Quebec, the tall windows, and the roof platform, all of which took advantage of the distant views over the Saint Charles River valley. The idea for the double balcony may well have been borrowed from a nearby villa "Bellevue," erected in 1847 by an as yet unidentified architect.[55] Baillairgé prepared detailed plans for Chinic's special balcony, which was sheltered beneath the broad cantilevered eaves of the hipped roof. Its exact appearance cannot be ascertained from the nineteenth-century photographs of the house, all of which were taken from a considerable distance. The house has been demolished, but judging from the detailed description of the balcony in the building contract, it probably resembled the balustrade on the verandah at the manor house of Saint-Roch-des-Aulnaies which Baillairgé designed in the same year.[56]

It was in this manor house that Baillairgé, though respecting an underlying classicism by the symmetrical plan, achieved his most complete expression of picturesque qualities in this period and indeed in his entire career. Perched on a height of land overlooking the seigniorial mill, the manor house at Saint-Roch-des-Aulnaies measured seventy feet by forty feet, with sixteen rooms including a library and sun room located in the two projecting end towers (fig. 85). No documentary proof has yet been discovered to identify positively the architect for the manor house. Historians have consistently accepted the initial attribution to Charles Baillairgé by Henri Têtu in 1898 in *Histoire des familles Têtu, Bonenfant, Dionne et Perreault* without offering any further evidence.[57] It is possible, however, to confirm Baillairgé's authorship, at least on circumstantial grounds, by comparing the manor house stylistically to the Têtu house, designed in the same year in Quebec. The social connections, moreover, make the choice of Charles Baillairgé a likely one: the young seigneur for whom it was built, Pascal-Amable Dionne, spent the winter of 1851 in Quebec City articling with a law firm and Pascal-Amable's sister, Caroline, was the wife of Cirice Têtu.[58]

The manor house at Saint-Roch-des-Aulnaies is a curious blend of influences. Some writers perceive it as a French château, probably because of its U-plan created by the end pavilions or towers which project in front of

FIG. 79. Overlooking the mouth of the Saint Charles River are two rather plain town houses that Baillairgé designed in 1857–8 for the notary Alexandre Lemoine. Just how consistent Baillairgé remained in his residential designs is shown by the almost identical row partly visible on the left–built a decade earlier for another Baillairgé client. Canadian Parks Service, Heritage Recording Services

FIG. 80. Inside the Leaycraft house, the staircase has fluted balusters with scrolled stringer motif so often seen in Baillairgé's 1850s residences. The use of round and semicircular panels on the door reflects the architect's growing interest in the Italianate style. CIHB

FIG. 81. This is one of seven rosettes to survive intact in the DeFoy house on the avenue Sainte-Geneviève. The circular bulbous form and wriggly acanthus leaves intertwined with flowers in cornucopias are characteristic of plaster rosettes of the mid-1850s. CIHB

FIG. 82. The capitals from the drawing-room arch at the DeFoy house serve as reminders of Baillairgé's admiration for Lafever's work. CIHB

FIG. 83. This trio of hall doors at the DeFoy house bears all the trademarks of Baillairgé's sumptuous interior work from his Greek Revival phase: six-panel doors, eared trim, and graceful carved scrolls that crown the lintels. CIHB

the main rectangle of the building (fig. 86). This plan was introduced in Quebec during the French regime by such a notable example as the Château de Vaudreuil (1723–6) in Montreal and later in the eighteenth century by the Aubert-de-Gaspé manor house (c. 1765) at Saint-Jean-Port-Joli.[59] This French influence may well have come to Charles Baillairgé through one of his newly acquired architectural books, *Paris moderne; ou, Choix de maisons construites dans les nouveaux quartiers de la capitale et dans ses environs*, by Louis-Marie Normand. In the second volume published in 1843, the plates illustrating the Château à la Roche-du-Veau, département de la Sarthe, designed in 1837 by an architect named Cannissié, include a ground plan which has corner towers and overall organization remarkably similar to the manor house at Saint-Roch-des-Aulnaies (fig. 87).[60]

If the ground plan and steep pavilion roof are features drawn from French prototypes, the clapboard exterior and decorative vocabulary are definitely American. The horizontal log construction of the wall, called *pièce-sur-pièce* – unusual for Baillairgé who preferred stone, but common in rural Quebec at the time – is covered by horizontal clapboarding which recalls buildings in the New England states. The Greek ornamentation hardly needs comment, dependant as it so obviously is on Lafever's books. The eared trim, anthemia scrolls, and rosettes are repeated inside and out to create a rich and well-integrated effect (figs. 88–9). At the edge of the eaves, Baillairgé used for the first time the scalloped trim that reappeared often in his later work. Unlike his earlier stolid attempts at villa design, the manor house of Saint-Roch-des-Aulnaies captured the fantasy and gaiety of the picturesque rural retreat. Enhanced by the careful siting of outbuildings in an identical style and the arrangement of gardens, pond, and waterfall, the seigniorial domain was, in the words of a contemporary witness, the parish priest and Cirice's brother, Henri Têtu, "a terrestial paradise.[61]

The most striking feature of Baillairgé's residential buildings from this period was the adaptation of Lafever's version of the Greek Revival style to create elegant, stately dwellings for gentlemen of standing. For the finest

FIG. 84. In 1853–4 Baillairgé captured the spirit of the picturesque in a suburban villa that he designed for hardware merchant Eugène Chinic. MAC, IBC 78–3163–45

FIG. 85. The manor house at Saint-Roch-des-Aulnaies, Baillairgé's most successful response to the picturesque aesthetic. CIHB

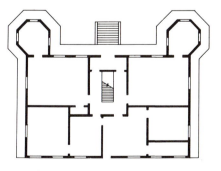

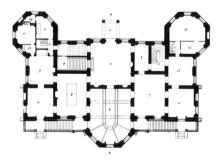

FIG. 86. The U-plan of the Manoir de Saint-Roch-des-Aulnaies, with its projecting corner towers or pavilions, may be drawn from eighteenth-century precedents in Quebec or Baillairgé may have been influenced by plans from French architectural books in his possession. Canadian Parks Service, Heritage Recording Services

FIG. 87. The U-plan for the Château à la Roche-du-Veau (1837), designed by the architect Cannissie, bears a striking resemblance to the plan of the Manoir de Saint-Roch-des-Aulnaies. This plate was photographed from Baillairgé's own copy of this book. Louis-Marie Normand, *Paris moderne*, vol. 2 (n.d.), plate 12

of these buildings, such as the Têtu and Légaré houses, the pervasive influence of neoclassical philosophy was reflected in the adoption of the centre-hall plan, a more harmonious solution to the distribution of space. But whether the entrance was at the centre or to the side, all the residences from this period featured refined ornamentation and modern conveniences that significantly improved their quality and comfort.

Baillairgé's outstanding architectural achievement in these years, the Quebec Music Hall, introduced a new stylistic vocabulary, Greek Revival, into his work. But the architect himself was dissatisfied. He felt that he had not yet been truly challenged, that his intellectual knowledge far outstripped the work he had so far undertaken. As he wrote to the secretary of the Department of Public Works in 1853: "I have never yet had a building to design where I had to deploy more than a small part of my ability; but if someone were to say to me that there is a certain building to erect, requiring so many rooms of such dimensions and for such purposes, I would know how to build, arrange, and decorate it. One must not believe that, to be an architect, one has necessarily to know everybody's needs; but if I am told what is required, I know that I am able to deliver it. In a word, I can state with confidence that I am master of all that one expects from a good architect."[62] Little did he know that the challenge he sought was about to materialize. It is mere coincidence that, on the same page of *Le Canadien* where a reviewer of one of his lectures prophesied that "a great career" was opening before Baillairgé, an article announced the granting of a royal charter for Laval University.[63] Baillairgé was to spend the following years designing and supervising the buildings for the first French-speaking university in North America.

FIG. 88. Inside the Manoir de Saint-Roch-des-Aulnaies, Baillairgé captures the fantasy and gaiety of the rural retreat in the richly carved capitals, anthemion scrolls, and rosettes. CIHB

FIG. 89. The freestanding staircase at the Manoir de Saint-Roch-des-Aulnaies echoes the interior decoration with its carved stringer ornaments and bold Baroque scroll newels. CIHB

5 Innovations in Construction Technology: Laval University Buildings

THE ESTABLISHMENT OF LAVAL UNIVERSITY could not have happened at a more propitious moment for Charles Baillairgé, who by that time had acquired broad experience in a variety of building projects and had justly earned his reputation as a competent and creative architect. The challenges that such an important project presented to the architect drew his attention away from further experimentation in architectural style and led to an exploration of new construction technologies, particularly the use of cast and wrought iron. This evolution in his career raises the complex issue – common in the nineteenth century – of whether his architectural pursuits led to his engineering bent, or vice versa. Although Baillairgé had occasionally introduced iron for decorative purposes during the Quebec Music Hall period, he now integrated cast and wrought iron into the structural fabric of Laval University and thereafter increased his use of the material for other projects such as the Monument aux Braves and several commercial buildings.

LAVAL UNIVERSITY

Pressure for a French-language university in Canada had been steadily mounting since the 1840s, culminating on 8 December 1852 when Abbé Louis-Jacques Casault received in London, England, the official charter for Laval University, the first French-speaking Catholic university in North America. Administration of the university was to be carried out by the Seminary of Quebec, the council being composed of the most senior professors. The rector of the university – in the first instance Abbé Casault – was the superior of the Seminary. Initially there were four faculties: theology, medicine (the university took over the *Ecole de médecine* founded in 1847), law, and arts (including science and literature).[1]

To accommodate these faculties, which were temporarily housed at the Seminary of Quebec, Abbé Casault set aside Seminary land on what was to become rue de l'Université and secured the services of two of the best architects of Catholic persuasion in Quebec City: Goodlatte Richardson Browne and Charles Baillairgé. Three buildings were to be erected: the main university building, a separate medical facility, and a student residence for about seventy-five students. Browne designed the medical school at 6, rue de l'Université, the smallest building on the site, a three-and-one-half storey stone structure measuring 75 feet in length. It was Charles Baillairgé who designed and supervised the two larger ones, the five-and-one-half storey *pensionnat* or residence, measuring 105 feet long by 40 feet wide, and the main building which was 300 feet long, 60 feet wide in the central section, and 54 feet wide at each end (figs. 90–2).[2] Total cost of the three buildings, according to one contemporary estimate, was $238,788.[3] Especially for the main university building, Abbé Casault could not have made a more astute choice of architect than Charles Baillairgé to transform his ambitious scheme into physical reality.

Baillairgé's involvement with the project probably began in 1853 when the building program was being formulated by Abbé Casault and his staff. General plans for the university building were certainly completed

FIG. 90. The pensionnat or residence that Baillairgé designed in 1855–7 for the students attending Laval University is a plain, functional building, remarkable mainly for its unusual size. MAC, IBC 13,896–98 C-6

FIG. 91. The façade elevation for Baillairgé's Laval University (1854–7). The stark unornamented façade is only slightly relieved by touches of neoclassical ornament around the doorways and some of the windows. AVQ, fonds Charles Baillairgé, no. 2–43

before September 1854, when the cornerstone was laid. Plans for the residence were ready in April 1855.[4] The project dragged on, however, far beyond the anticipated two years, sapping the architect's time and energy. Although the buildings were partially occupied in 1856 and officially opened on 9 September 1857, Baillairgé was still seeking payment of his fees – £400 for design and supervision of both buildings – a year later in September 1858.[5]

The Laval University project – by far the most comprehensive in Quebec City at the time – gave Baillairgé the civil engineer a chance to demonstrate how much technical and theoretical knowledge he had acquired. Just the dimensions of the university building reveal the structural challenge; its five-storey, eighty-foot height made it the tallest building in the city at the time and the most prominent, with the exception of the Citadel, when viewed from the river. Its most striking feature, the flat roof, an avant-garde feature drawn from European neoclassicism and the first of its kind in Canada, allowed for an open roof-top terrace that surpassed Durham Terrace in both height and length. Through a careful examination of this project, one

FIG. 92. This 1863 photograph shows the rear façade of Laval University and the rooftop promenade overlooking the magnificent panoramic view of the Saint Lawrence River. ASQ

can confirm Baillairgé's reliance on the Greek Revival phase of neoclassicism and explore his departure from traditional construction methods.

In terms of style, with the exception of the flat roof for the main building, Baillairgé's designs for Laval University did not introduce radical new stylistic features into his repertoire. The stark unornamented façade of smooth Deschambault greystone had already become a trademark of his best buildings. The central doorway with Doric columns *in antis* and carved wreaths on the frieze recalled similar motifs from the Greek Revival repertoire at the DeFoy store, Music Hall, and Têtu house (figs. 46, 56, 65, 93). What is new is the design for two flanking entrances of the main building where Baillairgé introduced for the first time a streamlined version of a Lafeveresque doorway, with an unusual irregular curve at the top and smooth shaped capitals and pilasters (fig. 94). This model, which Baillairgé had already sketched in 1853 in an unfulfilled housing project, reappeared in many of his other buildings of this period and appears to be his own invention.

What inspired Baillairgé to choose a flat roof for the university building? Was it an aesthetic concern for the overall appearance of the severely neoclassical design, or Baillairgé's known predilection for platforms and cupolas that allowed panoramic views? The available documents do not give an answer. What is clear, however, is Baillairgé's determination to have a flat roof. His long letters of explanation and justification indicate that the Seminary council did not readily accept his recommendation. He even made a comparative cost analysis between the sloped roof of G.R. Browne's medical school and his proposed platform, claiming that the latter would cost £1255.18.0 in comparison to £1536.10.0 for the former. He argued that a flat roof was more economical because it did not need roof framing, metal covering (which was more expensive than cement), raised gable walls, or high chimneys. He recommended Warren's cement from Montreal rather that asphalt roofing, at the time being used at the Citadel, because the latter required bricks as well as asphalt from the Jura region of France, making it a more expensive proposition.[6] Abbé Casault's hesitation in accepting the flat roof proved to be justified. Although he reluctantly gave his approval, he soon regretted it, for the roof began to leak almost immediately. In a letter written in June 1857, Baillairgé sought to justify his design by explaining why the roof was leaking and offered patchwork solutions to the problem. Although the roof was repaired, dissatisfaction continued until it was replaced by a mansard roof in 1876.[7] For the moment, however, Baillairgé could take comfort from the panoramic view atop the promenade, a vista which was said to be "equal to that of the bay of Naples."[8]

In terms of construction technology, the university building and residence were up-to-date in all respects; in terms of actual construction, the project was probably ahead of its time because, in collaboration with engineer and mechanic Phillip Whitty, who was responsible for all the iron work, Baillairgé designed and built a steam-driven hoist to lift materials efficiently into place.[9] The *Morning Chronicle* underscored the importance of this invention for future construction projects: "It was, we believe, on the suggestion of the Rev. Mr. Forgues, that the architect prepared plans for the steam elevating machine which has with such ease and rapidity raised the enormous weight of stone and other materials ... to the requisite height ... It raises about 160 tons weight of materials daily ... each load which it raises would

FIG. 93. The central doorway for Laval University. Christina Cameron

FIG. 94. One of two flanking doorways at Laval University. Christina Cameron

FIG. 95. The vestibule of the residence at Laval University reveals Baillairgé's skill at organizing space. The series of elliptical arched doorways, with a subtle curve below each fanlight, have disappeared in the recent renovation of the building. CIHB

take 16 men, and ten times as long to raise it. We cannot imagine that in future the erection of any large building will be attempted without the aid of this powerful machine."[10]

The buildings themselves were fitted up with the same modern conveniences found in his earlier work, such as central air ventilation systems made from Bell terra cotta pipes laid in the walls, central heating using Chartré's and Baillairgé's tubular system (with three furnaces per building), hot and cold running water, and gas lighting.[11] But it was especially in the use of iron for structural support at the university that Baillairgé broke away from the conservative building methods in which he had been schooled and allied himself with this progressive branch of technology. He probably acquired his theoretical knowledge about iron from the engineering books in his library, from his preparation as a civil engineer, and from the publicity surrounding the construction of Joseph Paxton's Crystal Palace in London in 1851, a vast structure of iron and glass that abandoned conventional materials and technology. No examples of iron construction existed in Quebec City at that time, however, to provide a practical illustration. One surmises that he probably first saw actual cast-iron buildings in New York City. By the middle of the nineteenth century, when Baillairgé began to visit the metropolis, New York had established, as construction historian Carl W. Condit states, "a pre-eminence in iron construction that was not to be challenged until the rise of the Chicago school in the 1880's."[12] The young Quebec architect was undoubtedly impressed by the work of James Bogardus and Daniel Badger who were, in Condit's opinion, "the two most ambitious and influential manufacturers of iron building components in the nineteenth century."[13] Wrought iron – a ferrous metal with a low carbon content which was worked or wrought at an anvil – had served for minor structural elements and decorative details from the eighteenth century on. Construction with cast iron – a ferrous metal with a high carbon content which was melted and poured into moulds – began in England in the late eighteenth century as an offshoot of the Industrial Revolution and rose to prominence as a building material in the second quarter of the nineteenth century. Though weaker in tensile strength than wrought iron, cast iron proved to be stronger in compression, with obvious advantages over traditional masonry of lighter weight, flexibility, and non-combustibility.[14]

Until the Laval University project, Baillairgé had dabbled in iron technology for decorative and minor structural elements only: cast-iron rosettes for the Music Hall doors; a wrought-iron balcony for Bilodeau's store; wrought-iron shutters for the Gibb and Têtu warehouses. While he never completely freed himself from traditional methods, as did his American counterparts when they developed full cast-iron façades or when they built classically camouflaged domes in iron, Baillairgé was nevertheless the first architect in Quebec City to introduce cast-iron columns as structural components of the building fabric.[15]

Because of the university building's unusual height, Baillairgé called for the insertion of iron columns into the walls in order to stabilize the structure.[16] Once again the Seminary council balked. In the interests of economy, columns were eliminated from some parts of the building, causing gradual sinking of the floor, particularly in the ceremonial hall. Forty years later Baillairgé did not hesitate to point out the result of that false economy and justified his original proposal by demonstrating that the central section, where iron columns *had* been retained, had never settled.[17] The Laval University project thus gave Baillairgé the opportunity to explore and apply current iron construction technology in his own work.

On the inside, the university buildings demonstrated Baillairgé's skill at spatial organization, as well as his on-going dependence on the Greek Revival style and his use of cast iron for structural and decorative purposes. Fate has not dealt kindly with the interior work of these two structures: the university building was redecorated near the end of the century and the residence has recently been stripped of most of its trim. While the woodwork was in general restrained and discreet, the principal public spaces such as the vestibule of the residence and the library and ceremonial hall at the university were more highly decorated. In the vestibule, the architect's sense of spatial organization and his love of curved forms were given full play, for the space was enclosed by a variety of graceful arched openings (fig. 95). The inner front doorway had a circular fanlight and a circular-headed door that in turn featured glazed round-headed upper panels in the Italianate manner of the 1850s. Opposite the main entrance is another arched doorway with a special Baillairgesque feature: a circular fanlight with a subtly curving bottom edge that received a similarly shaped door head. This type recurred in the corridor leading to the *salon*. On the west side of the vestibule opened a series of elliptical arched doorways with wide sidelights. The subtle Baillairgé curve below the fanlight was once again in evidence.

At the university building, the library and the ceremonial hall, known as the *salle des cérémonies* or *salle des promotions*, still reflected the influence of Minard Lafever (figs. 96–7). The ceremonial hall was a large room measuring 100 feet long by 50 feet wide by 25 feet high, and featuring a coved or slightly vaulted ceiling and a mezzanine supported by ornamental cast-iron columns.[18] Insofar as they can be seen in a late nineteenth-century photograph of the ceremonial hall, when several major changes had already occurred, the ceiling rosettes are based on a plate from Lafever's *The Beauties of Modern Architecture* (fig. 98). The detail that perhaps fascinated Baillairgé the most was the ornamental balcony in cast iron. This material suited the purpose well, for cast iron could adopt any form, no matter how intricate, and, once the basic mould had been created, it could be repeated many times with great precision at low cost. An early proposal for the wooden model to be used in casting the balustrade featured a serpent, eagle, and shell, and was signed "C. Baillairgé Arct. Del."[19] It shows how dependent Baillairgé was on his library, for it is an almost exact reproduction of plate 14 in *Knight's Scroll Ornaments* (1833?) by Frederick Knight (figs. 99, 100). Commenting on this proposal, Baillairgé recommended it to the Seminary council and added that the central panel could be changed to represent a lyre, a medallion, or some other allegorical figure.[20] Early sketches of this room show that it was the lyre motif which was chosen. Fortunately, the appearance of the ceremonial hall was recorded shortly after its completion when the Prince of Wales was received there in 1860 by the Roman Catholic bishop of Quebec.[21] *Le Journal de Québec*, in describing the event, inadvertently commented on the elegant classicism of the room: "The grand hall at University Laval ... was simply but richly decorated. A throne had been erected for the Prince, behind which hung a magnificent tapestry, surmounted by the Prince of Wales' crown. Everywhere there reigned elegance and a classic severity that indicated to all that they were in the sacred temple of Science."[22]

FIG. 96. Ceremonial hall. Laval University, during the visit of the Prince of Wales in 1860. ASQ

FIG. 97. The ornamental details of the cast-iron columns and balustrade of the ceremonial hall at Laval University are clearly visible in this composite photograph of the reception for the Prince of Wales. NA, C-9233

FIG. 98. As this late nineteenth-century photograph reveals, Baillairgé's original design for the ceremonial hall of Laval University was modified by the addition of columns at the mezzanine level. The Lafever-inspired plaster rosettes and ornamental iron balcony are still intact. ASQ

FIG. 99. Baillairgé's drawing for the balustrade of the ceremonial hall at Laval University. AVQ, fonds Charles Baillairgé, no. 2–39

FIG. 100. An 1833 drawing by British designer Frederick Knight, *Knight's Scroll Ornaments*, plate 14

The Laval University project showed Charles Baillairgé in his prime: confident, capable, innovative, and controlling an enormous site. His contribution was justly assessed by a contemporary article in the *Morning Chronicle*: "While proving by the present vast undertaking the comprehensiveness of his talents and genius, Mr. Baillairgé has also added much to his reputation as a practical architect, and reflects credit on Canada."[23]

MONUMENT AUX BRAVES

For the Monument aux Braves, Baillairgé predictably chose his preferred style, the Greek Revival, and applied his new knowledge of iron technology. What was important about this project was not the work itself – which was a handsome if predictable example of Baillairgé's production – but the prestige associated with the erection of the monument.

It all began with the discovery in about 1850 of skeletal remains on the property of Julien Chouinard, near the present site of the monument.

They were presumed to be the remains of French and British soldiers who had fought in the battle of Sainte-Foy in 1760, the last stand of French troops led by Lévis against the British under Colonel James Murray. Members of the *Société Saint-Jean-Baptiste*, under the leadership of three devotees of history, Dr Oliver Robitaille, François-Xavier Garneau, and Louis-de-Gonzague Baillairgé, arranged for the reburial of the soldiers and hit upon the idea of erecting a monument in their honour.[24] The pall-bearers who participated in the June 1854 ceremony to transfer the remains to their new resting place were the political and cultural leaders of French-speaking Quebec including Etienne-Pascal Taché, René-Edouard Caron, Augustin-Norbert Morin, de Sales Laterriére, Jean Chabot, P.-J.-O. Chauveau, and Jacques Viger, all members of parliament, Colonels de Salaberry and Charles Panet, as well as G.-B. Faribault, François-Xavier Garneau, Joseph Cauchon, Louis-de-Gonzague Baillairgé, and Joseph Légaré.[25] Many of them had been or would be clients of Charles Baillairgé.

It was probably through his uncle, lawyer Louis-de-Gonzague, that Charles Baillairgé became involved in the project. In 1855 he was named to a subcommittee of the *Société Saint-Jean-Baptiste*, set up to make arrangements for the monument. Charged by this committee with the task of producing a design and cost estimate, Baillairgé made an initial plan in a few days (fig. 101). The monument was built in stages: the stone base in 1855, the column in 1860-1, and the statue of Bellona, gift of Prince Jérôme-Napoléon of France, was put in place in 1863 (fig. 102).[26]

Baillairgé followed a well-established practice by selecting a column for his commemorative monument. The tradition came from British and French neoclassicism, but there were several early nineteenth-century examples in Canada, including the column for Simon McTavish (1804) and Nelson's column (1809) in Montreal, the monument to Wolfe and Montcalm (1828) in the governor's garden, and a restored version of the monument to Wolfe (1849) on the Plains of Abraham in Quebec.[27] Baillairgé's own version, however, shows his predilection for the Greek Revival style and his creative use of contemporary building materials; the forty-five foot fluted Doric column is a hollow shaft, composed of cast-iron sections bolted together (fig. 103). He made changes to his original proposal, including the addition of a decorative ring of mortar shells around the base of the shaft and, at least in one phase of the design's evolution, the incorporation of wreaths (like those at Laval University) for the statue pedestal above the column. Though not innovative in format, Baillairgé's Monument aux Braves was a graceful and characteristically stark rendition of Greek themes. James Macpherson Lemoine found it "decidedly the finest public monument in Quebec."[28]

The commission gave Baillairgé a high public profile. The cornerstone ceremony, postponed until 18 July 1855 so that officers from the French warship *La Capricieuse* could attend, gave him good public exposure. After a mammoth parade from the Esplanade to the site, the moment came to lay the cornerstone. Standing on the platform with the president and officers of the *Société Saint-Jean-Baptiste* and other dignitaries was Charles Baillairgé. It was he who handed the trowel to Governor General Sir Edmund Head to set the stone in place. To be associated with such august company could only enhance Baillairgé's reputation with his compatriots. A few years later an engraving of his monument, with an accompanying text in which the Cana-

FIG. 101. Baillairgé's preliminary perspective for the Monument aux Braves dates from 1855. He followed a well-established tradition for commemorative monuments by choosing a single column crowned by a military statue. AVQ, fonds Charles Baillairgé, unnumbered

FIG. 102. This photograph, taken soon after the completion of the Monument aux Braves in 1863, shows that Baillairgé's proposed military figure was replaced by the statue of Bellona, gift of Prince Jérôme-Napoléon of France. NA, C-84470

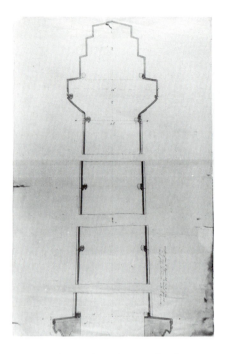

FIG. 103. This working drawing for the Monument aux Braves demonstrates Baillairgé's enthusiasm for contemporary technology. Though designed in the traditional Greek Revival idiom, the fluted Doric column is a hollow shaft of cast-iron sections, bolted together to create the illusion of carved stone. AVQ, fonds Charles Baillairgé, no. 7–75

dian architect was identified, appeared in the prestigious British publication the *London Illustrated News*.[29]

COMMERCIAL BUILDINGS

Most of the commercial and residential projects that Baillairgé undertook during the Laval University period revealed little stylistic change from his earlier work, being for the most part variations on the Greek Revival idiom. However, several of the commercial structures – in particular the Merrill, Desbarats, and Caisse d'économie buildings – revealed the influence of the more up-to-date Italianate style, at that time gaining popularity in the United States. These more modern buildings also afforded him the chance to implement his avant-garde ideas about construction technology.

One renovation project presented Baillairgé with a particularly good opportunity to demonstrate his new dexterity with cast iron. It was the shop for dry-goods merchant Alexander Merrill (fig. 104), to be built in the structure that Baillairgé had already renovated for René-Edouard Caron in 1851. The architect's task was to rebuild the lower two storeys for separate retail and wholesale functions and to design a modern eye-catching shop-front. Workmen had to prop up the house just below the third floor and demolish the lower two levels. The two-tiered shop-front that resulted was unusual in Quebec City, as comparison with neighboring stores in historical street views shows (fig. 105). So were the materials. The stone pilasters and cornice had an ornamental covering in cast-iron and the wide plate glass windows were protected by sliding shutters that moved up and down through manipulation of ropes and pulleys.[30]

But his two most important commercial projects from the period were the new savings bank, the Caisse d'économie on the rue Saint-Jean, and the Desbarats building on the rue Sainte-Anne, both of which survive in drastically modified condition. The Caisse d'économie Notre-Dame de Québec erected a building which was meant to house the bank and also to serve as an investment property (fig. 106). Consequently, the ground floor was reserved for the bank, the second level for offices, and the upper storeys for separate living quarters. Baillairgé's approach to the Caisse d'économie showed a transition in his stylistic evolution as well as an increased fascination with iron technology. Probably influenced by several recent buildings by local architect Edward Staveley in the more robust Italianate style, Baillairgé abandoned his customary Greek Revival idiom when he designed the Caisse d'économie. The Italianate mode introduced into his work a more relaxed tone, allowing for a greater play of light and shadow. The façade elevation and interior finish created textural effects by using such devices as an overhanging cornice with vigorous paired brackets, and the enriched decoration of scrolls, laurel wreaths, and leafy capitals.

The demands of the more fulsome aesthetic of the Italianate style dovetailed nicely with the rising popularity and availability of cast iron. This wealth of ornamentation demonstrated the economic advantage of the new technology of cast iron, for all the decoration of intricate detail could be mass-produced at low cost. Baillairgé specified cast iron for the pilasters for the façade, twenty-three-inch-long ornaments for the pilaster panels, garlands for the pedestals, consoles and moulding for the two cornices, and decorative motifs above the doors and windows.

It is the flat roof and the combination of materials that set the building apart from Baillairgé's earlier commercial production. Once the masonry walls were built, cast-iron decorations were fastened onto the stone surface using iron ties. This method applied to the pilasters (similar to Alexander Merrill's shop across the street), the headers over the windows, which were to be covered with "cast iron ornaments attached to the walls by hooks," the frieze and brackets, and the laurel wreaths to be bolted to the stone pedestals of the pilasters. Occasionally the two kinds of iron were even to be used together. The shutters were to be made of wrought iron and finished with ornamental cast-iron work attached to the panels. In a final gesture that would have horrified modern conservationists, Baillairgé gave instructions that all the iron and cut-stone work of the façade be painted a uniform grey(?) colour.[31]

His other important commercial project was the building that Georges Desbarats erected on speculation to house the printing shops of Derbyshire and Desbarats (fig. 107). Putting his faith in the myriad rumours that hinted that Quebec was about to be chosen for the permanent seat of government, Desbarats went ahead with construction, intending to print the *Canada Gazette* in this building. In the event that the government went elsewhere, it was designed in such a way that it could be subdivided into four separate dwellings. In spite of the size of the building, the builders broke all records by erecting it in little over ten weeks – and in the difficult months of November and December.[32] In keeping with his interest in the Italianate style and cast-iron technology, Baillairgé chose cast iron for the window decoration, this time introducing a design with a slightly curved shape and applied motifs. He used this model in the same year on Taché's building in the Lower Town (fig. 108).[33] The local newspapers reacted positively to Desbarat's building, noting that "the masonry is garnished with cast-iron ornaments which beautify the whole building" and calling the "vast construction ... an ornament for our city."[34] In a sense the Desbarats project was prophetic, because the building only served as a printing shop for a few brief years before the government left Quebec for good. Baillairgé's personal slump in business found its parallel in the general economic decline that Quebec suffered when the decision was finally announced that Ottawa would be the permanent seat of government.

In terms of achievements, the mid-1850s were remarkably successful years for Baillairgé. He produced a series of distinguished and innovative buildings including Laval University, the Monument aux Braves, and commercial structures such as the Merrill, Desbarats, and Caisse d'économie buildings, where he demonstrated his new awareness of the Italianate style and his grasp of current technology by incorporating iron into the structural fabric. But his architectural successes were to some extent mitigated by the fact that business was slowing down as the population grew cautious awaiting the government's decision about the choice of permanent seat. Lacking work, Baillairgé diversified his activities by undertaking projects and duties outside the practice of architecture. Yet he remained firm in his conviction that projects of a scale and importance commensurate with his skill and experience would only be found in the Department of Public Works. He therefore had little choice but to renew his efforts to become chief government architect.

FIG. 104. In 1854 Baillairgé renovated the shop-front for A. Merrill & Company on rue Saint-Jean. *Quebec Business Directory Compiled in June and July 1854* (Quebec: Bureau & Marcotte 1854), 118

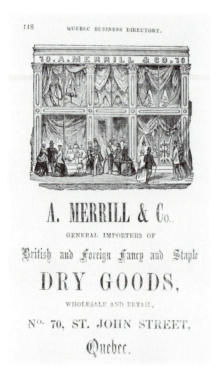

FIG. 105. This 1860s street view of rue Saint-Jean shows how unusual the two-tiered shop-front was in Quebec City at that time. NA, PA-12691

FIG. 106. Baillairgé's 1857–8 design for the Caisse d'économie Notre-Dame de Québec. NA, PA-24188

FIG. 107. This building was erected in ten weeks in the late fall of 1858, for the express purpose of housing the printing shop of Derbyshire and Desbarats. When Quebec failed in its bid to become the seat of government, Desbarats moved his presses elsewhere and the building was converted into a hotel. NA, PA-24160

FIG. 108. The modest shop on the rue Saint-Pierre in Lower Town, which Baillairgé designed in 1859–60 for Taché, echoes the decorative repertoire of the Desbarats building, particularly in the cast-iron lintels. The building was demolished in the late 1970s. Christina Cameron

6 Religious Commissions: Sainte-Marie de Beauce

THE ROMAN CATHOLIC CLERGY had been Baillairgé's first and most reliable client. But though in the latter part of the 1850s Baillairgé created some outstanding religious works including the church at Sainte-Marie de Beauce and the ornamental fence in front of Notre-Dame de Québec, this era marked a significant loss of patronage from the Roman Catholic establishment and a serious deterioration in Baillairgé's relationship with the clergy at both the diocesan and parish levels. What led to this antagonism is not certain; Baillairgé undoubtedly fueled the debate by his own unorthodox designs, by his irreverent attitude to church authorities, and by his frequent criticism of the conservative and oft-repeated formula for church architecture.

Of the work that he did for the diocese of Quebec, Baillairgé had the opportunity to superintend construction of only two of the buildings, the Notre-Dame-de-Grâce wing for the Ursuline Sisters and the parish church at Sainte-Marie de Beauce. The remainder were parish churches for which he merely prepared plans: l'Isle-Verte (1853),[1] Saint-Romuald (1854), Saint-Patrice de la Rivière-du-Loup (1855) (fig. 109), and Sainte-Marguerite de Dorchester (1856). In each case, the parish made an outright purchase of the plans without engaging the architect to supervise the works. His control over changes to his design and the quality of construction was thus minimal. The churches at l'Isle-Verte and Saint-Patrice were essays in the Gothic Revival style; the other two were in the more familiar neoclassical vein. For the former, Baillairgé used the Gothic idiom in much the same way as he had done for his church at Beauport, applying Gothic details to the surface of otherwise symmetrical – hence classical – buildings.

For the Notre-Dame-de-Grâce wing of the Ursuline convent, Baillairgé had little room to manoeuvre: the building had to be economical and the external design had to conform to the older wings of the convent, some of which had been erected during the French period. Linked to the older section by a covered walkway, the wing was a plain structure built in the traditional French Canadian way, with solid masonry walls of roughly coursed stone, window frames of smoothly dressed stone, and a steep gable roof with two rows of dormer windows. Only the large scale of the building and the spacious height of each storey – twelve and fourteen feet at different levels – betrayed its mid-nineteenth-century construction date.

Inside, the wing was equipped with modern conveniences, such as central heating and water closets, and recent technological innovations such as iron fire doors on each storey and iron bars that were introduced into the traditional wood roof frame for added strength. With his usual attention to detail, Baillairgé specified that the heating pipes rising to the third-storey dormitory were to be camouflaged beneath projections in the form of pilasters.[2] In spite of the relative simplicity of the classrooms, laboratories, and recreation rooms, the architect achieved gracious and well-lighted spaces through the repeated use of transom windows above the doors and the flanked end windows that illuminated the central corridors at each level.

FIG. 109. The church of Saint-Patrice at Rivière-du-Loup built in 1855–6. CIHB

FIG. 110. The parish church for Sainte-Marie de Beauce begun in 1854. ANQ, photothèque, GH-510-73

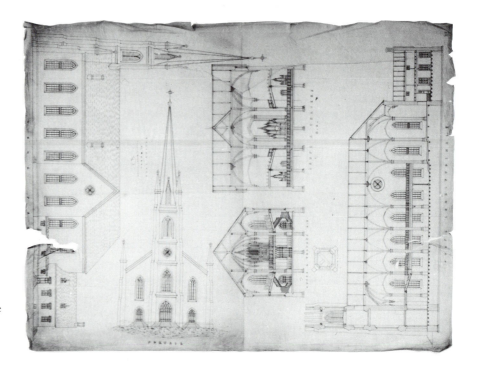

FIG. 111. The elevations and sections for the church at Sainte-Marie de Beauce show the care and attention to detail that Baillairgé put into his architectural drawings. AVQ, fonds Charles Baillairgé, no. 5-4

FIG. 112. The lavish interior of the church at Sainte-Marie de Beauce was completed in 1866. ANQ, photothèque, N-1175-114

In terms of business, the Ursulines' wing was not a profitable undertaking for the architect. In a letter to the archbishop several years after the completion of the building, Baillairgé was still chafing under the perceived injustice and berated the archbishop for withholding church contracts from him: "I am not bitter, Monseigneur, and yet I may perhaps be entitled to be so. You made me lose £23 at the Ursulines by denying that you had arranged for me to supervise the construction of the building. Since this time your Grace appears to have carefully avoided sending any clients to me for church designs."[3] The Notre-Dame-de-Grâce wing thus marked a new low in Baillairgé's relationship with the Roman Catholic clergy, a relationship which had begun to deteriorate at the time of the debate over the juxtaposition of a Gothic spire and classical dome at the asylum for the Soeurs de la Charité.

Baillairgé's major architectural triumph among his churches of this period was the parish church at Sainte-Marie de Beauce. In contrast to the others, for which Baillairgé did only exterior plans and no supervision, the project at Sainte-Marie included exterior and interior design as well as supervision. Family connections may once again have helped him to secure the commission, for François had carved the three altars for an earlier church in the parish in 1811–12 and Thomas had worked there in 1814.[4] For grandiose ambition, Baillairgé met his match in Sainte-Marie's parish priest, Curé Proulx, who was prepared to push his parishioners into raising the funds necessary to build the largest rural church in the diocese, measuring 180 feet by 73 feet (almost as big as Quebec's Saint-Jean-Baptiste church which was 180 by 80 feet). Although Baillairgé prepared his initial plans in 1854, construction was delayed for two years while difficulties over the legal boundaries of the parish – and hence the list of contributors – were sorted out. Work began in 1856, with the shell of the new church being built around the old one, which continued to serve the parish until its demolition in 1859. Lack of funds slowed progress. The vault and interior decoration were only carried out from 1861 to 1866.[5]

The stylistic idiom chosen for Sainte-Marie was Gothic Revival (figs. 110–15). Remarkably similar to Saint-Patrice at Rivière-du-Loup designed by Baillairgé at about the same time, the exterior was restrained, with Gothic features merely applied to the surface rather than integrated into the structure. The buttresses of the central tower were timid and those at the corners too insubstantial to be functional. The sources of inspiration for the specific interpretation of Gothic Revival at Sainte-Marie and Saint-Patrice may well have been two churches being built in Quebec City at that time by professional architects whom Baillairgé admired: Chalmers Free Presbyterian church on the rue Sainte-Ursule, begun in 1851 following the design of Montreal architect John Wells, and Saint-Colomb church at Pointe-à-Pizeau in Sillery, begun in 1852 using plans by architect G.R. Browne (of the earlier partnership of Browne & Lecourt).[6] All four churches shared common characteristics such as the plain rectangular plan with single central steeple, slender non-functional buttresses at the edges of the façades and projecting central towers, and pointed doors and windows arranged symmetrically on the principal façades.

It was on the interior that Baillairgé lavished much care and time, as the impressive number of working drawings shows. It has survived in an almost unaltered state, although other colours have been added to the original white and gold scheme. Details for the inventive arrangement of Gothic forms were drawn from the fourteenth-century English churches in the so-called Decorated style, exemplified by the choir at Ely Cathedral, the nave and cloister at Canterbury Cathedral, the presbytery and transepts of Gloucester Cathedral, Saint George's chapel at Windsor, and others. In this interpretation of Gothic forms, Baillairgé has gone beyond the pre-Puginesque Perpendicular phase of Gothic Revival. At Sainte-Marie de Beauce, he has created a church of soaring height and Decorated Gothic details that holds its own in the mature Puginesque tradition.[7] It is, however, unclear to what extent this may be attributed directly to the English leader of Gothic Revival, Augustus Welby Pugin. Baillairgé owned several books which advocated this aesthetic, but none by the master himself (though one by his father).

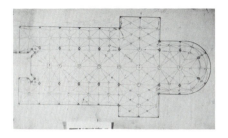

Fig. 113. The plan for the ceiling of the church at Sainte-Marie de Beauce. AVQ, fonds Charles Baillairgé, no. 5-11

Fig. 114. The bold profiles of these cluster colonnettes inside the church at Sainte-Marie de Beauce show the influence of the new robust Italianate style on Baillairgé's work. Christina Cameron

FIG. 115. The pulpit for the church at Sainte-Marie de Beauce reveals Baillairgé's discovery of bulbous and ornate forms. Christina Cameron

This particular phase of the Gothic style was first defined at the beginning of the nineteenth century and treated in at least two of Baillairgé's books: John Henry Parker, *An Introduction to the Study of Gothic Architecture* (1849), and Augustus Pugin and E. Willson, *Specimens of Gothic Architecture* (1821). The Decorated style featured rich mouldings and clustered shafts, and introduced the ogee arch, called the *arc en talon* or *arc en accolade*. These details all appear at Sainte-Marie. Most striking are the animated criss-cross patterns of ribs, meticulously laid out on a surviving drawing for the vault (fig. 113). They too first appeared in England in the fourteenth century. The description of Decorated Gothic vaulting in another of Parker's books matches Baillairgé's design exactly: "Ribs are introduced crossing the vaults in directions opposite to their curves, so as to form in some degree an appearance of net-work upon them ... The short ribs which connect the bosses and intersections of the principal ribs and ridge-ribs, but which do not themselves either spring from an impost or occupy the ridge, are termed *liernes*, and the vaults in which they occur, *lierne vaults*."[8] In general terms, the interior of Sainte-Marie church excels in its bold profiles – in marked contrast to the restraint of early nineteenth-century carving in Quebec – and its cleverly interwoven theme of quadrefoils, first stated on the exterior and repeated on the doors, balcony, pew, and altar (figs. 114–15). It is undoubtedly Baillairgé's masterpiece in the Gothic idiom.

Reaction to the church was mixed. Critics found it pretentious, though admitted its daring. Curé Proulx was accused of having burdened the parish with a substantial debt. The archbishop admitted in 1867, however, on completion of the interior, that it was "a grand and magnificent gothic church, well-finished ... and perfectly beautiful."[9] Baillairgé himself always considered it to be one of his major accomplishments. He unabashedly wrote on more than one occasion that Sainte-Marie church had "one of the finest gothic interiors in Canada."[10] A photograph of the interior appeared in the *Canadian Architect and Builder* in 1890 and architectural drawings of the interior were exhibited by Baillairgé at the third annual meeting of the Province of Quebec Association of Architects in 1892.[11]

About 1857 Baillairgé's contracts with the diocese decreased dramatically. In letters to his own parish, Baillairgé complained that he had little to do and pleaded for more work. The parish council of Notre-Dame de Québec responded by offering him a series of minor jobs. He surveyed two parcels of land for the cimetière Saint-Charles, begun in 1855, and the cimetière Belmont, exploiting the natural curves and ravines to create informal meandering paths in the manner of English gardens. He built a small brick funerary chapel for the latter,[12] and made two renovations, one an extension to the altar end of the chapelle de la Congrégation, the other the design of a small annex for the presbytery of Notre-Dame to house offices for the treasurer.

The parish also came forward with three more substantial projects: the fence in front of the cathedral, housing for the Jesuit priests, and the presbytery for the Saint-Jean-Baptiste church. With the first of these three major contracts, Baillairgé finally got his chance to erect an ornamental fence in full view of the public on prime land in the Upper Town. The fence (fig. 116) resembled an earlier one at the Marine Hospital. Both were designed with cut-stone base or wall with iron railing above. At Notre-Dame the iron work of the sequence of square piers composed of railing was lighter, and the gates with their circular motifs and free flowing scrolls were more delicate than the Marine Hospital example. Baillairgé once again drew inspiration from his library, modelling Notre-Dame's fence on the gates at the Royal Lodge, Hyde Park Corner, London, reproduced in his copy of *Knight's Scroll Ornaments* (fig. 117). The curved plan of the fence at Notre-Dame, in which the enclosure seemed to be wrapped around the cathedral façade, added a graceful elegance that was missing in the earlier version at Marine Hospital.

The residence for Jesuit priests, known as the Congrégation Notre-Dame de Québec, was the most substantial contract that Baillairgé enjoyed from the parish council during this period. In its exterior appearance and interior trim the residence resembled work of the same year at Laval University. The walls of the façade, for example, were of smooth Deschambault stone, finished in fine bush-hammered work and laid up with thin mortar joints. The doorway had the characteristic curved lintel with flowing tendrils that Baillairgé had introduced in the flanking doors of the main university building. The plainly finished interior had a refectory, library, oratory, recreation room, and two sacristies.

The third important contract was the presbytery for the Saint-Jean-Baptiste church which was erected in 1858. What should have been a straightforward commission eventually plunged Baillairgé into more controversy. His plan called for a two-storey structure with cast-iron decorations and a hipped roof with broad flattened roof ridge to be used as a balustraded terrace. Originally he had proposed a completely flat roof similar to that at Laval University,[13] but some unidentified builders criticized his plan and convinced the church wardens to remove the ornaments, arguing that they distracted from the neighbouring church. What was even more insulting to Baillairgé was their insistence that his avant-garde roof be replaced by a traditional sloped roof, because the cement for the flattened ridge was unreliable. Baillairgé dashed off an angry letter to the wardens, affirming the reliability of Warren's cement and explaining that the university roof had leaked because of the coping and not the cement. He remonstrated with the wardens on their lack of confidence in him as a professional architect and renewed his attack on builders with pretensions to being architects: "What other interest do I have than that of making good, solid buildings, as beautiful as possible within the means of the owners. But some prefer the ideas of any Tom, Dick or Harry. With this system, Quebec will always have the same dreadful style of buildings, always the same bad taste. When one hires a doctor, one follows his directions. Likewise, when one hires a good architect, one ought to act in the same way and not seek out the opinion of the first carpenter or mason to appear."[14]

Baillairgé's frustration with the clergy, clearly apparent in this letter from October 1858, developed into open warfare a year or so later over his plans for Sainte-Marguerite church. Though they had been made in 1856, construction was delayed until 1862. All seemed to be proceeding smoothly in February 1860 when the wardens called for tenders and advised that the plans and specifications could be seen in Charles Baillairgé's office.[15] What happened next is conjecture. Monseigneur Baillargeon appears to have intervened and refused to approve part or all of Baillairgé's plan. He had the proposal modified by another architect, Raphael Giroux (a former apprentice of Thomas Baillairgé), including the roof frame which Baillairgé judged to be so weakened in Giroux's plan that the roof would cave in. Incensed at

FIG. 116. The ornamental fence in front of Notre-Dame de Québec. (1857). Canadian Parks Service, Heritage Recording Services

FIG. 117. The model for the iron fence at Notre-Dame de Québec came from one of Baillairgé's architectural books. Knight, *Knight's Scroll Ornaments*, plate 29

this meddling and aware of the potential damage to his reputation if the roof collapsed, Baillairgé fought back by circulating a copy of the plan for the roof frame to Quebec's architects and builders. They in turn signed a petition endorsing Baillairgé's opinion that the "*entrait*" or collar tie was too high.[16] Baillairgé then sent the petition to Monseigneur Baillargeon, together with a long letter that voiced his concerns for the profession of architecture in Quebec and poured out his resentment at not being given his share of diocesan business. A few excerpts from this angry letter will suffice to summarize his arguments:

I ask you in grace not to force the parishioners of Sainte-Marguerite, against their wishes and in spite of the certificate of all the best builders of Quebec, to execute a plan which would cost them a great deal of money while at the same time endangering their lives and obliging them to rebuild in 20 years a church which ... ought to survive at least a century ....

You refer all the plans to Giroux or, if he is not available, to Bernard. Monseigneur, I declare before God that several priests (at least five or six) have complained to me about your requirement to have their plans done by Giroux or others ....

You persist in repudiating me, although I was employed for so many years by the Archbishop ... You have the misfortune of trusting too much in your own taste and judgement in this matter of church plans. I do not mean to insult you by saying that though you may be an excellent bishop, you may be very indifferent as an architect. Each to his own trade ... In all things related to religion and the church, I must bow to my bishop; but in matters of construction I think I know of what I speak; and I will prevent by all legal means the erection of buildings in this country from such defective plans.[17]

How the archbishop reacted to this challenge has not been recorded. The fact that Baillairgé never received any further commissions from the clergy speaks for itself. It is ironic that in the same era in which Baillairgé was producing his finest examples of church designs – especially the Gothic Revival church at Sainte-Marie de Beauce – he lost the patronage of the Roman Catholic clergy and thereby cut himself off from one of the most important employers of architectural services in Quebec City.

7   First Mishaps: Department of Public Works

OVER THE YEARS CHARLES BAILLAIRGÉ'S DEALINGS with the Department of Public Works fluctuated between intense satisfaction and keen disappointment. During the 1850s he attempted to prepare the ground work for his eventual appointment as chief architect. Despite his success in penetrating the charmed circle of government commissions by winning two relatively minor contracts for the Parliament House fence and the Marine Hospital bathroom wing, his relationship with the Department of Public Works was rife with misunderstanding and bitter hostility. His independent and assertive behaviour, following his unsuccessful bid for the Quebec Customs House, threatened to cause a permanent rupture with the department and ruin his chances for attaining the cherished post of chief architect.

But before one can properly understand Baillairgé's interaction with the Department of Public Works, a brief examination of departmental operations is necessary. His early misadventures with the department were the result of three problems endemic within the organization: frequent changes of ministers (a reflection of the political unrest of the period), repeated adjustments to the administrative structure, and strong personalities among some staff members.

The Department of Public Works had grown out of the Board of Works, an independent board established in the new United Province of Canada in 1841. It was created by Lord Sydenham in order to administer funds for roads, bridges, harbours, canals, and occasionally buildings required by the government. The most costly enterprise was the never-ending canal building. Poor organizational structure and administrative procedures, which resulted in serious overspending, led to the revamping of the Board of Works in 1846.[1]

Although this reorganization took place in 1846, the very year that Baillairgé began his architectural practice, it is important, in view of Baillairgé's later involvement with him, to linger over the personality of one of the members of Sydenham's original board, H.H. Killaly. Hamilton Killaly was an Irishman and an engineer, appointed by Lord Sydenham as chairman of his newly created Board of Works. Killaly was a colourful character, judging from a description by Lord Sydenham's chaplain, which portrayed him as a "jovial Irishman ... attired in tight satin breeches and patent leather dancing pumps ... the ensemble topped by a hat so dilapidated that it looked ... as if he had tumbled into the mud of a nearby ditch returning from an Irish fair."[2] He probably had a more conniving side – a prerequisite for survival in a public works department in the colonies – as a letter written in 1856 by John Langton suggests. He describes Killaly as "a jolly fellow brought out by Lord Sydenham and about as double dealing and corrupt a scoundrel as you will meet anywhere."[3] Even if this account is exaggerated, Killaly was clearly adroit in manipulating the Board of Works. Named as chairman, he at once assumed the added role of chief engineer, meaning in effect that in his role as political head he endorsed decisions that he made in his role as technical specialist. Expenditures were enormous and virtually uncontrolled.

The reorganization of the Board of Works in 1846 was the politicians' response to Killaly's amassing of power. Political scientist J.E. Hodgetts's important study of the nascent civil service from 1841 to 1867 has carefully examined the structural flaws inherent in the Board of Works and has isolated as the central issue the conflict between the political head (usually a layman) and the technical expert. The reorganization of 1846 was an attempt to redress the balance by severing the two functions. The political head was to become the chief commissioner, with a second political position, assistant commissioner. Technical staff positions included the chief engineer, the secretary, and so forth. The staff positions were of course permanent ones, as was the office of assistant commissioner, the latter for no obvious reason.[4] The chief commissioner changed frequently, subject to the vagaries of the electorate. Hodgetts has rightly concluded that it was inevitable that, while the legal authority rested with the chief commissioner, the real power fell to the key permanent positions – the assistant commissioner, secretary, and engineer.[5] From the 1846 reorganization until 1859 the official name was still the Board of Works, although it was just as often referred to as the Department of Public Works, perhaps because its structure was more closely allied to that of a department than an independent board.[6]

A digression from structure to personalities is once again instructive. The key post of assistant commissioner, which was a political appointment, was occupied from February 1851 to 1859 by the same H.H. Killaly who had been stripped of power by the 1846 reorganization. The secretary was Thomas A. Begley, who had held the position from its creation in 1841, survived the reorganization, and remained in that function until 1859. Together Killaly and Begley could sign contracts and make decisions in the name of the chief commissioner. For this reason, Hodgetts has argued that by 1859 Killaly exercised equal power with the political head.[7] Baillairgé's early dealings with the Department of Public Works should be viewed against this backdrop of strong personalities and bureaucratic confusion.

PARLIAMENT HOUSE WING

In 1850 the government of the Province of Canada announced its intention to rebuild the old wing of the legislative building in Quebec City, the former Episcopal Palace, which had not been used as the seat of government since the 1837 rebellion. When an earlier government had repaired the building in 1830, it had been Thomas Baillairgé who had produced the design. Twenty years later, Charles made an attempt to win the contract for the wing. He had not yet worked for the central government, although he had contemplated submitting plans for the new Montreal Court House.[8] In August 1850 *Le Canadien* reported the rumour that Charles's brother George-Frédéric, at that time an assistant draughtsman with the Department of Public Works based in Montreal,[9] was to supervise the construction of the new wing for the Parliament House.[10] Infuriated that his brother, who had not been trained as an architect, should receive the contract, Charles fired a letter off to the Department of Public Works offering his own services as a *qualified* architect and pointing out that "it is my cousin, Thomas Baillairgé, with whom I studied architecture, who erected the present wing of the Parliament house, and it ought to remain in the family."[11] But his appeal was to no avail, for the department, showing none of the loyalty that the Roman Catholic clergy had shown to the family, awarded the initial contract to Pierre Gauvreau and further work to George Browne.

PARLIAMENT HOUSE FENCE

Despite this initial rebuff, Baillairgé's innovative and ambitious character led him to renew his efforts to seek the challenges offered by the major undertakings of the Department of Public Works. For the Parliament House fence, Baillairgé was apparently invited to submit a proposal in the spring of 1853 by the chief commissioner of the Board of Works, Jean Chabot.[12] With the government located in Quebec, it may have been Baillairgé's success with the Music Hall and his other works that brought him to Chabot's attention. It may also have been Baillairgé's letter seeking employment – already cited at length in this study – that convinced Chabot to try out this young architect from Quebec.[13] By his own admission, Baillairgé was so anxious to have a chance to prove himself that he bid low in order to exclude other architects.[14]

As in the case of Laval University, Baillairgé was responsible for the design and supervision of the work. Board of Works' projects at that time were generally marked by intrigue, delays, extra payments, and the like, engendering massive volumes of paperwork. Baillairgé's commission was no exception. But the circumstances surrounding the fence project were even more convoluted than usual, creating grounds for suspicion and misunderstanding. After he had produced two series of plans for the fence – the first proposal being considered too costly – the Parliament House for which the fence was intended burned down in February 1854. Since the contracts for the stone and iron work had already been signed, the department chose to transfer the work to the Marine Hospital, another government property. The change of site delayed the works, for the plans had to be adjusted to the new terrain; it also entailed additional costs, for the fence required more piers, and the distance for workmen and materials to travel was greater.[15]

But there were problems of a greater magnitude than the time delays and escalating costs. In the confusion over the Parliament House fire and the selection of a temporary seat of government, the commission for the fence was transferred to the Marine Hospital without any written authority being transmitted to the architect. According to Baillairgé, the then chief commissioner of public works, Jean Chabot, gave him verbal instructions to make whatever adjustments were necessary and to submit extra charges on behalf of himself and the builders.[16] To make matters worse, Chabot also gave Baillairgé verbal authorization to design and build a new bathroom wing at the hospital. As Baillairgé explained in a letter to the Board of Works in 1855: "The small wing for the water closets and other works therewith connected were ordered (by the Hble J. Chabot, then chief commissioner of the Public Works) to be proceeded with by the day instead of by contract, and the several already paid on account of those works and still required to complete the works are as follows."[17] In the case of the fence, there was confusion about which works were part of the contracts and which were extra. In the case of the bathroom wing, they were all extra, to the tune of £2123! Baillairgé must have been naïve to continue on that basis. The board quite properly wanted nothing to do with an open-ended situation in which a young Quebec architect was signing an unending series of certificates for payment of works that had never been approved.

FIG. 118. The fence erected around Quebec's Marine Hospital in 1854 represents Baillairgé's first contract with the federal Board of Works. ANQ, photothèque, GH-970-147

The inevitable happened. Jean Chabot had been dismissed as chief commissioner. The department refused to pay the bills. Baillairgé wrote lengthy epistles of explanation and justification to the department. Costs escalated. The works were suspended, pending an investigation. Finally the fence and wing were completed in June 1855, at considerable cost to Baillairgé's reputation with the Board of Works.[18]

The fence itself was a highly successful design (fig. 118). It had a cut-stone wall or coping below and ornamental iron railing painted and bronzed above. The gate posts of cut stone featured flattened Greek capitals similar to those of the flanking doorways of Laval University. Above the gate posts were iron lamps with stained glass. Baillairgé himself was satisfied with the result, as his immodest comment illustrates: "I believe that anyone who sees the fence as built will not hesitate to say that it equals in appearance, taste and richness, and surpasses in solidity, anything of the kind in Canada and even in the United States."[19] The architect must have been disappointed that the fence was hidden away at the Marine Hospital and not in full view of the general public in the Upper Town of Quebec. Though Baillairgé may well have impressed government officials with his design, he did not realize the extent of damage that the untidy management of affairs had done to his reputation. It was hardly an auspicious beginning for a man who wanted to become chief architect of the government.

The February 1854 fire at the Parliament House involved Baillairgé in another way with the Board of Works, for it was his buildings which were chosen as the temporary seat of government. He therefore was hired to refit them for government use. The first building selected was the chapel of the Soeurs de la Charité. Though Baillairgé drew up plans for converting the chapel into a legislative assembly, this structure in turn caught fire in May 1854, before Parliament had even convened there.[20] Desperate to find another building to finish out the parliamentary term (for the government was scheduled to move to Toronto in the fall of 1855), public works officials opted for the Music Hall. Only minor changes were required to render it suitable for legislative purposes.[21]

QUEBEC CUSTOMS HOUSE

But Baillairgé did not consider such alterations worthy of his talents. What he sought was the contract for the new Quebec Customs House to prove his abilities and hence secure the job of chief government architect. His ambitions appear to have been well-founded, for two members of government, the Hon. Jean Chabot, chief commissioner of pubic works, and the Hon. Hamilton H. Killaly had privately encouraged him and offered their support.[22] Baillairgé elaborated his submission for the Customs House competition over a period of two years. Although the land was only acquired in 1855, he began his project in 1854, for the main elements of his design appear in a preliminary cost estimate in that year.[23] That his plans were not finalized early in 1856 is evident from a letter of introduction from the mayor of Quebec to the mayors of Boston, New York, and Portland. With characteristic thoroughness, Baillairgé intended to examine American examples of customs houses before completing his own design:

I am taking the liberty of presenting to you Charles Baillairgé, architect of this city, who intends to visit Boston, New York and Portland in the near future, charged with a special mission on behalf of the Canadian government.

FIG. 119. Baillairgé's proposal for a new Customs House, Quebec, 1856. AVQ, fonds Charles Baillairgé, no. 6A-78

Having decided to erect a Customs House in this city, the government is sending Mr. Baillairgé to examine similar structures in the United States, where major improvements have been effected, especially in the distribution of interior space.

The city of Quebec considers any help extended to Mr. Baillairgé in carrying out this mission a service to itself.[24]

Baillairgé's competition plans, "6 sheets on drawing paper marked 'fire proof' in red ink and bound with blue ribbon, and … one sheet of details on tracing linen,"[25] survive in the Quebec municipal archives (figs. 120–3). They show a large free-standing structure in the Greek Revival style. The cruciform ground plan creates four separate façades, each finished with classical pediments in the manner of Greek temples. The two principal façades with monumental colonnades composed of forty-foot-high Corinthian columns were inspired by architect John Wells's portico for the Bank of Montreal (1848) on the Place d'Armes in Montreal.[26] Certain details of the proposal recall Baillairgé's work at his Laval University buildings, including the smooth ashlar walls, the scrolled window decorations, and the semi-circular headed doorways. The interior was to be handsomely finished with panelled vaults in the rotunda and long room, sweeping staircases in the open central vestibule, and rich ornamental plaster and wood trim.

Baillairgé's belief that his Customs House design was fireproof, as indicated on the plans, probably stemmed from what appears to be an unusually early proposal for cast-iron I-beams for the floor joists, visible in the cross-section. When used as a horizontal structural member, cast iron had proved to be weaker than wrought iron, which had a higher tensile strength. For this reason, Baillairgé followed current American practice by reinforcing the beams with brick arches.

A controversial feature was the flattened dome, which was intended to lighten the central staircase. His clumsy manner of depicting this dome was a tactical error. Perhaps it was his lack of skill in drawing perspective views, or perhaps he assumed too much technical knowledge on the part of

FIG. 120. Baillairgé's Customs House proposal featured the semi-circular doorways and scrolled lintel ornaments reminiscent of his other work from the mid-1850s. AVQ, fonds Charles Baillairgé, no. 6A-71

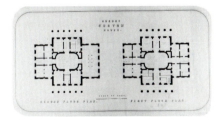

FIG. 121. The Customs House proposal featured a cruciform plan, with an open central vestibule enlivened by sweeping staircases crowned by a flattened dome. AVQ, fonds Charles Baillairgé, no. 6A-80

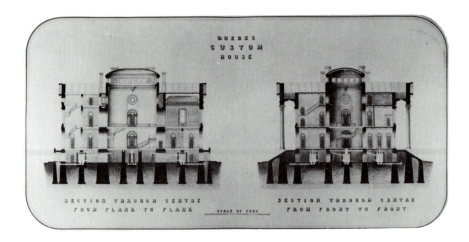

FIG. 122. The sections of Baillairgé's Customs House proposal reveal an unusually early attempt at fireproofing. AVQ, fonds Charles Baillairgé, no. 6A-82

the judges. Whatever the cause, his plans were misunderstood. Though the dome was never meant to be seen from ground level, the project was nevertheless criticized for its awkward, timid dome. Baillairgé hastened to explain to public works officials that he had never intended the dome to be seen from the street, as mathematical calculations would prove: "Without any doubt, if I had wanted to design a dome that would be visible from the outside and seen with the rest of the building, no doubt I have not succeeded. But ... I never had such an idea ... It suffices to place a ruler on top of the lantern and the edge of the cornice or covering of the roof and one will see how far this line has to be extended in order to reach a point above the ground equal to eye level ... The viewer would have to be far from the building to see even the top of the lantern."[27]

In general, his initial plans were well received in official circles and elicited high praise – at least privately – from the governor general and the prime minister, as this excerpt from an 1856 letter by Baillairgé reveals: "When I made my first plans for the Customs House ... everyone was delighted with me. There was talk of sending me to England at government expense – Mr. Chabot could tell you about it – the Governor and Mr. Hincks admired my plan and said at the time that they did not know that it was possible in this country to achieve as much."[28] Envisaging a successful bid for the Quebec Customs House as a major step towards establishing his reputation with the government, Baillairgé exploded with frustration when he placed fifth in the competition. Far from the government, which had moved to Toronto, he no longer had the pulse of the Department of Public Works and thus sorely misjudged the antipathy towards him that stemmed from the Marine Hospital problems. In a rancorous letter, which, he noted in a postscript, he had written in "a holy anger," Baillairgé tried to deal frankly with the real reason that he lost the Customs House competition, namely, government loss of confidence in him: "Since certain persons, whether badly informed or intent on destroying me, take pleasure in repeating that I recently cost the government £2500 for water closets at the Marine Hospital, and that this is the reason that I have lost the government's confidence and receive no more work, I must in justice to myself refute with all my strength such assertions."[29] The phrase "*ou pour me nuire* in this letter marks one of the earliest instances of Baillairgé's awareness – or paranoia, depending on one's point of view – of actively hostile forces working against his interests. Forthright, outspoken, and inflexible on questions of morality, Baillairgé began at this period to acquire "enemies" who would cause him considerable woe in the years to come. In his angry letter, he reported that an unnamed minister allegedly replied to those who were promoting Baillairgé as architect for the Customs House contract "not to talk of your Baillairgé. He cost the government £2500 for water closets and if he got a chance to build the Customs House, it would probably have a proportional overrun."[30]

This was probably Killaly, who was furious with Baillairgé for refusing to endorse his choice of site for the Customs House.[31] The anti-Baillairgé lobby was fueled by Pierre Gauvreau, a master mason in the 1840s who emerged as an architect in the 1850s. Baillairgé, it will be recalled, made a sharp distinction between architects like Gauvreau, who came from the trades, and "real" architects with academic training in design, draughtsmanship, mathematics, geometry, and so forth. That the two men were rivals for the job of government architect is apparent in Killaly's comments on a newspaper announcement. "Look at that!" Killaly reportedly said to Baillairgé, "this notice that Mr. Gauvreau has signed his name to as government architect. I am entirely against that, Mr. Baillairgé, Mr. Gauvreau does not have the education or the capacity to do this job. It is you Mr. Baillairgé who ought to be the government architect. I have already spoken two or three times to Mr. Chabot and I will do so again."[32] Even if there is some exaggeration in this report of Killaly's comments, the rivalry between Gauvreau and Baillairgé is clear. They tripped over each another's jurisdiction at the Marine Hospital, where Gauvreau in his capacity as "government architect" was supervising a major new wing at the same time that Baillairgé was supervising his fence and water closets. Just when this rivalry began is not clear, but it certainly existed by the time the competition for the Quebec Customs House was held. It is probably not mere accident that the drawings for the winning project, by William Thomas of Toronto, were displayed in the office of Pierre Gauvreau in Quebec.[33]

Disappointed by his failure to secure the Customs House commission and critical of the weaknesses he perceived in William Thomas's design, Baillairgé resolved to fight back. Determined to reinstate himself in the good graces of the Board of Works, Baillairgé vowed that he was ready "like the Phoenix, to arise from my ashes and to use my talents in the service of my country."[34] The opportunity did not present itself until 1860, when he secured the Quebec Jail commission which was to cause him so much woe.

8 Parliament Buildings Competition and the Quebec Jail

BY 1858 THE LAVAL UNIVERSITY BUILDINGS were completed and Baillairgé was faced with a dearth of contracts. Building activity in Quebec had slowly ground to a halt as the city, like other hopeful municipalities, awaited the final decision on the location of a permanent seat of government for the United Province of Canada. Faced with a dwindling number of projects from the religious and private sectors, Baillairgé was in a sense forced to renew his pursuit of government projects, in spite of his previous unhappy experiences with the Department of Public Works. Following new overtures to politicians and departmental officials concerning his possible appointment as chief architect, Baillairgé devoted his energies to the preparation of a grandiose Greek Revival design for the long-awaited permanent Parliament Buildings. Bitterly disappointed by his failure to win the competition, he received in 1860 a consolation prize in the form of the commission for the new Quebec Jail, a project which occupied him for almost three years until his nomination as associate architect of the Parliament and Departmental Buildings in Ottawa in April 1863.

In his campaign to become chief architect of the Department of Public Works, Baillairgé turned to H.H. Killaly for support. Killaly, it will be recalled, had initially been impressed with Baillairgé, envisaging for him the coveted job of chief architect. But Killaly had subsequently been annoyed by his independence and lack of flexibility when Baillairgé refused to rubber stamp Killaly's choice for the Quebec Customs House site.[1] Baillairgé evidently believed that that incident had been forgotten by 1858 when he wrote to Killaly, asking for his recommendation to the new chief commissioner, the Hon. L.V. Sicotte, whom Baillairgé did not know. In his letter, Baillairgé confessed that he was out of work, had "completed the university buildings in this city, and though I am always called on for any thing worth doing, I happen to be rather idle at the time." Baillairgé reminded Killaly of his earlier encouragement: "You may ere this, sir, have most probably forgotten me; but I can recall a circumstance which will prove that at the time you must have had a good opinion of me ... I happened [to be] in your office ... some 4 or 5 years ago. You held a newspaper in your hand and called my attention to an advertisement signed 'P. Gauvreau architect.' It was for some government work, and you remarked to me at the time how much you were annoyed that a person like Mr. Gauvreau, not being a gentleman, nor possessing any education should have signed his name as Government architect. You remarked at the same time that you had then already spoken to M. Chabot [chief commissioner] two or three times about making me Government architect."[2] The deep-seated rivalry that Baillairgé felt for Gauvreau, already discussed in relation to the Marine Hospital works, is plainly evident. In the accompanying letter to Chief Commissioner Sicotte, Baillairgé refers to Gauvreau as "the clerk of works for your department."[3]

Baillairgé's recourse to Killaly was an unlucky choice. Out of touch with departmental intrigues since the government had returned to Toronto, Baillairgé obviously was unaware that Sicotte was about to destroy Killaly's empire. In the autumn of 1858 Sicotte prepared a memorandum setting forth the weaknesses in the departmental organization that prevented the chief commissioner from exercising control and his legal responsibility. This led to another major reorganization of the department through an 1859 amendment which clarified the structure. The position of assistant commissioner was abolished and the new position, deputy commissioner, was clearly subordinate to the chief commissioner.[4] Sicotte also dismissed Killaly and Begley unceremoniously, in spite of their lengthy service. Hodgetts has described these events: "The informal compact between Begley, the Secretary, and Killaly, the Assistant Commissioner, was destroyed. Begley was the first to go, dismissed as 'inefficient, unfit and utterly incapable for the duties assigned to him.' Killaly thought 'poor Begley' had been sacrificed to the politicians, but perhaps his acid observations were attuned to the almost certain knowledge that his head would be the next to fall before the axe of the Chief Commissioner, as indeed it shortly did."[5] In view of this upheaval, the recommendation that Baillairgé sought from Killaly in September 1858 certainly would have fallen on deaf ears. His discovery that supervision for the court house and jail at Rimouski had been awarded to Pierre Gauvreau, junior, son of his nemesis, only added insult to injury.[6]

PARLIAMENT BUILDINGS COMPETITION

Baillairgé was probably able to contain his disappointment without much difficulty, for he considered this superintendant's job as a mere stop-gap measure to fill the interval until the competition for the Parliament Buildings was announced. This competition depended on the final resolution of the hotly debated issue over the location of the permanent seat of government. By 1856 the government, recognizing the intolerable financial burden that came from moving the government and its offices up and down the Saint Lawrence River every four years, decided to select one city as its permanent headquarters.[7] Which city would win? Throughout 1857 Quebec City newspapers printed well-substantiated rumours that their municipality would be chosen. In July *Le Canadien* reported that "our letters from *a very good source* assure us that Quebec has definitely been chosen as the capital" and in September the paper confirmed that "rumour has it that Quebec has been chosen as the permanent seat of government."[8]

Quebec's hopes were dashed in January 1858 when Queen Victoria named Ottawa as the capital of the United Province of Canada. But even then uncertainty prevailed. A vote the following July proposing an amendment to the effect that Ottawa ought not to be the permanent seat of government was carried by sixty-four votes to fifty. As late as November 1858 some remained convinced that the choice would still be Quebec. The government finally made its intentions unmistakably clear in February 1859, when, after narrowly winning a crucial vote on the question, the new chief commissioner of public works, the Hon. John Rose, advised the governor general to send officials to Ottawa to select the exact site for the new buildings.[9]

In anticipation of this competition, Baillairgé began working on his proposal in 1858. Although neither city nor site had been chosen at that point, Baillairgé seems to have drawn up his plans on the assumption that the city would be Quebec and the site would be the land occupied by the so-called Jesuit Barracks, the former Jesuit College.[10] In his letter of September 1858 to the chief commissioner of public works, the Hon. L.V. Sicotte, who was in

FIG. 123. Baillairgé's 1858–9 proposal for permanent Parliament Buildings for the Province of Canada. AVQ, fonds Charles Baillairgé, no. 6A-108

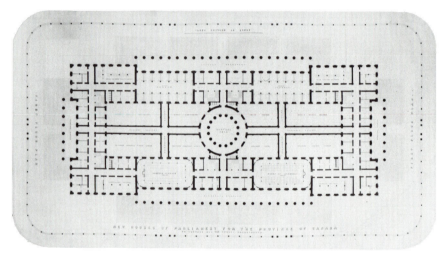

FIG. 124. The plan for Baillairgé's proposal for the Parliament Buildings competition arranges the two assembly halls symmetrically. AVQ, fonds Charles Baillairgé, no. 6A-112

fact replaced before the Parliament Buildings competition took place, Baillairgé unabashedly presented his credentials and referred to the plans that he hoped to show to the department: "I am considered a man of talent and of genius in architecture, surveying and civil engineering. I hope soon to have the opportunity to present to your department a plan for the Canadian Parliament Buildings and at that time I count on proving myself, I believe, the equal if not the superior to anyone in this field on the continent."[11] When in February 1859 the choice of Ottawa received legislative confirmation and funds were voted for the public buildings, Baillairgé was ready to spring into action. In a ploy to pre-empt the competition process, Baillairgé offered his plans to the government in March, before any competition had been announced: "Government having appropriated £225000 to the erection of public buildings, will be desirous, for that money, to procure a building affording the largest amount of accommodation and a monument of *grandeur* to the Province. I have lately completed a set of plans which I can safely challenge America or even Europe to surpass. I made them expressly to suit the sum of money voted and earnestly beg of you to command my presence at Toronto to explain my views. If the expense of new plans is an object to Government I am ready to make a present of mine to your department provided I have the superintendence of the work, or provided only they be paid for if they are adopted."[12]

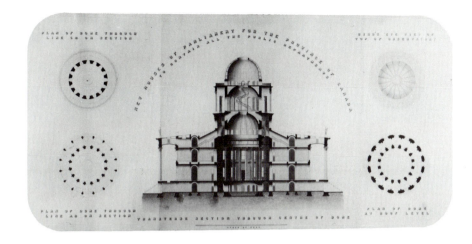

FIG. 125. In this transverse section through the centre of the dome, the grace of Baillairgé's proposed Parliament Buildings is apparent. The Corinthian colonnade around the main rotunda is echoed by the central circular foyer below. AVQ, fonds Charles Baillairgé, no. 6A-109

Baillairgé's plans – though not his wooden model – for the Parliament Buildings have survived in the Quebec municipal archives (figs. 123–5). They reveal a monumental design in the neoclassical style. Each façade of the rectangular building, which measured 500 feet by 250 feet, had Baillairgé's familiar recessed or *in antis* entrance with many steps and an imposing colonnade in the Corinthian order. On top of the columns were bronze statues of Canada's founding fathers and famous men, inspired by British and French public buildings in the neoclassical style. The walls flanking the peristyles were treated with two-storey fluted pilasters of the same order. Crowning the composition was a rotunda, whose lowest drum, as Baillairgé pointed out, would not be seen from the ground level and was hence quite plain.[13] The Corinthian colonnade around the main section of the rotunda found its echo inside in the central circular hall below, which was eighty feet in diameter and an overwhelming ninety-six feet high. Certain Baillairgesque features are recognizable, in such details as the scrolled lintels above the windows, reminiscent of the Têtu and Leaycraft houses, and the semi-circular doorways like those at the pensionnat of Laval University.

The building was meant to house the legislative assemblies and all the government departments. There were two assembly halls and an open rooftop terrace. Baillairgé tried to make it fireproof by applying his civil engineer's knowledge to the task. He subdivided the space into fifteen sections that were separated by solid walls and iron fire doors, allowed for eight staircases for rapid egress, used iron strapping in the roof frame, and incorporated cast-iron columns into the fabric of the building.

Baillairgé considered his project "bold and grand," believing that "it is highly important to the province that we should possess at least one building worthy of the United Provinces of Canada."[14] He stated that he drew his inspiration from some of the finest and most recent buildings in England and France such as the British Museum, London (Sir Robert Smirke, architect, 1847), St George's Hall, Liverpool (Harvey Lonsdale Elmes, C.R. Cockerell, and Robert Rawlinson, architects, 1841–54), La Bourse, Paris (A.-T. Brongniart and others, 1808–15), and part of the Louvre,[15] all of which (except the Louvre) were imposing Greek Revival structures with grandiose colonnades. The closest parallel is with St George's Hall, described by architectural historian J. Mordaunt Crook in his study of the Greek Revival as a building "of monumental strength and grandeur."[16] By choosing such models, Baillairgé clearly allied himself with the contemporary European neo-classical movement, which was at that point reaching the end of its popularity. Believing that it was the only proper style for public buildings because it relied on fundamental principles of eternal beauty, Baillairgé explained his philosophic position by comparing buildings of monumental design – that is to say, neoclassical buildings with imposing colonnades – to Niagara Falls: "Do you want to know what effect is produced by grand and monumental architecture? It is like the impression that Niagara Falls makes on us when at first we cannot grasp its total effect. Man needs to be prepared for this masterpiece of nature. Yes, he must see these eternal falls again and again to understand fully their grandeur. The more he sees them, the more he admires them, the more he is impressed and overwhelmed. He may see them a thousand times and the charm will always seem new, always inexplicable."[17]

In response to Baillairgé's offer to show his plans to officials, the department sent a standard non-commital acknowledgement.[18] In view of the recent reorganization, the new team – Chief Commissioner John Rose, Deputy Commissioner Samuel Keefer, and Secretary Toussaint Trudeau – wanted to avoid the kind of irregular behaviour which had led to the ouster of Killaly and Begley. On 7 May 1859 the Department of Public Works published the rules and requirements for a competition for "plans and designs for the several Public Buildings proposed to be erected in the City of Ottawa," with three distinct parts: Parliament Building, Departmental Buildings, and governor-general's residence.[19]

Baillairgé entered two sets of plans for the Parliament and Departmental Buildings competitions, an "Italian" one with the motto "Stadacona," which has not survived, the other listed as "No motto or name" in the "Classic" style.[20] This is presumably the proposal developed in 1858, since it was automatically eliminated for not conforming to requirements. The two evaluators for the competition were Keefer and F.P. Rubidge, the assistant engineer. Keefer evidently left the first screening to Rubidge, for he only scored three out of the sixteen entries for the Parliament Building and three out of seven for the Departmental Buildings. Rubidge eliminated the two entries from "No motto or name" on the grounds of "non compliance with separating buildings and considered too costly" and "Parliament House and Departments in one building contrary to requirements." Baillairgé's other proposal "Stadacona" fared little better. Rubidge allotted a score of forty-three out of one hundred points for the Parliament Building, and fifty out of one hundred for the Departmental Buildings, both among the lowest scores of all the candidates. Rubidge was especially severe on "Stadacona" in the categories of adaptation to site, beauty of design, and conformity with conditions.[21] Although little more is known about the "Stadacona" proposal than Rubidge's vague label of it as being in the "Italian" manner, it is clear that the classical repertoire used in both Baillairgé's entries ran counter to the judges' obvious predilection for the more up-to-date Gothic Revival idiom, which had been given official sanction at the new Parliament Buildings at Westminster.

The winners were approved by the governor general on 29 August 1859 and Baillairgé's plans were returned to him in January and February of 1860.[22] It was a bitter defeat. Little did he imagine at that moment that his entanglement with the public buildings at Ottawa was far from over.

QUEBEC JAIL

Baillairgé was still smarting from the loss of the Parliament competition when the Department of Public Works offered him a consolation prize: the design and supervision of the new Quebec Jail. He threw himself into the project with fervour, hoping that he might still have a chance to win the coveted chief architect's position. From his previous experience, Baillairgé should have known that the terms of reference under which he agreed to work were well-nigh impossible to fulfil. Ambition clouded his judgment, however, and he accepted the commission. The difficulties that ensued continued to plague him, even after he went to Ottawa, and were the direct cause of his ignominious dismissal.

The Quebec Jail project began in a climate of confusion and indecision. In 1855 *Le Canadien* deplored the poor condition of the district jail and predicted that the government would build a new one on a site outside the city in the immediate future.[23] This rumour was well-founded, for in January 1856 the Department of Public Works published a call to architects to participate in a competition for the new prison at Quebec City. The vague wording of the announcement – only the prize money was mentioned, significantly not any specific site nor funds available – suggested that the department was responding to public pressure and was not wholly committed to immediate action. As if time were not important, the deadline for submissions was extended in April of the same year.[24]

Contrary to some accounts of these events, Baillairgé did not win this competition.[25] He did not even enter it. Although he prepared plans for the new jail in the spring of 1856, he missed the deadline. He intended to submit them late, knowing full well that rules were often bent in such matters, but decided against it after he lost the Quebec Customs House competition.[26] He feared that his plans would be judged on the quality of the architectural drawing (which he acknowledged to be less artistic than the work of some architects) and not on the architectonic merits of the building.[27]

It was perhaps a reflection of government upheaval and departmental turmoil following the establishment in 1857 of a Board of Prison Inspectors that the competition drifted for four years before the winners were announced. Still undecided in early 1860, the Department of Public Works asked for advice from the Board of Prison Inspectors, which had been constituted in 1857. The board's approval had to be obtained for construction of all prisons.[28] The board, headed by Dr J.C. Taché, sent a report on the competition plans in March 1860 and forwarded a lengthy memo two months later containing draft specifications along with rudimentary architectural plans and elevations (figs.126, 127). The department now had a series of competition plans on the one hand and the Board of Prison Inspectors' conditions on the other, causing Deputy Commissioner Keefer to inform the chief commissioner in a note jotted on the incoming memorandum from the prison inspectors: "These conditions should be put into the hands of an architect to have a detailed plan and specification prepared for His Excellency's approval ... The first thing to be done it appears to me is to have a decision as to which of the competition plans is entitled to the premium. Then the successful competitor, if approved, might be put in communication with the Prison Inspectors to mature the working plans."[29] The intention then, as of 21 May 1860, was to award the prizes for the competition and then ask the winning architect to

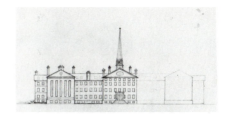

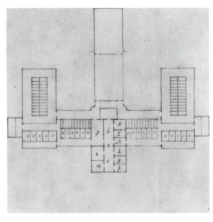

FIGS. 126–7. In 1860 the Board of Prison Inspectors developed a working plan for the Quebec Jail to serve as a guide for the winning architect. Their plan conformed to current ideas about prison design, particularly the flanking cell wings which are separated from the common services area in the centre. NA, RG II, vol. 276, no. 47,129, plates I, 3

abandon his project and rework that proposed by the Board of Prison Inspectors! One wonders why the department had bothered with a competition at all. Perhaps it was the departmental reorganization of 1859 which affected the proceedings.

Since Baillairgé had not entered the competition, how did he end up winning the job? The process is mysterious, but correspondence files of the department provide a few clues. Baillairgé must have heard unofficially that action was about to be taken on the proposed new jail, for in April 1860 he suddenly sent his set of plans for the prison to the department. Secretary Trudeau wrote back: "I have the honor to acknowledge receipt of your letter of the 13th instant, transmitting a sett [sic] of Plans prepared by you for the Jail proposed to be erected in Quebec, and offering your services to prepare the designs and to superintend the work, and to inform you that the matter has been referred to the Prison Inspectors."[30] His plans must have impressed departmental officials – or perhaps they were close in thinking to the plans proposed by the Board of Prison Inspectors – for an order in council followed swiftly. In it the first prize for the competition was awarded to R.C. Messer of Toronto and the second place to Thomas Ellis of Kingston. But it went on to state that neither proposal was considered satisfactory and finished by naming Charles Baillairgé as the architect to draw up plans and supervise construction.[31]

During this phase of curious manoeuvring, a crucial decision was made which influenced the subsequent course of events. This was the fixing of the sum of £16,000 as the total appropriation for the new prison at Quebec. How was this figure reached? No cost had been mentioned in the competition notice in 1856. The first time that a precise figure appeared was in the report on the competition plans by Dr Taché and Dr Nelson, written in March 1860. The estimated cost was set at £25,000.[32] Two months later, in the official report of the Board of Prison Inspectors, Dr Taché had lowered the figure to £15,000. "As for the cost of the projected building," he wrote, "it needn't be larger than a vast establishment built in Quebec ... which has many interior divisions and one of the most beautiful buildings in the country. This building cost only about £15,000 if I am well-informed, which I believe I am."[33] Dr Taché was not well informed, for the building in question was Baillairgé's Hospice des Soeurs de la Charité which had cost not £15,000 but £21,000. Deputy Commissioner Keefer jotted a note to the chief commissioner that sheds some light on the matter: "My own estimate of a Jail of the dimension herein given is £25,000. I understand the sum to be expended is limited to £16,000."[34] How the £16,000 figure was derived is uncertain, but Baillairgé may well have been correct when he stated that it was based on the estimate of the winning architect in the competition: "The second prize plan, that of Ellis, is estimated by him at £39,500 and Browne's at £91,336. Considering that the estimated cost of the competition plans sent in ranges as high as £177,000, it is not unfair to suppose that Messer's estimate of £16,600 is entirely out of the question; in the same way as, of a number of tenders varying greatly in amount, the lowest is generally considered too low, and the highest as much the contrary."[35] Despite these obvious danger signals, the allocation for funds for the new Quebec Jail was left at £16,000.

An appreciation of Baillairgé's final plan depends on an understanding of the evolution of prison architecture in the middle of the nineteenth century. Radical changes in prison design were linked to a reform movement which began at the end of the eighteenth century and which aimed at not merely the punishment but the rehabilitation of criminals. In England the movement was led by John Howard, who wrote several books on the deplorable conditions in British and European prisons, and in the United States by two groups, the Quakers and the Boston Prison Discipline Society. Reformists promoted the concept that criminals could be improved through education, contemplation, and work in an artificially controlled environment. They stressed the need to segregate prisoners by sex, age, and type of offence, to maintain silence and individual confinement so that inmates might reflect on their offences, and to provide work to occupy prisoners' time and make them useful to society.[36] The challenge for architects was to combine these theories with security requirements.

By the time that Baillairgé undertook the Quebec Jail, the Americans had taken a clear lead over Europe in the application of reform theories to prison design. In the first half of the nineteenth century two prisons in the United States emerged as models, the Auburn Prison plan, which was encouraged by the Boston Prison Discipline Society, and the Eastern Penitentiary plan, supported by the stricter Quakers. Auburn Prison, New York State (1816–25), had distinct wings for administrative services and prisoners' cells. It followed the principle of individual cells for night lock-up combined with common workshops and dining rooms where prisoners carried out daytime activities in silence. For security reasons the cells did not line the outer walls, as in earlier prisons, but were centred within the wing – a sort of structure within a structure. Iron grills allowed for light and surveillance, and balconies at each level permitted the entrance and egress of inmates. Since prison guards could observe more than one level of cells at a time, surveillance was good. The second model, the Eastern Penitentiary, Cherry Hill near Philadelphia (1825), was designed in the belief that solitary cellular confinement and total isolation from fellow prisoners were the most effective means of rehabilitation. Consequently, prisoners were locked up twenty-four hours a day in cells that were slightly larger than those of the Auburn plan. There were no workshops and no common rooms. The Eastern plan, considered by many to be too severe and psychologically damaging, served less frequently as a model for other prisons.

Baillairgé was aware of current theories of penology and prison design, not only from Kingston Penitentiary (1832–49), which adopted the Auburn system, but also from his visits to these American prisons in January 1856. With characteristic thoroughness, he presumably carried out this inspection tour from Boston to Washington in response to the call for plans for the Quebec Jail. In a letter of May 1856 to Chief Commissioner Lemieux, explaining why he could not make the competition deadline, Baillairgé confidently claimed he could design a superior prison: "As for the prison, I am unable to send my plans in time, and I am angry about it. After having seen and visited all the prisons and penitentiaries from Quebec to Washington and chatting with the superintendants of all these buildings about their good and bad points and about the improvements that could be made, and after having brought back a suitcase half-full of descriptions of all these buildings – and we know that on this subject the United States are more advanced than Europe – (since the best prisons in England are modelled on those in Philadelphia, etc.), I am convinced that I can produce a prison design that is superior

FIG. 128. Except for the choice of stylistic idiom, the road front elevation for Baillairgé's 1860 design for the Quebec Jail in the National Battlefields Park bears a strong resemblance to the working model from the Board of Prison Inspectors. SIQ

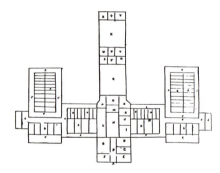

FIG. 129. Baillairgé's plan for the Quebec Jail, like the plan produced by the Board of Prison Inspectors, calls for cell blocks inset from the walls of the flanking wings. *Le Journal de Québec*, 10 Jan. 1861, 2

– at least in terms of discipline, separation of prisoners and interior arrangement – to all that I have seen."[37]

What Baillairgé's original Quebec Jail design of April 1860 looked like is not known. It presumably incorporated details from both American models. His final plan, for which drawings and specifications survive, is probably an amalgam of his ideas and those presented by the Board of Prison Inspectors in May 1860, as a comparison of the plans and elevations makes clear (figs. 126–30). Although the Prison Inspectors' elevation is superficially different in that it is clothed in neoclassical garb, the overall layout of central administrative block with flanking cell-block wings, the distribution of window openings (including the three-storey windows for the front cell blocks), and the internal arrangement of cell blocks (inset from the walls) all show the close interdependence of the two plans and their mutual derivation from the Auburn plan. The Board of Prison Inspectors considered that the Quebec Jail was constructed on "the great social principle 'that Society is bound to take every possible precaution to prevent those whom ... she thrusts into prison from coming out thence worse than when they entered it, in other words she must look to it that her Gaols do not become moral pest-houses, and nurseries of vice.'"[38]

Baillairgé's central block contained administrative services, the kitchen, chapel, and so forth, while the flanking wings had an assortment of cells, 66 large ones for debtors and 210 ordinary 3-foot by 8-foot cells (Auburn cells measured 3 1/2 feet by 7 feet, Kingston's 2 1/2 feet by 9 feet). The regular cells were stacked in one, two, and three tiers to suit requirements for segregation of inmates by groups. Workshops were located in the basement of the cell-block wings, which were made fireproof throughout by the vaulted brick ceilings at each level.

A long description of the Quebec Jail plan in *Le Journal de Québec* early in 1861, presumably prepared from Baillairgé's notes, revealed a thorough awareness of the reformist wave of prison architecture in the United States, in particular the Auburn model:

The other 210 cells will serve to detain at night prisoners who work during the day in the workshops ....

One will note that the cells are everywhere separated from the exterior walls by corridors, this system offering the greatest security against prisoner escape, since a prisoner who succeeds in getting out of his cell will still find himself within the walls of the prison and will still have a three-foot thick stone wall to pierce before reaching the outside.

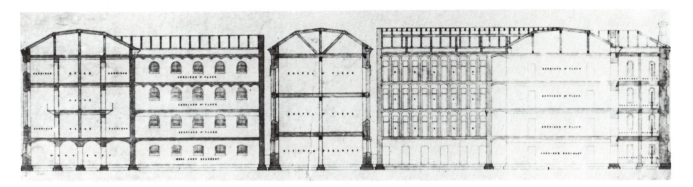

The central section is separate from the wings by iron fire doors to prevent any communication in case of fire.

The architectural style is necessarily severe as is appropriate for buildings of this type, with decoration reduced to a minimum.[39]

The semi-circular openings for some windows and the centre door, and the rugged appearance of the masonry walls, drawn from the Italian Renaissance *palazzi*, may have been borrowed from the infamous Newgate Prison in London (1770–85) and was in keeping with Baillairgé's new interest in the Italianate idiom, as shown at the Caisse d'économie and the Desbarats block.

That, then, was Baillairgé's plan. But what about cost? Baillairgé was given two stipulations when he received his instructions in June 1860 to prepare plans and specifications: to comply with the conditions set out in the Board of Prison Inspectors' memorandum and to limit the cost to £16,000.[40] By October of that year Baillairgé realized that it was impossible to meet both criteria. When he submitted the final working drawings, he explained to the department: "That I have complied with those *principles and conditions*, is manifest from Mr Meridith's letter of the 30th July last ... and, that I have been unable to suit my labour to the second requirement, as to cost, will not be wondered at, when it is considered that accommodation had to be provided (one of the P.I. conditions) for nearly 300 prisoners."[41] He estimated that the building would cost £30,300. To soften the blow, Baillairgé hastened to reassure the department that there would be no bills for extras: "I have specified everything – eschewing all ornaments to be of the most economical nature, with a due regard to the solidity and durability of the structure; and, *with a competent Contractor* [my italics] under my superintendance I am bold to promise the Department a building of appropriate style ... which ... will endure."[42]

Baillairgé was pragmatic enough to know that the allocation of £16,000 would not be changed quickly. He therefore proposed that the government construct only one cell-block wing and a scaled-down central block in an initial phase, estimating by no coincidence the cost at £16,000. He was banking on the probability that at a future date the prison would be completed as originally planned. Baillairgé's attempt to comply with an arbitrary sum and hence reach an estimate in reverse, as it were, showed poor judgment on his part. His proposal, unfortunately for him, was accepted.

Construction got off to an inauspicious beginning with the selection of Thomas Murphy and Thomas Quigley as general contractors. It will be recalled that Baillairgé had emphasized that success depended on the choice of a good contractor. In view of the subsequent deterioration of their rela-

FIG. 130. In this sectional drawing for the Quebec Jail, Baillairgé followed the reformist Auburn Prison model for the separation of common services such as the kitchen, chapel, and workshop from the cell wings. The stacking of the cells in the centre of the block is a security device. SIQ

FIG. 131. Only the centre block and one cell wing of Baillairgé's Quebec Jail were built in the 1861–6 period. This early photograph shows the severity of the exterior design and the rugged appearance of the masonry wall. ANQ, photothèque, N-1073-54

tionship it is important to note that Baillairgé and Murphy were good friends of long standing at the outset of this project. With his partner John O'Leary, Murphy had worked as a master plasterer on several of Baillairgé's important buildings of the mid-1850s, including the Saint-Jean-Baptiste church and the Trudelle, Têtu and Bilodeau houses. The problem with Murphy and his new partner Quigley was their lack of experience as general contractors. In all the projects they had worked on in 1858 and 1859, including the parish churches at Beauport and Sainte-Anne-de-la-Pocatière, and a convent at Rivière-Ouelle, it was always in their capacity as associated master plasterers.[43] The Department of Public Works' choice of contractors did not bode well for the project.

Construction began in the spring of 1861. What ensued will be set down briefly, followed by the conflicting interpretations of those events. During the first year the works appear to have proceeded on schedule, although the contractors' costs far outweighed their revenue.[44] During the 1862 season the works began to fall behind schedule, until Baillairgé finally reported to the department in July that the works had not caught up to his progress reports and that at that moment the contractors in fact owed money to the government. Moreover, the architect severely reduced a bill for extra work submitted by the contractors in July.[45] The department responded by withholding the contractors' monthly payment. Murphy and Quigley could then not pay their workmen. Labour relations degenerated to the point where the government's treatment of the workers was decried as harsh in the local press and Baillairgé was physically beaten on the construction site.[46] In the fall of 1862 the workmen quit, construction ground to a halt, and the building was left exposed for the winter, thereby suffering significant damage.[47] In April 1863, in the midst of these troubles, Baillairgé resigned from the project, having been called to Ottawa to supervise construction of the Parliament Buildings.[48] The Quebec Jail was turned over to architect Joseph-Ferdinand Peachy, a former apprentice of Charles Baillairgé who was about to become his partner during the latter's absence in Ottawa. Four months later Peachy was out, and the central block and one cell wing were terminated under the supervision of departmental employee and Baillairgé's enemy Pierre Gauvreau, at a final cost of about $130,000 or £31,500, close to Baillairgé's original estimate for the *entire* building.[49]

The two protagonists in the case, Baillairgé and the contractors, held opposing views as to what had gone wrong during these three years. Murphy and Quigley believed that the architect demanded an excessively high quality in the work, that he refused legitimate demands for extra charges for works not specified in the original contract, and that he under-measured the completed parts of the building. They blamed delays in construction on lack of instructions from the architect. In short, they accused Baillairgé of protecting his own professional reputation at the expense of the contractors by delivering to the government at the original estimate a building worth much more than £16,000.[50]

Baillairgé viewed the events differently. He blamed the inexperience of the contractors for the slow progress. He cited several examples. He had, for instance, to write out all the subcontracts with estimates (a function normally carried out by the contractor), for which service he charged the contractors professional fees, an act which he no doubt regretted later. Costs for the contractors increased when they hired a foreman to do part of their own work.[51]

But Baillairgé also realized that Murphy and Quigley were losing money on the venture. In his role as superintending architect he was caught between delivering the product at the agreed price and allowing legitimate extra charges to help the contractors out of their financial troubles. By December 1862 he had approved £6000 extra work, which included the addition of the fourth storey as originally planned.[52] He considered that he had been generous to the point of putting himself in a compromising position, so that when criticism grew in the fall of 1862 he wrote a letter defending himself which he intended to publish in the local papers. In the letter, which was not published until after his dismissal from Ottawa, he listed what concessions he had made to help the contractors:

Numerous minor concessions and alterations have been allowed by me, in every case for the benefit of the contractors, such as the substitution of fire brick for hammer-pointed stone, in the interior arches, over windows and doors, etc.; the use of stone spalls in the thicker brick walls; a redistribution of the saddle bars in the windows ... stone spalls and refuse instead of broken stone for the concrete ....

In fact there is not a clause in the contract that can be said to have been carried out to the letter, almost every alteration having been made for the direct benefit of the builders, while such as may have caused any extra labour or material have been fully allowed for.[53]

It is difficult to judge who was truly responsible for this debacle. Baillairgé had his share of responsibility, for it was he who had pared down the original plans to match the £16,000 allocation and it was he who had convinced Murphy and Quigley that this estimate was satisfactory – even though he later hypocritically referred to their estimate as "a notorious inadequate price."[54] If any doubts existed about Baillairgé's role in this matter, the secretary's letter to Murphy and Quigley in November 1860 clearly puts the responsibility on his shoulders. The letter contained a sketch plan of the original proposal, on which the contractors had based their bid, and proceeded to cite the architect's report on reductions which concluded that the plans, as modified, could be implemented for £16,000.[55] Perhaps Baillairgé had been too exacting in the interests of his own professional status. Perhaps Murphy and Quigley did deliberately bid low, as Baillairgé suggested, intending to make their profit on the extras. With hindsight and in light of the documents assembled together, it would seem fairer to view both sides as victims in an ill-conceived venture, one in which there were no winners, only losers, because the original terms of reference were impossible to meet.

How Baillairgé would have resolved the problems is an intriguing question which will never be answered. In the period just prior to his resignation, his inclination to seek replacement of the contractors was tempered by the realization that no other contractor would complete the work for the amount left in the original allocation. One can only imagine his relief when he received the call to Ottawa, allowing him to leave the problems to someone else, at least for the time being. He ought to have been sobered by the knowledge that unresolved issues and bitter animosities could be like slowly ticking time-bombs, awaiting the appropriate moment to explode.

WHEN BAILLAIRGÉ WAS CALLED TO OTTAWA in April 1863, he encountered firsthand the difficulties of controlling the country's largest construction project within the chaotic political and administrative framework of the Department of Public Works. To his detriment, he concentrated on the technical issues and ignored the political reverberations of the scandals and controversies then raging over the fiasco.

In 1863 construction on the Parliament and Departmental Buildings had been in abeyance for over a year while a Commission of Inquiry investigated the state of the works and sorted out the claims of the architects and contractors. In order to complete the buildings, the government drew up new and more stringent contracts for the remaining work. Baillairgé was appointed as joint supervising architect to carry out these second contracts. Had his task remained at that, he probably would have completed the job successfully and possibly would have attained his goal of becoming chief architect. His misfortune was to be asked by the department early in 1865 to take on an additional chore, that of collecting technical evidence on the site for the impending arbitration on the first contracts. With the high stakes involved in these settlements, Baillairgé thus became a threat to politicians and contractors alike, especially since it was well known that he was not afraid to speak forthrightly on such matters. His testimony had to be eliminated. Less than three months after the request to help prepare evidence for the arbitration hearing, Baillairgé was unceremoniously dismissed.

To understand Baillairgé's participation as associate architect for the public buildings at Ottawa from 1863 to 1865 and as a potential witness at the arbitration hearings, it is necessary to summarize briefly the events preceding his arrival. Although the history of the Parliament Buildings has been studied by several historians,[1] the initial construction phase has been particularly well analysed by political scientist J.E. Hodgetts who used it as a case study to demonstrate the structural and administrative deficiencies of the Department of Public Works at the time.[2]

The architectural competition, which it will be recalled was held in the summer of 1859, required that certain conditions be met, including cost restrictions of $300,000 for the Parliament Buildings and $240,000 for the two Departmental Buildings.[3] When plans by Fuller and Jones (under the motto "Semper Paratus") and Stent and Laver ("Stat nomen in umbra") were chosen, no one in the department bothered to test the plans for cost – nor for completeness, as proven by the omission of heating and ventilation systems from the original plans (although specifically mentioned in the notice to architects). This oversight necessitated a separate contract and afforded the contractors ample opportunity to make extra charges. Already the die was cast. The architects and deputy commissioner later readily admitted before the inevitable Commission of Inquiry that the winning designs in the expensive Gothic Revival style could never have been built for the announced appropriations.

In addition to this basic contradiction, the tendering process itself guaranteed that the project would end in calamity. In spite of the requirement for each tender to be accompanied by a detailed schedule of prices – to enable the department to measure the work for monthly progress reports and to assess the value of extra work not specified in the contract – the winning tender of contractor Thomas McGreevy from Quebec City had no schedule. Hodgetts has clearly explained the events which followed the awarding of the contract:

McGreevey [sic] obviously had friends at court for he was permitted to supply the required schedule some time after his tender had been accepted. It even appears that officials of the department accommodatingly made up the missing schedule by using prices taken from tenders that had been rejected ... Nor did this exhaust Mr. McGreevey's ingenuity, for we find that after the contract had been drawn up by the Law Officers, he asked that the work be split up – the firm of Jones, Haycock & Company to undertake the construction of the departmental buildings. In the process of redrawing the contract somehow the schedule of prices was left out and no reference at all made to what would constitute "extra" or "additional" work. Mr. McGreevey even arranged to have his contract exclude the clause that would have given him no claim for compensation had he exhausted the appropriations.[4]

Speculating on the identity of departmental officials who might have been party to this intrigue with McGreevy, Hodgetts has narrowed the choice to Chief Commissioner John Rose, who resigned in 1861, or Deputy Commissioner Samuel Keefer, who was fired in 1864.[5]

The incomplete plans, loosely worded contracts, and absence of price schedules ensured that when construction on the Parliament Buildings began in 1860 the monthly estimates would be swollen with extras and the appropriation would be swallowed up quickly. Indeed, by the end of 1860 over $423,000 (out of the total allocation of $540,000) had been expended and the walls were scarcely above ground.[6] How could this have happened? The Department of Public Works lacked the communication and administrative procedures to control this vast project. The politically responsible person, Commissioner Rose, who alone had the authority to approve extra work, complained that he was kept in the dark by Keefer and Assistant Engineer Rubidge. The most serious example of this mismanagement, according to the subsequent royal commission, was that the works for the heating and ventilation systems were carried out and paid for without estimates, contracts, or price schedules. Rose claimed that he had been unaware that such extra charges were being incurred until months afterwards.[7] The superintending architects, Thomas Fuller and Stent & Laver, also shared responsibility for these expenditures. Hired to supervise construction at the usual rate of 5 per cent on monthly estimates (up to an authorized maximum of $33,000), they interpreted this to mean 5 per cent on all extra work as well. Although the architects were meant to act as impartial enforcers of the contracts, with no authority to approve extras without written permission from the chief commissioner, they in fact had a financial stake in approving extra work and did so frequently.

The resignation in June 1861 of Commissioner Rose, who could no longer cope with the mounting bill of extras and dwindling appropriations, is of particular significance to Baillairgé's career, because his replacement was the fiery and outspoken founder and editor of Le Journal de Québec and member for the county of Montmorency, the Hon. Joseph Cauchon. It was Cauchon who was to play an instrumental role in orchestrating Baillairgé's dismissal in

1865. Cauchon did not last long in the post of chief commissioner of public works but, under the pretence of hastening the works to an early conclusion, he ignored his deputy commissioner and personally authorized in only four months the expenditure of $295,700 to the contractors, without receiving the ordinary or usual vouchers.[8] With the initial and supplementary appropriations gone, the government had no choice but to stop the works in September 1861. Cauchon resigned in May 1862 when his colleagues in the Cartier-Macdonald government were defeated.

The department halted the works in Ottawa and appointed a special investigator to examine the situation and propose a course of action to extricate the government from this untenable situation. He was none other than Hamilton Killaly, a man of great familiarity with public works who, it will be recalled, had been dismissed in the reorganization of the department in 1859. Hodgetts has accurately described Killaly as a man whose "own lengthy experiences with departmental practices apparently had left him with an extremely lenient attitude toward the contracting profession."[9] Killaly proceeded to measure all work done and materials delivered to the site, in a report on 11 March 1862, he generously concluded that the government still owed the contractors almost $500,000.[10]

The government rejected Killaly's findings, aware that the contractors were overcharging but realizing that the vague contracts and lack of schedules made it almost impossible to prove. In June 1862 a royal commission was appointed "to inquire into all matters connected with the Public Buildings in Ottawa." At the time of its nomination, $994,554 (compared with the original tendered price of $627,310) had been expended. The commission was composed of four well-known and impartial professionals: John Wilson, a lawyer from London; Victor Bourgeau, an architect and builder from Montreal; Joseph Sheard, an architect and builder from Toronto; and Joseph Stark, a civil engineer from Sorel. They came to a very different conclusion from Killaly, deciding that the contractors had been overpaid by more than $70,000 and that they in fact owed money to the government.[11] The commission's conclusions were of course rejected by the contractors who had nothing to lose by demanding – and eventually receiving – a hearing before an arbitration board. In the meantime, despite the implications of the Commission of Inquiry which put in doubt the department's ability to carry off such an enormous enterprise, the department merely drafted new contracts with proper schedules and offered them to the old contractors.

BAILLAIRGÉ AS ASSOCIATE ARCHITECT

When the works started up again in April 1863, the department set in place what it believed to be strict controls to avoid the pitfalls of the first contract. Reporting to the political head, now the Hon. U.J. Tessier, commissioner of public works in the newly formed John Sandfield Macdonald administration, was a triumvirate of technical experts composed of a superintendent and two associate architects. The superintendent was a departmental employee and assistant chief engineer, F.P. Rubidge; the architects were Thomas Fuller and Charles Baillairgé. They were put on salary, instead of the professional fee of a percentage of the expenditures, in order to remove any incentive for approving extra work.[12] The salary of £1000 or $4000 a year plus expenses was considered by Fuller to be a "comparatively high official salary,"[13] although it hardly matched the 5 per cent of $300,000 or $400,000 which the architects had received under the first contract. The new contracts with McGreevy and Jones, Haycock & Company were iron-clad, with little room for ambiguity since detailed schedules of prices for measurement were appended to the contracts. Even the proviso that the contractors would not be paid if the appropriations were exhausted was included. Final authority was given to the associate architects and the superintendent, as clause 14 from the contract made clear. But there was a loophole at the end of this clause which McGreevy eventually turned to his advantage: "But nothing herein contained shall prevent the Commissioner from reviewing any such determination of the Superintendent and Architects if he shall desire so to do, and of modifying, altering or revoking the same by any writing under his hand to such effect."[14]

By what process were Fuller and Baillairgé chosen to carry forward this project? Commissioner Tessier decide for unstated reasons that Fuller was the only architect from the original foursome to be retained: "After mature examination, he [Tessier] submits that the Architects who had charge of the works during their progress under the late Contracts, (with the exception of Mr. Thomas Fuller) should not be employed to continue the works under the proposed Contracts; and that another Architect, not previously connected with these works should be appointed to act in conjunction with Mr. Fuller."[15] As for Baillairgé, he met at least one of Tessier's criteria for the other appointment: he had no previous connection with the works. How his name came to Tessier's notice is unclear. There are no grounds for believing that the nomination was gained through political influence. It is more likely that departmental officials at the technical level put forward his name. They were, after all, seeking not a designer but a controller, a competent technical man who had experience in supervising important construction sites in Canada. Baillairgé's superintendence of major projects such as the Hospice de la Charité, Laval University, and the Quebec Jail qualified him on this basis. Perhaps it was Baillairgé's reply to a departmental query in 1861 about systems of measurement in Canada which impressed officials. In a twelve-page letter he gave a virtuoso display of technical knowledge and practical experience, comparing the different measurement systems used in Lower Canada and Upper Canada and demonstrating by mathematical calculation their application in terms of estimates and progress reports. Baillairgé's clear grasp and articulation of his subject, in marked contrast to his rival Pierre Gauvreau's two-page reply to the same question, must have convinced the department that this man had sufficient expertise and experience to deal effectively with the contractors' demands for extras.[16]

On the envelope of the order in council authorizing the appointment of the architects and superintendent, the commissioner scribbled:

Prepare letter of appt to Ths Fuller & Chs Baillairgé, as architects separately according to this order in council and ask an answer to it to be kept as an acceptance.
9 April/63
U.J.T.[17]

The choice, then was ultimately made by Tessier. Baillairgé accepted the appointment on 16 April 1863, moved his family to his parent's home in Quebec City, and took a room in Kavanagh's Boarding House in Ottawa.[18]

FIG. 132. This official portrait of public works employees at their headquarters in front of the old barracks on Parliament Hill was taken between April 1863 and August 1864. *Seated left to right*: Charles Baillairgé, associate architect; Frederick Preston Rubidge, superintendant; Thomas Fuller, associate architect. *Standing left to right*: John LeBreton Ross, clerk of works; René Steckel, assistant to the architect of the Departmental Buildings; William Hutchison, clerk of works for Eastern Block; George B. Pelham, clerk of works for Western Block; John Bowes, measurer for Parliament Buildings; John H. Pattison, measurer for Departmental Buildings; Joseph Larose, clerk of works for Parliament Buildings; King Arnoldi, assistant to the architect of the Parliament Buildings; and John Kelly, clerk of works. OMA, CA-0161

Far from the seat of government in Quebec City, the new team installed itself in Ottawa. The playing field was rough, as views taken during construction by photographer Sam McLaughlin reveal: acres of stone, brick, lumber, metal, and glass (fig. 134). But the opposing team – the contractors – was even rougher. A recently discovered photograph, probably taken in 1863, captured the government squad in formal attire at its headquarters on Parliament Hill (fig. 132). If they look grim-faced, it is perhaps a reflection of the awesome task that confronted them.

What precisely was Baillairgé's role? As associate architect with Fuller, he had a legal obligation to superintend the completion of all three structures. He and Fuller invariably both signed official correspondence, plans, and instructions, often with Rubidge's signature as well. In practical terms, however, the workload was divided between the two architects, Fuller resuming supervision of his own design for the Parliament Buildings, and Baillairgé assuming responsibility for the Eastern and Western Blocks of the Departmental Buildings as designed by Stent & Laver.

Baillairgé had to work from Stent & Laver's original drawings which had been brought forward as part of the second contract of April 1863 and countersigned by Jones, Haycock & Company and the associate architects. From these general plans, Baillairgé and his assistant René Steckel prepared working drawings for specific details, always identified by the letter B for Baillairgé after the drawing number (figs. 133–4). He also issued written instructions to guide the contractors, sometimes making reference to books by Gwilt, Weale, and Nicholson, part of his library which he had brought with him to Ottawa.[19] Though his scope for real change in Stent & Laver's design was obviously limited, Baillairgé proposed and had approved some modifications of a practical sort. For example, he insisted on raising the chimney stacks on both blocks of the Departmental Buildings "for, not only will they be altogether too low, both as regards draught and appearance, if carried out as now intended, but also out of keeping with the style of the Buildings" (fig. 135). He undertook a major redistribution of interior space to provide more office accommodation by utilizing the basement of the Western Block and the vast attic spaces of the Eastern Block. He increased the number of windows on the rear façade and removed some of the leaded windows in order to improve the lighting. The most significant difference between Stent & Laver's elevations and the Western Block as completed was the row of basement windows which replaced the simple plinth of the original design (figs. 136–7).[20]

Baillairgé's changes led to a nasty encounter with one of the original architects, Thomas Stent. But before examining this exchange one should consider an incident involving Stent & Laver which would be comical if it did not reveal such lamentable confusion – or hypocrisy – within the Department of Public Works. When construction was halted in autumn of 1861, the architects and contractors remained in Ottawa, waiting for the government to tidy up its paperwork and raise more funds, fully expecting to resume where they had left off. A year and a half later, when the second contract was signed and the associate architects appointed, Stent & Laver still had an office in the lower storey of the stone building on Barrack Hill belonging to the government. As late as November – seven months after Baillairgé and Fuller had assumed responsibility for the Departmental Buildings – Stent & Laver were still roaming around the site and had actually issued written orders to the clerk of works, William Hutchison, to knock down the new chimney shaft that the associate architects had designed. What was worse, Stent & Laver actually forced him to remove part of it on the spot![21]

What followed is as crafty a sleight of hand as one could ever hope to see. The clerk of works duly reported the unauthorized order from Stent & Laver to his superiors. From Quebec the commissioner, through his secretary, confessed himself "much surprised." "This action on your part," he wrote to the architects, "appears the more inexplicable in view of the fact that your connection with the buildings ended on the 2nd April last, when an order in council was passed dispensing with your services."[22] Stent & Laver pleaded innocence. They denied ever receiving notification of this order in council and added that no one had collected from them the books and official documents belonging to the government. Their letter is full of innuendo, with

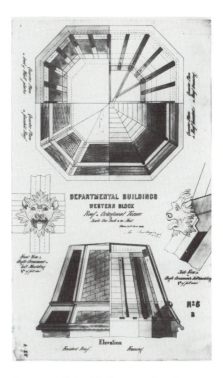

FIG. 133. Baillairgé had to complete Stent & Laver's design for the Western Block on Parliament Hill. This architectural drawing, dated June 1863 and identified by the B for Baillairgé, shows the plan, elevation, section, and details for the octagonal tower. NA, NMC-18062

FIG. 134. This early photograph of Parliament Hill shows the Western Block under construction in 1863. Baillairgé's octagonal tower is on the left. NA, C-18011

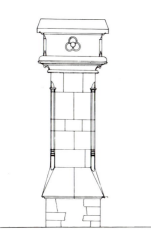
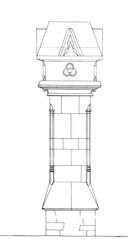

FIG. 135. Baillairgé's practical knowledge of building led him to propose changes to Stent & Laver's chimneys for the Departmental Buildings. NA, RG 11, vol. 422, no. 64, 860

FIG. 136. Photograph of the Western Block taken in 1864, during Baillairgé's stint as supervising architect. NA, C-7715

FIG. 137. Photographed soon after its completion in 1866, the Western Block of the Departmental Buildings bears the traces of several changes to Stent & Laver's 1859 design, in particular the added basement storey and heightened chimneys. The decorative slate roof, part of the original concept, was later replaced by copper, thereby diminishing the picturesque effect. NA, C-135

suggestions of political influence at Quebec and scarcely veiled attacks on the competence and honesty of Rubidge, Fuller, and Baillairgé. If this exchange between the commissioner and Stent & Laver lacks credibility, what about the masterpiece which Rubidge sent to Secretary Trudeau? In reading this extract, one should keep in mind that all the participants had been working on the same site for eight months:

In reply to your letter of the 23rd Instant directing me to enquire whether any correspondence or communication has taken place between the officers on the works and messrs Stent & Laver ....

I have the honor to report that Messrs Fuller and Baillargé [sic] distinctly deny having had any official communication, or correspondence with these Gentlemen, since the resumption of building operations; as do likewise all the Measurers and Clerks of Works.[23]

This is the background against which to evaluate Stent's attacks on Baillairgé in the *Montreal Gazette* in December 1863 and Baillairgé's equally virulent reply. In a bid to win back his job as supervising architect, Stent publicly accused Baillairgé of ruining his design, citing changes to the chimneys, windows, joists, cresting, and so forth as examples of this treachery.[24] In conjunction with these newspaper attacks, Stent carried his campaign to Barrack Hill, standing before the Departmental Buildings, stamping his foot and stick upon the ground, and asking aloud "if it were not enough to make a man shed tears to see his buildings disfigured with such work."[25] In Baillairgé's printed rebuttal, his "maiden essay on these buildings" written in January 1864 and addressed to the commissioner of public works, he countered by listing the errors he had been obliged to correct in the interests of safety and suitability. In the case of the chimney stacks, which were shown in the original design twice as far apart as they would have to be in execution, Baillairgé returned to a familiar theme by accusing Stent of "architectural humbug and dishonesty of purpose, in showing things on paper, not as they really will appear in execution, but as they should appear to suit the eye of those who have to pronounce upon the merits of competition drawings."[26] Baillairgé's heated response to Stent's claim that he alone understood the intricacies of Gothic Revival is worth close attention, for it revealed Baillairgé's values as an architect and his adherence to French academic training, especially as expressed by the *école polytechnique* in Paris,[27] which emphasized appropriate distribution of space and construction technology: "As to gothic art, Sir, supposing what you say be true; think you I would exchange my knowledge of construction, distribution, decoration, my familiarity with works and material of every kind, my practical experience in almost every branch of building, my knowledge of the value of all kinds of work and of the strength of materials and calculations applicable thereto, for the doubtful quality which you pride yourself upon and which is perhaps the only one you possess, if even that, of being able to tell whether some two-penny ornament or other pertains to the 13th rather than to the 15th century of Gothic history."[28]

One final aspect of Baillairgé's printed reply to Stent should be examined: his attitude towards corruption. After only six months on the site, Baillairgé had picked up enough information on the enormity of the scandal to make public statements on the dishonesty of the architects and contractors during the first contract: "Had I been here in time, [my integrity] might have helped to save the country the extra half a million or it may be more, which has so foolishly and unblushingly been lavished in the making of cut stone ducts, and drains and boiler houses, and dummy chimneys ... and useless excavations twice or thrice the size required filled in with solid masonry to boot, and all the host of unheard blunderings, incompetence and jobbery that Canada was ever destined to be made acquainted with and pay the price of.''[29] It was perhaps Baillairgé's technical knowledge and his evident distaste for corruption that led the commissioner to ask him, a year later, to collect evidence for the official arbitration.

But before that happened, Baillairgé devoted most of his effort to controlling expenditures, deadlines, and workmanship. The scenario was predictable. Right from the first progress report under the new contract of April 1863, the contractors challenged the fairness of the measurement system and made claims for extras.[30] The triumvirate of superintendent and associate architects responded quickly by issuing explicit instructions with drawings to explain how to measure intricate Gothic mouldings and decorations (fig. 138).[31] They came to the defence of John Bowes, measurer of the Parliament Buildings, insisting on his impartiality.[32] The government team stood firm despite some "dirty tricks" such as the erasing of the measurer's mark from the stones and the removal of scaffolding before the measurer could take his dimensions *in situ*, forcing him into approximate – hence vulnerable – estimates.[33] As the 1863 building season drew to a close, the government recognized the contractors' shortage of funds and in October approved the request of Jones, Haycock & Company to include 60 per cent of the value of raw and wrought materials (the contract had specified only "fixed and finished" work) in the monthly estimates.[34]

In spite of this concession, trouble was brewing. The contractors continued to have cash-flow problems. Labour disputes erupted with the carpenters and stone cutters. Materials were delayed in reaching the site and were often of unacceptable quality when they finally arrived. McGreevy threatened to pull off all day labourers as a gesture of defiance.[35] By April the situation had deteriorated to the point that Jones, Haycock & Company exercised their right of appeal as set out in clause 14 of the contract and complained to the commissioner about the unfairness of the decisions on measurements made by the government team.[36]

Evidently afraid that the works could be delayed yet again, another new commissioner of public works, the Hon. J.C. Chapais, through the secretary, asked for Baillairgé's suggestions in relation to the "vigorous prosecution of the Buildings during the ensueing [sic] summer, the proper organization of the staff & a close and rigid inspection of the works."[37] Baillairgé first asked for additional staff, claiming that he and the others were working overtime to keep on top of the situation. This demand was met in part by the assignment of the department's chief engineer, John Page, to the works in May 1864. But Baillairgé's fiery letter to the commissioner captured the explosive atmosphere on the site – threats, bribes, conspiratorial alliances, manoeuvres – all normal practices in a game with such high stakes:

The whole staff is constantly met and endeavoured to be influenced by the insertion on part of the Contractors that their Contract is a *hard* one; that Government desires to deal liberally with them and does not want "cheese paring" of their accounts.

Need I remind you Sir in how many other ways Contractors endeavour to

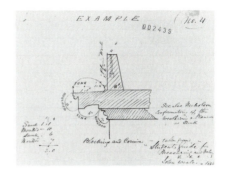

FIG. 138. In an attempt to control expenditures in the construction of the Parliament and Departmental buildings, Baillairgé resorted to his architectural library for examples of measuring Gothic mouldings. Issued in 1863 by the superintendent and associate architects, this measurement system makes reference to two of Baillairgé's architectural books by Nicholson and Weale. NA, RG II, vol. 417, no. 10,788; C-118097

obtain their ends. "They have friends in the Government, say they, and they can have this one dismissed and that one taken on at their desire" ....

Delay in the works from the employment of an insufficient number of hands or from strikes & other causes with which the Contractors themselves have alone to do, is also translated ... into delay for want of plans and orders ....

I need hardly advert to the more ordinary and "persuasive" kinds of pressure which men with insufficient salaries are sometimes tempted to yield to ....

Yes, Sir, Government I believe does desire to deal liberally with their Contractors & wants no "cheese paring," and the whole staff I sincerely think is acting towards them in this spirit of liberality, so far at least as is consistent with their duties as honest men & justice towards their employers; but they can not accept that interpretation of the word "liberal" which nothing short of from 100 to 1000 per cent will satisfy ....

Any *strict* management of works like these is sure to be objected to, and I take it rather as a compliment to any of the staff when complained of by the Contractors, as it is generally a sign that they are doing their duty in an impartial manner.[38]

Baillairgé's statement portrays him as an honest man with a keen sense of duty and the tenacity to uphold what he considered proper. He did admit, however, his vulnerability in the face of such powerful contractors in a paragraph which proved to be prophetic:

Nor is it mere conjecture on my part to say that fear of dismissal is constantly held out and repeated through contractors or their foremen or other trumpeters obedient to their bidding, for 'tis only yesterday one of our Clerks of works was told by a Contractor's foreman, that: now the new ministry [Taché-Macdonald] was formed Rubidge and Baillairgé would have to go. And in the same way with the new Quebec Jail, the Contractors boasted of the friends they had in the Government and said "Let Baillairgé take care, for we can get him out in twenty four hours." The pressure as you see was great, great as the interests at stake, and yet I dared in face of it to reduce an exorbitant bill of extras ... and hoped I may yet be honest & independent enough to do the same when circumstances offer.[39]

In spite of these forebodings, the works continued during the 1864 season, though the government was forced in August to make new concessions to bail Jones, Haycock & Company out of their perennial monetary problems.[40] None of the buildings was ready for the winter session as planned, but the work was well advanced and Baillairgé had every reason to expect a successful end to the project when, in February 1865, he was asked to collect evidence for the upcoming arbitration.

While work on the buildings continued under the terms of the second contract, the arbitration process was set in motion in October 1864 to settle the claims made by the architects and contractors for the first contract. Arbitration was required because they had all refused to accept the findings of the Commission of Inquiry of 1863. This time the settlement was to be binding on all parties. The board was composed of one government nominee, one member named by the contractors, and a third person chosen by the first two.[41] Government named as its member the competent and reliable John Page, chief engineer of the Department of Public Works. The contractors' nominee was Toronto-based architect and civil engineer Frederick Cumberland. Together they finally agreed on Judge James Robert Gowan, of the county court of Simcoe County, as the third member. In January 1865 the arbitration board was ready to begin work.[42]

The arbitration need not have affected Baillairgé, since it dealt with events that occurred before he came to Ottawa. But the stakes were high (the claims mounting to over half a million dollars), and the battle promised to be tough. Government needed all the help it could get. John Page, the government's nominee on the board, warned the department in December 1864:

The two principal claimants (Mr McGreevy and Messrs Jones, Haycock & Co.) have each employed *two eminent counsel*, who have no doubt already given much time and consideration to their respective cases.

The Department will of course select Counsel of at least equal experience and standing and it is desirable this should be done at once, so as to give the Gentleman chosen an opportunity of considering in advance the main questions at issue.[43]

The "eminent counsel" were the Hon. Charles Alleyn and Frederick Vannovous of Quebec City, who acted on behalf of McGreevy, and Thomas Galt and John H. Cameron of Toronto, who represented Jones, Haycock & Company.[44]

The government lawyers, Richards and Scott, needed technical experts who could testify with credibility about costs, measurements, and the construction process. Preparation of the technical aspect of the case fell under the responsibility of Rubidge, assistant engineer of public works during the first contract and superintendent of the Parliament and Departmental Buildings under the second. To help Rubidge, the government named John Bowes, measurer of the Parliament Buildings under the new contract, and Charles Baillairgé.[45]

Why was Baillairgé asked? He was technically competent and the only architect intimately familiar with the buildings who had not been part of the first contract, so his nomination was predictable. But government may also have chosen him because, through his letters and actions, going back to his denial of extras to Murphy and Quigley in July 1862 and continuing during his control of the works in Ottawa, he had clearly demonstrated a crusader's distaste for dishonesty. Baillairgé found himself in a delicate position, working on the one hand with Fuller and the contractors, while collecting evidence against them. Page and Rubidge sought to relieve his discomfort by requesting that the department send him an official letter, "to relieve Mr. Baillairgé from any invidious reflections which might be cast upon him when affording assistance to resist claims of Parties with Whom he is in daily business."[46] Thus it was that on 17 February 1865 Baillairgé received instructions from the commissioner of public works, the Hon. J.C. Chapais, "to render Mr Rubidge all the assistance in your power in furnishing such information and evidence as may be necessary to enable the Crown Counsel to conduct their cases."[47]

Needless to say, Baillairgé attacked the problem with energy and determination, his natural predilection for honesty and his outrage at corruption perhaps supplemented by the hope that a job well done might secure him the treasured position of public works architect. He worked long into the nights with the measurers, clerks of works, and lawyers, preparing sheet upon sheet of figures and calculations.[48] Predictably, interpersonal relationships on the construction site degenerated to the point that, as Baillairgé himself reported to the minister, "the contractors hate me on sight."[49] Pressure intensified as rumours abounded that the contractors were going to force his dismissal in order to prevent his giving evidence at the arbitration hearings. According to these rumours, letters written by Baillairgé during the erection of the Quebec Jail were to be released by the contractors, Murphy and Quigley, to prove that Baillairgé had accepted kickbacks from the contractors in return for approving extras. Knowing that he was innocent, Baillairgé decided to take the initiative and put the matter to rest once and for all by publishing a brochure on the Quebec Jail that would explain the context in which the letters had been written. By so doing, he believed that his honesty and ethical behaviour would be apparent to all, thereby undermining any potential damage caused by citing the correspondence out of context. In a confidential letter to the minister, the Hon. J.C. Chapais, on 3 April 1865 – a letter which shows that Baillairgé still did not realize his vulnerability – he reported the rumours, sketched a sombre scenario orchestrated by his enemy Pierre Gauvreau that would have obliged Chapais to dismiss him, and hastened to reassure the minister that his publication would clarify the matter and furnish him with all the ammunition he would need to defend Baillairgé:

They tell me that Murphy and Quigley are still at work with their threats. It's Mr. Gauvreau's son who is working for them, with the father no doubt applauding anything that could harm me and blacken my name. To assuage his jealousy and hostility, they say he sought you out and, with a protective air, said that poor Mr. Baillairgé had been seriously compromised. You replied that "it was sad that French Canadians knew so little about how to do things, always putting the department in the position of having to fire them to save appearances." "An Anglophone," you apparently added, "can steal as much as he likes and everyone will respect him, so crafty is he." And Gauvreau firmly approved this line of thinking.

    That is the worst of it, Sir, but frank dealing and truth, as you will soon see from a letter that I am sending you on the subject, will have no difficulty in triumphing over lies and specious appearances.[50]

Oblivious to the danger, Baillairgé then dropped the matter, preferring to brief the minister on the contractors' abuses and claims at the Ottawa buildings.

DISMISSAL

Was Baillairgé naïve? Did he underestimate the degree of political involvement in the payment of extras on Parliament Hill? Events unfolded quickly. Chapais played the exact role that Baillairgé had outlined in his fictitious scenario some three weeks earlier. In a memorandum on 28 April 1865 to the governor general, Chapais recommended his dismissal:

The undersigned has the honor to represent to Your Excellency that a correspondence written and signed by Mr Chas Baillairgé, ... in 1861 whilst he was employed ... upon the new Jail of Quebec, has lately been placed in his hands.

    That this correspondence, a copy of which is herewith submitted, clearly shews that Mr Baillairgé has been guilty at that time of gross derilection of duty, and rendered himself wholly unworthy of confidence.[51]

An order in council was passed on 1 May 1865 dispensing with his services, a mere two-and-a-half months after his assignment to the arbitration process.

What fury and disillusionment must have passed through Baillairgé when he received official notification of his dismissal from the secretary of public works. How ironic that he should be considered unworthy of government confidence![52]

One will never know what was in the "correspondence" that Chapais saw and considered so damaging, for the copy is no longer with Chapais's memorandum and the order in council has not survived. Indeed, there may have been an attempt to alter the record, for a note in a public works ledger against the date 24 June 1865 reads "Papers respecting C. Baillairgé's dismissal taken by Hble Sol: Gen¹ E."[53] This was the Hon. Hector-L. Langevin. Although the exact nature of the correspondence is not known, Baillairgé's brochure and the ensuing attacks by *Le Journal de Québec* showed that it concerned an alleged $500 kickback that Baillairgé was purported to have received from Murphy and Quigley in exchange for falsifying the monthly estimates in their favour and for allowing them to substitute materials of an inferior quality during construction of the Quebec Jail. Without repeating the charges and counter-charges which are argued at length in Baillairgé's brochure and in newspaper articles, one need only note that Baillairgé did not deny the payment nor the letters but claimed that the latter had been cited out of context and that the former had been legitimate payment for professional services that he had performed for Murphy and Quigley, including an arbitration hearing at Sainte-Claire, plans for Murphy's house, and extra work that Baillairgé had had to do for them at the Quebec Jail.[54]

Where does the truth lie? Although one can never be entirely certain, the weight of evidence is in Baillairgé's favour. It is inconsistent with his keen sense of duty that he would have participated in a kickback scheme. Public works records confirm that he reported changes to the jail contract as they were made and did not hide them, as Murphy and Quigley suggested. The contractors' complaints to the department against Baillairgé's hard estimates during his tenure as supervising architect contradict the later accusations that he was collaborating with them in a scheme to defraud the government. Baillairgé's claim that the charges stemmed in part from house plans for Murphy can be verified independently, since the plans have survived, unexecuted, in the Quebec municipal archives.[55] The evidence against Baillairgé, as published by *Le Journal de Québec*, was a scissors-and-glue exercise, with parts of letters quoted out of context. Indeed the most damaging letter, which gave permission to the contractors to use inferior materials but to be sure to hide them from "traitors" who could inform the government, and ended with "brulez ceci," was unsigned and, although attributed to Baillairgé by the paper, is not in his writing style and was probably a fabrication.[56] A final consideration is a comparison of the stakes for the participants; Baillairgé had little to gain from a paltry $500 bribe, but Murphy and Quigley had much to gain by his dismissal and loss of reputation, for their own claims for extras from the Quebec Jail contract – claims which had escalated from $22,000 in Baillairgé's time to an astronomical $97,000 – were soon to be submitted to arbitration.[57] With the information available today, all these factors tend to support Baillairgé's protestations of innocence. But at the time, his trial by press – for no official charges were ever laid against him – succeeded in seriously damaging his professional reputation.

It is evident that two minor contractors from Quebec could not by themselves have waged such an effective campaign against Baillairgé. Support and encouragement had to come from those who had a stake in eliminating a stubborn and inflexible witness. Who were they? The contractors at Ottawa are the most obvious immediate beneficiaries of his removal. McGreevy, who as part of the Irish community in Quebec knew Murphy and Quigley well, undoubtedly urged them on. But some politicians may also have participated in this character assassination. One was the Hon. Joseph Cauchon who had spearheaded the anti-Baillairgé campaign in *Le Journal de Québec*. Cauchon had been minister of public works during that crucial summer of 1861 when McGreevy had succeeded in having an outrageous $300,000 of work approved. Given Cauchon's apparent insensitivity to conflict of interest on the question of receiving government funds while serving as a member of the parliament, as shown by his involvement in the Beauport asylum scandal of the same years, he may have had much to lose by a close examination of financial matters connected with the Parliament and Departmental Buildings in Ottawa.[58]

A second politician whose motivation is less clear but whose name keeps appearing on crucial documents relating to the arbitration process and Baillairgé's dismissal is the Hon. Hector-L. Langevin, solicitor-general east at the time of these events. When John Page and Frederick Cumberland were attempting to select the third member for the arbitration board, they sent a telegram to Chapais with a short list of proposed names. In public works files there is a cryptic handwritten note attached to that telegram which indicates that, although the question was directed to Chapais, it was Langevin who had an influence on the composition of the board: "Une réponse a été faite. H.L.L. Sol: Genl E."[59] Langevin – and not Chapais – may also have been the moving force behind Baillairgé's dismissal, for it was he who showed the letters to the governor general and executive council and, as noted above, later removed the compromising documents.[60] In 1871, when McGreevy was seeking arbitration for the second contract, John A. Macdonald, in his capacity as minister of justice, overruled civil servant John Page's recommendation to proceed to independent arbitration and gave *carte blanche* to Langevin, then minister of public works, to settle the case within the department.[61] What was Langevin's motivation? He had not, after all, been directly involved in the construction of the public buildings in Ottawa. One might perhaps speculate on whether his unholy alliance with McGreevy, which led thirty years later to Langevin's political disgrace and McGreevy's imprisonment, may have begun at this period.[62]

As the public battle raged in Quebec City between the attacker, *Le Journal de Québec*, and the defender, *Le Canadien*, an anonymous letter to the editor of *Le Canadien* signed "Justice" gave a balanced assessment of the case, eventually siding with the architect. Claiming that he scarcely knew Baillairgé but that he represented general public opinion, "Justice" saw the architect as a fundamentally honest man whose forthrightness worked to his detriment. He described Baillairgé as "a man who writes too much and clumsily, who is always putting his head in the wolf's mouth."[63] "Justice" saw the fight as unequal, the single honest citizen against a group of dishonest schemers, and viewed the crusader's ouster as inevitable, unless he had abandoned his high principles and joined the scheme:

We know that Mr. Baillairgé set himself the mission, when he accepted the associate architect's job in Ottawa, of stopping the speculation, of introducing honesty into a system where waste had reigned for such a long time. Consequently he automatically made enemies with people with whom he worked. Did he measure the difficulty of the task and did he never anticipate what is now happening to him? In any case, those clever men whom he hoped to stop must have smiled once they got to know him a bit, seeing the role he was undertaking. They must have said that he was not a force to match them, that he was too maladroit, and that they would get rid of him when they wanted.

It is my firm conviction ... that Mr. Baillairgé fell victim to very dishonest men, against whom he wanted to fight in the public interest. If he had wanted to conspire with them, he would still be in place and would pass for the most honest man in the world.[64]

In 1873 Baillairgé came close to the truth when, with hindsight, he described his removal as a political necessity in a published letter to Langevin, whom Baillairgé obviously did not suspect of any collusion.[65]

The arbitration hearings were held late in 1865. On 8 March 1866 Jones, Haycock & Company were awarded $88,176 and soon after McGreevy settled for $61,785 in additional extras on the first contract.[66] When construction of the Departmental Buildings was completed in 1867, John Page in his role as superintendent arranged a settlement with Jones, Haycock & Company for the second contract to the tune of $436,199.[67] Work was halted on the Parliament Building in 1867, with the library left unbuilt. McGreevy (by this time Robert, for Thomas had transferred the contract to his brother when he became a member of parliament) refused to settle, having discovered the advantages of arbitration, particularly when one had friends in power. For his claim for damages suffered by the cancellation of the contract before the library was built, McGreevy received $29,245 through an order in council in 1870. Two years later government settled his claim for work done under the second contract for $620,760.[68] The Department of Public Works had paid dearly for its mismanagement; the final tally for the Parliament and Departmental Buildings, minus the library, was a whopping $2,572,194 as of June 1867 – five times higher than the original estimate.[69]

As for Baillairgé, on receipt of the letter informing him of his dismissal, he calmly listed all the plans, documents, and books in his possession and turned them over to Page. By 10 May he had left Ottawa and returned to Quebec to face the malicious attacks from *Le Journal de Québec*. He submitted demands for a year's salary, and overtime for arbitration work, and asked for an inquiry into the causes of his dismissal. Each time he made a claim, it landed on the desk of John A. Macdonald who immediately forwarded it to Langevin. No action was taken during the Conservatives' reign; it was only ten years after the events, when Alexander Mackenzie and the Liberals took power, that Baillairgé's case was finally settled by the payment of a mere $650 for overtime work for the arbitration hearings. No inquiry was ever held into the causes of his dismissal.[70]

BAILLAIRGÉ & PEACHY

Although most of Baillairgé's energies from 1860 to 1865 were devoted to the service of the Department of Public Works, he did manage to keep up a skeletal private practice. While engaged as supervising architect of the Quebec Jail he continued to accept other commissions; but when he moved to Ottawa in 1863 he tried to maintain a presence in Quebec City by forming a partnership with Joseph-Ferdinand Peachy, his former apprentice and trusted

FIG. 139. Interior of the church at Saint-Laurent, Île d'Orléans. ANQ, photothèque, N-374-12

friend. Together they worked on the church interior at Saint-Laurent, the école Saint-Jean-Baptiste, and the Petry house, under the name Baillairgé & Peachy, operating from Baillairgé's home and office at 30 [now 58], rue Saint-Louis until it was rented in 1864, at which time the firm moved to Peachy's office at the corner of the rues Saint-Jean and Sutherland.[71] Even during their partnership, however, each architect worked independently on other projects.

The fact that Baillairgé & Peachy won the contract for the interior of the church at Saint-Laurent, Ile d'Orléans (fig. 139) was unusual, at least in Baillairgé's repertoire; he habitually designed church exteriors, sometimes leaving the interior decoration to a former Thomas Baillairgé apprentice, François-Xavier Berlinguet. After Baillairgé's flirtation with Gothic Revival in the 1850s, Baillairgé & Peachy returned to a classical vocabulary at Saint-Laurent, no doubt dictated by the neoclassical shell of the church designed prior to their involvement in the project. The interior has much in common with Baillairgé's masterpiece at Sainte-Marie de Beauce, despite the obvious fact that the latter adopted the Gothic idiom (figs. 184–8). Although the initial plans for Sainte-Marie were drawn up in 1854, work on the interior was only being carried out in the early 1860s, at the same time as the interior of Saint-Laurent, and by the same firm of contractors, Breton & Frère. Perhaps these factors account for the close similarity in taste, the heavy bulbous profiles, and the repeated use of twisted cable mouldings, signs of Baillairgé's interest in the fuller Italianate forms. Art historian Gérard Morisset's preference for the simple and delicate work of the eighteenth and early nineteenth centuries permeates his severe condemnation of Saint-Laurent's decoration, which he characterized as being "of a pretentious and insupportable Roman style," with exaggerated mouldings and robust but heavy decoration.[72] The heaviness that Morisset disliked was part of a general evolution of taste noticeable in the 1860s and consistent with Baillairgé's work at the Caisse d'économie and Merrill buildings, and at the Quebec Jail.

During this period Baillairgé worked alone on two important religious commissions: the Venner tomb and the Aylmer convent. The mausoleum for wealthy merchant William Venner (fig. 140) was the most sumptuous one in Quebec at that time. The stone and iron fence which enclosed Venner's plot at the cimetière Saint-Charles was put up in 1857-8, an exact match with Baillairgé's fence in front of Notre-Dame Cathedral of the same date. The monument itself was built several years later in 1861-2, though still during Venner's lifetime. It adopted the Corinthian order, built by the finest craftsmen with materials including marble, copper, and Montreal stone. Baillairgé prepared full-size drawings for such details as the wreaths, capitals, and modillion blocks – all characteristic of his repertoire – and gave instructions that the most skilled craftsmen be engaged to carve wooden models to guide the stone cutters.[73] His design for the Aylmer convent, a three-storey stone building of extensive proportions, was "worthy of a large city." A fire in 1866 utterly destroyed the convent, all the walls caving in so that not a stone was left.[74]

It was perhaps a reflection of poor economic conditions in Quebec, caused in part by the irrevocable decision to move the seat of government to Ottawa, in part by the shift in trade patterns, that contracts for quality housing were scarce. Baillairgé designed brick town houses for Dr Baillargeon and Ferdinand Hamel, each one carefully finished in his usual manner and fitted up with running water, gas lighting, Chartré's tubular furnace, and bell system. Baillairgé alone, and Baillairgé & Peachy together showed greater innovation in the suburban verandahed houses that they designed in these years. The Whitty and Blaiklock houses (fig. 141) were standard Baillairgé fare, but "Elm Grove" and the Petry house, which break with earlier tendencies to use smooth surfaces and a strict rectilinear arrangement of forms, demonstrate the Italianate influence. The Petry house possessed more texture and variety through the use of brick quoins, arched openings, and overhanging eaves with modillion cornice; "Elm Grove" (fig. 142) achieved a textured effect through the rustic quoins, the two bay windows that extended up the entire three storeys, and the picturesque verandah roof which was to be painted in alternate stripes of light and dark green.[75]

It is clear that Baillairgé concentrated on the public works commissions in the early 1860s to the detriment of his private practice, which he no doubt found dull and repetitive. He forged ahead towards his goal of becoming chief architect of public works. During these years, he only occasionally designed buildings himself, but instead devoted most of his professional time to the supervision of works and the technical problems encountered on the construction sites. By his own admission he considered that his move to Ottawa would be of long duration.[76] His abrupt dismissal from the Ottawa Parliament Buildings and subsequent character assassination in the Quebec papers proved to be a crucial turning point in his career. The thrust that he had maintained since youth was suddenly thwarted and, at the age of thirty-nine, he was forced to return to Quebec, crestfallen, his dream of becoming chief architect turned to ashes.

FIG. 140. Venner tomb. CIHB

FIG. 141. Only half of the double house that Baillairgé designed in 1862–3 for F.W. Blaiklock has survived at 20, rue Grande-Allée ouest. Originally situated in the outskirts of the city, it has the scale and simplicity of a suburban cottage. Christina Cameron

FIG. 142. Elm Grove, located at 1045, boulevard Saint-Cyrille. NA, C-19, 110

FIG. 143. Chapel for the Soeurs du Bon-Pasteur, situated at 1080, rue de la Chevrotière. The illustration comes from the corner of a portrait of Monseigneur Charles-Félix Cazeau, painted in 1880 by Soeur Marie Jésus. ANQ, photothèque, N-78-Q-80-6

FIG. 144. Interior of the Chapelle du Bon-Pasteur. CIHB

ON HIS RETURN FROM OTTAWA, BAILLAIRGÉ briefly attempted to rebuild his private practice until he entered the municipal service in October 1866. Although he did not intend to stay, he in fact remained with the city for the rest of his professional career until he was forced to retire in 1898 at the age of seventy-two. He found the daily routine unchallenging, but a number of special projects that the city undertook sparked his imagination and provided him with occasional opportunities to design important structures: market halls, the Dufferin Improvements, and iron staircases. From time to time he supplemented his city work with private commissions, but his combined architectural output never came close to the complexity and productivity of the earlier years.

PRIVATE COMMISSIONS

Following his dismissal as associate architect of the Parliament and Departmental Buildings in Ottawa in May 1865, Charles Baillairgé returned to Quebec to face the music. He was virtually unemployed, since his £1000 governmental salary had been cut off and his private practice of £1100 per annum, which he claimed to have enjoyed prior to the move, had been diverted into new channels during his absence.[1] He had to join his wife and five children in his father's home on the rue Saint-François, for his own house had been rented out and most of the furniture sold when he went to Ottawa. To make matters worse, his prospects for rebuilding his private practice were not good, for the newspaper campaign being waged against him over the Quebec Jail made it difficult for him to attract prospective clients. It was finally the Soeurs du Bon-Pasteur who rallied to his cause by offering him his first commission, the design and superintendence of their chapel.

Baillairgé's choice of the classical idiom for the chapel marked a return to the teachings of Thomas Baillairgé and Abbé Jérôme Demers and a rejection of his own experimentation in the Gothic Revival style which he had used for his churches at Beauport, the Hospice de la Charité, l'Isle-Verte, Rivière-du-Loup and Sainte-Marie de Beauce. Perhaps his experience with the buildings at Ottawa had soured his taste for Gothic forms. At the Bon-Pasteur chapel Baillairgé overcame the disadvantages of the narrow fifty-foot wide lot and created a dignified, unified façade through the wise choice of a single central spire – modelled on Gibbs's St Martin-in-the-Fields, just like the steeple that Baillairgé had designed twenty years earlier for the church in Saint-Roch – and the thematic use of circular and semi-circular motifs (fig. 143). These curved forms were repeated inside the chapel, from major components such as the vaults and arcades along the nave to specific details such as the round windows and semi-circular doors and windows (fig. 144). Two special features contributed to the soaring beauty and ephemeral effect of the chapel: double galleries and the glazed apse. Over fifteen years earlier, Baillairgé had already formulated a solution to the problem of easy access at different levels with his triple galleries at the chapel of the Soeurs de la Charité. At the Bon-Pasteur chapel, he simply adopted a double-gallery solution in neoclassical garb. The treatment of the apse wall, however, required more creativity on his part (figs. 145–6). Set within a rectangular end wall were two curved walls which formed an apse at the end of the nave. What was unusual about these curved walls was that they were not solid partition walls with applied decoration, as was usually found in Quebec churches. Instead, they were formed by rows of graceful arcaded windows, a shimmering insubstantial surface. This was Baillairgé's response to the cloistered nuns' requirement to have a private view of the altar for themselves and for the delinquent girls that they sheltered. Though hardly representing the degree of challenge that Baillairgé was seeking, the Bon-Pasteur chapel afforded him an opportunity to create a graceful and harmonious structure that was a tribute to his knowledge and skill as a designer.

Before Baillairgé entered the municipal service as the superintendent of works, he was hired by the city as a private consultant to draw up plans and specifications for three new market buildings and to take over the faltering Saint John Gate project. The brick buildings for the Berthelot and Jacques Cartier Markets were plain functional structures which Baillairgé surely found boring; indeed, he presented the same plan for both market halls. But the engineering problems at Saint John Gate were challenging, although the final result proved a disappointment. The design of the gate as built actually came from the original proposals made in 1863 by the associated architects Tate and Lecourt.[2] This was the same J.P.M. Lecourt who had earlier worked in partnership with George Browne. The slow progress and evident problems with the contract, remarked upon in a series of articles in *Le Journal de Québec* in October 1865, led the city to appeal to the more experienced Baillairgé for help.[3] The works must have been sufficiently advanced to oblige him to adhere to Tate and Lecourt's design, a stiff interpretation of classical forms with two arched carriageways flanked by footpaths (fig. 147).[4] The challenge came from the three-dimensionality of the project, for unlike a simple masonry wall, in which the courses were all equal and stones could be transposed indiscriminately, the size of each stone for Saint John Gate had to be individually calculated to ensure the proper opening and closing of the iron gates. Baillairgé claimed that errors at the point of springing of several of the arches in Tate and Lecourt's original plan would have prevented the gates from folding back in their recesses when open.

He attacked the problem with characteristic vigour and prepared eighty-three sheets of detailed plans "of each course of masonry, showing headers and stretchers, skews and voussoirs on arch stones, cornices, etc.," some of which have survived in the Quebec municipal archives.[5] Although the design was acceptable, Saint John Gate was never a success from an engineering standpoint, despite Baillairgé's intervention. While the gates did function properly, the vaulted roofs of the arches dripped constantly from want of proper drainage and the southwest wall steadily shifted from the pressure of the earthworks uphill.[6] It was Baillairgé himself who began a campaign for its demolition only five years after its completion, not just because of its defects but because the federal government had neglected the fortification walls, rendering the gate "more ornamental than useful."[7] Influenced by the progressive spirit towards urban renewal exemplified by Baron Haussmann's improvement in Paris, he agreed with those merchants and property owners who wanted to open up the old walled city through a

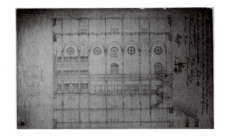

FIG. 145. This longitudinal section of the Chapelle du Bon-Pasteur shows the rounded apse wall, set within the rectangular outer walls. AVQ, fonds Charles Baillairgé, no. 4–24

FIG. 146. The interior glazed wall of the apse at the Chapelle du Bon-Pasteur which has been designated as a National Historic Site. Christina Cameron

FIG. 147. Photograph of the Saint John Gate taken after completion in 1867. NA, C-80179

network of broad boulevards. His repeated urging only took hold in 1897 when Saint John Gate was finally torn down.[8]

CITY ENGINEER

Building activity in Quebec in the 1860s was clearly not what it had been in the 1850s, when important government, religious, and commercial structures were being erected. An occasional chapel, market hall, or city gate could not provide Baillairgé with an adequate income, so it was probably with mixed emotions of reluctance and relief that he learned that his application for the post of superintendent of works had been accepted by the municipality in October 1866.[9] Ironically it may have been the accidental death of his father which created an opening at the city; Pierre-Théophile Baillairgé, assistant city engineer, died on 3 November 1865 from a fall through a trap door while on duty in a Lower Town store.[10]

The vacancy left by his father's death provided the opportunity for a reorganization of the municipal Public Works Department. The city attempted to combat uncontrolled spending by creating the job of superintendent of works in 1866. Expenditures which had previously been authorized by various committees without any coordination were to be channelled through a Board of Works, managed by a superintendent of works, whose responsibilities included the roles of city inspector, inspector of roads, streets, bridges and chimneys, and water works engineer. The superintendent of works was to be entrusted with all the disbursements of the corporation except contingencies.[11] This scheme was the brainchild of the then mayor of Quebec, Joseph Cauchon, the previous owner of *Le Journal de Québec* who had played a key role in securing Baillairgé's dismissal in Ottawa and whom Baillairgé referred to as "the one sworn enemy of my peace."[12] As mayor, Cauchon stood to gain more power over the distribution of municipal funds, provided that the appointee in the position of superintendent of works was malleable. The last person he wanted there was the inflexible Charles Baillairgé. But Baillairgé had his own supporters on the council, including his former partner Peachy, and in spite of Cauchon's opposition he succeeded in winning the nomination over the only other qualified candidate, none other than his rival L.P. Gauvreau. It goes without saying that *Le Journal de Québec* seized every opportunity to undermine the new superintendent of works.[13]

From the outset Baillairgé considered the work and the salary beneath him. The salary was set at £500 per annum – only half his Ottawa remuneration. What was worse, the city only paid him £400 in the first year because he was to receive £100 from his contract with the city for Saint John Gate. The continuation of the £400 salary for years provided the grounds for Baillairgé's vocal and strident monetary grievances against the corporation.[14] His responsibilities included roads, wharves, municipal services, public buildings, and public places, work which he referred to as "this city drudgery" with its "trumpery repairs and small jobs" and "its hosts of malcontents and grumblers."[15] In his first published report in 1868, Baillairgé gave an exemplary display of performance measurement by itemizing his average annual duties:

Of letters, notices, protests, subpoenas and references from City Council, etc., the yearly average has been 464. Of permits given to open drains, empty cesspools, to build, repair or impede the way, notices to renew sidewalks, fence in vacant lots, repair leaky gutters, remove dangerous walls ... 216. There have been 256 pay-lists to examine, certify and enter, of the men employed on the roads and markets and in the fire and water works departments, also of chimney sweeps, coal oil lamp lighters, health officers and stone breakers ... The average yearly number of tenders advertised for in French and English have been 15 and of separate tenders sent in 66, written orders given for works and materials 148, committee meetings held and minutes entered 27, reports ... 26, reports ... 23, sets of plans, specifications and estimates prepared 13, ... calls to have water pipes thawed 888. The average yearly number of persons calling on me has been 4050 or from 13 to 14 per diem.[16]

While he was obviously kept busy, the only project of a clearly architectural nature was the establishment of six fire stations to house the equipment and some of the men of the new permanent municipal fire brigade which had been formed following the disastrous Saint-Roch fire of October 1866 which destroyed 2000 houses.[17] Three of the stations were merely enlargements of existing city structures; the other three were new plain brick buildings with large functional doors, with only a hint of aesthetic concern in features like the cornice with frieze and moulding.

In 1870 Baillairgé was stripped of significant powers with the repeal of the municipal act channelling all expenditures through him. In his 1878 report entitled *The Municipal Situation*, in which he attempted to prove through charts and tables the disastrous financial consequences of the reorganization, he explained that the committees were "jealous of my prerogatives and displeased at not having as theretofore any patronage at their disposal."[18] From that moment Baillairgé lost his title of superintendent of works and signed himself city surveyor, water works engineer, city inspector, and most often, city engineer. This loss of power inevitably brought on boredom and restlessness, recalling that earlier phase of Baillairgé's career when he insisted on his love of hard work and need for challenge. He readily admitted that his own workaholic nature was in part responsible for the fact that he was overworked at the city. Recalling how his father had regularly laboured from dawn until midnight, he added: "This mania for work seems to me a disease which I would that I could master. It runs in the family as the saying is, and yet I know, I am told it every day, I never shall get any thanks for it. I have a brother now 20 years in the government service at Ottawa ... he too has the execrable habit of working out of office hours, t'is in the nature of the animal."[19] But he resented the pettiness of most of his city work, and by 1872 his frustration was such that he made his complaints public in a self-pitying preface to his printed annual report: "Whether I shall survive to write another is more than I can tell; for, there is an end to all things, and the unfed, overburdened beast must give way rapidly under such inhuman treatment ... Because I have the misfortune to be architect and engineer as well as surveyor, I am looked to to perform the work of all three for the salary of one. I do not regret the experience of men and things thus acquired by being brought into contact with all the world and his wife; but I have enough of it now and nothing more to learn at it."[20]

A brief survey of his projects in the early 1870s helps to explain Baillairgé's discontent in these years. He built a wing to the overcrowded City Hall in 1871, designed a wooden staircase from Champlain Street to Cove Field, proposed in 1875 a plan for the Montcalm Market Hall that was reminiscent of his proposals for the Saint Paul Market Hall thirty years

Fig. 148. Wire dome, Place d'Armes, 1874. NA, PA-66,869

earlier, and intervened in architect Paul Cousin's winning design for the Montcalm Market Hall, by orchestrating a public write-in campaign to impose his proposal for a mansard roof.[21] Slightly more appealing was the dome for the Place d'Armes, erected in 1874 to mark the city's celebration of the second centennial of the episcopal foundation of Quebec by Monseigneur de Laval. Baillairgé was able to indulge his love of fantasy and technical experimentation by creating a 25-foot high ribbed wire dome that was illuminated on the night of the festivities by fourteen dozen hanging Chinese lanterns, the whole event being described by historian Lemoine as the "grandest spectacle ever witnessed in Quebec" (fig. 148).[22] In a vain attempt to recycle his cherished 1858 plans for the Parliament in Ottawa, Baillairgé proposed that the provincial government, which was preparing in 1875 to erect a legislative building, construct his plan on the site of the Jesuit barracks. He circulated a printed memorial describing the merits of his design accompanied by a Livernois photograph of the façade elevation.[23]

On the engineering side, Baillairgé participated in the initial phase of the Quebec Harbour Improvements, a project that had interested him since 1859 when he first proposed a comprehensive scheme for the estuary of the Saint Charles River.[24] He represented the city's interests as joint engineer of the preliminary survey in collaboration with the representative of the federal government, none other than René Steckel, his former apprentice and assistant at the Ottawa buildings. Baillairgé's two reports of 1875 and 1876, which promoted a large harbour and graving dock, did not prevent the ensuing fiasco.[25] The harbour works, carried out by a British firm with little experience of the North American scale of shipping, were later characterized by Baillairgé as "the most profound stupidity,"[26] for the harbour had "an enclosure so small that an ocean steamer will not be able to turn about within it." To add insult to injury, the graving dock was built in Levis.[27]

So great was Baillairgé's discontent that he swallowed his pride and once again appealed to the federal Department of Public Works for a job. In a printed letter in 1873 addressed to his former classmate Hector Langevin, then minister of public works, Baillairgé declared that he was wasting his time at the city, that he had nothing more to learn there, and that his talent and experience could be put to better use in the service of Canada:

There is not, Sir, so much distance between us. We were once schoolboys together. You are in a sphere where you make good use of your talents and knowledge. Place me somewhere where I can use mine. I have already earned £1000 per year, not just in Ottawa but before going there; I can earn it again and with interest.

I am abused here in the Corporation of Quebec's employ by the quality and quantity of work that I am doing and by a salary unworthy of a self-respecting city. I do not regret having spent several years here, in view of the practical experience gained in engineering of all sorts and in the waterworks, but there is nothing more here for me to learn and I consider myself far above the position that I hold.[28]

Baillairgé believed that this appeal had been heard, for it was rumoured in Quebec during the summer of 1874 that he had obtained the position of federal architect for the province of Quebec. His disgust on discovering that it was Pierre Gauvreau, not he, who had been chosen was summed up in a note to his friend Nazaire Levasseur. Comparing his own watchdog role at Ottawa with Gauvreau's attempt to reward the contractors at the Quebec Jail with government funds, Baillairgé decried the ways of the world: "Those who wished to enrich the country receive nothing, not even their due. While he who wanted to be overpaid by $80,000 is rewarded by a lucrative job."[29]

DUFFERIN IMPROVEMENTS

While seeking employment elsewhere, Baillairgé made the best of his present job in the 1870s by throwing himself into a campaign for urban improvements. Although Quebec's population had stabilized by 1860, the city still required changes to make it more efficient and modern, without which, Baillairgé contended, it "will continue to be called, as it deserves to be, the most backward [sic] city in the Dominion."[30] His approach to city embellishment reflected nineteenth-century progressive thinking. He fell squarely into the anti-heritage camp, showing little sensitivity for the romantic and sentimental values associated with landmarks and historic buildings. In this way he shared the views of Emperor Napoleon III's celebrated urban improver, Baron Georges Haussmann, who razed entire wards in Paris to create wide tree-lined avenues, boulevards, and public squares.

When the British army turned over the fortifications of Quebec to the dominion government in 1871, a city improvement scheme became possible. With the support of the business community, Baillairgé as city engineer initiated proposals, listed in his annual report of 1871-2, to facilitate communications, to develop tourist potential, and to create attractive public spaces. He called for demolition of the city gates, the lowering of the fortification walls, the removal of the Upper Town market in favour of a public square complete with garden and fountain, and the extension of Durham Terrace.[31] Although fortifications were the responsibility of the federal government, Baillairgé and the city were able to intervene because municipal roads and, by entension, the gates fell under city jurisdiction. Consequently, Baillairgé set out to demolish the gates and guard houses, removing Saint Louis and Prescott Gates in 1871, Hope and Palace Gates in 1873, and calling for the demolition of Saint John Gate.[32] A sense of the progressive spirit in which these improvements were made is revealed in his report on Saint Louis Gate: "The awkward, narrow and dangerous sinuosities in the St Lewis road outside the City Walls, have at length been made to disappear, and after them the gate itself, thus shortening the distance through, by about 400 feet ... the thoroughfare now presents one grand and uninterrupted vista stretching away in the distance as far as the eye can reach ... Property in the vicinity has already been thereby enhanced in value."[33]

Baillairgé's favourite project, however, was the proposed prolongation of Durham Terrace to the King's Bastion, making a cliffside terrace over one quarter of a mile in extent. He developed this scheme between 1869, at which time he was only calling for minor repairs to Durham Terrace, and 1872, when he sought public support for this "grandest of improvements" on the basis of city beautification and tourism: "Such a walk ... would of itself be sufficient to attract annually thousands of additional tourists to Quebec ... Every Quebecer should have this improvement at heart and I have no doubt that half the cost of the work could be raised by subscription. I would willingly subscribe $50. myself for the enjoyment of such a luxury as a level walk a quarter of a mile long facing on one of the most magnificent harbours in the world and hope sincerely to see it carried out before I am ten years older."[34]

But Baillairgé's progressive spirit was not universally shared. Historian James Macpherson Lemoine, a lover of tradition and heritage, spearheaded opposition to these improvements, or "vandalism" as he preferred to call them, nostalgically lamenting the "sad and unnecessary destruction, and an irreparable one, of very costly monuments of national history" and decrying "the unsightly gap in our city walls, of yore yclept Palace Gate." Baillairgé countered by arguing that "for one traveller we may lose who would have come here merely to see our Gates and city walls, a thousand will call, were it but to enjoy the unrivalled luxury of a walk a quarter of a mile long over a level flooring on the brink of the cliff."[35]

How this debate would have been resolved if left to local conflict and limited municipal resources will never be known, for the ground rules shifted with the unexpected intervention of the newly appointed governor general, Lord Dufferin. A sensitive cultivated Irishman, Dufferin arrived in Canada in April 1872 and was immediately taken with Quebec, deeply appreciating its dramatic topography and the historical associations of its walled city. Saddened by the destruction of the gates and part of the fortification walls, and disturbed by demands for further demolition, he intervened late in 1874. In a letter to the Earl of Carnarvon, secretary of state for the colonies, Dufferin outlined his actions and inadvertently described Baillairgé – among others – as a "wretched inhabitant," "goth," and "vandal":

Quebec is one of the most picturesque and beautiful cities in the World, not only from its situation, but also from the diadem of wall and towers by which it is encircled. Its wretched inhabitants, however, who are all of them pettifogging shopkeepers, would willingly flatten out their antique city into the quadrangular monotony of an American town. With this intent they have come to the Government to ask leave to level with the ground their ancient fortifications and the ministers have shown a lamentable indifference on the subject. I have however put my foot down, and by dint of using the most abusive language, calling them Goths and Vandals, and telling them that the next generation, being better educated than themselves, will blush for what their forefathers have done, I have succeeded in compelling them to agree to a compromise, namely, – to leave the walls, to be content with a fewer number of outlets ... and to allow me to send them a very clever architect I happen to know at home, who has a *specialité* for picturesque mediaeval military construction, and who is to be allowed to finish off the breeches ... with tourelles, towers, turrets, etc, as may best preserve the ancient character of the enceinte.[36]

He then summoned one of his compatriots, architect William Lynn, to come out from Ireland for the summer of 1875 in order to visit Quebec and draw up a suitable plan for what came to be known as the Dufferin Improvements. In the autumn of 1875 Lord Dufferin presented his proposal to the city and received official sanction. By 1878, following preparation of detailed plans and the securing of funds, the works began in earnest.[37]

"The key to the plan for the embellishment of Quebec," wrote Lord Dufferin to his successor, the Marquis of Lorne, "is the maintenance of a pathway round the entire circuit of the Walls, and this 'motive' should never be lost sight of."[38] In addition to the uninterrupted promenade atop the fortifications and the boulevard outside the walls, Dufferin's scheme called for the prolongation of Durham Terrace and the construction of a new château Saint-Louis at the Citadel, to be used as a vice regal residence in the summer. Lord Dufferin and architect Lynn successfully steered a narrow course between the progressive position of city boosters like Baillairgé and the preservationist desires of the historical contingent led by Lemoine. Dufferin and Lynn planned to keep the streets between the city and the suburbs wide and unencumbered – even promoting further penetration of the fortification walls – while at the same time encouraging reconstruction of the city gates in pseudo- historical styles.[39] The solution satisfied all parties. Describing the initial plan in glowing terms, Lemoine concluded: "History speaks from every stone of its [Quebec's] frowning battlements, from every tortuous winding of its antiquated streets … from its quaint buildings and generally from the many monuments and relics of an eventful past, which crowd each other within its hoary walls. All these, it is the commendable desire of Lord Dufferin not only to carefully preserve, but to improve as far as possible without obstructing the growth and advanced ideas of modern Quebec."[40]

What was Baillairgé's participation in Lord Dufferin's scheme? As city engineer, he would automatically have had some involvement in the implementation, if not the planning, of the improvements. But in this particular case, Lord Dufferin's special interest in Quebec was a stroke of luck for Baillairgé who saw in the governor-general the ideal promoter and fundraiser for the grandiose plans he had already formulated for his native city. Even though Baillairgé did not share Lord Dufferin's romantic vision of an historic walled city, he was evidently ready to pay lip service to this aspect of Dufferin's plan in exchange for the unexpected influx of federal and British funds to make city improvements that normally would have been carried by the municipality alone. On a personal level, the two men appear to have struck up a relationship of friendship and mutual respect, for Dufferin even called Baillairgé to Ottawa to discuss part of the project.[41] How Baillairgé must have enjoyed discussing the project with Lord Dufferin, not to mention being seen by Quebec's citizens as he roamed around the city and fortifications in the company of the governor- general! In a letter to John A. Macdonald, minister of militia and defence, written shortly after Lord Dufferin's departure, Baillairgé underscored this relationship: "I am the only person thoroughly acquainted with Lord Dufferin's views and desires, His Excellency having on more than one occasion walked around the City with me and pointed out in detail all he desired to have done."[42] In case one suspects Baillairgé of exaggeration, Lord Dufferin corroborated this account in a confidential memorandum to Lord Lorne: "The improvements of Quebec ought to be placed under the superintendence of some trustworthy person, who being upon the spot could attend to details as they proceeded. I have explained my ideas to Mr Baillairgé, the City Engineer, who appeared to me to be a suitable person."[43]

After architect Lynn returned to Ireland in the fall of 1875, he continued to send sketches and plans to the governor general. But it fell to Baillairgé to prepare detailed estimates of the cost, calculated at $93,500, and to rework and refine Lynn's drawings.[44] Since the dominion government assumed responsibility for reconstructing the gates, the city's participation in the design and execution of part of the Dufferin Improvements was limited to Baillairgé's cherished project, the extension of Durham Terrace.

Although Baillairgé had proposed work on Durham Terrace in 1872, it was not until 1878 that the design was finalized and construction actually began. The main architectural features of the plain wooden deck were the

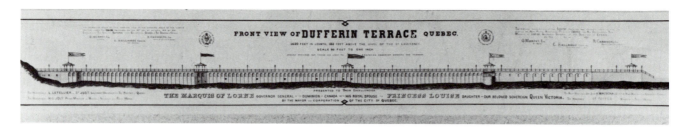

Fig. 149. Presentation drawing of Dufferin Terrace made for the Marquis of Lorne and Princess Louise. ASQ

Fig. 150. Taken before 1892, when the Château Frontenac replaced the old Normal School, this photograph shows Baillairgé's Dufferin Terrace with its ornamental iron railing and row of picturesque kiosks along the frontage. The grandeur of its cliffside siting, nestled beneath the Citadel while dominating the river, made it – and continues to make it – one of the most magnificent terraces in the world. ANQ, photothèque, GH-371-22

Fig. 151. The kiosks on Dufferin Terrace. ANQ, photothèque, N-80-1-184

iron railing and five kiosks along the frontage (figs. 149–51). The kiosks illustrated Baillairgé's continuing attraction to metal as a building material, for they were made from cast and wrought iron.[45] The ogee profile and delicate eaves trim of the green-and-white striped roof and the lacy interwoven national emblems in the spandrels of the arches lent a gay and picturesque air appropriate to an open pleasure walk. Iron plaques affixed to the deck identified the authors: "Dufferin Terrace, H. Hatch, contractor; C. Baillairgé, engineer." Carried away by the success of the embellishment scheme, Baillairgé went so far as to suggest that an aquarium with horticultural and zoological gardens be installed under the terrace (fig. 152), a concept that he had seen at Brighton, England, during his European trip in 1874. He claimed that Lord Dufferin had said of his aquarium that "There will be nothing of its kind like it in the world." The aquarium was never built.[46]

Lord Dufferin's improvements gave Baillairgé a chance to mingle with British aristocracy and won him praise and appreciation from the mayor, aldermen, and citizens of Quebec. He took an active part in the official ceremonies when Lord Dufferin laid the corner stone for the new terrace on 18 October 1878, just before his return to Britain, and when the new governor general and his wife, the Marquis of Lorne and Princess Louise, officially named and inaugurated Dufferin Terrace on 9 June 1879.[47] He proudly recalled the moment when Princess Louise congratulated him and shook his hand saying, "This is the finest promenade in the world."[48] Two days later he had a second occasion to rub shoulders with royalty at the corner stone ceremony for the new Kent Gate. What associations the event must have held for Baillairgé, who surely recalled his ancestor François Baillairgé's collaboration with Princess Louise's grandfather, the Duke of Kent, when he lived in Quebec at the end of the eighteenth century.[49] In his capacity of city engineer, Baillairgé opened the proceedings by reading the inscription tablet and enumerating the contents of the leaden box which was to be placed in the stone. Princess Louise then set the corner stone using an ebony-handled silver trowel on which was engraved "Foundation Stone, Kent Gate, Quebec, Laid by H.R.H. Princess Louise, 11th June, 1879. R. Chambers, Esq., Mayor. C. Baillairgé, Chevalier, City Engineer."[50]

FIG. 152. Baillairgé's proposed aquarium under Dufferin Terrace. CAB, 13 (1900): 93

The exhilaration that Baillairgé undoubtedly experienced during these events was reinforced by the homage paid him by Quebec residents like Lemoine who publicly credited him with "many of the boldest and most striking features of the Dufferin plan of embellishments."[51] But his enthusiasm was short-lived, for the Dufferin Improvements slowly lost impetus with the departure of their promoter. Armed with Lord Dufferin's assurance that John A. Macdonald had promised to carry through the plan, Baillairgé pestered the federal government to push ahead, but to little avail. On the back of Baillairgé's demand for authority and funds to proceed with the construction of arches and piers under the terrace, following Lord Dufferin's ideas, Chief Architect Thomas S. Scott scribbled, "I know nothing of the Dufferin Terrace arrangement mentioned; nor do I understand what wall Mr. Baillairgé desires to have proceeded with."[52] The Dufferin Improvements ceased with the completion of the Saint-Louis and Kent gates and Dufferin Terrace, "lasting proof of his Lordship's interest in the welfare of Quebec."[53] Sensing that the spurt of activity stimulated by Lord Dufferin had come to an end, a deflated Baillairgé once again applied for work as chief architect of the Department of Public Works in Ottawa. Though his brother George-Frédéric was by then deputy minister of public works and his classmate Hector Langevin was minister of public works, Baillairgé's application was unaccountably disregarded.[54]

He remained in Quebec, attending to the small jobs and endless boring repairs and additions to aging municipal buildings. An exception to this dull parade of utilitarian structures was the series of kiosks for carters and bands that Baillairgé designed in the 1880s and 1890s for different locations in the city; though the construction material was wood, not iron, these attractive octagonal buildings followed the general outline of the Dufferin Terrace kiosks, thereby creating a corporate image associated with municipal public works.[55]

QUEBEC CITY HALL

One project that stirred Baillairgé's imagination was the possible expansion of City Hall. Expecting to design and supervise construction, he mounted a campaign against the overcrowded conditions at the old City Hall, the former residence on the rue Saint-Louis which had been refurbished following designs by architects Browne & Lecourt in 1850. In response to a demand from city council in 1885, Baillairgé made a preliminary plan – including seventy-one pages of specifications – for enlarging the old City Hall, proposing an extension to the west in the same comfortable and familiar style. It was a symmetrical composition using motifs that matched Browne & Lecourt's section, including a second frontispiece with a portico in the Greek Doric order. The new roof was to be crowned by an octagonal cupola with a small open terrace. Though practical and relatively inexpensive, this proposal failed to gain support, presumably in part because the reworked neoclassical façade was hopelessly out-of-date by 1885 and unsuitable as a symbol for any aspiring municipality.

Undaunted, Baillairgé kept up the pressure in his annual reports: "Last Thursday I was at my office window when a carriage passed by, with four to six Americans aboard. The driver said to them when they reached the building, "This is the City Hall" – "Where?" cried our cousins from across the border – "Here," replied the driver – "What!!! that little house" – "Yes" ... "Oh! Shame!!!"[56] Such tactics bore fruit, for city council opted in 1889 to construct an entirely new City Hall on the site of the former Jesuit Barracks which had been demolished about a decade earlier. Instead of asking the city engineer to prepare the design, the council decided to hold an international architectural competition. Baillairgé was probably furious and, judging from what ensued, he did his best to at least salvage superintendence of the first major construction project to come within his grasp since Dufferin Terrace a decade earlier. His first task was to draw up a notice to architects that set forth the conditions of the competition and outlined the city's needs. To do so, he made, by his own admission, a complete set of plans, causing a correspondent in the Canadian Architect and Builder to remark in March 1890 that the instructions read "more like a description of a design already prepared, than as a basis of designs yet to be elaborated."[57]

His voluminous Instructions to Architects Submitting Competing Designs for the New City Hall Quebec (1889), curiously printed in English only, had an unprecedented sixteen pages of specific details, full of what the Canadian Architect and Builder called "fatherly advice."[58] There were to be three prizes offered, $1500 for the best design, $1000 for second place, and $500 for third place. Plans, including elevations, ground plans, and sections to a scale of one-eighth inch to one foot, as well as specifications, bills of quantities, and estimates, were to be submitted by each competitor. The city was to take ownership of the premiated designs. After being exhibited to the public for a week, the designs were to be judged by an as-yet unnamed jury. The city reserved the right to award superintendence of construction as it wished – not necessarily to the winning architect.[59]

Baillairgé's terms of reference caused a furore in the fledgling professional journal, the Canadian Architect and Builder. The editors smelled a rat and called on all self-respecting architects to boycott the competition.[60] They interpreted the narrow and explicit instructions as proof that "Quebec does not wish to discover a good design ... so much as they desire to secure a set of plans which can be placed in the hands of the City Engineer." They claimed that the prize money was inadequate since it would cost each participant more than that to prepare such detailed plans, specifications, and estimates. Though the journal considered that the total cost estimate of $200,000 contained in Baillairgé's instructions was far too low, they argued that the value of such plans was at least $5000.[61]

Since the city would retain ownership of the three winning designs, it would have all that it required to erect the building, without further participation from the winning architect. The loss of superintendence, which brought in 5 per cent of construction costs, would prevent the architect from making any money on the venture. A Quebec correspondent writing in February 1890 was clearly cynical about the reason: "It is to be noted that the advertisement distinctly says that the architect securing first prize will not necessarily be allowed to secure the larger plum-commission for superintendence. Why, each one may guess for himself."[62] The editors of the *Canadian Architect and Builder* opposed on principle the public exhibition of designs prior to the awarding of prizes, fearing that public pressure could influence the jury. They also criticized the city's failure to identify the members of the jury at the time the competition was announced, arguing that architects had the right to know if the judges were competent or not before undertaking the preparation of plans. They ended their attack by stating that the conditions were "most unreasonable and unfair" and that the amount of work was "out of all proportion to the rewards offered."[63]

One suspects that Baillairgé, armed with detailed plans from the competition, intended to persuade city council that he could do a better job of supervision, being familiar with Quebec building conditions, than an outsider. Was this the reason why the specifications were never published in French? Moreover, he could argue that it would not entail any capital outlay since he was already on salary. Baillairgé's letter in the March 1890 edition of the *Canadian Architect and Builder*, in which he responded to criticism about the City Hall competition, appears to be laying the groundwork for such an argument: "It is possible that the premiated plan may be from an architect not thoroughly conversant with all the requirements of solidity of construction, not thoroughly possessed of all the qualifications necessary to carry out the work, or whose terms might be incompatible with the means at the disposal of the committee."[64] There was something unorthodox about the jury too. Officially its members were Eugène-Etienne Taché, architect and deputy minister of crown lands (and, it might be added, a former apprentice of Baillairgé), Harry Staveley, architect from Quebec City, and Victor Roy, architect from Montreal. These are the three who signed the judges' report.[65] Yet the latter wrote to the *Canadian Architect and Builder* stating that "Mr. Staveley, Mr. Baillairgé, of Quebec, and myself, were the judges to decide on the merits of the plans submitted."[66]

Although more than fifty architects applied for the *Instructions to Architects*, the boycott was effective. Only six designs were entered in the competition. First place went to "Stadacona" (Elzéar Charest, Quebec), second to "Escutcheon" (Cirius Porter & son, Buffalo), and third to "Fides" (Joseph-Ferdinand Peachy, Quebec).[67] The city purchased the remaining three entries for $300 each, giving further substance to the *Canadian Architect and Builder*'s case. The fiasco continued. No design was found entirely satisfactory. The city authorized Peachy – a local boy, former city councillor, and Baillairgé's former apprentice and partner – to prepare plans for the proposed City Hall, appropriating any good points that he might find in any of the competition drawings; supervision was to be carried out by Baillairgé. Reacting to this turn of events, the *Canadian Architect and Builder* lashed out: "The competition for the proposed new City Hall at Quebec has resulted in the usual fizzle ... One of the competitors is handed all six sets of plans with instructions to draw up new plans embodying the best points of each, the whole to be done under the superintendence of the city engineer. And so it goes. When will the profession awake to a sense of their humiliating position,

FIG. 153. Built in 1882–3, the Saint-Augustin staircase was the most attractive of the several iron staircases that Baillairgé designed in this decade. ANQ, photothèque, N-80-1-235

FIG. 154. The iron entrance arch at the foot of the Saint-Augustin staircase is vaguely neoclassical, with Ionic pilasters and Greek scrolls. CIHB

and insist, as a condition of their entering a competition, that a proper code be drawn up and that competent judges be appointed."[68] When Peachy's compromise was rejected, city council turned the project over to Tanguay & Vallée, architects, in 1893. Their design was an amalgam of the Châteauesque, Romanesque, and Second Empire features of the several competition plans. Contracts were signed in December 1894 and construction began in the spring of 1895, under the supervision of Tanguay & Vallée.[69] Baillairgé was the big loser, since he did not get to superintend construction. Commenting on Tanguay & Vallée's project for City Hall, he complained with self-pity that "architects from outside the city got everything (more than $8,000.00). The engineer: nothing, as usual."[70]

ENGINEERING WORKS

The municipal government became involved in public works that were not strictly buildings, although they required expertise in design as well as construction techniques. One such example was the series of staircases built to link the heights of the old city to the Lower Town and low-lying suburbs. Over the years Baillairgé had been responsible for building several wooden staircases, some of them, like those at Cove Field and the Mariners' Chapel, of considerable scale. Beginning in the 1880s, he was able to indulge his love of iron as a construction material when the city set about replacing the plain wooden staircases with five handsome cast and wrought iron ones. The first and most attractive was the Saint-Augustin staircase which ran between the rue Saint-Augustin and the rue Saint-Vallier. Built in 1882–3, it featured rows of delicate scroll brackets along its outer railing, custom-made benches at each landing, and an arched entrance on the lower street (figs. 153–4). A variant of neoclassicism with its Ionic pilasters and Greek scrolls, the arch was encrusted with interwoven national symbols – roses, shamrocks, thistles, maple leaves – and the names of the city councillors stamped onto the winding ribbon. The designer identified himself by "Baillairgé CE" printed beneath the names of Mayor François Langelier and the builder, Antoine Rousseau, on the circle in the centre:

ERIGE SOUS L'HON FR LANGELIER	
PAR	
ANT ROUSSEAU	
BAILLAIRGE CE	
BOURGET	HON HEARN
CHOUINARD	RHEAUAME
GINGRAS	RINFRET
GUAY	VALLIERE
CANNON GR	LAFRANCE T

The Saint-Augustin staircase pleased the city's road committee, who publicly praised its solidity and elegance.[71] The second iron staircase, which descended from the rue Sainte-Claire to the rues Saint-Vallier and de la Couronne, had a projecting observation deck in the shape of a half moon, flanked by arches which no longer drew on classical prototypes but were frankly modern in design (fig. 155). The motif of varied circles punched through the metal, illustrating the strength of the iron even when not solid, was used for the arches and beneath the stair treads to give a buoyant picturesque effect. At the summit of each arch was a portrait bust in relief of Mayor Langelier. The staircases built in the 1890s continued to exploit the design potential of iron, permitting wide staircases with ornamental yet functional railings and risers (fig. 156). To further the city's embellishment, Baillairgé even dreamed of creating an elegant spiral staircase in iron and steel to plunge down from Dufferin Terrace to the street below, but this dramatic concept was never realized.[72]

During the 1880s Baillairgé participated as an inspector of works on two major projects undertaken by the city: the aqueduct and the Lake Saint John Railway. Though evidently satisfied with this role in the case of the railway – having no pretensions to being a railway engineer[73] – he considered himself fully competent to build the new thirty-inch waterworks main from Lorette to the city. He even presented detailed plans and specifications for the aqueduct in a report to the city in 1881, obviously expecting to carry out the works.[74] But politics intervened and the hefty contract, worth $455,500, was awarded to Montreal contractor Horace Janson Beemer on 10 July 1883.[75] Baillairgé complained bitterly to the city administration, demanding in an open letter to the mayor that he be paid on a professional scale for his 1881 report, pointing out flaws in Beemer's plan and criticizing "the folly of paying strangers" to do city work.[76] When his protests were ignored, Baillairgé carried his campaign to the newspapers, accusing the mayor and city councillors of corruption or stupidity for wishing to adopt Beemer's plan for the waterworks. Mayor Langelier retaliated. Even though he had once praised Baillairgé as "one of the best-educated engineers in the country … one of the most industrious and hardworking men we have,"[77] Langelier suspended Baillairgé for going to the press. In a letter written in June 1883, the mayor explained his action to Baillairgé, pointing out his lack of politeness and his disregard for the council's opinion:

You are not polite enough for the councillors and the public. Courtesy in a public servant is a quality that excuses immense defects and that the most solid competence can with difficulty replace. You have no idea of the negative image that you project on the corporation by your brusque actions and bad dealings which, I know, do not come from bad intentions.

Another reproach that I have often made to you is that you don't pay enough attention to the council, which after all is your master. On several occasions you have stirred up a great deal of discontent, which took all my efforts to qualm, because you did the contrary of what was decided by council or by some committees.

That is the criticism I made of you and I repeat it frankly to your face for your own good. But I have always recognized your great learning and your rare work habits.[78]

Langelier finished by suspending him, stating that as long as he was mayor of Quebec, he would not allow an employee to insult the city council. Before Baillairgé was reinstated, he was forced to make two written apologies, the first being considered by Langelier as lacking sufficient humility![79]

Despite his protests over the aqueduct contract, Baillairgé found himself inspecting Beemer's work and signing off certificates for payments. The only reward for Baillairgé from the aqueduct, in addition to the innumerable small branching operations between the old and new systems, was the iron tubular bridge over the Saint Charles River which he designed and superintended. Baillairgé no doubt searched in his books such as *The Theory, Practice and Architecture of Bridges of Stone, Iron, Timber, and Wire, with Examples on*

FIG. 155. The 1888 Sainte-Claire staircase, seen here from the rue Saint-Vallier. NHPS

FIG. 156. Baillairgé continued to embellish Québec City with iron staircases. This grand staircase from 1893, linking côte de la Montagne with rue Buade, has recently been refurbished. Canadian Parks Service, Heritage Recording Services

FIG. 157. The tubular bridge over the Saint Charles River. Baillairgé, *Rapport de l'Ex-Ingénieur 1866 à 1899*, opp. 19

FIG. 158. This 1883 photograph shows Charles Baillairgé (second from right) as the city's representative on the team that inspected the progress of the Lake Saint John Railway. The inspection party, which included the wives, is examining the clearance of the hinterland during the construction of the track somewhere in the vicinity of Rivière-à-Pierre en route to Roberval. NA, PA-124263

FIG. 159. The Taschereau arch at the junction of rues Saint-Louis and Sainte-Ursule (1886). ANQ, photothèque, N-277-112

the *Principle of Suspension* (1855-6), Clark and Stephenson's *The Britannia and Conway Tubular Bridges* (1850), and *Fairbairn's Construction of Conway and Britannia Bridges* (1849) for a solution to the problem of running both old and new pipes over the river in a safe, fireproof manner, without interrupting navigation. The result was an arched tubular bridge of iron, lined with wood to protect against frost, with its novel feature of a reversed curve in the vertical plane at each stone abutment (fig. 157).[80]

The city's involvement in railways began in the 1870s when the municipality subscribed to the North Shore Rail Road to run between Quebec and Montreal, and the Lake Saint John Railway to link Quebec to the hinterland. Since the city had contributed one-third to the cost of the latter, Baillairgé was instructed to represent the city's interest on the inspection team in his capacity as a trained civil engineer. Though the work progressed slowly, activity picked up in 1883 when contractor Horace Janson Beemer, the man who had won the Quebec aqueduct job, took over the railway contract and pushed the line through to Roberval by 1888.[81] Baillairgé wrote frequent progress reports for city council; in addition to verifying the progress of construction, he displayed great enthusiasm for these outings which enhanced his appreciation of the region's mineral wealth and colonization potential (fig. 158).

FESTIVAL DESIGNS

But these assignments were insufficient to keep the indefatigable Baillairgé busy. Always quick to spot an opportunity for some new venture, he used public festivals and carnivals as pretexts to create imaginative arches, towers, fountains, and other monuments that required modern materials and technology. When the city celebrated the investiture of native son Elzéar-Alexandre Taschereau as the first Canadian cardinal in July 1886, Baillairgé came up with a triumphal arch in front of City Hall and an illuminated cone for the Place d'Armes. The Taschereau arch at the intersection of the rues Saint-Louis and Sainte-Ursule (fig. 159) was unusual in the way it straddled the juncture of the two streets, like a transept crowned by an inner dome, and allowed traffic to circulate through the arches in four directions. The illuminated cone (fig. 160), a wooden tower 100 feet high, was lit on the night of the celebration by a thousand Chinese lanterns wound around the tower from top to bottom. Though not attached to the ground, the cone stood for four years before a cyclone destroyed it.[82]

From this moment, Baillairgé's public monuments became more fanciful, more experimental. His electro-chromatic revolving fountain, for instance, which he apparently invented before 1871 although he only promoted and patented it in April 1889,[83] grew out of a lecture by Laval University's Professor Laflamme on the reflection of light. Working from the premise that light could be made to follow a curved path, Baillairgé added water, colour, electricity – and conventional sculptured putti – to produce what he claimed was the "most beautiful and fairy-like" electric fountain ever conceived.[84] The cylindrical fountain (fig. 161) had three tiers or series of water jets, twelve jets to a tier; the middle tier was to remain stationary, while the upper and lower tiers rotated in opposite directions. In the centre was a brilliant source of light (aluminium, oxy-hydrogen, or acetylene were recommended fuels), which passed though lenses and small tramways carrying pieces of coloured glass.[85] Vaunting that his invention would surpass anything similar in Chicago or Paris, Baillairgé described the anticipated effect in glowing terms: "The jets thus appear to be constantly playing at leap frog the one over the other, while the receiving basin gleams during the play of jets with coloured fire as if of melted gold, silver, ruby, topaz, sapphire, etc."[86] Although he intended the fountain to be erected as a city attraction at the Place d'Armes, Quebec never rose to the occasion and the fantastic scheme remained on the drawing board.

The same year Baillairgé submitted plans for a competition to build a tower in London, England. This project followed hard on the heels of the successful opening of the Eiffel Tower in Paris in the spring of 1889. On seeing the technical, scientific, and commercial success of the French venture, a group of British businessmen formed the Tower Company, Limited, and initiated an international competition for a tower even taller than Eiffel's unprecedented 300 metres (984 feet). Modern in its multi-functional conception, the London Tower was intended to contain restaurants, shops, theatres, public baths, winter gardens, and a meteorological observatory, all serviced by banks of elevators.[87] Baillairgé's participation gave further proof that he kept himself up-to-date on the international scene and that he allied himself to the general nineteenth-century quest for technological advancement. Examining the nineteenth-century phenomenon of the pursuit of height for its own sake, architect Frank I. Jenkins observed that "the tower became a symbol of the optimism and technical endeavour of the era, a monument to man's mechanical progress and his belief in that progress."[88] Baillairgé's career had been marked by the use of contemporary construction technology, but further proof of his curiosity came from his pilgrimage to Sydenham during his European trip in 1874 to examine for himself the reconstituted Crystal Palace from the 1851 exhibition, about which he had read so much.[89]

Unlike many of the sixty-eight entries in the competition, Baillairgé's proposal for the London Eiffel Tower (figs. 162–3) shed the last vestiges of conventional stylistic theory and was frankly modern in design, its structure clearly revealed without reference to associative values. The motto that he inscribed on each sheet of plans, "circumferentially, radially and diagonally bound," suggested a simultaneous interlocking of all dimensions that foreshadowed the spatial concepts of cubism. His tower was a staggering 1600 feet high, over 600 feet higher than the Eiffel Tower. Circular in plan and adopting the same construction principles as Baillairgé's much smaller illuminated cone, this cast- and wrought-iron frame ascended in sections which could be dismantled – a condition of the competition in case the venture failed and the owners opted to sell segments for local exhibitions. Each successive tier decreased in diameter until the open gallery at the top was reached. The webbed structure was then to be enclosed with glass and illuminated with electric lights on the overhanging galleries every two hundred feet. Double staircases and multiple elevators completed the scheme.[90] As Jenkins has pointed out, Baillairgé's "telescope" solution resembles curiously an earlier tower project by an English architect C. Burton, who in 1852 proposed in the *Builder* a 1000-foot tower to be built from the glass and iron salvaged from the demolition of the Crystal Palace.[91] Baillairgé may possibly have seen this plan in the English magazine but, given his interests and career evolution, there is no reason to believe that his London Eiffel Tower design was not his own invention.

FIG. 160. At the Place d'Armes, Taschereau's investiture was also marked by Baillairgé's creation of a wooden tower, which was illuminated on the night of the festivities with 1000 Chinese lanterns. NA, PA-23624

FIG. 161. Baillairgé's electro-chromatic revolving fountain. Baillairgé, *Rapport de l'Ex-Ingénieur 1866 à 1899*, opp. 81

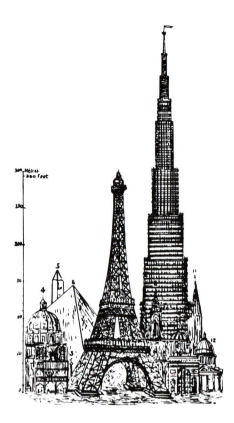

FIG. 162. The London Eiffel Tower project, 1889–90. This sketch compares Baillairgé's 1600-foot high tower to other world monuments such as the Eiffel Tower, Cheops's pyramid, the Washington Monument, and Saint Peter's in Rome. Baillairgé, *Rapport de l'Ex-Ingénieur 1866 à 1899*, opp. 90

The competition attracted a truly international crowd, with designs coming from the United States, Great Britain, Germany, Austria, Italy, Sweden, Australia, and Turkey. Baillairgé was the only Canadian entry. Among the sixty-eight competitors he placed fifth, a respectable showing when one considers that he stuck with the (by that time) more traditional iron instead of steel, which the promoters preferred, and when one compares his cautious, monolithic design to some of the startling and eccentric entries.[92] In later years he insisted that he ought to have been awarded first prize because the first four place winners had defaulted by not designing structures capable of subdivision. The tower was never built, presumably for financial reasons, although Baillairgé attributed it to "its savouring too much of an idea borrowed from the French, and the English being too proud and conservative to encourage any thing of the kind."[93]

An offshoot of the London Eiffel Tower design was Baillairgé's proposal for the Victoria Jubilee Tower (fig. 164). He wanted the city to celebrate the Queen's jubilee by building this permanent structure over the fountain at the Place d'Armes, in place of his earlier wooden illuminated cone which had blown over. Circular in plan like his earlier towers, the Victoria Jubilee Tower was to be an iron and steel structure 150 feet high with ten tiers or storeys, each one illuminated with electric arcs or incandescent lighting. In a description intended to persuade city council, Baillairgé indulged in a boyish science-fiction fantasy: "The crow's nest ... would afford a commanding view of the whole surrounding country, and in the case of an illumination with fireworks, a hundred or more set around its periphery or two or three hundred of them in double or treble tiers, all slightly inclined outwards at an equal angle to the vertical, if simultaneously or together fired by electricity, and soaring skyward another hundred and fifty feet or more, would thus form a sheaf, a monster parachute, opening at some 600 feet above the St.Lawrence, and their component vari-colored stars lighting up the heavens and descending in a fiery shower ... of blessing for a munificent reign of 60 years."[94] Although he continued to lobby for its construction until his death, the Victoria Jubilee Tower was never built.

The winter carnivals of 1895 and 1896 provided another opportunity for Baillairgé to give free rein to his imagination. When the carnival committee was formed late in 1893 by merchants anxious to stimulate tourist business, Baillairgé became secretary of the construction committee chaired by architect François-Xavier Berlinguet.[95] He dashed off reams of sketches for snow and ice sculptures, ranging from variations on the theme of triumphal arches to entire complexes of ice, such as the reconstruction of the fortification walls and historic gates of Quebec (figs. 165–6). As secretary, he sent off suggestions to the students at the Ursulines, Seminary, and Laval University, encouraging them to make fortresses, obelisks, columns, urns, and statues "like the gardens of the Trianon at Versailles,"[96] and snowmen with pumpkin heads lit by lamps or candles. He even lapsed into amusing plays on words, as in the proposed log cabin to be erected opposite the railway station, which announced such delicacies as "rat gout de mouton," "vins feints," and "fruits qu'on fit." But the idea that clearly fascinated him the most was the slide. Among the many sketches one finds different versions of this classic symbol of winter carnivals, including the multi-lane straight slide for Dufferin Terrace – a forerunner of the one that still operates during Quebec's winter carnivals – the star or radiating slide, and especially the spiral slide (figs. 167–8). For the 1896 carnival, Baillairgé had a ten-foot high model of his spiral slide built and mounted on one of the parade floats. As it was pulled through the streets of Quebec, boys showed how it worked by climbing up the ladder inside and sliding down the spiral track around the cone to re-enter the structure at its base. The idea was inspired by the laying of train tracks on curves. Its inventor boasted that there was nothing like it in the world, and the *Canadian Engineer* agreed that it was a "novel conception."[97] His ambition to erect a full-scale spiral slide 50 feet high on Dufferin Terrace or at Victoria Park was never realized.

In a final fling before his retirement from the city in 1898, Baillairgé conceived and implemented a plan for the development of a public pleasure ground at an elbow of land formed by a meander in the Saint Charles River. He had already shown himself sensitive to city embellishment schemes in general, as exemplified by his role in the Dufferin Improvements and the opening up of the Grande Allée. He also supported the growing park movement, as shown by his creation of the broad tree-line boulevard Langelier in 1883, which featured parks for local citizens and a promenade route for visitors. At Victoria Park he laid out the ring road and meandering paths, and sited the buildings; he also designed and supervised construction of two small swing bridges of iron that provided access to the peninsula at avenue Parent and rue Gignac, as well as two conservatories for the park's planting stock.[98] Victoria Park, or Parent Park as it was sometimes called in honour of the mayor, was opened in 1898. Several years later Baillairgé was still suggesting improvements and additions for the facilities and gardens.[99] His whimsical projects for civic decoration – towers, fountains, slides, parks – suggest that he was relieved of much of the drudgery in his final years as city engineer and left free to dream up schemes for making his beloved Quebec a more attractive urban space.

There were no more private commissions for Baillairgé in these years. The only buildings that he designed were for his own use. In about 1886 he added a private chapel to the summer house he had bought in 1867 at Saint-Michel de Bellechasse and then sought permission from church authorities to hold mass there (fig. 169).[100] The chapel, named Sainte-Alice, perhaps in honour of his daughter, has recently been moved from its original location to La Guadeloupe in Frontenac County. In Quebec in 1887 he received as a gift from his wealthy bachelor uncle Louis-de-Gonzague Baillairgé the property situated at 72, rue Saint-Louis known as the Montgomery house. It was in this one-storey wooden house that the body of General Richard Montgomery had been laid out in 1776 following the unsuccessful American assault on Quebec. When Louis-de-Gonzague Baillairgé acquired the property, his sensitivity to these historical associations led him to mount a commemorative tablet on the wall of the house. Aware of his nephew's iconoclastic bent, he gave Charles permission, in the legal document of donation, to rebuild the house on condition that the inscription to General Montgomery remain perpetually on display.[101] Baillairgé did demolish the house, to the disgust of heritage buffs like Charlotte Macpherson who complained: "Why, to think Americans should have been permitted to carry off bodily the house where Montgomery's body was laid, and are making a fortune out of it, having set it up as an Indian curiosity shop in some part of the States."[102] He then designed and supervised construction of the present 72, rue Saint-Louis in 1890, using the hard Rivière-à-Pierre granite that he had discovered on his inspection tours

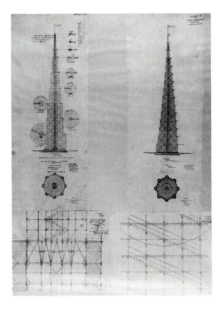

FIG. 163. Elevations, plans, and details for Baillairgé's London Eiffel Tower proposal. AVQ, fonds Charles Baillairgé, no. 8–sheet B

FIG. 164. Baillairgé's 1894 proposal for the Victoria Jubilee Tower. Baillairgé, *Rapport de l'Ex-Ingénieur 1866 à 1899*, opp. 84

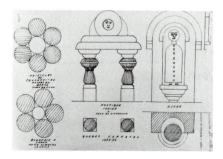

FIG. 165. Baillairgé produced many imaginative proposals for snow and ice sculptures for the Quebec Winter Carnival in 1895, including this Indian arch and niche. The colonnettes were to be made from empty nail barrels, whitewashed to simulate snow. ASQ, Séminaire 38, no. 95

for the Lake Saint John Railway (fig. 170.)[103] It was a solid, modest house, well-finished in an unobtrusive way. Baillairgé eventually died in this house and his widow remained there until about 1925.

Immediately following his retirement from the city in December 1898, Baillairgé briefly turned developer, exploiting the courtyard and stable area behind his house as a site for a second dwelling, fronting onto the ruelle des Ursulines. It broke with his traditional house type by having a mansard roof and an oriel window. The architect considered that it was "an example of what may be done on a narrow lot ... when a porch or carriage way is to run through it to rear of house on opposite street."[104] To solve the problem, he made the house deeper and ran the stair hall across the building, or parallel to the front and rear walls (fig. 171).

Apart from these structures, the only other non-city designs that Baillairgé produced in these last decades were for his Baillairgé-Hurly Safety Raft and the North Pole explorer ship *Indestructible*. He entered the Pollok prize competition in September 1901 for the best life-saving apparatus in case of disaster at sea. Baillairgé's solution – steel spring buffers in the stern of the vessel to neutralize collisions at sea and a system of side rafts pierced with embrazured openings to match the portholes – was inspired in part from a crude exhibit by a Mr Hurly in the Paris 1900 exhibition.[105] Although 400 proposals were submitted to the Pollok prize jury in Le Havre, France, no award was ever made. His proposal for a polar vessel called the *Indestructible* was based on his experience in constructing shock-resisting wharves for the city. Since his pontoons had withstood the blows of ferry boats and ice pressure in the Quebec context, Baillairgé was convinced that –

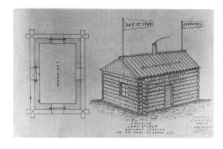

FIG. 166. Baillairgé's proposed log house for the winter carnival of 1895–6, opposite the Lake Saint John Railway station. AVQ, conseil et comités, carnaval de Québec 1895–6, 3

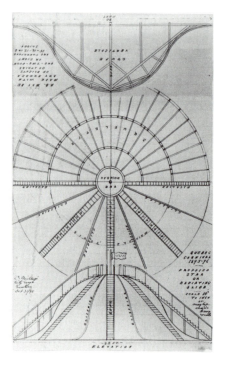

FIG. 167. Baillairgé's star or radiating ice slide, planned with an 80-foot height. AVQ, conseil et comités, carnaval de Québec 1895–6, 3

FIG. 168. Baillairgé's spiral slide, shown in a photograph of the 10-foot high wooden model that toured the city on a parade float. Baillairgé, *Rapport de l'Ex-Ingénieur 1866 à 1899*, opp. 86

despite his lack of experience as a naval architect – his wood and iron vessel would be able to withstand the crushing force of polar ice. Although he explained his concept in professional journals and to the members of the Royal Society of Canada in May 1903, no action was ever taken on his suggestion.[106]

As city engineer, Baillairgé's greatest contribution was urbanistic rather than architectural in nature. The endless parade of fire stations, market halls, and hay-weighing stations took second place to such accomplishments as Dufferin Terrace, the iron staircases, boulevard Langelier, and Victoria Park. Had some of the inventions such as the electro-chromatic revolving fountain and the Victoria Jubilee Tower been built, Baillairgé would have left the city with some unusual and eccentric landmarks. What does emerge from Baillairgé's long career as city engineer is his unfailing enthusiasm for his native Quebec.

FIG. 169. Baillairgé designed this private chapel for his summer house at Saint-Michel de Bellechasse in about 1886. Simple in design, decorated by stained glass windows, the chapel was moved in the 1970s to La Guadeloupe, Quebec. Canadian Parks Service, Heritage Recording Services

FIG. 170. Baillairgé's house at 72, rue Saint-Louis, 1890. Canadian Parks Service, Heritage Recording Services

FIG. 171. An early example of infill in the courtyard of Baillairgé's house, 1898. Canadian Parks Service, Heritage Recording Services

11 Baillairgé the Educator

DURING THE YEARS that Baillairgé worked as city engineer, he actively promoted the dissemination of scientific and technical knowledge through his own lectures, publications, and inventions. It was his significant contribution in this sphere, rather than his production as city engineer, that won him local, national, and even international recognition in the form of medals, diplomas, titles, and enhanced social standing.

His interest in communicating technical information can be traced to the beginning of his career when, immediately upon completion of his own training, he began to accept apprentices in architecture, civil engineering, and surveying. He did not limit himself to teaching other aspiring professionals, however, for he gave during the 1850s many public lectures before audiences of several hundred persons at the *Institut canadien*, the *Association de la chambre de lecture de Saint-Roch*, Saint Patrick's Catholic Institute, and the meeting hall of the Parliament Building. Although the listeners were not specialists, the topics that Baillairgé chose came from the disciplines of mathematics and the physical sciences: astronomy, optics, pneumatics, acoustics, atmosphere, winds, currents, steam and steam engines, and so forth.[1] Even the annual reports that he produced for the city in later years went beyond the usual scope of such documents, ressembling general research studies on specific subjects. His 1872 and 1878 reports, in particular, were so thorough and comprehensive that they were sought after by city engineers in Canada and the United States.[2]

So active was Baillairgé's career in the 1850s that he only found time late in 1859 to begin work on a textbook of geometry, trigonometry, and mensuration, subjects that were familiar to him through study and practical experience.[3] Begun during the lull in business between the loss of the Ottawa Parliament Buildings competition and the winning of the Quebec Jail commission, and completed during his two years at Ottawa, the *Nouveau traité de géométrie et de trigonométrie rectiligne et sphérique, suivi du toisé des surfaces et des volumes* (1866) was published the year after Baillairgé had returned to Quebec. It was a lengthy book, nearly 900 pages long, in which the propositions of the Greek geometer Euclid were reduced by half, without affecting his deductions and conclusions. Baillairgé's intended readership were architects, surveyors, engineers, teachers, and students.[4] Although other geometry textbooks existed, including a recent one by Dr John Playfair in 1856, his purpose in producing yet another version was to save time because, as he argued, there were "too many other sciences to learn now a-days to devote a year or more to the study of the olden master." The redundancy in Euclid's work, according to Baillairgé, was the result of his having "to deal with a set of obstinate sophists."[5]

In writing this book, Baillairgé demonstrated his ability for analysis and synthesis rather than creative thought. By grouping together all problems linked to a specific principle, he was able to eliminate the entire fifth book of Euclid. He occasionally challenged existing theory – as in the case of Thorpe's trisection of an angle – and even contributed some original ideas. One new formula, number 1521, was found in the section on the theory and practice of mensuration – the *bête noire* of Baillairgé's experiences in Ottawa. Theorem 1521, which provided a mathematical formula for determining the volume of any solid, contained the germ of a concept that Baillairgé was soon to exploit in his so-called invention, the Stereometrical Tableau. But for the moment the mathematical treatise received good press on its own merits. Reviewers invariably remarked on the usefulness of the book, and in particular the simplicity and universal application of formula 1521.[6] Recognizing the enormous labour involved in producing the treatise, the *Quebec Mercury* paid tribute to Baillairgé's desire to make technical information more accessible to the public and concluded that "it is evident that in writing such a book the author has had no other object in view than that of being useful to his fellow men."[7]

The Stereometrical Tableau grew out of theorem 1521 of Baillairgé's treatise on geometry, trigonometry, and mensuration. It applied to prismoids, solid bodies which had parallel end areas bounded by parallel sides. The prismoidal formula, which calculated the volume of certain prismoids, was not discovered by Baillairgé but by a Dr Simpson before him.[8] What Baillairgé did was to enlarge this theorem, prove that it worked in almost all instances (with certain specific exceptions), and then apply it in a practical way so that it was accessible to professionals and laymen alike. His contribution, therefore, was in the broad practical application of a previously obscure and restrictive geometric formula. His invention – or generalization – was aimed at "architects, engineers, surveyors, students and apprentices, customs and excise officers, professors of geometry and mathematics, universities, colleges, seminaries ... mechanics, measurers, gaugers, ship-builders, contractors, artisans"[9] – in short, all those practical men who often had to calculate the solid content or volume of any body.

It is obvious that he had been led to this problem through his years of experience as an architect, when he had so often been required to produce estimates and measurements of work, the payment being made in accordance with the *volume* of the work. His familiarity with different measurement systems has already been demonstrated in his comprehensive analysis of them for the Department of Public Works in 1861 and his written instructions to tradesmen during construction of the Ottawa buildings. It was his belief that geometry was the basis of all public works and the constructive arts.[10]

The prismoidal formula as expounded by Baillairgé stated that the volume of a solid object could be calculated by the following method: "to the sum of the parallel end areas, add four times the middle area, and multiply the whole by one sixth part of the height or length of the solid."[11] While making the theory available in a number of publications, he went further by embodying the theory in physical, three-dimensional form as a teaching aid that he called the Stereometrical Tableau (fig. 172). This was a wooden box or case, five feet long, three feet wide, and five inches deep, containing 200 wooden models comprising all the elementary, geometrical forms, their segments and sections, and numerous other solids, simple and compound. The case was covered by a hinged glass cover to keep out dust while exhibiting and allowing access to the wooden models, each of which was attached to the board by a wire peg and could be removed and replaced as needed.

Through its visual appeal to uneducated persons, the Stereometrical Tableau was intended to simplify the study and teaching of solid geometry, its nomenclature and the development of surfaces, perspective, planes, and spheres. For more sophisticated users, the combined use of the prismoidal formula and the wooden models, which helped in the analysis of the component forms of any solid body, reduced the science of mensuration from the study of many complex formulae to one universal and generally applicable rule. Baillairgé claimed that his invention considerably shortened the time needed to study this science: "The whole difficulty is, therefore, reduced by my system to measuring the areas of the opposite bases and the middle section, the remainder of the work being mere multiplication; so that the proposed formula renders this branch of study of such easy and general application that the art or science may now be taught in a few lessons where it formerly required months and even years."[12]

Baillairgé worked on the development of the prismoidal formula and its universal application from 1866 until 1871, when he had the actual boxes with wooden models manufactured. He then set about marketing his invention. He began by displaying the Stereometrical Tableau in the provincial exhibition of 1871, accompanied by a free pamphlet explaining the prismoidal rule. According to one reviewer, the wooden box, which hung, significantly, on the wall of the corridor linking the arts and industry sections, aroused great public curiosity.[13] At the same time he sought the endorsement of expert mathematicians and educators, testimonials which he could then use to support his subscription drive. He started the ball rolling by sending the prospectus with a photograph of the Stereometrical Tableau to the Council of Public Instruction for the province of Quebec, which in turn asked committee members, including Bishop Jean Langevin of Rimouski, to evaluate the worthiness of the invention.[14] Not being a mathematician, Bishop Langevin asked the Seminary of Quebec for a written opinion on the exactitude of Baillairgé's rule for measuring solids.[15] Whether Baillairgé had deliberately planned it that way or not, it was a flattering scenario. The superior of the Seminary of Quebec, Monseigneur Thomas-Etienne Hamel, accompanied by the institution's most reputed professor of mathematics, Abbé Napoléon Mainguy, trudged over to Baillairgé's house at 14, rue Ferland to inspect for themselves the Stereometrical Tableau.[16] They were reportedly well-satisfied with their visit, a fact confirmed by Abbé Mainguy's book demon-

FIG. 172. An advertising flyer announcing Baillairgé's Stereometrical Tableau, invented in 1871. The wooden box and objects were mass-produced for Baillairgé by joinery contractors François Godin and Ferdinand De Varennes. Baillairgé, *Key to Baillairgé's Stereometrical Tableau*, fly leaf inside front cover

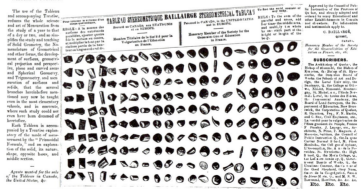

strating the validity of the prismoidal formula, *Démonstration générale et discussion de la formule stéréométrique Baillairgé* (1872), and his letter praising the invention for the simplicity, clarity, and universality of the formula and expressing his wish that "your efforts be fully crowned with success."[17] Bishop Langevin added his congratulations, crediting Baillairgé with authorship of the formula.[18] The Council of Public Instruction officially recommended his invention for all Quebec schools and the experts unanimously substantiated the theoretical basis of Baillairgé's invention, joining in a chorus of praise for its simplicity, utility, and general applicability.[19]

Baillairgé's next step was to discuss his invention in a public forum. He got his chance on 20 March 1872, when he appeared before the Literary and Historical Society of Quebec, of which he was a member, to give a lively and successful lecture before "the *elite* of the scientific and well read men of this community." His skill as an orator and teacher served him well. By comparing with "poetic imagination" abstract geometrical forms to everyday objects, and using large drawings and scale models as teaching aids, he reportedly "kept [the] audience entranced for two whole hours with such unflagging interest, that the two hours had passed as though but one."[20] On completion of his presentation, society members congratulated him for having removed a great obstacle from the path of education.[21] The president concluded by stating "that in his recollection, he had never been so pleased or gratified with a lecture ... and that ... Mr. Baillairgé should be considered the real discoverer" of the formula.[22]

Buoyed up by such a positive reception, Baillairgé sent his prospectus to the United States and France, achieving a break-through in marketing strategy and incidentally confirming that time-worn adage that a prophet – especially a Canadian one – is only truly recognized outside his own country. In New York he made the front page of the 1 June 1872 issue of *Scientific American*, complete with an illustration of his tableau.[23] In France he had even greater success, for he penetrated the ranks of some of the many literary and scientific societies then in existence. It is unclear whether he made contact through his friend the minister of public instruction for Quebec, who seems to have been known in France, or whether it was merely his application for a French patent that brought him to the attention of Auguste Humbert, secretary-general and founder of the *Société de vulgarisation pour l'enseignement du peuple*.[24] Humbert actively promoted Baillairgé's interests in France, obtaining for him memberships in his own society in August 1872 and in the *Société libre d'instruction et d'éducation populaire* in 1873.[25] Baillairgé's delight was obvious. He dashed off a letter to his friend Nazaire Levasseur, editor of *L'Événement*, asking him to mention the nomination in his paper, and ending with false modesty: "put that in your miscellaneous column if it is worth mentioning."[26]

Humbert also arranged to exhibit the Stereometrical Tableau in the international exhibition at the Palais de l'industrie, taking place in Paris in 1873 and 1874. This was the turning point for Baillairgé. First his invention was awarded top marks in the instruction category. This diploma was handed to Baillairgé's representative, Humbert, on 5 January 1874 (fig. 173).[27] Then it received the highest award offered by the *Société de vulgarisation pour l'enseignement du peuple*: the bronze medal called the "médaille d'honneur en vermeil." In his capacity as secretary-general of the society, Humbert extended an official invitation to Baillairgé to attend the presentation ceremony in Paris

FIG. 173. Diploma awarded to Charles Baillairgé in 1873–4 at the international exhibition at the Palais de l'industrie, Paris. MQ, cahier Charles Baillairgé, photograph by Patrick Altman

on 15 March 1874, promising that "society is preparing a brilliant reception for you."[28]

How could Baillairgé resist? Despite his modest income, he resolved to visit France to receive the prize in person and to enjoy the attention of this circle of admirers. Having obtained a three-month leave of absence from the city on the grounds that he would gain knowledge useful for Quebec's public works during his trip, Baillairgé set out for Portland, Maine, on February 20.[29] There he boarded the *Circassian*, one of the newest and largest vessels of the Allan line, and crossed the Atlantic in fourteen days. En route to Paris he made a brief stopover in England, taking time to visit the royal pavilion and cliff-side aquarium in Brighton, the South Kensington Museum and Saint Paul's Cathedral in London, and Paxton's Crystal Palace at Sydenham.[30]

In Paris Baillairgé's reception exceeded even his expectations. Not only was he to receive the bronze medal and diploma from the *Société d'éducation*; he discovered on his arrival that he would be the recipient of a special prize – the Philippe de Girard medal – given by Madame la Baronne de Pages in honour of her grandfather, a celebrated engineer, and awarded for the most useful invention or discovery of the year.[31] Thus on 15 March 1874, in the grand hall of the Conservatoire des arts et métiers, Baillairgé gathered with the dignitaries, society members, and other award winners. A letter written the following day to a Quebec newspaper (probably from Baillairgé himself) described the occasion:

Each prize-winner came forward and heard the recital of his achievement, then received his diploma, book, medal, etc., from the hands of the President or other persons ... bowed and retired.

Finally it was the turn of a distinguished Canadian, Mr. Baillairgé, to be called. The presence of a Canadian prize-winner in this context was so unusual that it was remarked upon. It was in the midst of a most perfect silence that Mr. Baillairgé advanced to accept the prize which he had been awarded. Before taking his seat, he thought that he ought to address a few words to the audience. His happy improvisation was strongly applauded.[32]

In the *Quebec Mercury*, the exact nature of this "happy improvisation" was made explicit: "A perfect burst of applause greeted him when, in returning thanks for the honour done him, he said that 'It was with legitimate pride and most lively feelings of emotion that he, a grandson of Old France, had such a flattering occasion accorded him of speaking publicly for the first time on the cherished soil of that country which his ancestors had proudly claimed as the land of their nativity.' "[33] How Baillairgé must have delighted in the events following the ceremony, when he was presented to Madame la Baronne de Pages and other artistic and literary celebrities. Such a day undoubtedly went far to compensate him for the bitter defeats and petty disputes of bygone years. His official portrait by Quebec photographer J.E. Livernois, taken soon after his return from France at the age of fifty-two, shows him proudly wearing his Paris "médaille en vermeil" (fig. 174).

He remained in France for almost two months, consolidating his new friendships among the intellectual elite, observing architectural monuments and engineering projects, and seeking out his French relatives. He spent five weeks in Paris, attending theatrical performances in Garnier's new Opera Hall, visiting the Pantheon and other historic examples of neoclassicism so familiar to him through his books, and witnessing first-hand the dramatic

FIG. 174. Baillairgé posed for this official portrait by Quebec photographer J.E. Livernois soon after his return from Paris in 1874. ASQ

changes to the city's infrastructure brought about in the previous twenty years by Napoleon III's dynamic urban planner Baron Haussmann.[34] With his characteristic fascination for technical details, he even inspected the Paris sewer system in a boat that floated along on top of the *grand collecteur* "with a party of 100 gentlemen and ladies – english, french, german [sic] and other … and no one had even to raise his kerchief to his nose."[35] What seems to have impressed him the most were the refined eating habits of the French, in particular their custom of matching the liquid refreshment to the meal. "The French are right," he commented. "Wine with meals, coffee with milk for cakes, black coffee with a liqueur after meals, beer while smoking – nothing sweet with meat."[36] Baillairgé later confessed to having some difficulty in readjusting to the plainer habits of Quebec! His only excursion was a boat trip down the Loire River from Paris to Angers in search of descendents of his ancestors. At Blois he queried the parish priest over lunch, then proceeded to Tours where he discovered Alphonse J. Baillairgé, an architect who was also, like his Canadian relative, a literary man.[37] They obviously struck up quite a friendship, judging by the engravings of Tours that Charles received as part of Alphonse's bequest in 1882.[38]

Baillairgé returned to Quebec in May 1874. Although the mayor and local citizenry did not immediately perceive his new status, outsiders like Lord Dufferin and visiting French naval officers apparently did. Writing to his friend Nazaire Levasseur, Baillairgé described a picnic that he arranged that summer for the captain and officers of the *Adonis* and the *Majestueux*, and revealed his irritation at being excluded from the mayor of Quebec's dinner in their honour:

My dear Levasseur,
I went yesterday to your office. I wanted to invite you to celebrate at my house. We all went – P. Huot, Evanturel, P Chauveau, Alvanez, Chevalier Jr., Fiset and I – on a picnic to Lake Beauport with the captain and officers of the Adonis, and the officers of the Majestueux and came back around 10 P.M. to my house. A pleasant supper with champagne. In replying to a toast made to me by the captain, I had to say that as a prize-winner from France I had the honour to receive them in my home. We had a charming evening and we all went our separate ways saying that it was much more amusing than the mayor's dinner. We agreed among ourselves that it had been mean not to invite me, not because of my position as a citizen of Quebec but, because of my prizes, as a link between France and Canada.[39]

Another indication of Baillairgé's increased social standing was his membership in the *Club des 21*, a group of artistic, literary, and learned gentlemen who occasionally met for dinner and debate in Quebec's Russell House. Led by the comte de Prémio Réal – consul-general for Spain, personal friend of Lord Dufferin, civil engineer, and distinguished mathematician, the *Club des 21* included poet Louis-Honoré Fréchette, musician Calixa Lavallée, and Baillairgé's friend and newspaper editor Nazaire Levasseur. In 1879 Baillairgé entertained them with an amusing after-dinner speech in which he poked fun at each member's foibles through clever verbal caricature.[40]

For the next ten years, Baillairgé and his Stereometrical Tableau received recognition from learned societies in Canada and abroad, so that by 1886 he could proudly boast that he was the recipient of thirteen medals and seventeen diplomas from France, Belgium, Italy, Russia, Japan, Brazil, Canada, and the United States.[41] These honours included la Société de vulgarisation pour l'enseignement du peuple, Paris, member (1872); la Société libre d'instruction et d'éducation populaire, Paris, member (1873), diploma and bronze medal (1874); l'exposition internationale et universelle du pavillon de l'Enfance, Paris, diplôme d'honneur (1874); la Société des sciences industrielles, arts et belles lettres, Paris, member (1874); Philippe de Girard medal, Paris (1874); l'Association des amateurs des arts et métiers, Québec, honorary member (1874);[42] la Société centrale des architectes de France, member (1875);[43] l'Institut Confucius, Bordeaux, bronze medal (1875);[44] l'Université Laval, Quebec, honorary Master of Arts degree in science (1876);[45] international exhibition, Philadelphia, medal (1876);[46] l'Académie Christophe Colomb, Marseille, corresponding member (1877); la Société de géographie, member (1877); la Società scientifica litteraria artistica Voltri, Italy,[47] member and title of *Chevalier de l'ordre de Saint-Sauveur de Monte Real* (1877);[48] la Société des Sauveteurs de France et de l'étranger, Paris, diploma "en souvenir de ses belles actions" (1877);[49] l'Académie ethnographique de la Gironde, honorary corresponding member (1877);[50] universal exhibition, Paris, honorable mention in class 7, organization and appliances for secondary education (1878);[51] l'Institut protecteur de l'enfance, Paris, honorary member as a "bienfaiteur de l'humanité" (1878);[52] and the Society of Science, Letters and Arts of London, honorary member (1886).[53] Of special importance among these awards was the Order of Saint-Sauveur, for it carried with it the title "Chevalier." From that moment on, Baillairgé often signed himself as the "Chevalier Baillairgé."

The Stereometrical Tableau, priced at $50 a unit, was eventually distributed to dozens of institutions, for the most part in the province of Quebec, though some were shipped to Ontario, New Brunswick, and as far afield as the United States. Baillairgé's invention even became a recommended part of the curriculum for all elementary and polytechnical schools in the Russian Empire.[54] He kept up promotional activities through public lectures, an attempt at franchising through Thomas Whitty, a professor from Montreal, and a belated entry in the London Colonial Exhibition of 1886.[55] The unit in London was then donated to the South Kensington Museum.[56] But interest in the Stereometrical Tableau had by that time faded.

His invention did, nonetheless, bring him honour and recognition in the form of titles, medals, and diplomas from fashionable learned societies. It also ensured him significant coverage in nineteenth-century biographical dictionaries. The first biography appeared not in Canada but in Italy, in the *Rivista universale* in February 1878.[57] Two months later the Montreal-based *L'Opinion publique* carried a long biographical sketch, complete with portrait, praising him for his remarkable discovery in the field of geometry:

He made a discovery in a field of science where one would have said it was impossible to go farther. He found the secret for measuring all solids by one and the same formula.

His stereometrical tableau is a masterpiece that places him in the first rank of scholars the world over ... It is curious that learned gentlemen in Europe have been bypassed by a French-Canadian in a field of science so little cultivated among us. He is an honour to himself and his country.[58]

When the Canadian Academy of Arts, soon known as the Royal Canadian Academy of Art, was founded in 1880 by the Marquis of Lorne and Princess Louise, Baillairgé was named an associate architect by the president,

Lucius O'Brien, and exhibited a drawing in the inaugural exhibition.[59] It was perhaps the fine arts orientation of the association or the requirement to exhibit every three years that caused Baillairgé to lose interest. In any event, he tactfully if untruthfully withdrew from active participation in 1885 "on account of advancing years" and was transferred to the roll of honorary members.[60] In 1882 the Royal Society of Canada was founded, again under the patronage of the governor-general, the Marquis of Lorne, for the purpose of stimulating learned discussion among the country's one hundred leading scholars as well as for disseminating information about Canada's progress in the arts and sciences. Baillairgé's reputation was by this time so secure that he was again nominated as a founding member of Section III of the Royal Society of Canada, the group which concerned itself with the mathematical, physical, and chemical sciences.[61] He obviously enjoyed this fraternity, for he often attended the annual meetings at Toronto, Ottawa, Montreal, or Halifax, and regularly presented papers on a variety of technical subjects, usually in Section III but occasionally in Section II, which dealt with English literature, history, and allied subjects.[62] He went to his last meeting and gave his last paper in 1903 at the age of seventy-seven. His major grievance against the Royal Society was its failure to publish *all* the papers read before its four sections; but he solved this problem by privately printing his own papers in Quebec and distributing them free of charge.

It could be argued that Baillairgé coasted on the benefits of his idea or invention of the Stereometrical Tableau for well over twenty years. Having extracted all the honours and publicity possible from his prismoidal formula and Stereometrical Tableau by the mid-1880s, he turned to another discipline, that of etymology or the study of words. His complete mastery since childhood of both English and French made him particularly sensitive to the nuances of the sounds and meanings of words. As in the case of the Stereometrical Tableau, his particular angle was education. Part of his daily routine with his own children was a half-hour session of word games – which he dignified with the phrase "educational system." The players discovered words with the same sound – homonyms – and then explained their different meanings.[63] The success of this system in imparting a general and practical education to his children led him to gather the material together in the *Nouveau dictionnaire français; système "éducationnel," rimes, consonnances, homonymes, décomposition des mots, combinaisons variées de leurs éléments et équivalents, jeux de mots* (1888), *Vocabulaire des homonymes simples de la langue française* (1891), *Vocabulary of English Homonyms* (1891), and *Educational: Word Lessons* (1899).

In the introduction to the *Nouveau dictionnaire* the author made his purpose clear. Though the collection of words would be useful for poets and writers, his principal objective was to place the dictionary in homes and schools "where there are children to instruct ... for both educational and recreational purpose."[64] For his dictionary Baillairgé received testimonials praising the work as original, the result of years of research and observation;[65] in 1889 he also received a diploma and first-class medal from yet another Parisian learned society, the Académie des palmiers, founded in 1880 and dedicated to the expansion of literature and the encouragement of study travel, as well as the suppression of slavery and war. His fascination with language persisted for the rest of his life; as late as 1903 he was still working on what he called "a labor of love," a book on the *Origin, Signification, Translation, Classification and Etymology of Proper Names*, which remained incomplete at his death. More than anything he had done in the field of architecture or engineering, Baillairgé's initiatives in the field of education and the dissemination of technical subject matter – in particular the Stereometrical Tableau and to a lesser extent the dictionaries – guaranteed him a secure place in Canadian biographical literature.

12 Professional Standards

AT THE BEGINNING of his career Baillairgé had trained as an architect, civil engineer, and land surveyor through traditional apprenticeships with an established master, Thomas Baillairgé. At that time this was the only way to enter such professions. When poorly trained or unscrupulous architects and engineers flooded the market during the boom period in the second half of the nineteenth century, pressure mounted for the establishment of professional standards and licences. Baillairgé played an important role in the formation of professional associations in the three disciplines in which he had practised.

With his interest in education, he was naturally inclined to define the problem, at least initially, as a lack of technical schools where prospective architects, engineers, and surveyors could be properly instructed. He consequently took an active part in promoting the Quebec School of Arts and Trades which opened its doors in 1870. During the winter of 1872 Baillairgé taught evening classes twice a week on geometry, industrial design, perspective, mensuration, and related subjects. At the end of the year the students presented him with a carefully drawn diploma thanking him for the course, testifying to his "perfect mastery of the subjects" and "the clear and concise manner in which you enunciated and demonstrated the several propositions introduced to our notice," and confirming the fact that their comprehension "has been greatly facilitated by our access to the models of your 'TABLEAU.'"[1]

In 1880 he donated batches of his architectural drawings to the various schools of the *Académie commerciale des frères*, in the conviction that skill in drawing formed the basis of the industrial arts. He believed that, by copying models of Greek and Roman columns, doors, windows, and so forth, students would acquire a clearer perception of the aesthetic and practical requirements of design. In a newspaper communiqué announcing this gift of drawings, probably written by Baillairgé himself, the benefits to the industrial designer of studying historical examples are explained: "Initiated early in the study of diverse decorative styles – the majestic simplicity of antiquity, the delicate arabesques of the Middle Age, the rich and elegant ornamentation of the Renaissance – the artisan knows how to apply them often or to create multiple combinations of them, which are always based on the underlying principles understood by artistic men."[2] This improvement in taste, according to Baillairgé, would revolutionize Canadian industry and inaugurate an era of prosperity.

In the same year he was named chairman of a task force sponsored by the Société Saint-Jean-Baptiste, charged with making a report on the current state of science, literature, and the fine arts in Quebec and the means by which they could be advanced. In his report, Baillairgé concentrated on his own particular area of concern – the building arts – and made an ardent plea for the establishment of technical schools like the École polytéchnique in Montreal. He no longer believed that classes in linear drawing were sufficient to train students in this field, though he added that such classes should be part of the curriculum of all normal schools; instead, he called for well-staffed polytechnical schools with a complete roster of technical and scientific courses.[3] He took up the cause again in 1887 in a paper that he read before the newly formed Canadian Society of Civil Engineers.[4] He opened by stating that, in his opinion, no definite line could be drawn between architects and engineers since both professions required training in construction technology and aesthetics. He once more appealed to government to establish much-needed technical schools, citing specific examples where builders had shown a lack of training in mathematical calculation, construction technology, and design principles. In regard to design, Baillairgé remained faithful to a belief in certain innate proportions or ratios, which he defined as "a true aesthetic sentiment, a true appreciation of what is proper," and an insistence on visual logic. He decried what he perceived to be the defects in contemporary Quebec buildings; poorly proportioned rooms at the new provincial legislature, the top-heavy upper storey of the new Post Office, and the awkward ratio of openings to masonry wall at the new Court House. To improve the quality of construction and design, he repeated his demand that legislators create schools of art "where the rising generation of engineers and architects may study and make themselves acquainted with all that is essential to an intelligent appreciation of the necessity of being guided in constructions of all sorts by the well known rules which should be followed out to prevent disaster and the waste of public money."[5]

But the establishment of technical schools was not enough to set and enforce standards of quality. What was needed were professional associations with power to license individuals and regulate educational requirements through an examination process. Baillairgé played a leading role in the creation of such an association for surveyors. He himself had become a provincial land surveyor in 1848, with the right to practise anywhere in Lower Canada. He had obtained this licence by carrying out an apprenticeship with a certified surveyor who then supported his application by signing a legal document called a "bond."[6] Baillairgé then belonged to an informal group of provincial land surveyors and served on its Board of Examiners as a member and then as chairman in 1875.[7] In 1859 an attempt was made to found the Association of Architects, Civil Engineers and Provincial Land Surveyors of Canada based in Toronto, the first formal association of architects, engineers, and land surveyors in Upper and Lower Canada. Though it did not endure, Baillairgé was sufficiently well known to become vice-president in 1861.[8] The limited authority of these early associations led to the legal incorporation of land surveyors in the province of Quebec in 1882, the origin of what is now known as the Ordre des arpenteurs-géomètres du Québec. Baillairgé's stature in the field was reflected by the fact that he was elected as this group's first president from 1882 to 1885. He maintained his membership until 1903, at which date he became an honorary member.[9]

In the discipline of civil engineering, Baillairgé had never actually carried out a formal apprenticeship; like so many others at that time, he had trained himself through study, observation, and experience. The establishment of a permanent professional organization for engineers did not occur until February 1887, when the inaugural meeting of the Canadian Society of Civil Engineers was held in Montreal under the leadership of Ottawa engineer Thomas Coltrin Keefer. Although Baillairgé was one of the founding members and gave a paper in the first year, he only occasionally attended meetings of this highly specialized society which subdivided the field of engineering into a number of technical branches; hydraulic, mechanical,

FIG. 175. American and Canadian engineers in front of the New England Gas and Coke Company in Boston, 1900. An elderly Charles Baillairgé stands at the extreme right. *CE*, 7 (April 1900): 324

civic, railway, mining, and electrical engineering.[10] A notable exception was his attendance at the annual meeting of the Canadian Society of Civil Engineers in Boston in the spring of 1900, at which time Baillairgé was seventy-three years old (fig. 175). This explains why, despite his limited participation in this group, he was curiously named to the executive council in 1902 and a lengthy obituary was published after his death in the society's transactions.[11]

Although it would appear that the official engineering association was in some ways too specialized for Baillairgé's training and experience, he nevertheless contributed regularly to the trade paper the *Canadian Engineer*, begun in 1893 with an initial circulation of 3000 subscribers. Published to meet special Canadian requirements in the field of engineering, the *Canadian Engineer* gave Charles Baillairgé excellent coverage, honoring him with the first full-length biography and portrait of any Canadian engineer, calling him one of the "leading scientists of the world," reprinting (for the first time in the magazine's history) his article on the ball-nozzle mystery because of public demand, supporting his demand for higher wages from the city of Quebec, and featuring some of his inventions such as the spiral slide and Jubilee Tower.[12] Baillairgé was a major contributor to this journal, sending in over thirty articles in little more than ten years. The subject matter covered a broad range of practical engineering observations that grew out of his personal experiences in Quebec, including wind pressure, municipal lighting, drainage canals, steam boiler explosions, dam constructions and failures, landslides, aerial navigation, tidal power, polar navigation, road building, and metric measurement. Thus his contribution to the profession of engineering could be considered one of popularization and dialogue rather than academic exchange and standard setting.

This was not true of his major sphere of activity, namely architecture. In response to a general malaise about the architectural profession in the 1880s, Canada saw the birth of a professional magazine called the *Canadian Architect and Builder* in 1888 as well as the rise of provincial associations, in particular the Ontario Association of Architects in 1889, and the Province of Quebec Association of Architects in 1890.[13] Given Baillairgé's previous involvement in the short-lived Association of Architects, Civil Engineers, and Provincial Land Surveyors of Canada, he no doubt delighted in this increased concern for the profession. The impetus for organizing the Quebec association came from a steering committee of Montreal architects who sent out a circular asking for interested persons to attend an inaugural meeting in

Montreal in the fall of 1890. Only four architects came from Quebec City: Charles Baillairgé, François-Xavier Berlinguet, Georges-Emile Tanguay, and Harry Staveley. The draft constitution approved at this meeting stated that the purpose of the association was "to facilitate the acquirement and interchange of professional knowledge among its members; to promote the artistic, scientific and practical efficiency of the profession, and to endeavour to obtain by legislation the power to regulate future admissions to the study and practice thereof." It went on to define the role of the architect in terms remarkably close to Baillairgé's views: "An Architect is a professional person, whose occupation consists in the artistic and constructive designing of buildings and in supplying the drawings, specifications and other data required for carrying such design into execution; also in exercising administrative control over the operations of contractors employed in the construction of said buildings; in officiating as arbitrator of contracts, and stipulating terms of obligations between proprietor and contractor."[14] The constitution also gave the association the power to expel architects for professional misconduct. The proposed constitution and by-laws received legislative approval from the provincial government on 30 December 1890. The preamble to the Province of Quebec Architects Act explained that it had been passed to protect public interests, to enable persons to distinguish between qualified and unqualified architects, and thereby to ensure the advancement of the art of architecture.[15]

The rapport among the architects at the inaugural meeting surpassed the steering committee's most optimistic expectations. The format of business and academic sessions followed by a tour to points of interest and a formal luncheon on the second day became the model for ensuing annual meetings held alternately in Quebec City and Montreal. Following the generous repast at the Windsor Hotel, Baillairgé rose to his feet to repeat in English Berlinguet's reply to a toast to the Quebec contingent. A sense of the spirit of conviviality that presided over the first meeting is captured by the image of the whole troupe parading down to the wharf to see the Quebec members off on the steamer with "three cheers and one cheer more" (fig. 176).[16]

Baillairgé was an active and loyal member of the Province of Quebec Association of Architects. He held a number of offices: auditor from 1890 to 1892, first vice-president in 1894, president in 1895, and a member of council from 1896 to 1898.[17] In addition, he played a key role in the control of educational standards by serving as part of a three-man Board of Examiners for the Quebec region, appointed by the association's executive on a yearly basis. Baillairgé was on the board from 1890 to 1898 and participated in the elaboration of a program of examinations. Needless to say, his own *Stereometricon* was put on the curriculum.[18]

With the exception of 1897 and 1903, he attended every annual meeting of the association. Perhaps because he was more experienced at preparing and delivering academic papers than most of his colleagues, Baillairgé was one of the few to make regular presentations at the yearly gatherings; among the papers that he presented were "Escape from Buildings in Case of Fire" (1892), "A Plea for a Canadian School of Architecture" (1893), "Foundations in Deep and Unreliable Soils" (1894), "A Quick and Easy Way of Getting at the Weight of Iron Scantlings, Girders, Columns, etc." (1894), "On the Bearing and Resisting Strength of Structures and that of their Component

The vitality and *esprit de corps* of the early years of the Province of Quebec Association of Architects is well-illustrated by an incident involving Baillairgé at the second annual meeting in Quebec City in 1891. During the sumptuous banquet at the Florence Hotel, he was called upon to respond to the toast "Canada, our Country." In evident high spirits, Baillairgé gave a brief preamble concerning American doubts about annexing Canada and then addressed one of his pet issues – bribery or boodling. He spoke of the difficulty of making a living and, by way of illustration, suggested that the audience might "like to know the way the miller advised his sons to manage when they could not make a dollar honestly." Then, to the astonishment and delight of members, he broke into a humorous rendition of a song called "The Miller."[21] This boisterous enthusiasm had faded by 1900 when the annual meeting was poorly attended and no papers were given. Baillairgé attended his last meeting in 1904. On learning of his death, the Province of Quebec Association of Architects passed a motion of regret which was published in the local newspapers and sent an official delegation to his funeral.[22]

Another response to the unsettled state of the architectural profession was the launching of the *Canadian Architect and Builder* in 1888 by Toronto Parts and Materials" (1895), and "On Bribery and Boodling" (1895).[19] For the exhibitions that were held spasmodically in conjunction with these meetings, he recycled some of his earlier work, showing an interior of a church (presumably the church at Sainte-Marie de Beauce) and an elevation of the Monument aux Braves in 1892 and his old proposal for the Parliament Buildings in 1904.[20]

FIG. 176. This group portrait by Joseph Beaudry depicts the Quebec City founding members of the Province of Quebec Association of Architects. Leaning back in his chair, third from the right is Charles Baillairgé. Seated in front of the table is his apprentice Joseph-Ferdinand Peachy. Standing, fifth from the left, is Georges-Emile Tanguay, one of Peachy's own apprentices and a practitioner of architecture in the Baillairgé tradition. Archives de l'Université Laval, fonds 214, no. 21–27

publisher C.H. Mortimer. Baillairgé no doubt heartily approved of its first editorial stating that "the profession of architecture in Canada requires to be raised to a higher level," grouping practising architects into varying shades of aesthetic and/or mathematical competence, and concluding that only by careful selection and education of students could "the architects of the future ... become a much superior body of men ... to those now practising."[23] When the provincial associations in Ontario and Quebec were incorporated, the *Canadian Architect and Builder* became their official paper. Baillairgé corresponded incessantly with this magazine from its beginning until his death in 1906, sending over forty letters and articles on a broad spectrum of professional and technical matters. Most touched on architectural subjects such as drafting tables, the Quebec City Hall competition, mensuration, quantity surveyors, monuments, fire escapes, the London City Hall disaster, kiosks, bay and oriel windows, aquariums, ice houses, and skyscrapers; some belonged more clearly to civil engineering, such as the articles on boiler explosions, wind velocity, and dam construction; others concerned landslides, crystalline bodies, and the Chicago drainage canal.

For its part, the *Canadian Architect and Builder* gave Baillairgé regular coverage. In 1890 it illustrated with a full-page photograph the interior of Baillairgé's Sainte-Marie de Beauce church; in 1891 it published a major biography of him with portrait, and in 1894 a brief biographical sketch, again with portrait, on his nomination to the presidency of the Province of Quebec Association of Architects.[24] From time to time the magazine announced Baillairgé's latest publications – even in unrelated fields such as the ventilation of sewers, Hudson Bay explorations, and a polar vessel – adding that the author was "a versatile and prolific writer upon scientific subjects" and that the works "will well repay perusal." About his pamphlet on bribery and boodling, the editors noted that "Mr. Baillairgé's words of warning are ... well timed ... though somewhat too forcibly expressed in places, and partaking to some extent of a personal character" and expressed appreciation for his "boldness in dealing with such a subject."[25] The *Canadian Architect and Builder* publicly supported his request for a salary increase in 1895, giving a flattering assessment of his contribution to the city: "It is to be hoped the Council will recognize Mr. Baillairgé's able and faithful services to the city during the 29 years he has occupied his present position, by acceding to his request. Such versatility of talents as he possesses are rarely combined in one individual, and at one time or another the City of Quebec has received the benefit of them all."[26] Finally, the magazine supported his causes, including the campaign for proper fire escapes which Baillairgé promoted to the point of writing to the prime minister of Canada and the president of the United States, and ran articles on his inventions and his entries for the Paris 1900 exhibition.[27] The magazine therefore served to bolster Baillairgé's reputation as an elder statesman and experienced master in the architectural profession while it provided a vehicle through which he could communicate with the rising generation of architects.

Baillairgé could look back over his career with legitimate pride. Not only had he left a legacy of public and private buildings to his native city, he had played an important role in promoting education and the dissemination of technical knowledge and in advancing the professional stature of the three disciplines in which he had been trained. He enjoyed a national and international reputation for his technical, scientific, and literary achievements. With

FIG. 177. On the eve of the new century, Baillairgé hosted a formal dinner to celebrate the accomplishments of the nineteenth century and the aspirations for the twentieth. His printed menu is full of whimsical word plays as well as references to outstanding discoveries and events from his lifetime. ASQ, Polygraphie 35, no. 16

a conscious sense of history, he culminated his career by giving an extraordinary formal dinner for his colleagues and friends at the new Château Frontenac. He chose as the appropriate occasion the beginning of the twentieth century – which he obstinately insisted, against conventional wisdom, began at midnight on 31 December 1900 (and not 1899). Heading the official guest list was the prime minister of Canada, Sir Wilfrid Laurier, to whom Baillairgé, in his role as president of the Quebec Geographical Society, had so often appealed for funds on behalf of Bernier's expedition to the North Pole.[28] Over fifty gentlemen – the political, intellectual and professional elite of Quebec and Ottawa – attended the banquet.[29] The printed menu showed Baillairgé at his most whimsical, being full of plays on words and references to past and current events of particular significance to him (fig. 177). After a sumptuous meal, Baillairgé delivered an address to his captive audience, using the words in the menu as spring boards to review the remarkable progress of the nineteenth century by way of inventions and discoveries and to predict developments in the new century such as aerial and submarine navigation, the discovery of the North Pole, the horseless carriage, and the colonization of James Bay.[30] According to a local newspaper, "Mr. Baillairgé delivered a very appropriate address, which was frequently applauded ... full of interesting facts and historical data, showing deep study."[31] Given Baillairgé's love of gadgetry, one should not be surprised to learn that at precisely midnight, during his speech, the wall at the head of the room burst into electrically lit letters "1901."[32] One can only surmise the sense of satisfaction that the seventy-four year old man felt as he surveyed the scene in the tapestry-lined dining room. It was a fitting climax to an arduous and remarkably productive professional career.

Conclusion

MEMBER OF THE FOURTH GENERATION of an exceptional cultural dynasty in Canada, Charles Baillairgé enjoyed a long career which spanned almost sixty years. His accomplishments in his chosen field of architecture and engineering can be measured in terms of his actual practice as well as his contribution as a writer and theoretician. He created a corpus of work that few of his contemporaries could have matched either in scope or sheer volume. By the end of his life, recognition of his achievements had extended far beyond his native Quebec City to national and even international spheres. In this sense Baillairgé, though his career was largely local, represented important intellectual, cultural, and social trends of the nineteenth century in North America and Europe.

Baillairgé's major accomplishments as a practising architect were concentrated for the most part in the early years of his career – between 1846, when he received his certification from Thomas Baillairgé, and about 1866, when he assumed his duties as city engineer. In spite of his immense efforts as associate architect in Ottawa during his two years there from 1863 to 1865, his achievements as a practising architect were slight and his impact on the Parliament and Departmental Buildings minor. He did, however, learn to his peril the cost of ignoring the political dimensions of his job.

In his architectural practice, Charles Baillairgé's fundamental response to design problems demonstrated his adherence to the neoclassical tradition of the earlier Baillairgés. He habitually adopted the classical vocabulary of forms and steadfastly clung to values of symmetry, balance, and just proportion. Yet superimposed upon this basic cultural reflex towards neoclassicism was an experimentation with different stylistic idioms in vogue in the middle of the nineteenth century: Greek Revival as shown in his designs for the Quebec Music Hall, the Bilodeau and DeFoy stores, the Têtu, Leaycraft, and DeFoy houses, the manor house at Saint-Roch-des-Aulnaies, and his proposals for the Quebec Customs House and the Parliament for the Province of Canada; Gothic Revival as exemplified by the chapel for the Soeurs de la Charité and the parish churches at Beauport, Isle-Verte, Rivière-du-Loup, and Sainte-Marie de Beauce; Italianate as seen in the Caisse d'économie and the Desbarats buildings, the Quebec Jail, "Elm Grove," and the Petry house. His Gothic churches never fully exploited the chromatic and picturesque potential of the Gothic Revival idiom, however, underscoring his loyalty to the symmetrical proportions associated with neoclassical principles.

The sources of inspiration for these design experiments came from books in his architectural library and from personal observation of Canadian and American buildings, especially those erected in Quebec City in the first half of the nineteenth century. The very act of turning to such sources could also be considered as a manifestation of his early training in neoclassical methodology, for a trademark of neoclassicism was the accurate imitation of the works of the great masters of ancient Greece and Rome. Although with his characteristic inventiveness Baillairgé chose to imitate modern masters, be it plates from his copies of Gibbs, Knight, or Lafever, or actual buildings by architects George Browne or John Wells, the instinct to seek inspiration from worthy prototypes grew out of the neoclassical tradition.

Baillairgé appears to have worked his way through the questions of style and design during his early years as a practising architect. He soon settled into a pattern of predictable design solutions and shifted his attention to the more challenging problems of construction technology. His innate interest in technical matters, coupled with his preparation in civil engineering, led him to strive for the incorporation of current building technology into his own work. Thus his houses began to feature gas lighting and indoor plumbing, as well as central hot-air heating systems of his own invention. More significantly, his major commissions such as the Laval University buildings, the Merrill store, the Caisse d'économie, and the Monument aux Braves showed the results of his study of technical and engineering subjects, for they adopted the latest technology, especially in the use of cast and wrought iron for decorative and structural purposes. His dependence on iron for his Quebec Customs House proposal was so extensive that he claimed that his building, if constructed, would be fireproof. His attention remained focused on the field of construction technology in later years, as confirmed by the architectural and engineering works he produced during his stint as city engineer: the Dufferin Terrace, the iron staircases, the Victoria Jubilee Tower, the tubular bridge, the Victoria Park swing bridges, and the London Eiffel Tower proposal. These projects, more urbanistic than architectural in nature, revealed his unflagging curiosity for the technical problems associated with building and exemplified the nineteenth-century tendency to fuse traditional architecture with engineering. Indeed, the trend for architecture to become intertwined with technology, evident in Baillairgé's work, foreshadowed the twentieth-century development of modern architecture.

In his practice as an architect, Baillairgé had a major impact on the physical appearance of Quebec City and the nearby parishes, leaving a legacy of well-designed and carefully constructed buildings and street furniture, and several broad boulevards which still form part of the city's communications network. To this day, in the Upper Town of the city in particular, a pedestrian cannot wander far afield without encountering a building or urban feature created by Charles Baillairgé.

But how did he compare to other architects of his time and place? At the outset of his career in the middle of the nineteenth century, Baillairgé's academic training and knowledge of the traditional and current literature in this discipline set him apart from native Quebec City architects such as Michel Patry, Narcisse Larue, and Pierre Gauvreau, who possessed only a smattering of architectural and mathematical theory and who had graduated from the ranks of the building trades. Patry and Larue had relatively minor careers, designing only a few buildings, while Gauvreau had an extensive career as a practical builder who assumed without much success the role of architect. Gauvreau worked in the 1830s and 1840s as a master mason, usually building plain but solid structures and occasionally implementing designs by architects like Thomas Baillairgé. Late in the 1840s, Gauvreau ventured into architectural design, including 46–8, avenue Sainte-Geneviève (1848) for Jean Langevin. A comparison with Charles Baillairgé's Hamel house next door reveals the lack of refinement and sophistication in Gauvreau's design. In 1850 he found his true calling as a government overseer or clerk of works, first for the federal and later for the provincial Department of Public Works, a position he occupied until shortly before his death in 1882. Although he occasionally got the chance to produce designs, Gauvreau usually implemented those of government architects, including Charles Baillairgé in the case of the Quebec Jail.

Among Baillairgé's contemporaries, a more meaningful comparison can be drawn from the group of British architects, such as Edward Staveley and George Browne, who had emigrated to Canada after receiving their training in the United Kingdom. Like Baillairgé, both Browne and Staveley were professionals who produced technically proficient drawings and specifications, supervised construction of the work, and acted as liaison between the client and builders. George Browne, born and trained in Belfast, had mastered current British architectural trends and fashions, thereby easily surpassing Staveley and Baillairgé in versatility of design, be it the dignified neoclassicism of Kingston Town Hall (1842-4) and the Quebec Parliament Building (1850-2), or the Gothic Revival of suburban cottages and churches. Edward Staveley and Baillairgé, however, kept apace with each other in their neoclassical villas and timid Italianate designs, although Staveley, well-versed in the Gothic repertoire, clearly made his influence felt through such buildings as the entrance lodge of Mount Hermon cemetery (1848) in Sillery. Though Baillairgé rarely used Gothic Revival for public or domestic buildings, he appears to have modelled his Gothic churches on those of Staveley and especially G.R. Browne: his chapel for the Soeurs de la Charité and his Beauport church reflected the influence of Staveley's Wesleyan church in the superimposition of Gothic forms on an essentially classical skeleton, and his single-towered church type, erected at Isle-Verte, Rivière-du-Loup, Sainte-Marie de Beauce, and elsewhere, clearly imitated the general form and specific details of Browne's earlier Saint-Colomb church at Sillery. In his use of Greek Revival, Baillairgé differed from the work of his colleagues in two respects: the degree of austerity with which he handled his façades, probably under the influence of European neoclassicism as set forth by authors such as Durand, and the almost literal adoption of graceful Greek motifs from the American pattern books of Lafever.

In a moment of introspection late in his life, Baillairgé appears to have realized that his strength did not lie as much in design creativity as in critical analysis: "Your ex-engineer believes ... that he has the intuition for good and beautiful things; but perhaps less talent to conceive them himself than to judge them in the work of others."[1] But even though Browne and Staveley matched and often surpassed him in creative design, Baillairgé's training in civil engineering and mathematics meant that he outstripped them both in his superior knowledge of building methods and construction technology in British North America. Baillairgé's contribution as a practising architect was summed up with penetrating concision in an obituary published by the *Canadian Architect and Builder*, which properly emphasized his capability as a constructive architect: "Mr. Baillairgé had the energetic and inventive mind that gives eminence in any walk of life, but his mathematical and scientific attainments made him a constructive architect *par excellence*. He had the proper combination of original thought and technical skill, and worked with freedom and facility."[2]

Did Charles Baillairgé have an impact on future generations of architects in Quebec City? What became of the apprentices who trained under his guidance? At least two of them, René Steckel and Eugène-Etienne

Taché, had outstanding careers as government employees, with an emphasis on the engineering aspect of architecture. Steckel had apprenticed with Baillairgé in 1862 and assisted him at the Parliament and Departmental Buildings in Ottawa (fig. 206). Steckel remained in Ottawa with the federal Department of Public Works after Baillairgé's downfall, reappearing at Quebec in the 1870s in his capacity as federal hydraulic engineer to work with Baillairgé, representing the city's interests, on the survey for the Quebec Harbour Improvements. That Baillairgé held his former pupil's mathematical abilities in high regard is illustrated by the fact that he read one of Steckel's papers before the Royal Society of Canada and that he recommended his appointment to Section III of that learned group. Taché, son of one of Baillairgé's clients and ten years his junior, had articled with him in 1860 in the field of surveying. Like his master, Taché became a civil servant, occupying the posts of assistant commissioner of the Department of Crown Lands and later deputy minister of the Department of Lands and Forests. Although his surveying background stood him in good stead in the execution of his duties, Taché occasionally carried out the architectural design of major government projects such as the provincial Parliament Building (1878–84), the Quebec City Armouries (1884), and the Court House (1887) on the Place d'Armes.[3]

But the true successors to Baillairgé's architectural legacy were Joseph-Ferdinand Peachy and, through him, Georges-Emile Tanguay, both of whom followed more orthodox career paths as private practising architects. Peachy, after a brief stint under Pierre Gauvreau, had studied with Baillairgé in the middle of the 1850s, and, except for his partnership with him under the firm name of Baillairgé & Peachy from 1863 to 1866, enjoyed a bountiful individual practice for almost half a century. At first, Peachy adhered closely to Baillairgé's model, producing impeccable architectural drawings and specifications for buildings of smooth Deschambault stone in a neoclassical vein that make visual separation of the two architects' work in the 1850s and 1860s difficult. Under the influence of new stylistic currents and tastes, however, Peachy's designs from about 1870 became more textural and full-blown, borrowing the rough-dressed stone effects and heavier details of the Baroque Revival idiom and promoting the robust mansard roof from the Second Empire influence. By the end of the century, Peachy was reputed to have the largest clientele in Quebec City. This encompassed most of Baillairgé's former clients, including the church wardens of Notre-Dame de Québec, the Roman Catholic diocese of Quebec, religious institutions such as the Ursulines, the Seminary of Quebec, the Hôtel Dieu, and the Soeurs de la Charité, and francophone mercantile groups such as the Caisse d'économie. As Baillairgé's immediate successor, Peachy took over work on Baillairgé's buildings, including the supervision of the Quebec Jail project, the addition of a mansard roof to the central pavilion at Laval University, and the design of a new steeple for the chapel for the Soeurs de la Charité. Peachy's technical competence revealed the influence of his teacher, for the dizzying height of the nave vault of his Saint-Jean-Baptiste church (1882), rebuilt when Baillairgé's version burnt down, and the impressive cast-iron spiral staircase (1875) at the Seminary, demonstrated his mastery of construction technology. Like Baillairgé, Peachy was a founding member and active participant in the Province of Quebec Association of Architects, following him to the presidency in 1898.[4]

Born in 1857, Georges-Emile Tanguay, a member of the next generation, articled under Peachy in the 1870s, thereby inheriting the essence of Baillairgé's professional principles and procedures. From Peachy, Tanguay gained access to the same network of clients, including the French-Canadian religious and commercial establishment. It must have given Baillairgé no small measure of satisfaction to see Tanguay, his professional descendant, participate in his schemes for Quebec's embellishment, for it was Tanguay, in partnership with Alfred-N. Vallée, who made the final design for the new Quebec City Hall and the main restaurant pavilion at the new pleasure ground at Victoria Park. In keeping with the due rights of succession, Tanguay in his turn became president of the Province of Quebec Association of Architects in 1900 and 1901.[5]

Although his achievements as a practising architect were important, it might well be argued that Baillairgé's contribution to the evolution of the profession had even greater significance. During his lifetime he witnessed a radical change in the architectural profession, a movement towards formal education, standards, and codes of ethics. Trained in the traditional manner as an apprentice to a recognized master architect, Baillairgé may be seen as a transitional figure between the apprenticeship system and formal schools of architecture, between uncontrolled practice and formal licensing procedures. He consistently promoted the improvement of the architectural profession by personal example, by the dissemination of technical knowledge through his lectures and writing, by his relentless advocacy for technical schools, and by his participation in professional associations.

Baillairgé set a high standard in his own practice, establishing from the beginning a pattern of behaviour from which he never wavered and which anticipated the future evolution of the role and responsibilities of the professional architect. Unlike François and Thomas Baillairgé and some of his own contemporaries, Charles never executed any of the works himself. Instead, he chose to remain aloof as the educated professional man, the supervising architect, the controller of the project, the liaison between client and contractors. In this respect he diverged from local practice and adopted the model set forth in his books and followed by the British-trained architects. His influence extended to members of the next generation of architects for, from 1850 on, he inculcated these same liberal arts values in those who were apprenticed to him.

The driving force behind Baillairgé's frequent public communications – whether they were lectures, formal classes, pamphlets, articles, or books – was his commitment to the dissemination of technical knowledge to a broad spectrum of society, including fledgling architects and builders. This lifelong pursuit became apparent early in his career, for in 1848 at the age of twenty-two he gave his first series of public lectures on scientific subjects, discovering that he had a good speaking voice and assured delivery, and in 1853 he published his first brochure. It was this concern for making technical information accessible to those who needed it, and specifically his response to the problems of measurement that he had encountered during the Parliament and Departmental Buildings project at Ottawa, that led to his geometry textbook and the subsequent invention of the Stereometrical Tableau. This preoccupation accounts for his repeated demands for polytechnical schools and his own brief career as a teacher at the Quebec School of Arts and Trades. Through his own voluminous written work, amounting to over 250 books, articles, and pamphlets, and including regular submissions to technical journals such as the *Canadian Architect and Builder* and the *Canadian Engineer*, Baillairgé contributed significantly to the corpus of knowledge then available in the architectural and engineering disciplines.

In yet another way, Baillairgé had a direct influence on the development of the architectural profession in Canada, namely, his participation in the establishment of the Province of Quebec Association of Architects in 1890. He provided leadership as a member of the initial steering committee and as an executive member, occupying at different times the offices of auditor, vice-president, president, and council member. But he undoubtedly made the most direct impact on the careers of architectural students through his appointment as head of the Board of Examiners for the Quebec section from 1890 to 1898. In this position he was able to work towards one of his primary objectives: the control of the architectural profession by setting academic standards and thereby regulating the licensing procedure. By his own example, by his dissemination of technical knowledge, and by his activities in the Province of Quebec Association of Architects, Baillairgé played a major role in the development and improvement of the architectural profession in the province.

Although Baillairgé acknowledged frankly that he resided in "an end-of-the-world sort of place" far from the centre of world affairs, he refused to be limited by this circumstance and immodestly regarded himself as a participant in the national and international forum. Right from the start he took part in world-class exhibitions, entering his marine revolving steam express in the Industrial World's Fair at New York City in 1853, his Stereometrical Tableau in the international exhibition at the Palais de l'industrie at Paris in 1873-4 and in the world exhibition at Philadelphia in 1876, his tower proposal in the London Eiffel Tower competition in 1889, posters depicting his inventions in the universal exhibition at Paris in 1900, and his Baillairgé-Hurly Safety Raft in the Pollok prize competition at Le Havre in 1901. These grand ambitions explain why he so readily left the comfort of his home and family in 1863 to go to Ottawa in pursuit of the elusive job of chief architect in the Department of Public Works. It was on this national and international level, moreover, that he received the most praise and recognition for his achievements. He was nominated as a founding member of the two most prestigious learned societies in Canada: the Canadian Academy of Arts (later called the Royal Canadian Academy of Art) and the Royal Society of Canada. He received many awards, memberships, and honorary titles from Canadian and European institutions and learned societies. His geometry textbook and stereometrical system were adopted in the polytechnical schools of Russia. Articles on his work appeared in Canadian, American, and European scientific publications. Like a self-fulfilling prophecy, Baillairgé's conscious participation in the broad sweep of current intellectual movements and events, well beyond the limits of his native city, brought in return encouragement and appreciation from national and international organizations.

How did he achieve all this? How could one man have accomplished so much in his lifetime? A clue lies in Baillairgé's personal habits, for he loved to study and work hard, and he had little need of sleep. His assertion that he required only four or five hours of sleep daily has been corroborated by his grandson, who recounts the family tradition which claims that Charles Baillairgé was rarely seen in bed. He had, in addition, a pronounced aptitude for scientific matters and an intelligence that absorbed voluminous quantities of detail. Yet he also enjoyed social events, if one can take at face value his descriptions of champagne parties for French naval officers, dancing parties that went on until three in the morning, and large-scale picnics or *fêtes champêtres* at his summer house at Saint-Michel. Baillairgé's grand-daughter, Marie Brewer, offers confirmation, reporting that "Charles was a true gourmet and was always invited to carve when a guest at dinner parties." His character might be described by a group of somewhat contradictory adjectives: on the one hand curious, energetic, inventive, unorthodox, indefatigable, confident, enthusiastic, honest, and humourous; on the other hand, aggressive, forthright, outspoken, ambitious, tenacious, disputatious, and proud. These qualities help to explain much of his activity, such as his creation of a comprehensive architectural and engineering library, his comic play, his difficult working relationships with some clients and employers, his staggering productivity, his support of Bernier's expedition to the North Pole, his intention at the age of seventy-seven to attend the exhibition of aerial vehicles at St Louis, Missouri, and so forth. In realizing the breadth and scope of Baillairgé's career, one returns again and again to Francis Bacon's characterization of the Renaissance man who takes all knowledge to be his province.

Charles Baillairgé's death came in his seventy-ninth year on 10 May 1906, the result of an unspecified "long and painful illness."[6] Lengthy obituary notices in honour of this distinguished citizen of Quebec City appeared in local newspapers and later in professional journals.[7] The Quebec section of the Province of Quebec Association of Architects held an unscheduled meeting, honouring their late colleague by publishing a special tribute expressing regret at the loss of "one of its most devoted members and the most ardent defender of its rights," and by resolving to attend his funeral as a group.[8] Along with this delegation of architects, the service was attended by family members, city and church officials, professionals, and business men. The funeral mass took place in Notre-Dame de Québec, where Baillairgé had been a regular parishioner and which bore the mark of four generations of Baillairgés. In the front pew sat his son, William-Duval, city engineer and member of the fifth generation of this cultural dynasty. After the service, the funeral procession wound its way to the Saint-Charles cemetery, which he had laid out almost half a century earlier. There, the Chevalier Baillairgé was buried beside his first wife. As a lasting symbol of his independent thought, Baillairgé's grave, like that of his brother George-Frédéric, who had died in 1896, and unlike all the neighbouring plots, was marked not with a traditional tombstone but by a simple yet massive granite boulder inscribed with the words "famille Baillairgé."

Appendix 1   Summary Catalogue of Architectural Works by Charles Baillairgé

The summary catalogue is meant to provide a schematic overview to Baillairgé's architectural career. The chart is organized in chronological order and by functional type, arranging in separate groups all the commercial, educational, religious, residential, social/recreational, and governmental buildings.

To give an idea of the relative scale and importance of particular projects, the figures in brackets indicate the cost of the project, when known, expressed in pounds (£) or dollars ($) according to the source. The exchange value at that time was approximately £1 to $4. Figures are most often taken from building contracts, parish registers, and institutional records. Not included are the architect's fees, 1 to 1½ per cent of total cost for the plans alone and 5 per cent for plans, specifications, and supervision of construction. An asterisk preceding a project indicates that Baillairgé was engaged as supervising architect.

When comparing these figures, one should keep in mind that there was an inflation factor. According to some sources, the cost of materials and manpower rose between 1850 and 1855 by almost 30 per cent.

Year	Commercial	Educational	Religious	Residential	Social/Recreational	Governmental
1845						Saint-Paul Market Hall [proposal]
1846			Église de Saint-Roch steeples (£280)			Saint-Paul Market Hall [proposal]
1847	Drolet (£567)		*Église Saint-Jean-Baptiste (£7200)			Pump house Saint-Paul Market Hall [proposal]
1848	Brunet/Glackemeyer (£80) Lawlor (£155 joinery)			"Clermont" (£121 plasterwork) *Dean *A. Hamel (£1000) *J. Hamel Trudelle		
1849	*Bilodeau (£5000) De Blois (£2225) Tessier (£375) *Woolsey (£900)		*Église de Beauport (£13,000)	Corriveau (£975) Douglas *Hôtel-Dieu (£2809) Parent/Têtu (£724) "Ravenswood" Roy (£235 joinery) Gethings		
1850	Baillargeon (£525 joinery) Benjamin (£220) DeFoy (£474) *Hamel (£800)		*Hospice des Soeurs de la Charité (£21,012)	Méthot (£615) Turcot (£850)		City Hall [proposal]
1851	*Caron (£900) Dean DeFoy (£145) Ross			Légaré (£434)	*Quebec Music Hall (£9890)	
1852	Bérubé (£416) Holmes (£236)		Église de Saint-Elzéar	Black (£1075) Dorion (£120 masonry) Jackson (£515) Manoir de Saint-Roch-des-Aulnaies *Têtu (£1575)		

Year	Commercial	Educational	Religious	Residential	Social/Recreational	Governmental
1853	*Fréchette *Gibb Taché (£900) *Têtu (£3686)	*Notre-Dame-de-Grâce wing (£7782)	Église de l'Isle-Verte	*Bilodeau (£720 joinery) *Chinic (£1710) Drolet (£660) *Phillips		*Marine Hospital wall and railing (£3029)
1854	Bilodeau/Murray (£2700 joinery) Hardy (£600) Laterrière (£197) *Merrill (£900) O'Neill [proposal]	*Central Pavilion, Université Laval (£40,000 approx. for both buildings)	Église de Saint-Romuald (£5540) *Église de Sainte-Marie de Beauce (£10,000 approx.)			*Marine Hospital wing (£2123) Quebec Customs House [proposal]
1855		*Pensionnat, Université Laval	Église Saint-Patrice	Petitclerc	*Monument aux Braves ($5344)	
1856	Grégoire (£285 without bricks) Talbot (£1500)		Église Sainte-Marguerite	*Baillairgé (£180 painting) *Congrégation Notre-Dame de Québec (£4799) DeFoy (£1340) *Johnston *Morin (£1740) *Hamel (£1504) *Morrin (£1505)		
1857	*Caisse d'économie (£4068)		*Chapelle de la Congrégation (£754) *Notre-Dame de Québec (£350)	Chartré (£891) *Leaycraft (£2388) Lemoine (£1852) *Moisan (£580) Scott (£575)		
1858	*Desbarats Labrecque (£400) Taché		*Chapelle de Notre-Dame de Belmont (£381) *Presbytery of Saint-Jean-Baptiste (£1159)			Parliament House [proposal]
1859			Treasury of Notre-Dame de Québec			
1860	Cap Rouge pottery *Simard (£4125)			Baillargeon (£525) Murphy [proposal]		*New Quebec Jail (£16,000 plus extras)
1861			*Venner tomb ($5000)			
1862				*Blaiklock Hamel (£755) *Whitty (£610)		
1863	Quebec Bath House (£1250)	École Saint-Jean-Baptiste (£1422)	*Église de Saint-Laurent	"Elm Grove" (£2750) *Petry ($5183)		*Departmental Buildings
1864	Moffat/Chabot		Aylmer Convent ($15,000)			
1866			*Chapelle du Bon-Pasteur (£3427)			Berthelot Market Hall ($8500) Berthelot Weighing House ($1000) Jacques Cartier Market Hall ($8500) Saint John Gate ($35,000)
1867						Fire Station no. 1 ($1000) Fire Station no. 2 ($2350) Fire Station no. 3 ($2000) Fire Station no. 4 ($500) Fire Station no. 5 Fire Station no. 6 ($1175)

Year	Commercial	Educational	Religious	Residential	Social/Recreational	Governmental
1868				Ryan		
1871			Église de Sainte-Anne de Beaupré			*Cove Field Staircase ($550) *Old City Hall Wing ($480)
1872			Église de Saint-Nicolas			
1873						Aqueduct Bridge ($13,944)
1874						*Dome
1875						*Montcalm Market Hall ($45,500)
1878	Dufferin Terrace Restaurant ($5000)					Dufferin Terrace ($20,000)
1879						*Weighing house ($398)
1881						*Fire Station no. 2 ($894)
1882						Saint-Augustin Staircase ($4135)
1883						*Berthelot Market Weighing House ($430) *Champlain Market Hall *Tubular Bridge
1884						*Salle Jacques Cartier ($1606)
1885			*Chapelle Sainte-Alice ($909)			City Hall [proposal] Quarantine Station ($4052)
1886				*Baillairgé		*Finlay Market Hall *Illuminated Cone *Taschereau Arch
1888						*Bandstand Kiosk *Sainte-Claire Staircase ($3186)
1889				*Aqueduct ($777)	London Eiffel Tower [proposal]	*Buade Staircase ($3065) *Champlain Staircase ($3171) Electro-Chromatic Revolving Fountain [proposal] *Fire Station no. 7 *Police Station no. 3 ($3676) *Police Station no. 15 *Saint-Pierre Market Hall
1890				*Baillairgé ($7694)		*Berthelot Market Hall ($2555) *Fire Station no. 8 *Saint-Pierre Weighing House ($2289)

Year	Commercial	Educational	Religious	Residential	Social/Recreational	Governmental
1893						*Civic Hospital ($3357) *Disinfection Station ($1980)
1894			Chapelle du Séminaire			*Carters' Kiosks *Police Station no. 7 Victoria Jubilee Tower [proposal]
1895						*Fire Station no. 4 *Fire Station no. 5 Palace Market ($649) Spiral slide Winter Carnival sculptures
1896						*Conservatory ($815) *Swing bridges ($26,913)
1897						Arago Staricase
1898						*Conservatory ($1674) Ice house [proposal]
1899				*Baillairgé		

Appendix 2   Genealogy of Charles Baillairgé

The genealogical charts found in Appendix 2 are not comprehensive ones for the entire Baillairgé family, since these have been published elsewhere in George-Frédéric Baillairgé's biographical series. The three genealogies appended to this study have as their focus Charles Baillairgé. The first chart, *Selected Genealogy of Charles Baillairgé, Showing Architects and Engineers*, illustrates the five generations of Baillairgés active in the building trades in Canada. Appendix 2.2, *Selected Genealogy of Charles Baillairgé, Showing his Surviving Brothers and Sisters*, concentrates on his parents and siblings. Appendix 2.3, *Selected Genealogy of Charles Baillairgé, Showing Descendants*, charts the eleven and nine offspring from his two marriages. I am indebted to Baillairgé's great-grandson, Paul Lafontaine of Montréal, for information on the family descendants.

2.1 Selected Genealogy of Charles Baillairgé, Showing Architects and Engineers

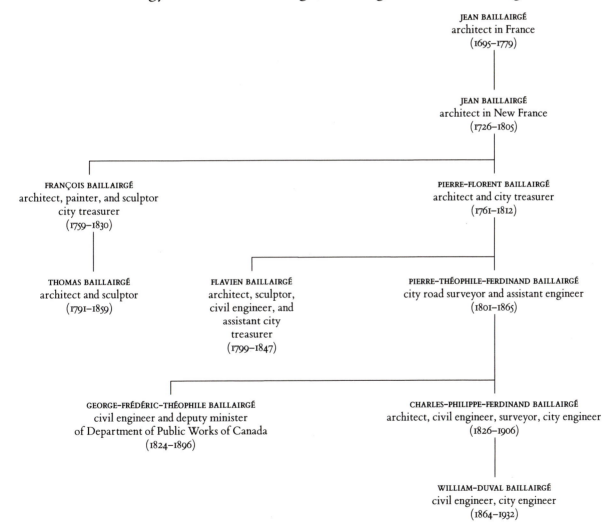

JEAN BAILLAIRGÉ
architect in France
(1695–1779)

JEAN BAILLAIRGÉ
architect in New France
(1726–1805)

FRANÇOIS BAILLAIRGÉ
architect, painter, and sculptor
city treasurer
(1759–1830)

PIERRE-FLORENT BAILLAIRGÉ
architect and city treasurer
(1761–1812)

THOMAS BAILLAIRGÉ
architect and sculptor
(1791–1859)

FLAVIEN BAILLAIRGÉ
architect, sculptor,
civil engineer, and
assistant city
treasurer
(1799–1847)

PIERRE-THÉOPHILE-FERDINAND BAILLAIRGÉ
city road surveyor and assistant engineer
(1801–1865)

GEORGE-FRÉDÉRIC-THÉOPHILE BAILLAIRGÉ
civil engineer and deputy minister
of Department of Public Works of Canada
(1824–1896)

CHARLES-PHILIPPE-FERDINAND BAILLAIRGÉ
architect, civil engineer, surveyor, city engineer
(1826–1906)

WILLIAM-DUVAL BAILLAIRGÉ
civil engineer, city engineer
(1864–1932)

2.2 Selected Genealogy of Charles Baillairgé, Showing his Surviving Brothers and Sisters

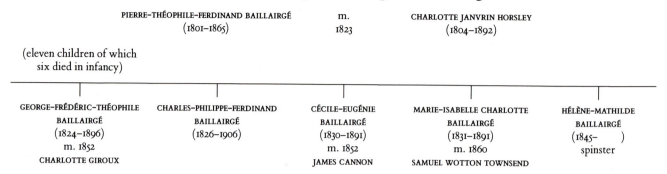

PIERRE-THÉOPHILE-FERDINAND BAILLAIRGÉ   m.   CHARLOTTE JANVRIN HORSLEY
(1801–1865)   1823   (1804–1892)

(eleven children of which
six died in infancy)

| GEORGE-FRÉDÉRIC-THÉOPHILE BAILLAIRGÉ (1824–1896) m. 1852 CHARLOTTE GIROUX | CHARLES-PHILIPPE-FERDINAND BAILLAIRGÉ (1826–1906) | CÉCILE-EUGÉNIE BAILLAIRGÉ (1830–1891) m. 1852 JAMES CANNON | MARIE-ISABELLE CHARLOTTE BAILLAIRGÉ (1831–1891) m. 1860 SAMUEL WOTTON TOWNSEND | HÉLÈNE-MATHILDE BAILLAIRGÉ (1845–) spinster |

2.3 Selected Genealogy of Charles Baillairgé, Showing Descendants

First marriage (eleven children of which six died in infancy)

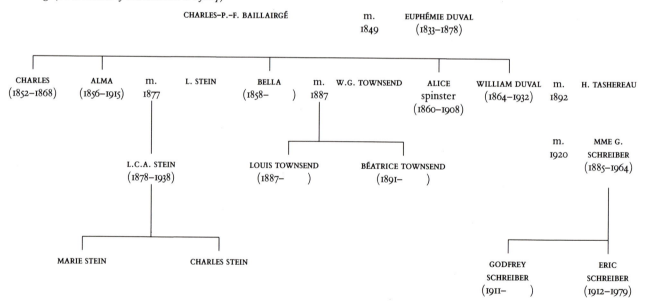

CHARLES-P.-F. BAILLAIRGÉ   m.   EUPHÉMIE DUVAL
1849   (1833–1878)

| CHARLES (1852–1868) | ALMA (1856–1915) m. 1877 L. STEIN | BELLA (1858–) m. 1887 W.G. TOWNSEND | ALICE spinster (1860–1908) | WILLIAM DUVAL (1864–1932) m. 1892 H. TASHEREAU |

L.C.A. STEIN (1878–1938)

LOUIS TOWNSEND (1887–)   BÉATRICE TOWNSEND (1891–)

m. 1920   MME G. SCHREIBER (1885–1964)

MARIE STEIN   CHARLES STEIN

GODFREY SCHREIBER (1911–)   ERIC SCHREIBER (1912–1979)

(continued) 2.3 Selected Genealogy of Charles Baillairgé, Showing Descendants

Second marriage (nine children)

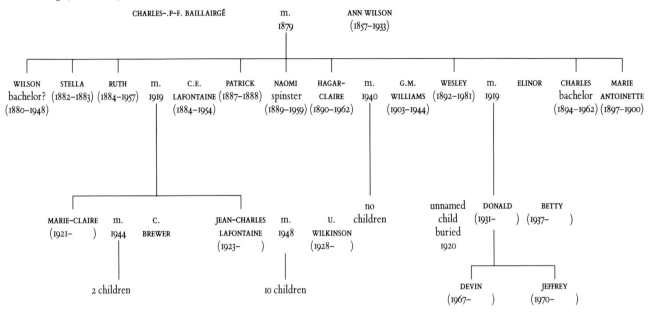

Appendix 3 Bibliography of Primary Source Material

This bibliography is limited to primary source material, namely Baillairgé's own writings, manuscript collections, and his architectural library. References to secondary sources are found in the notes.

PRINTED WORKS BY CHARLES BAILLAIRGÉ

Architecture

Description et plan d'un nouveau calorifer [sic] à air chaud, sur le système tubulaire, pour chauffer les édifices privés et publics. Quebec: Bureau et Marcotte 1853.

The Public Buildings. [Ottawa]: n.p. 1864.

"Lettre de M. Baillargé [sic]." *Le Canadien*, 24 May 1865, 1–2.

The New Jail, Quebec. Quebec: n.p. 1865.

Honble H.L. Langevin G.B. Ministre des Travaux Publics. Quebec: n.p. 1873.

Les édifices publics pour la province de Québec. [Quebec]: n.p. [1875].

The Public Buildings for the Province of Quebec. [Quebec]: n.p. [1875].

"Rapport sur l'état actuel de l'art de bâtir dans la Province de Québec, et des moyens à prendre pour y remédier." In H.-J.-J.-B. Chouinard, *Fête nationale des canadiens-français célébrée à Québec en 1880.* Quebec: A. Côté et Cie. 1881, 429–36.

A Practical Solution of the Great Social and Humanitarian Problem: Escape from Buildings in Case of Fire. A Paper read before the Royal Society of Canada during its May Session 1887. Quebec: n.p. 1887.

M. Le Rédacteur du Journal "Paris Canada." Quebec: n.p. 1887.

On the Necessity of a School of Arts for the Dominion: A Paper read before the Canadian Society of Civil Engineers at their Meeting of the 26th May 1887. Quebec: n.p. 1887.

Visite de M. Baillairgé à l'École industrielle des Glacis. Quebec: n.p. 1887.

Visit of Mr. Baillairgé to the School of Industry Glacis Street. Quebec: n.p. 1887.

"On the Necessity of a School of Arts for the Dominion." *Transactions of the Canadian Society of Civil Engineers* 1, no. 2 (1887): 68–76.

"Information Wanted." *CAB* 1 (Dec. 1888): 6.

Instructions to Architects Submitting Competing Designs for the New City Hall Quebec. [Quebec: E. Vincent 1889].

Baillairgé's London Eiffel Tower. [Quebec]: n.p. [1890].

Une Tour Eiffel pour Londres: projet de M. Baillairgé. [Quebec]: n.p. [1890].

"Employment of a Quantity Surveyor." *CAB* 3 (1890): 30.

"Methods of Mental Computation." *CAB* 3 (1890): 29.

"Quebec City Hall Competition." *CAB* 3 (1890), 28.

Baillairgé, Charles, F.H. Berlinguet, and David Ouellet. "Canadian Building Stones." *CAB* 3 (1890): 138–9.

"Designs for World's Fair Monument." *CAB* 5 (1892): 5.

"Escape from Buildings in Case of Fire." *CAB* 5 (1892): 122–3.

"Fire Escapes for Public Buildings." *CAB* 5 (1892): 88.

"A Plea for a Canadian School of Architecture." *CAB* 6 (1893): 105–8.

"A Quick and Easy Way of Getting at the Weight of Iron Scantlings, Girders, Columns, etc." *CAB* 7 (1894): 154–5.

"Canadian vs. Foreign Cement." *CAB* 7 (1894): 15.

"Foundations in Deep and Unreliable Soils." *CAB* 7 (1894): 128–30.

Adresse de Bienvenue par M. Baillairgé à la Section de Montréal des Architectes du Canada. Quebec: n.p. [1895].

Bribery and Boodling, Fraud, Hypocrisy & Humbug, Professional Charges and Pecuniary Ethics. Quebec: n.p. 1895.

Mr. Baillairgé's Address of Welcome to the Montreal Section of Canadian Architects. Quebec: n.p. 1895.

On the Bearing and Resisting Strength of Structures and that of their Component Parts and Materials. Read before the Province of Quebec Association of Architects at their Annual Meeting – October 2, 1895 – at the Château Frontenac –' Quebec. [Quebec: C. Darveau 1895].

"Escape in Case of Fire." *CAB* 8 (1895): 77.

"On the Bearing and Resisting Strength of Structures and that of their Component Parts and Materials." *CAB* 8 (1895): 122–4.

La glissoire spirale. Toronto: n.p. 1896.

Baillairgé's Electro-Chromatic Revolving Fountain. [Quebec]: n.p. [1897]. (No author listed).

La Fontaine Rotative Electro-Chromatique Baillairgé. [Quebec]: n.p. [1897].

Monsieur le Président du Comité de chemins. Quebec: n.p. 1897.

"Reasons for a Dominion Association of Architects." *CAB* 10 (1897): 2–3.

Fires and Fire-Proof Construction. Quebec: n.p. 1898.

"Fires and Fire-Proof Construction." *CE* 6 (May 1898): 30, xv.

"Foundations." *CE* 6 (May 1898): 5–6.

"The London Building Disaster." *CAB* 11 (1898): 25.

Bilan de M. Baillairgé, comme Architecte, Ingénieur, Arpenteur-Géomètre, durant les 21 ans, avant d'entrer au service de la Cité, ès-qualité d'Ingénieur des Ponts et Chaussées, ou de 1845 à 1866. Puis – entre heures – de 1866 à 1899, mais non compris les Travaux Civiques relatés dans un rapport supplémentaire. [Quebec]: n.p. [1899].

Exposition universelle à Paris, an 1900: Exhibits de M. Chs. Baillairgé, Arct. et Ing. de Québec, Canada: divers. [Quebec: n.p. 1899]. (No author listed).

Exposition universelle de Paris, an 1900: Seule solution du grand problème humanitaire du siècle: évasion sure – simultanée – instantanée en cas de feu des étages supérieurs. Quebec: n.p. 1899. (No author listed).

"A Caution to Architects and Builders." *CAB* 12 (1899): 8.

"Words of Appreciation." *CAB* 12 (1899): 74.

"A Proposed Aquarium under Dufferin Terrace, Quebec." *CAB* 13 (1900): 93.

" 'Bay' and 'Oriel' Windows." *CAB* 13 (1900): 41–2.

"Design of Kiosks on Dufferin Terrace, Quebec." *CAB* 13 (1900): 40.

"Some Novel Architecture Features." *CAB* 13 (1900): 40.

"Un projet inoui: pourquoi ne pas installer un aquarium sous la terrasse." *Le Soleil*, 26 April 1900, 5.

Escape in Case of Fire. Quebec: n.p. 1901.

Évasion en cas de feu. Québec: n.p. 1901.

"The Construction of Ice Houses." *CAB* 14 (1901): 8.

"Originality of Design in Architecture at the Expense of Beauty (Slater) – How Skyscrapers can be made more Aesthetic." *CAB* 15 (1902): 144.

"The Park Avenue Hotel Fire." *CAB* 15 (1902): 41.

"A Possible Solution of the Sky-scraper Question as bearing on the subject of City Hygiene." *CAB* 16 (1903): 78.

"The Flat Iron Building, New York." *CE* 10 (1903): 100.

"Correspondence." *CAB* 17 (1904): 198–9.

"The Chicago Theatre Fire." *CAB* 17 (1904): 56–7.

Engineering

Rapport du surintendant des travaux de la corporation de Québec pour l'année 1868. Québec: C. Darveau 1869.

Report of the Superintendent of Works of the Corporation of Quebec for the Year 1868. Quebec: C. Darveau 1869.

Rapport du surintendant des travaux de la corporation de Québec pour l'année 1869. Québec: C. Darveau 1870.

Rapport du surintendant de la Cité et de l'Ingénieur de l'aqueduc pour l'année 1872–73. Québec: C. Darveau 1873.

Report of the City Surveyor and Waterworks Engineer for the Year 1872–73. Quebec: C. Darveau 1873.

Rapport de C. Baillairgé, Ecr. ingénieur du chemin de fer du nord pour la corporation de Québec. Québec: n.p. 1874.

Report of C. Baillairgé, Esq., Corporation Engineer of the North Shore Rail Road. Quebec: n.p. 1874.

Report of the City Engineer, Quebec, on the Pro-posed Improvements in the Mouth of the River St. Charles. Quebec: n.p. 1875.

Supplementary Report of the Quebec Corporation Engineer of the North Shore Railway. Quebec: n.p. 1875.

Report of the City Engineer, Quebec, on the Proposed Dry Dock in the Mouth of the River St. Charles. Quebec: [C. Darveau] 1876.

The Municipal Situation. Quebec: P.G. Delisle 1878.

Rapport du Chevalier C. Baillairgé, Ingénieur de la Cité de Québec sur l'Amélioration de son Aqueduc. Quebec: Elzéar Vincent 1881.

Report of Chevalier C. Baillairgé, Engineer, of the City of Quebec, on the Amelioration of its Aqueduct. Quebec: Elzéar Vincent 1881.

Aux entrepreneurs d'aqueducs: avis public. Quebec: n.p. 1883.

Opinions of the People. Quebec: n.p. 1883.

A Particular Case of Hydraulic-ram or Water-Hammer: A Paper read by the Undersigned before the Mathematical, Physical and Chemical Section of the Royal Society of Canada, May 1884. Quebec: n.p. 1884.

Rapport de Charles Baillairgé, Ingénieur de la Cité de Québec, section de 10 milles chemin de fer du lac St. Jean au nord de St-Raymond. Quebec: George Vincent 1884.

Report of Charles Baillairgé, Engineer of the City of Quebec, on the 10 Mile Section of the Lake St. John Railway North-ward of St. Raymond. Quebec: George Vincent 1884.

"A Particular Case of Hydraulic-Ram or Water-Hammer." *Proceedings and Transactions of the Royal Society of Canada* 2, first series, sect. 3 (1884): 81–6.

Rapport de M. Baillairgé, Ingénieur des ponts et chaussées, sur la 3ième section du chemin de fer de Québec & Lac St-Jean au nord de St-Raymond. Quebec: Georges Vincent 1885.

Rapport de M. Baillairgé, ingénieur du nouvel aqueduc de Québec, sur la terminaison du contrat Beemer, 30 oct. 1885. [Quebec: n.p. 1885].

Rapport du comité de l'aqueduc sur les taux proposés pour l'usage de l'eau. Quebec: C. Darveau 1885.

Report by Charles Baillairgé, City Engineer, to the City Council on the 3rd Section of the Quebec & Lake St. John Railway Northward from St. Raymond. Quebec: Georges Vincent 1885.

Report of Mr. Baillairgé, City Engineer, on the 5th–10 Miles – Section of the Railroad from Quebec to Lake St. John. Quebec: n.p. 1885.

Report of Mr. Baillairgé, Engineer of the New Quebec Aqueduct on the Completion of the Beemer Contract 30th Oct. 1885. [Quebec: n.p. 1885].

Report of the Water Works Committee on the Proposed Water Rates. Quebec: C. Darveau 1885.

The Aqueduct, Quebec. Quebec: [G. Vincent] 1885.

City Engineer's Office. Quebec: n.p. 1886. (No author listed).

Rapport de M. Baillairgé, Ingénieur de la Cité, sur la 5ème section du chemin de fer Québec & Lac St. Jean au nord de St-Raymond. Quebec: Georges Vincent 1886.

Rapport de l'ingénieur de la cité (gérant de l'aqueduc) sur les ouvrages faits durant la saison des travaux de 1887. Quebec: Georges Vincent 1887.

Report of the City Engineer and (Water-Works Manager) on the Works performed during the Season of 1887. Quebec: Georges Vincent 1887. (No author listed).

"The Quebec Disaster." *CAB* 2 (1889): 114.

An Attempt to deduce the Pressure per Square Inch under which a Steam Boiler explodes from the Effects produced by the Explosion: A Paper read by Mr. C. Baillairgé before the Royal Society of Canada, Section III, at its Yearly Sitting in Montreal, May 27 1891. [Quebec]: n.p. [1891].

Rapport de l'Ingénieur de la Cité pour 1890–91. [Quebec]: n.p. [1891].

Report of the City Engineer for 1890–91. [Quebec]: n.p. [1891].

Tentative de déduire des effets d'une explosion de chaudière à vapeur, la pression par pouce carré sous laquelle la chaudière a cédé. Étude lue par M.C. Baillairgé devant la Section III de la Société Royale du Canada, à sa séance annuelle du 27 mai 1891, à Montréal. [Quebec]: n.p. [1891].

"A Difficult Problem." *CAB* 4 (1891): 32.

La ventilation libre des égouts en rapport avec l'hygiène de l'habitation. Lu par M. Baillairgé devant la Section III de la Société Royale du Canada à sa séance du 31 mai 1892, Ottawa. Joliette: Imprimerie de l'étudiant, du couvent et de la famille 1892.

The Free and Liberal Ventilation of Sewers in its Relation to the Sanitation of our Dwellings. Quebec: C. Darveau 1892.

"Cost of Electric Lighting in all the Principal Cities of North America." *Water and Gas Review* (Feb. 1892): 7–10.

The Quebec Land Slide of 1889. Montreal: n.p. 1893.

"The Quebec Land Slide of 1889." *Transactions of the Canadian Society of Civil Engineers* 7 (1893): 140–52.

Rapport de l'Ingénieur de la cité pour les années 1892–93 – 1893–94, Quebec: Georges Vincent 1894.

Report of the City Engineer for the years 1892–93 – 1893–94. Quebec: Georges Vincent 1894.

"The Landslide at St. Alban's, Que." *CAB* 7 (1894): 77.

"The Fall of the Louisville and Jeffersonville Bridge." *Engineering Record* 35 (Jan. 1894): 113.

"The Pressure of Wind on Bridge Structures." *CE* 1 (March 1894): 328–9.

"Anent the Ball Nozzle 'Mystery.'" *Western Fireman and Journal of Public Works* 15 (March 1895): 253.

"An Invasion of Our Riparian Rights." *CE* 2 (April 1895): 349.

"Effect of American Drainage Works on Canadian Interests." *CAB* 8 (1895): 48.

"Effect on the St. Lawrence of the Proposed Deviation of a Portion of its Waters towards the Gulf of Mexico, by the Chicago Canal now in Process of Execution." *CAB* 8 (1895): 5.

"Municipal Control of Electric Lighting." *Canadian Electrical News* 5 (Feb. 1895): 19.

"Municipal Electric Lighting." *CE* 2 (Jan. 1895): 262.

"Solution of the 'Ball-Nozzle Fire Jet' Paradox." *CE* 3 (May 1895): 5.

"The Allard Process of Hardening Copper and Aluminium." *CE* 2 (April 1895): 348–9. (No author listed).

"The Ball-Nozzle Mystery." *CE* 3 (Aug. 1895): 97.

"The Ball-Nozzle 'Mystery.'" *CE* 3 (Nov. 1895): 186.

"The Bouzey Dam Failure and the Quebec Landslide." *CE* 3 (July 1895): 59–61.

"The Piston Problem." *CE* 3 (June 1895): 31–2.

"The Prevention of Steam Boiler Explosions." *CE* 3 (May 1895): 5–6.

"The Proposed Maritime Canal." *CE* 3 (May 1895): 19.

"The Swelling and Shrinkage of Excavated Materials." *CE* 2 (April 1895): 338–40.

"Velocity and Pressure of the Wind." *CE* 2 (Feb. 1895): 291.

City of Quebec: Municipal Engineering Statistics. Quebec: Vincent & Frère 1896. (No author listed).

Ville de Québec: Génie municipal, statistiques. Quebec: Geo. Vincent & Frère 1896. (No author listed).

"Effect of the Chicago Canal on Canadian Water Levels." *CAB* 9 (1896): 117.

"Le Cinématographie." *L'Evénement,* 7 Nov. 1896, 2. (Listed under J. Baillairgé).

"Le Cinématographe." *Le Trifluvien,* 20 Nov. 1896, 5. (Listed under J. Baillairgé).

Baillairgé's Marine Revolving Steam Express. N.p. [1897].

Le Pont proposé sur le St-Laurent devant Québec. Quebec: n.p. [1897].

The Navigation of the Air. [Quebec]: n.p. 1897.

"Baillairgé's Marine Revolving Steam Express." *CE* 5 (Oct. 1897): 166–7.

"Growth of Crystalline Bodies." *CAB* 10 (1897): 94.

"Suggestions aérostatiques." *La Presse,* 20 Nov. 1897, 2. (Author's name spelt Baillargé).

"The Navigation of the Air." *CE* 5 (Nov. 1897): 196–8.

"La perte de la Bourgogne." *L'Evénement,* 23 July 1898, 3. (Author's name spelt Baillargé).

"Tidal Motors." *CE* 6 (July 1898): 82.

"Wind Pressure, Actual and Estimated." *CE* 6 (Dec. 1898): 229–30.

"Wind Pressures on Surfaces of Different Areas." *Engineering Record* 39 (Dec. 1898): n.p.

Asphalt Block Pavement. [Quebec]: n.p. [1899]. (No author listed).

Exposition universelle à Paris, an 1900: exhibit de M.C. Baillairgé arcte. et ingr. de Québec, Canada: Système de fonder des piliers de ponts à eau profonde de 100 à 200 pieds ou plus. Quebec: n.p. 1899. (No author listed).

Rapport de l'Ex-Ingénieur de la Cité, des travaux faits sous le Maire, Hon. S.N. Parent et le Conseil-de-Ville actuels et sous leurs prédécesseurs durant le dernier tiers de Siècle: 1866 à 1899.

Quebec: C. Darveau [1899].

The Asphalt Block. [Quebec: n.p. 1899].

"Dam Building." *CE* 7 (May 1899): 18–19.

"Retaining Walls." *CE* 6 (Jan. 1899): 251.

"Rolling or Ramming in Road Building." *CE* 6 (April 1899): 351–2.

"The Asphalt Block." *CE* 7 (Sept. 1899): 146–7.

"Longitudinal Bulk Heads in Ocean Liners." *CE* 8 (Dec. 1900): 159–60.

"The Boston Gas Works." *CE* 7 (April 1900): 313–14.

"The Engineer, the Master Spirit of the Age." *CE* 8 (May 1900): 55–6; 8 (Oct. 1900): 133–4.

"The Floating of the 'Scottish King.'" *CE* 8 (Nov. 1900): 154.

"Written Comments on Thos. Drummond's 'The Miners' Inch and the Discharge of Water Through Various Orifices under Low Heads.'" *Transactions of the Canadian Society of Civil Engineers* 14 (1900): 149–55.

"Accidents to Reservoir Dams." *CAB* 14 (1901): 120.

"Friction in Water Pipes." *CE* 8 (March 1901): 243–4.

"Masonry Dams and Retaining Walls in General, Concrete Works, etc." *CE* 8 (Feb. 1901): 219–22; 8 (March 1901): 233.

"Masonry Dams and Retaining Walls in General, Concrete Works, etc." *Transactions of the Canadian Society of Civil Engineers* 15 (1901): 49–66.

"The Chicoutimi Dam Failure." *CE* 8 (June 1901): 310.

"The Instructiveness of Failure." *CE* 8 (Jan. 1901): 178–80.

"Boiler Explosion at Lebanon, PA." *CE* 9 (1902): 337.

"Discussion of A.W. Robinson's 'The Economy of Large Ships.'" *Transactions of the Canadian Society of Civil Engineers* 16 (1902): 155–6.

"Discussion of Chas. H. Rust's 'Sewage Disposal.'" *Transactions of the Canadian Society of Civil Engineers* 16 (1902): 194–5.

"Discussion of H.J. Cambie's 'An Unrecorded Property of Clay.'" *Transactions of the Canadian Society of Civil Engineers* 16 (1902): 211–13.

A Paper read before the Royal Society of Canada and before the Can. Soc. of Civil Engineers on the Construction of an Indestructible Vessel for a Voyage to the North Pole and how to reach it. Quebec: Imprimerie Darveau [1903].

"A Vessel for North Polar Navigation and Discovery." *CE* 10 (1903): 40–1.

"Dam Construction and Failures During the Last Thirty Years." *Transactions of the Canadian Society of Civil Engineers* 17 (1903): 270–82.

"Dam Construction and Failures of Thirty Years." *CE* 10 (1903): 131–4.

"Metric vs. English Measures." *CE* 10 (1903): 301–2.

"The Failure of the Chambly Dam." *CE* 10 (1903): 65.

"The Land Slide at Frank, B.C.." *CE* 10 (1903): 246–7.

"The Weight of Ice-Laden Telegraph and Other Wires." *CE* 10 (1903): 100.

"Prevention of Hot Air Explosions." *CAB* 18 (1905): 6–7.

"The Revetment Wall at the Quebec Docks." *CE* 12 (1905): 185–6.

Language

Nouveau dictionnaire français: système "éducationnel," rimes, consonnances, homonymes, décomposition des mots, combinaisons variées de leurs éléments et équivalents, jeux de mots. Quebec: C. Darveau 1888.

Dictionnaire des homonymes par Charles Baillairgé: appréciations. Joliette: Imprimerie de l'étudiant et du couvent 1889.

Vocabulaire des homonymes simples de la langue française. Joliette: Atelier typographique de l'étudiant, du couvent et de la famille 1891.

Vocabulary of English Homonyms. Quebec: C. Darveau 1891.

Technical Education of the People in Untechnical Language. Read before Section III Royal Society of Canada, May 1894 by C. Baillairgé. Quebec: [C. Darveau] 1894.

Educational: Word Lessons. Quebec: C. Darveau [1899].

Le grec – le latin. Leur utilité pour apprécier la signification des mots actuels de la langue, et dans la composition de nouveaux mots … Mémoire lu par l'auteur, Chs. Baillairgé, devant la Société Royale du Canada, à Ottawa, le 23 mai 1899. [Quebec], n.p. [1899].

An Introduction to the Author's Forthcoming Volume on the Origin, Signification, Translation, Classification and Etymology of Proper-Names to be read before Section II of the Royal Society of Canada at its May Meeting at Toronto, Ont., 1902. [Quebec: n.p. 1902].

Introduction au futur ouvrage de l'auteur sur l'origine, la signification, la traduction, classification et étymologie des Noms-Propres, à être lu devant la section II de la Société Royale du Canada, à Toronto, en mai 1902. [Quebec: n.p. 1902].

Mathematics

Nouveau traité de géométrie et de trigonométrie rectiligne et sphérique, suivi du toisé des surfaces et des volumes. Quebec: C. Darveau 1866.

Prospectus du Tableau Stéréométrique Baillairgé. [Quebec]: n.p. [1871]. (No author listed).

Prospectus of the Baillairgé Stereometrical Tableau. [Quebec]: n.p. [1871]. (No author listed).

"Geometry, Mensuration, and the Stereometrical Tableau." *Transactions of the Literary and Historical Society of Quebec*, new series, no. 9 (1871–2): 73–115.

Lecture by Mr. Baillairgé. Baillairgé's Stereometrical Tableau. [Quebec: n.p. 1872].

Géométrie, toisé et le tableau stéréométrique, lecture faite devant la société littéraire et historique de Québec 20 mars 1872. Quebec: C. Darveau 1873.

Geometry, Mensuration, and the Stereometrical Tableau, Lecture read before the Quebec Literary and Historical Society 20th March 1872. Quebec: C. Darveau 1873.

Clef du tableau stéréométrique Baillairgé. Quebec: C. Darveau 1874.

Clef synoptique ou abrégée du tableau stéréométrique Baillairgé. Nouveau système de toiser tous les corps-segments, troncs et onglets de ces corps par une seule et même règle. Quebec: C. Darveau 1874.

Key to Baillairgé's Stereometrical Tableau: New System of Measuring all Bodies – Segments, Frusta and Ungulae of such Bodies by One and the Same Rule. Quebec: C. Darveau 1874.

Appréciations du tableau stéréométrique Baillairgé. Quebec: C. Darveau 1875.

Clef du nouveau système de toiser tous les corps-segments, troncs et onglets de ces corps par une seule et même règle. Quebec: C. Darveau 1875.

Key to Baillairgé's Stereometrical Tableau; New System of Measuring all Bodies – Segments,

Frustra and Ungulae of such Bodies by One and the Same Rule. Quebec: C. Darveau 1876.

Key to the Stereometricon or Application of the Prismoidal Formula to All Solids. Quebec: C. Darveau 1876.

Nouveau système de toiser tous les corps par une seule et même formule, à l'usage des écoles élémentaires. Quebec: n.p. 1878.

The Stereometricon. Originator: C. Baillairgé, [sic] M.S. … Promoter: Thomas Whitty. Montreal: John Lovell & Son 1880.

Le Stéréométricon. Nouveau système de toiser tous les corps par une seule et même règle: Application générale de la formule prismoidale. Quebec: C. Darveau 1884.

The Stereometricon. New System of Measuring all Bodies by One and the Same Rule: General application of the Prismoidal Formula. Quebec: C. Darveau 1884.

The Stereometricon. Originator: C. Baillairgé, M.S. … Promoter: Thomas Whitty. Quebec: C. Darveau 1884.

Exposition coloniale de Londres, 1886: exhibit éducatif du Canada. Géométrie dans l'espace: stéréométrie, stéréotomie, le toisé des corps mis à la portée de toutes les intelligences: le stéréométricon Baillairgé. [Quebec]: n.p. 1886. (No author listed).

Géométrie dans l'espace: stéréométrie et stéréotomie. Le stéréométricon couronné en France, en Belgique, en Italie, en Russie, au Japon, au Brésil, au Canada, aux États-Unis d'Amérique. Quebec: n.p. 1886.

London Colonial Exhibition 1886: Canadian Educational Exhibit. Solid Geometry Made Easy: The Baillairgé Stereometricon. [Quebec]: n.p. 1886. (No author listed).

Solid Geometry Made Easy: The Stereometricon. N.p. 1886.

To the Jurors of the Educational Department of the Colonial Exhibition of London. Quebec: n.p. 1886.

[Suggestion aux géomètres à propos d'une nouvelle édition d'Euclide], Mémoire lu par l'auteur, C. Baillairgé, devant la Société Royale du Canada, durant sa séance de mai 1888. [Quebec]: n.p. [1888].

"Révision des Éléments de Géométrie d'Euclide." *Proceedings and Transactions of the Royal Society of Canada* 6, first series, sect. 3 (1888): 64.

"An Easy Method of Calculation." *CAB* 3 (1890): 44.

Étude ayant trait à la solution du problème de déterminer la hauteur atteinte par un projectile qui en retombant au niveau dont il a été lancé, a produit un effet connu. Lue par M. Baillairgé, devant la Section III, de la Société Royale du Canada à sa séance du 27 mai 1891, à Montréal. [Quebec]: n.p. [1891].

Miscellaneous

Lettre au maire de Québec. Quebec: n.p. 1884.

Mémoires lus devant la Société Royale du Canada, 1882 & 1883. Quebec: C. Darveau 1884.

Papers read before the Royal Society of Canada, 1882 & 1883. Quebec: C. Darveau 1884.

Québec, passé, présent, futur. Quebec: Jos.-G. Gingras & Cie. 1885.

La baie d'Hudson: Exploitation proposée de ses ressources de terre et de mer: nouvelle colonie: chemin de fer pour s'y rendre. Joliette: Imprimerie du bon combat, du couvent et de la famille 1893.

"Quebec in 1894." *CAB* 7 (1894): 16–17.

Hudson Bay: Proposed Utilization of its Land and Water Resources: A New Colony – A Railway to Reach it. Read before the Literary and Historical Society of Quebec, 7th March, 1895, by C. Baillairgé. [Quebec: C. Darveau 1895].

Le Communisme. [Quebec]: n.p. 1895.

MM. les Rédacteurs de "La Semaine." Quebec: n.p. 1895. (No author listed).

Oeuvres diverses – Sundry Works. [Quebec: C. Darveau 1895].

"On veut nous voler le Saint-Laurent!" *Le Naturaliste canadien* 22 (May 1895): 69–74.

"L'Oeuvre des étrennes aux enfants pauvres." *La Presse,* 5 Dec. 1896, 16.

Address by Mr. Baillairgé, delegate of the Quebec Geographical Society on presentation to the Royal Society of Canada, at its annual meeting at Halifax, N.S., of the Society's last Bulletin or illustrated volume of Transactions. N.p. 1897.

Bulletin de la Société de Géographie de Québec 1893 a 1897/Transactions of the Geographical Society of Quebec 1893 to 1897. Quebec: n.p. 1897. (No editor listed).

Les RR. Dames Ursulines de Québec. Quebec: n.p. 1897.

Divers, ou les enseignements de la vie. Quebec: C. Darveau 1898.

Divers ou les enseignements de la vie: style familier EGRIALLIAB. Quebec; n.p. [1898].

Exposition universelle à Paris, an 1900: exhibits

de M. Chs. Baillairgé, arcte. et ing. de Québec, Canada. Divers. Quebec: n.p., [1899].

L'antiquité de la terre et de l'homme: mémoire lu devant la Société Royale du Canada en mai 1899. [Quebec]: n.p. [1899].

La vie, l'évolution, le matérialisme: Mémoire lu par l'auteur, Chs. Baillairgé, devant la Société Royale du Canada, à Ottawa, à la réunion annuelle de la Société, le 23 mai 1899. [Quebec]: n.p. [1899].

Oeuvres diverses – Sundry Works. [Quebec: C. Darveau 1899].

Société Royale du Canada, 23 mai 1899: Rapport de la Société de Géographie de Québec. [Quebec: n.p. 1899].

20 ans après: Le Club des 21 en 1879. [Quebec]: n.p. [1899].

Amélioration, adoucissement possible du climat d'Anticosti par la fermeture du Détroit de Belle-Isle. [Quebec]: n.p. [1900].

Anticosti en 1900. [Quebec]: n.p. [1900].

Exposition universelle, Paris, an 1900. Canada, Ville de Québec, bâtisse coloniale, terrain de Trocadero – en face le champ de mars. Exhibits de M. Chs. Baillairgé, Ingénieur, Architecte, etc. N.p. [1900]. (No author listed).

Les oeuvres de M. Baillairgé. [Quebec: n.p. 1901].

Les progrès du XIXᵉ siècle. [Quebec]: L'Événement 1901.

Mr. Baillairgé's Writings. [Quebec: n.p. 1901].

Radeau de sauvetage Baillairgé-Hurly. [Quebec: n.p. 1901].

The Baillairgé, Hurly Safety Raft. [Quebec: n.p. 1901]. (No author listed).

The Human Mechanism the Most Marvelous … to be read by C. Baillairgé before Section III of the Royal Society of Canada at its May Meeting 1901. [Quebec]: n.p. 1901.

The Progress of the Nineteenth Century. Quebec: Quebec Daily Telegraph 1901.

"Discours de M. Baillairgé." *L'Événement,* 2 Jan. 1901, 2. (no author listed).

Baillairgé, Charles, N. Levasseur, and O. Frechette. *Expédition Bernier au pôle nord (1902–5).* Quebec: n.p. 1901.

Appréciations des oeuvres de M.C. Baillargé [sic]. [Quebec: n.p. 1902].

Prôtet de C. Baillairgé I.C.M.S.R.C. Québec contre la décision du comité d'adjudication du prix Pollok de $20,000.00. Quebec: n.p. 1902.

A Summary of Papers read at Different Times before the Royal Society of Canada, the Canadian Association of Civil Engineers and Architects, and Literary, and Scientific Societies, or which have appeared occasionally in Scientific and Other Publications. Quebec: H. Chassé Printing [1903].

"Chicoutimi." *CE* 10 (1903): 135–6.

"Mechanical Problem of the Flight of Birds." *CE* 10 (1903): 304.

MANUSCRIPTS

Major archival holdings of manuscripts relating to Charles Baillairgé are located in Quebec City and Ottawa. Other less extensive holdings, though important, are mentioned in the notes.

Of prime importance is the collection of over 500 architectural drawings for the period 1845–94 which constitute the fonds Charles Baillairgé at the municipal archives at Quebec City (AVQ). This repository also possesses thirty-three letterbooks containing copies of Baillairgé's correspondence as city engineer and subject files on municipal buildings from Baillairgé's tenure (1863–98).

Of equal significance are the notarial files held by the Archives nationales du Québec (ANQ), where all the building contracts with their richly informative specifications are located. The notarial records also contain documents on property, apprenticeship contracts, wills, and inventories after death, all sources unique to the province of Quebec with its French civil law tradition. This provincial repository also holds an outstanding collection of historic photographs, maps, and architectural drawings invaluable to any in-depth study of Quebec City.

The archives at the Seminary of Quebec (ASQ) holds significant Baillairgé material, including full documentation on the construction of the Laval University buildings, information on the Stereometrical Tableau, and the unusual scrapbook put together by the editor of *L'Événement,* Nazaire Levasseur, containing letters from Baillairgé and his wife during the 1870s.

Less extensive but still important are the archives of Notre-Dame de Québec (ANDQ), which contains drawings and correspondence relating to religious buildings and cemeteries; the Musée de Québec (MQ) to which Naomi Baillairgé donated her father's scrapbook containing newspaper clippings, letters, diplomas, photographs, and sketches covering his entire career; and the archives of the archdiocese of Quebec

(AAQ), which holds some key correspondence on Baillairgé's disputes with the Roman Catholic clergy.

In Ottawa, the principal resource for Baillairgé material is the extensive collection of public works records in the federal archives of the National Archives of Canada (NA). Records include correspondence, registers, minutes, letterbooks, reports, and commissions of inquiry covering the Board of Works and the Department of Public Works for the period under study (1845–1906). The National Map Collection, now known as the Cartographic and Architectural Archives Division, contains working drawings by Baillairgé for the Departmental Buildings, Ottawa, 1863–5, as well as other significant nineteenth-century cartographic evidence on Quebec City. The National Photography Collection, now known as the Documentary Art and Photography Division, holds a rich collection of period views of Quebec City and its environs essential for documenting Baillairgé's buildings as originally constructed.

Mention should also be made of the sparse but unique Barbeau collection, housed at the Canadian Centre for Folk Culture Studies (CCFCS), Canadian Museum of Civilization, which contains this pioneering ethnographer's hand-written list of architectural books still on the shelves of the widow Baillairgé's library in the 1920s.

Finally, an overview of manuscript sources would be incomplete without mentioning the Lafontaine Collection in Montreal, a private collection held by a grandson of Charles Baillairgé in which are found land deeds, drawings, and other family papers covering the period c.1836–c.1930.

ARCHITECTURAL LIBRARY OF CHARLES BAILLAIRGÉ

For the first time in Canada, research sources have been sufficient to permit the reconstruction of a major nineteenth-century architectural library. What the 126 titles demonstrate is the scope of scholarly and technical books – ranging from standard texts to the most up-to-date fashions – available to any Canadian professional determined to acquire them. In addition to revealing specific borrowings in Baillairgé's work, this collection tempers a parochial interpretation of the subject and orients the historian towards an examination of Canadian architecture in a national and international context.

This reconstitution of Baillairgé's architectural library is at best incomplete, based as it is on lists contained in Thomas Baillairgé's testament, the inventory made after the death of Charles' first wife (*inventaire* 1878), Marius Barbeau's notes in the 1920s (Barbeau list), and miscellaneous archival documents. In all cases, bibliographic information in these lists was partial, although currently available bibliographic tools have permitted identification of most of the items. One will never know, however, what other books might have been part of this collection, but were omitted from any of these lists.

This bibliography is arranged in alphabetical order, each entry being followed by an indication of the present location of the actual book, when found, and/or the source(s) in which it was listed.

A Selection of Sixty Subjects from the Works of the Best Ancient & Modern Sculptors. London: Charles Murton, n.d. QQLA, NB/450/S464; *inventaire* (1878), Barbeau list. Inscription on title page: "Chs. Baillairgé"; "Ecole des Beaux-Arts de Québec Bibliothèque."

Aide-mémoire to the Military Sciences, 2nd ed., 3 vols. London: John Weale, Lockwood & Company 1853–62. Not located; *inventaire* (1878).

American Encyclopedia, 16 vols. N.p.: 1860. Not located; *inventaire* (1878).

American Encyclopedia, 16 vols. N.p.: 1873. Not located; *inventaire* (1878).

Annual Report of the Minister of Public Works for the Fiscal Year 1890–91, part 2. Ottawa: S.E. Dawson 1893. QQLA, uncatalogued [bound with G.F. Baillairgé, *Alphabetical Record*].

Arnot, David Henry. *Gothic Architecture applied to modern residences containing designs of all the important parts of a private dwelling, exhibited in elaborate perspective drawings; together with large and copious details*. New York: D. Appleton & Company 1850. Not located; *inventaire* (1878), Barbeau list.

Baillairgé, George-Frédéric. *Alphabetical Record; Engineers and Superintendents, etc. and the Principal Public Works on which they have reported or been employed, Canada, 1779 to 1891*. [Ottawa: S.E. Dawson 1891]. QQLA, uncatalogued [collection code 105–7/33/13]. Unsigned.

Barnard, Henry. *School Architecture; or Contributions to the Improvement of School-houses in the United States*, 5th ed. New York: Charles B. Norton 1854. Not located; Barbeau list.

Bélidor, Bernard Forest de. *La science des ingénieurs dans la conduite des travaux de fortifications et d'architecture civile*. Paris: Claude Jombert 1775. Not located; *inventaire* (1878).

Bell, Thomas J. *History of the Water Supply of the World*. Cincinnati: Peter G. Thomson 1882. AVQ, rare books, TD/219/B433/1882. Inscription on title page: "Chs. Baillairgé."

Benjamin, Asher. *The American Builder's Companion; or, a System of Architecture, particularly adapted to the Present Style of Building*. Boston: R.P. & C. Williams 1827. Not located; *inventaire* (1878).

Blondel, Jacques-François. *Cours d'architecture, ou traité de la décoration, distribution et construction des bâtiments contenant les leçons données en 1750, et les années suivantes, par J.F. Blondel, architecte ... dans son école des arts*, 6 vols. Paris: Desaint 1771–7. QMM, Blackader; Barbeau list, Thomas Baillairgé will.

Bonneval, Claude Alexandre. *Antiquités romaines expliquées dans les mémoires de comte de B-, contenant ses aventures; un grand nombre d'histoires et anecdotes du tems très curieuses, ses recherches et ses découvertes sur les antiquités de la ville de Rome et autres curiosités de l'Italie; divisés en trois parties, et enrichis de plus de cent belles planches en taille-douce*. The Hague: Jean Neaulme 1750. Not located; Thomas Baillairgé will.

Borgnis, J.-A. *Traité élémentaire de construction appliquée à l'architecture civile*. Paris: Bachelier 1823. Not located; *inventaire* (1878).

Brandon, Raphael, and J. Arthur Brandon. *Parish Churches; being Perspective Views of English Ecclesiastical Structures*, vol. 1. London: David Bogue 1851. QQLA, NA/5463/B819/1851/1; *inventaire* (1878), Barbeau list. Inscription [beneath modern covering] on inside front cover: "Chs. Baillairgé $20. 2 vols."

——— *Parish Churches; being Perspective Views of English Ecclesiastical Structures*, vol. 2. London: David Bogue 1851. QQLA, NA/5463/B819/1851/2; *inventaire* (1878), Barbeau list. Inscription on inside front cover: "Chs. Baillairgé $20."

——— *The Open Timber Roofs of the Middle Ages, Illustrated by Perspective and Working Drawings of some of the Best Varieties of Church Roofs, with Descriptive Letter-Press*. London: W. Kent and Co. (late D. Bogue) 1860. Not located; *inventaire* (1878), Barbeau list.

Brees, S.C. *First Series of Railway Practice: A Collection of Working Plans and Practical Details of Construction in the Public Works of the Most Celebrated Engineers*, 3rd ed. London: John Williams and Co. 1847. QQLA, uncatalogued [collection code 105–7/33/17]; *inventaire* (1878). Inscription on inside front cover: "Chs. Baillairgé. For this and folio of plates £10.0.0"; signed on title page. "Chs. Baillairgé."

Buchotte. *Les règles du dessein et du lavis, pour les plans particuliers des ouvrages & des bâtimens, & pour leurs coupes, profils, élévations & façades, tant de l'architecture militaire que civile*. Paris: Charles-Antoine Jombert 1743. QMM, Blackader, WFD/B85; Barbeau list. This book is listed in François Baillairgé inventory. Inscription on title page: "C. Venner[?] [stroked out], L.G. Baillairgé à Charles Baillairgé 1894. Mme. A.W. Baillairgé."

Buildings for Mechanics' Institutions, comprising lithographic designs and ground plans of Buildings adapted for Institutes in small towns. London: Longmans & Company 1860. Not located; *inventaire* (1878).

Byrne, Oliver, ed. *A Dictionary of Machines, Mechanics, Engine-Work, and Engineering: Designed for Practical Working Men and Those Intended for the Engineering Profession*, 2 vols. New York: D. Appleton & Company 1851. QQLA, uncatalogued [collection code 105–7/33/31] (vol. 2 only); *inventaire* (1878). Inscription on inside front cover: "Chs. Baillairgé 60/ for 2 vols."; signed on title page. "Chs. Baillargé."

Castieau, William, and Percival Proctor. *The Modern Dictionary of Arts and Sciences*, vol. 1. London: G. Kearsly 1774. QQLA, uncatalogued [collection code 105–7/33/9]. Inscription on title page: "L.G. Baillairgé. 1894. à Charles Baillairgé."

Chamber's Encyclopedia; a Dictionary of Universal Knowledge for the People, 10 vols. London: W. and R. Chambers 1860–8. Not located; *inventaire* (1878).

Clark, Edwin, and Robert Stephenson. *The Britannia and Conway Tubular Bridges*, 2 vols. London: Day and Son and John Weale 1850. QQLA, uncatalogued [collection code 105–7/33/20] (vol. 1 only); *inventaire* (1878). Inscription on inside front cover: "Chs. Baillairgé 2 vols. text 1 do plates $36."

Colton, George Woolworth. *Colton's General Atlas, containing one hundred and seventy steel plate maps and plans ... accompanied by descrip-tions, geographical, statistical and historical by Richard S. Fisher*. New York: J.H. Colton & Company 1859. Not located; *inventaire* (1878).

Cowper, Charles. *The Building erected in Hyde Park for the Great Exhibition of the Works of Industry of all nations, 1851. Illustrated by twenty-eight large plates, embracing plans, elevations, sections and details, laid down to a large scale from the working drawings of the contractors, Messrs. Fox, Henderson, and Co. by Charles Downes with scientific description by Charles Cowper*. London: J. Weale 1852. QMM, Blackader, NA 6750/L6D7 [disappeared]; Barbeau list.

Cresy, Edward. *Encyclopaedia of Civil Engineering, Historical, Theoretical and Practical*, 2 vols. London: Longman, Brown, Green and Longmans 1847. Not located; *inventaire* (1878).

Croes, J.J.R. *Statistical Tables from the History and Statistics of American Water Works*. New York: Engineering News 1883. AVQ, rare books, TD/487/C939/1883. Inscription on title page: "Chs. Baillairgé."

The Cyclopaedia of Machine and Hand-Tools: a Series of Plans, Sections, and Elevations of the most approved Tools for working in iron, wood and other materials ... To which are added an Essay on the Strength and Qualities of Wood and Metals, embracing a sketch of the manufacture of iron and steel, by W.J. Macquorn Rankine ... and an Essay on the Puddling of Iron, by St. John Vincent Day. London: William Mackenzie 1869. Not located; *inventaire* (1878).

De l'Orme, Philibert. *Le premier tome de l'architecture de Philibert de l'Orme conseiller et aumosnier ordinaire du Roy*. Paris: Fédéric Morel 1568. BSQ, 203; *inventaire* (1878). Inscription on title page: "François Baillairgé, 1784." Inscription on inside front cover: "Chs. Baillairgé. New binding"; inscription on fly leaf: "Chs. Baillairgé £2.10.0"; inscription opposite title page: "L'Université Laval. Hommage du Chevalier Baillairgé 6 Oct. 79."

Dempsey, G. Drysdale. *The Practical Railway Engineer*. London: John Weale 1847. QQLA, uncatalogued [collection code 105–7/33/18]; *inventaire* (1878). Inscription on inside front cover: "Chs. Baillairgé £2.16.0."

Desargues, Gérard. *Manière universelle de Mr. Desargues, pour pratiquer la perspective par petit-pied, comme le Geometral*. Paris: Pierre Des-Hayes 1648. QQLA, NC/749/D441/1648. Inscription on title page: "Chs Baillairgé $1½."

Dilworth, Thomas. *The Young Book-keeper's Assistant: shewing him, in the most plain and easy Manner, the Italian way of stating Debtor and Creditor*. London: Richard and Henry Causton 1790. QQLA, uncatalogued [collection code 105–7/33/25]; *inventaire* (1878). Inscription on inside front cover: "F. Baillairgé."

Dupain de Montesson. *L'art de lever les plans de tout ce qui a rapport à la guerre et à l'architecture civile et champêtre*, 2nd ed. Paris: Ch. Ant. Jombert, père 1775. Not located; François Baillairgé inventory, Barbeau conversation. [Inscription on title page: "Thomas Baillairgé 1806"].

Durand, Jean Nicolas Louis. *Précis des leçons d'architecture données à l'École royale polytechnique*. Liège: D. Avanzo & Cie 1840. Not located; *inventaire* (1878), Barbeau list.

Duval, Charles Jérôme Alphonse. *Petites maisons de plaisance et d'habitation choisies aux environs de Paris et dans les quartiers neufs de la capitale présentées ... par C. Duval*. Liège: D. Avanzo & Cie. 1852. Not located; Barbeau list.

The Expositor; a Weekly Illustrated Recorder of Inventions, Designs and Art Manufactures, vol. 1. London: J. Clayton 1850. Not located; *inventaire* (1878).

Fairbairn, William. *Construction of Conway and Britannia Bridges*. London: John Weale 1849. Not located; *inventaire* (1878).

[Félibien, André]. *Des principes de l'architecture, de la sculpture, de la peinture, et des autres arts qui en dépendent, avec un dictionnaire des termes propres à chacun de ces Arts*, 2nd ed. Paris: Veuve Jean-Baptiste Coignard et Jean-Baptiste Coignard fils 1690. QMM, Blackader Rare Books, W/F33; *inventaire* (1878), Barbeau list. Inscription on inside front cover: "Chs. Baillairgé 1858 $15"; Inscription on title page: "Chs. Baillairgé."

Fergusson, James. *The Illustrated Handbook of Architecture; being a concise and popular account of the different styles of architecture prevailing in all ages and countries*. London: John Murray 1855. Not located; Barbeau list.

Ferrerio, Pietro. *Palazzi di Roma de piu celebri architetti disegnati da Pietro Ferrerio pittore et architett*, vol. 1. Rome: Gio Jacomo de Rossi [170–?]. QQBS, 203. Inscription on title page [scratched out]: "Thomas Baillairgé aoust 1821."

Foulke, William Parker. *Remarks on the Penal System of Pennsylvania, particularly with refer-*

ence to county prisons. Philadelphia: Philadelphia Society for Alleviating the miseries of public prisons 1855. Not located; Barbeau list.

Foulston, John. *The Public Buildings Erected in the West of England as Designed by John Foulston F.R.I.B.A.* London: J. Williams 1838. QMM, Blackader, WH45/11 F825; *inventaire* (1878), Barbeau list. Inscription on inside front cover: "Chs. Baillairgé £5.0.0."

Gibbs, James. *A Book of Architecture, containing Designs of Buildings and Ornaments*, 2nd ed. London: W. Innys and R. Manby, J. and P. Knapton, and C. Hitch 1739. QMM, Blackader, WF/11 G352; *inventaire* (1878); Barbeau list. Inscription on title page: "John Cannon 1806' [crossed out]; "Thomas Baillairgé 1833"; "Chs. Baillairgé 1858 $15."

Gould, Lucius D. *The American House Carpenter's and Joiner's Assistant*. New York: Daniel Burgess & Company 1853. Not located; *inventaire* (1878).

Great Exhibition of the Works of Industry of all Nations, 1851, 2 vols. London: Dickinson 1854. Not located; *inventaire* (1878).

Gwilt, Joseph. *An Encyclopaedia of Architecture, Historical, Theoretical and Practical*. London: Longman, Brown, Green and Longmans 1842. QQLA, NA/31/G994/1842; *inventaire* (1878). Inscription on inside front cover: "Chs. Baillairgé £4.2.?/binding 0.5.?/ £5.7.?"; inscription on title page: "Chs. Baillairgé."

Hamel, Joseph. *Rapport de l'inspecteur des chemins sur la canalisation de la cité de Québec/ Report of the Road Surveyor on the Drainage of the City of Quebec*. Quebec: Bureau & Marcotte 1852. QQLA, uncatalogued [bound with Sanderson, *Rural Architecture*].

Hope, Thomas. *Histoire de l'architecture*, 2 vols. Translated from English by A. Baron. Brussels: Meline, Cans et compagnie 1839. QMM, Blackader, WFII/H77F; *inventaire* (1878), Barbeau list. Vol. 1 inscription on title page: "Chs. Baillairgé in 2 vols. $9"; vol. 2 inscription on title page: "Chs. Baillairgé 2 vols. $9."

Hoppus, F. *The Gentleman's and Builder's Repository: or, Architecture Display'd, containing the most useful and requisite Problems in Geometry*. London: C. Hitch and L. Hawes, S. Crowder, B. Cole 1760. QMM, Blackader, WF/H77; *inventaire* (1878), Barbeau list. Inscription on title page: "François Baillairgé 1800"; ""Chs. Baillairgé 1858"; "Jan.

21/26 Mme. A.W. Baillairgé, Blackader."

The Imperial Journal of the Arts and Sciences, 3 vols. Glasgow: W. Mackenzie [1858–66?]. Not located; *inventaire* (1878).

Jackson, George, and Sons. *Part of the Collection of Relievo Decorations as Executed in Papier Maché et Carton Pierre*. London: George Jackson and Sons, n.d. [185?]. QQLA, NK/8555/J12/1856/Ex.B; *inventaire* (1878), Barbeau list. Inscription on inside front cover: "Chs. Baillairgé £2.12.6."

Jamieson, Alexander. *A Dictionary of Mechanical Science, Arts, Manufactures, and Miscellaneous Knowledge*, 2 vols. London: H. Fisher, Son and Co., 1827 [1837?]. Not located; *inventaire* (1878).

Jeaurat, Edme-Sébastien. *Traité de perspective à l'usage des artistes ... où l'on démontre géometriquement toutes les pratiques de cette science, et où l'on enseigne, selon la méthode de M. LeClerc, à mettre toutes sortes d'objets en perspective, leur réverbation dans l'eau, et leurs ombres, tant au soleil qu'au flambeau*. Paris: Charles-Antoine Jombert 1750. QQBS, 203. Inscription on title page: "F."; "Séminaire de Québec."

Jebb, Joshua. *Modern Prisons: their Construction and Ventilation*. London: John Weale 1844. Not located; *inventaire* (1878).

Johnson, William. *The Practical Draughtsman's Book of Industrial Design and Machinist's and Engineer's Drawing Companion, forming a Complete Course of Mechanical, Engineering and Architectural Drawing*. New York: Stringer & Townsend 1854. Not located; *inventaire* (1878).

Knight, Frederick. *Knight's Heraldic Illustrations, designed for the use of herald painters and engravers*. London: F. Knight [1843]. Not located; Barbeau list.

—— *Knight's Scroll Ornaments designed for the use of Silversmiths, Chasers, Die-Sinkers, Modellers, etc. etc.* London: J. Williams, T. Griffiths and Ackerman & Co. [1833?]. QMM, Blackader, NK1580/K7/1833/c.1; *inventaire* (1878), Barbeau list. Inscription on title page: "Chs. Baillairgé."

—— *Knight's Unique Fancy Ornaments*. London: J. Williams [1835?]. Not located; *inventaire* (1878), Barbeau list.

Lafever, Minard. *The Beauties of Modern Architecture*. New York. D. Appleton & Co. 1835. Not located.

—— *The Modern Builder's Guide*. New York: William D. Smith 1841. Not located;

inventaire (1878).

—— *The Young Builder's General Instructor, containing the Five Orders of Architecture*. Newark, NJ: W. Tuttle & Co. 1829. Not located.

Lardner, Dionysius. *Popular Lectures on Science and Art; delivered in the principal cities and towns of the United States*. New York: Greeley & McElrath 1846. Not located; *inventaire* (1878).

Leeds, Lewis W. *A Treatise on Ventilation, comprising seven lectures delivered before the Franklin Institute, Philadelphia, 1866–68*. New York: John Wiley & Son 1871. Not located, Barbeau list.

Letarouilly, P[aul-Marie]. *Édifices de Rome moderne ou recueil des palais, maisons, églises, couvents et autres monuments publics et particuliers les plus remarquables de la ville de Rome*, vol. 1. Liège: D. Avanzo & Cie. 1843. QQLA, NA/1120/L645a/1843/1 [collection code 105–7/33/6]; *inventaire* (1878), Barbeau list. Inscription on inside front cover: "Chs. Baillairgé $20 avec un vol. de texte"; inscription on title page: "Chs. Baillairgé."

—— *Édifices de Rome moderne*. Liège: D. Avanzo et Cie. 1849. QQLA, uncatalogued [collection code 105–7/33/14]; *inventaire* (1878), Barbeau list. Inscription on inside front cover: "Chs. Baillairgé £5.00 pour ce vol. et le vol. in folio de planches"; inscription on title page: "Chs. Baillairgé."

Lynde, Frederick Charles, ed. *Descriptive Illustrated Catalogue of the Sixty-eight Designs for the Great Tower for London, compiled and edited by Fred. C. Lynde for the Tower Company, Limited*. London: Industries 1890. Not located; Baillairgé, *Baillairgé's London Eiffel Tower*, 2.

[Meikleham, Robert]. *A Dictionary of Architecture; historical, descriptive, topographical, decorative, theoretical, and mechanical*, 3 vols., by Robert Stuart (pseud.). Philadelphia: A. Hart 1851. Not located; *inventaire* (1878), Barbeau list.

Meyer, Franz Sales. *A Handbook of Ornament, a grammar of art, industrial and architectural designing in all its branches, for practical as well as theoretical use*. New York: B. Hessling and Spielmeyer 1894. Not located; Barbeau list.

The National Portrait Gallery, 4 vols. London and New York: Cassell, Petter & Galpin 1875–7. Not located; *inventaire* (1878).

Newton, Isaac. *Optics or a Treatise on the*

Reflections, Refractions, Inflections and Colours of Light. London: W. & J. Innys 1718. Not located. Inscription: "F. Baillairgé 1804 Quebec"; "L.G. Baillairgé 1859 Charles Baillairgé"; as noted in MAC, IBC, fonds Morisset, 2/B157/C 475, p. 15.

Nicholson, John. *The Operative Mechanic and British Machinist, being a practical display of the Manufactories and Mechanical Arts of the United Kingdom.* London: Knight and Lacey 1825. Not located; *inventaire* (1878).

Nicholson, Peter. *Encyclopedia of Architecture. A Dictionary of the Science and Practice of Architecture, Building, Carpentry, etc. from the earliest ages to the present time forming a comprehensive work of reference for the use of architects, builders, carpenters, masons, engineers, students, professional men and amateurs*, ed. Edward Lomax and Thomas Gunyon, 2 vols. New York: Martin and Johnson 185?. Not located; *inventaire* (1878), Barbeau list.

Normand, Louis-Marie. *Monuments funéraires choisis dans les cimetières de Paris et des principales villes de France, dessinés, gravés et publiés par L. Normand, aîné.* Liège: D. Avanzo & Cie. 1852. *inventaire* (1878), Barbeau list.

———— *Paris moderne; ou, Choix de maisons construites dans les nouveaux quartiers de la capitale et dans ses environs,* vol. 1. Liège: D. Avanzo et Cie. n.d. QQLA, NA/7346/P232/1, Barbeau list. Inscription on inside front cover: "Chs. Baillairgé £10.0.0 pour les 3 vols."

———— *Paris moderne; ou, Choix de maisons dans les nouveaux quartiers de la capitale et dans ses environs*, vols. 2 and 3. Liège: D. Avanzo & Cie., n.d. Not located; Barbeau list.

Notman, William, and Thomas D. King. *Photographic Selections*, vol. 1. Montreal: William Notman 1863. Not located; *inventaire* (1878).

Official Reports of Various Duty Trials of the Gaskill Pumping Engine. Buffalo: Courier Company 1890. AVQ, rare books, TJ/770/1890. Inscription on title page: "Chs. Baillairgé."

Ornaments of all Nations. N.p., n.d. Not located; *inventaire* (1878).

Owen, Robert Dale. *Hints on Public Architecture, containing, among other Illustrations, Views and Plans of the Smithsonian Institution.* New York and London: George P. Putnam 1849. QQLA, NA/2540/O97/1849, Barbeau list. Inscription on inside front cover: "Chs.

Baillairgé £1.12.6."

Parker, Charles. *Villa rustica: Selected farm buildings and scenes in the vicinity of Rome and Florence, and arranged for rural and domestic dwellings, with plans and details,* 2nd ed. London: John Weale 1848. Not located; *inventaire* (1878), Barbeau list.

Parker, John Henry. *An Introduction to the Study of Gothic Architecture.* Oxford and London: J.H. Parker 1849. Not located; Barbeau list.

Pattisson, William. *Plans and Elevations of Cottage Villas and Country Residences, with parsonage houses, lodges, and other domestic buildings; also, various details and general estimates.* London: Atchley and Co. 1852. Not located; *inventaire* (1878), Barbeau list.

Pictorial Gallery of Art, 2 vols. London: Charles Knight and Co. 1845?–7. Not located; *inventaire* (1878).

Picturesque America; or, The Land we live in, ed. William Cullen Bryant, 2 vols. New York: D. Appleton and Company [1872–4]. Not located; *inventaire* (1878).

Piganiol de la Force, [Jean Aymar]. *Nouvelle description des chasteaux et parcs de Versailles et de Marly; contenant une explication historique de toutes les peintures, tableaux, statues, vases et ornemens qui s'y voyent … enrichie de plusieurs figures en taille douce,* 2 vols. This book had at least nine editions in the 18th century. The first was Paris: Florentin & Pierre Delaulne 1701. The edition that François Baillairgé brought back with him from France in 1782 was probably the ninth edition, Paris: Étienne-François Savoye 1764. Not located; François Baillairgé inventory, Thomas Baillairgé will.

Practical Mechanic's Journal, 3rd ser. London: Longmans 1864. Not located; *inventaire* (1878).

Proulx, Louis. *Hospice des Soeurs de la Charité à Québec.* Quebec: Aug. Côté et Cie. 1851. QQLA, uncatalogued [bound with Sanderson, *Rural Architecture*].

Pugin, Augustus C. and E.J. Willson. *Specimens of Gothic Architecture, accompanied by historical and descriptive accounts by E.J. Willson,* vol. 2. London: M.A. Nattali 1821. QQLA, NA/445/P978. Inscription [effaced] on inside front cover: "Chs. Baillairgé 2 vols. £?"; "J.P.E. Dussault, architecte, No. 253 rue St. Jean Quebec."

Rondelet, Jean. *Traité théorique et pratique de*

l'art de bâtir, 10th ed. Paris: Firmin Didot Frères 1843. QQLA, NA/2520/R771/1843/6; *inventaire* (1878), Barbeau list. Inscription on title page: "Chs. Baillairgé $32 et 5 vols. de texte."

Rondelet, Jean-Baptiste. *Traité théorique et pratique de l'art de bâtir,* 5 vols. Paris: Firmin Didot 1843. Not located; *inventaire* (1878), Barbeau list.

Rondelet, Jean. *Traité théorique et pratique de l'art de bâtir,* supplément par G. Abel Blouet. Liège: Dque Avanzo & Cie., n.d. QQLA, NA/2520/R771/1843/Suppl/2; *inventaire* (1878), Barbeau list. Inscription on inside front cover: "Chs. Baillairgé $15. avec un vol. de texte"; inscription on title page: "Chs. Baillairgé."

Rossi, Domenico de. *Studio d'architettura civile sopra gli Ornamenti di Porte Finestre Tratti da alcune Fabbriche insigni di Roma con le Misure Piante Modini e Profili: Opera de piu celebri architetti de nostri tempi,* part 1. Rome: Domenico de Rossi 1702. QMM, Blackader, WF36R/II R735; *inventaire* (1878), Barbeau list. Inscription on inside front cover: "Chs. Baillairgé 1858. 2 vols. $40.", inscription on title page: "Chs. Baillairgé 1858"; "Thomas Baillairgé aoust 1821."

———— *Studio d'architettura civile sopra varj Ornamenti di Cappelle, et diversi sepolcri tratti da piu Chiese di Roma colle loro Facciate, Fianchi, Piante, e Misure: Opera de piu celebri architetti de nostri tempi,* part 2. Rome: Domenico de Rossi 1711. QMM, Blackader, WF36R/II R735; *inventaire* (1878), Barbeau list. Inscription on title page: "Chs. Baillairgé 1858 en 2 vols. $40"; "Thomas Baillairgé aoust 1821."

———— *Studio d'architettura civile sopra varie Chiese, Cappelle di Roma, e Palazzo di Caprarola, et Altre Fabriche con le loro Facciate, Spaccati, Piante, e Misure: Opera de piu celebri architetti de nostri tempi,* part 3. Rome: Domenico de Rossi 1721. QMM, Blackader, WF36R/II R735 [bound with part 2]; *inventaire* (1878), Barbeau list.

Sanderson, James. *Rural Architecture; being a Series of Designs for Rural and Other Dwellings.* London: Wm. S. Orr & Co. n.d. QQLA, uncatalogued [collection code 105–7/33/7], Barbeau list. Inscription on inside front cover: "Chs. Baillairgé"; inscription on title page: "Chs. Baillairgé."

Sanderson, Nicolas. *Elements of Algebra for the Use of Students at the Universities,* 2nd ed. London: A. Millar, J. Whiston and B.

White, L. Davis and C. Reymers, Thuribourn and Woodyer 1761. QQLA, uncatalogued [collection code 105–7/33/8]. Inscription on inside front cover: "Chs. Baillairgé."

Sandrart, Joachim von. *Insignium Romae templorum prospectus, exteriores et interiores a celebrioribus architectis inventi nunc tandem suis cum plantis ac mensuris, septuaginta tribus figuris aeri incisis, in luce editi,* 2 vols. Norimbergae: Joannis Jacobi de Sandrart 1684. Not located; Barbeau list [inscribed on title page: "Thomas Baillairgé 1821"; "Charles Baillairgé 1858 $20."]

[Scott, David]. *Examples of Machinery and Mill-work; being Plans, Sections and Elevations, of Works in Several Departments of Machinery, Mill-work and General Engineering.* Glasgow: Blackie and Son 1845. Not located; *inventaire* (1878).

[Sears, F.L. *Famous American Buildings.* London?: Hinton & Simpkin & Marshall 1832.] QMM, Blackader WH83/11 H59, Barbeau list. Inscription on inside front cover: "Chs. Baillairgé £1.5." Title page is missing.

Sganzin, Joseph Mathieu. *Programme, ou résumé des leçons d'un cours de construction, avec des applications tirées spécialement de l'art de l'ingénieur des ponts et chaussées,* 5th ed. by Félix-Jean-Baptiste Reibell. Liège: D. Avanzo & Cie 1840–4. QQLA, TA/144/5523; *inventaire* (1878). Inscription on inside front cover: "Chs. Baillairgé £7.15.0. 2 vols de texte"; inscription on title page: "Chs. Baillairgé."

Sharpe, Samuel. *Egyptian Antiquities in the British Museum.* London: J.R. Smith 1862. Not located; *inventaire* (1878).

Silliman, Benjamin, and C.R. Goodrich, eds. *The World of Science, Art and Industry Illustrated from Examples in the New York Exhibition, 1853–1854.* New York: G.P. Putnam and Company 1854. Not located; *inventaire* (1878).

Sloan, Samuel. *The Model Architect. A Series of original designs for cottages, villas, suburban residences, etc.,* 2 vols. Philadelphia: E.S. Jones & Co. 1852. Not located; *inventaire* (1878), Barbeau list.

Smith, James. *The Dictionary of Arts, Sciences and Manufactures ... embracing in all nearly three thousand articles on Arts and Sciences,* 2 vols. Boston: Phillips, Sampson & Company 1854. Not located; *inventaire* (1878).

Soane, John. *Plans, Elevations and Sections of Buildings erected in the counties of Norfolk, Suffolk, Yorkshire, Staffordshire, Warwickshire, Hertfordshire, etcaetera.* London: Messrs. Taylor at the Architectural Library, Holborn 1788. QMM, Blackader, WF45/11 S676; *inventaire* (1878), Barbeau list. Inscription on inside front cover: "Chs. Baillairgé $10."

Switzer, Stephen. *An Introduction to a General System of Hydrostaticks and Hydraulicks, Philosophical and Practical.* London: T. Astley, S. Austen and L. Gilliver 1729. QQLA, uncatalogued [collection code 105–7/33/12]. Inscription on title page: "Chs. Baillairgé."

Tattersall, George. *Sporting Architecture.* London: R. Ackermann 1841. Not located; *inventaire* (1878).

Taylor, Michael. *Tables of Logarithms of All Numbers, from 1 to 101000; and of the Sines and Tangents to every second of the Quadrant.* Preface by Nevil Maskelyne. London: Christopher Buckton 1742. QQLA, uncatalogued [collection code 105–7/33/16]. No inscription.

Telford, Thomas. *On Bridges,* 4 vols. N.p., n.d. Not located; *inventaire* (1878).

Templeton, William. *The Operative Mechanic's Workshop Companion and the Scientific Gentleman's Practical Assistant,* 2nd ed. London: John Weale 1847. Not located; NA, RG 11, vol. 417, no. 10,788.

Tomlinson Encyclopedia, 2 vols. N.p. 1851. Not located; *inventaire* (1878).

Ure, Andrew. *A Dictionary of Arts, Manufactures and Mines: containing a clear exposition of their principles and practice,* 4th ed., 2 vols. London: Longman, Brown, Green and Longmans 1853. Not located; *inventaire* (1878).

Vignola, Giacomo Barozzio. *Le grand Vignol augmenté.* Paris: N. Berey 1664. Not located; François Baillairgé inventory, Thomas Baillairgé will.

Ville, Antoine de. *Les fortifications du chevalier Antoine de Ville, contenant la manière de fortifier toute sorte de places.* Paris: Toussainct Quinet 1636. Lyon: J. Barlet 1628. Not located; François Baillairgé inventory.

Vitry, Urbain. *Le propriétaire architecte, contenant des modèles de maisons de ville et de campagne, de fermes, orangeries, portes, puits, fontaines dessiné et rédigé par Urbain Vitry avec gravures par Hibon,* 2 vols. Paris: Audot 1827. Not located; *inventaire* (1878), Barbeau list.

Weale, John, ed. *Designs of ornamental gates, lodges, palisading and iron work of the Royal Parks; with some other designs equal in utility and taste; intended for those designing and making parks, terraces, pleasure walks, recreative ground, etc. etc.; principally taken from the executed works of Decimus Burton, arch., John Nash, arc. [and others].* London: J. Weale 1841. Not located; *inventaire* (1878), Barbeau list.

———— *Student Guide [for Measuring and Valuing].* London: John Weale 1843. Not located; NA, RG 11, vol. 417, no. 10,788.

———— *The Theory, Practice and Architecture of Bridges of Stone, Iron, Timber, and Wire, with Examples on the Principle of Suspension,* 4 vols. [vols. 1 and 2 bound together]. London: John Weale 1855–6. QQLA, uncatalogued [collection code 105–7/33/30]. All three volumes inscription on inside front cover: "Chs. Baillairgé £7.10 for the 3 vols." inscription on title page: "Chs. Baillairgé."

Wickersham, John B. *A new phase in iron manufacture, embracing a description of its use for enclosing public squares, cemetry lots, dwellings, cottages, offices, gratings for stores, prisons etc., window guards, bedsteads, tree boxes, verandas, etc.,* 2nd ed. New York: Wm. C. Bryant & Co. 1853. Not located; Barbeau list.

Willis, Nathaniel Parker. *Canadian Scenery Illustrated, from Drawings by W.H. Bartlett.* London: G. Virtue 1842. Not located; *inventaire* (1878).

Wood, John. *The Origin of building; or, the Plagiarism of the heathens detected, in five books.* Bath: S. and F. Farley 1741. Not located; *inventaire* (1878), Barbeau list.

Worthen, William Ezra, ed. *Appleton's Cyclopaedia of Drawing, designed as a textbook for the Mechanic, Architect, Engineer and Surveyor.* New York: D. Appleton & Company 1857. Not located; *inventaire* (1878).

Yearly Encyclopedia. N.p., 1861–8. Not located; *inventaire* (1878).

Notes

INTRODUCTION

1 See Appendix 2, genealogy of Charles Baillairgé.

2 Robert C. Tuck, *Gothic Dreams: The Life and Times of a Canadian Architect William Critchlow Harris 1854–1913* (Toronto: Dundurn Press 1978); Terry Reksten, *Rattenbury* (Victoria: Sono Nis Press 1978); Anthony Barrett and Rhodri Liscombe, *Francis Rattenbury and British Columbia: Architecture and Challenge in the Imperial Age* (Vancouver: University of British Columbia Press 1983). Although not yet published, a number of scholarly biographies on nineteenth-century architects practising in Canada have been completed or are in preparation, including a Master of Arts thesis on William Thomas by Neil Einarson of Winnipeg, a doctoral thesis by Ellen James of Concordia University on John Ostell, a study on George Browne by J. Douglas Stewart of Queen's University, a Master of Arts thesis on Thomas Fuller by Christopher Thomas of the University of Toronto, a Master of Arts thesis on Percy Nobbs by Susan Wagg of Concordia University, and a doctoral thesis by Raymonde Gauthier on Victor Bourgeau for Laval University. Exhibition catalogues include Geoffrey Hunt, *John M. Lyle: Toward a Canadian Architecture/Créer une architecture canadienne* (Kingston: Agnes Etherington Art Centre 1982), Ellen James, *John Ostell: Architecte, Arpenteur/Architect, Surveyor* (Montreal: McCord Museum 1985), and Susan Wagg, *Ernest Isbell Barott: Architecte/Architect* (Montreal: Canadian Centre for Architecture 1985).

3 See Appendix 1, Summary Catalogue of Architectural Works by Charles Baillairgé. For a complete catalogue of architectural works see Christina Cameron, "Charles Baillairgé, Architecte," doctoral thesis, Laval University, December 1982, Appendix II.

4 See Appendix 3, Bibliography, Printed Works by Charles Baillairgé.

5 Reference to the proposed volume is made in another work in the same series, George-Frédéric Baillairgé, *Notices biogra-*

phiques. Fascicule no. 1: Jean Baillairgé, 2ᵐᵉ du nom (Joliette: Bureaux de l'étudiant, du couvent et de la famille 1891), 5.

6 Marius Barbeau, "Les Baillairgé, Ecole de Québec en sculpture et en architecture," *Le Canada français* 33 (1945): 249–50; Gérard Morisset, "Jean Baillairgé (1726–1805)," *Technique* 22 (1947): 415–25; Ramsay Traquair, *The Old Architecture of Quebec* (Toronto: Macmillan Company of Canada 1947), 287–9; Gérard Morisset, "Pierre-Florent Baillairgé (1761–1812)," *Technique* 22 (1947): 603–10; Gérard Morisset, "François Baillairgé (1759–1830)," *Technique* 23 (1948): 27–32, 159–63; Gérard Morisset, "François Baillairgé 1759–1830: le sculpteur," *Technique* 24 (1949): 89–94, 187–91, 233–8; Alan Gowans, "Thomas Baillairgé and the Québécois Tradition of Church Architecture," *Art Bulletin* 34 (1953): 116–37; David Karel, Luc Noppen, and Claude Thibault, *"François Baillairgé et son oeuvre (1759–1830)* (Quebec: Le groupe de recherche en art du Québec de l'Université Laval et le Musée du Québec 1975), 1–84; Luc Noppen, "Le renouveau architectural proposé par Thomas Baillairgé au Québec, de 1820 à 1850," doctoral thesis, Université Toulouse-Le Mirail, 1976.

7 NA, RG 11, vol. 19, no. 19,850, letter from Charles Baillairgé to Hon. Jean Chabot, Quebec, 7 Jan. 1853.

8 George-Frédéric Baillairgé, *Notices biographiques*, vols. 1–4 (Joliette: Bureaux de l'étudiant, du couvent et de la famille 1891); ANQ, P 0092/3, fonds Jean-Jacques Girouard, journal de la famille Baillairgé, Quebec, 1854.

9 ASQ, exercices publics: Séminaire de Québec, collection of programmes of studies, Quebec, 1830–42.

10 Luc Noppen, "Le rôle de l'abbé Jérôme Demers dans l'élaboration d'une architecture néo-classique au Québec," *JCAH* 2, no. 1 (1975): 19–33; Noppen, "Le renouveau architecural."

11 A suggestion I owe to the late Eric Schreiber in a telephone converseation in 1971.

12 Partial research results have been released in A.J.H. Richardson, Geneviève Bastien, Doris Dubé, and Marthe Lacombe, *Quebec City: Architects, Artisans and Builders* (Ottawa: National Museum of Man 1984), and Christina Cameron and Monique Trépanier, *Vieux Québec: son Architecture intérieure* (Ottawa: National Museum of Man, 1986).

13 Christian Morissonneau, "Charles Baillairgé, architecte," *La Société de géographie de Québec 1877–1970* (Quebec: Les Presses de l'Université Laval 1971), 53. The exact phrase is "l'un des oubliés de l'historiographie canadienne-française."

CHAPTER 1

1 ANDQ, Registre Notre-Dame de Québec, 1826, no. 878, p. 207, "Charles-Philippe-Ferdinand Baillairgé, né avant hier, 1ᵉʳ oct. 1826." George-Frédéric Baillairgé, *Notices biographiques. Fascicule no. 4: Théophile Baillairgé … et Charlotte-Janvrin Horsley* (Joliette: Bureaux de l'étudiant, du couvent et de la famille 1891), 109–28. Théophile Baillairgé is identified as a "bookbinder, 1 St. Jean St." in John Smith, *The Quebec Directory or Strangers' Guide in the City for 1826* (Quebec: T. Cary & Co. 1826), 9. See Appendix 2, Genealogy of Charles Baillairgé.

2 ANQ, P 0092/3, fonds Jean-Jacques Girouard, journal de la famille Baillairgé, Quebec, 1854.

3 George-Frédéric Baillairgé, *Notices biographiques. Fascicule no. 1: Jean Baillairgé, 2ᵐᵉ du nom* (Joliette: Bureaux de l'étudiant, du couvent et de la famille 1891), 3; "Pierre-Florent Baillairgé," BRH 8 (1902): 26–7.

4 G.-F. Baillairgé, *Notices biographies no. 4*, 119.

5 Ibid., 122; "Baillairgé, George Frederick," *A Cyclopaedia of Canadian Biography being Chiefly Men of the Time*, ed. Geo Maclean Rose (Toronto: Rose Publishing Company 1888), 70.

6 ANQ, P 0092/3, fonds Girouard, journal de la famille Baillairgé; G.-F. Baillairgé, *Notices biographies no. 1*, 2; Marius Barbeau,

"Les Baillairgé: École de Québec en sculpture et en architecture," *Le Canada français* 33 (1945): 249–50; Doris Drolet Dubé and Marthe Lacombe, *Inventaire des marchés de construction des Archives nationales à Québec, XVIIᵉ et XVIIIᵉ siècles*, in *Histoire et archéologie*, 17 (Ottawa: Parks Canada 1977), 24, 98, 125, 148, 179, 203, 231, 249; Gérard Morisset, "Jean Baillairgé (1726–1805)," *Technique* 22 (1947): 415–25; Gérard Morisset, "Pierre-Florent Baillairgé (1761–1812)," *Technique* 22 (1947); 603–10; Gérard Morisset, "François Baillairgé (1759–1830)," *Technique* 23 (1948): 27–32, 159–63; Gérard Morisset, "François Baillairgé 1759–1830: le sculpteur," *Technique* 24 (1949): 89–94, 187–91, 233–8; Luc Noppen, *Notre-Dame de Québec (1647–1922), son architecture, son rayonnement* (Quebec: Ed. du Pélican 1974), 150–1.

7 David Karel, Luc Noppen, and Claude Thibault, *François Baillairgé et son oeuvre (1759–1830)* (Quebec: Le groupe de recherche en art du Québec de l'Université Laval et le Musée du Québec 1975), 1–84.

8 The drawings, which are dated 1780 and 1781, belong to the collection of the Musée du Québec; at least two of the perspective drawings of spiral staircases were originally part of the cahier Charles Baillairgé, which was acquired by the museum in 1959 from Naomi Baillairgé. One of the other drawings is reproduced in Karel et al., *François Baillairgé*, 68.

9 Luc Noppen, "François Baillairgé, architecte," in Karel et al., *François Baillairgé*, 67–84; Luc Noppen, *Les églises du Québec (1600–1850)* (Quebec: Fides 1977), 248–50.

10 Luc Noppen, "Le rôle de l'abbé Jérôme Demers dans l'élaboration d'une architecture néo-classique au Québec," *JCAH* 2, no. 1 (1975): 19–33. See also Olivier Maurault, "Un professeur d'architecture à Québec en 1828," *Marges d'histoire*, vol. 1 (Montreal: Librairie d'action canadienne-française 1929), 93–113.

11 His career is carefully studied in Luc Noppen, "Le renouveau architectural proposé par Thomas Baillairgé au Québec, de 1820 à 1850," doctoral thesis, Université Toulouse–Le Mirail, 1976.

12 George-Frédéric Baillairgé, *Notices biographies. Fascicule no. 3:Thomas Baillairgé … et François-X. Baillairgé* (Joliette: Bureaux de l'étudiant, du convent et de la famille 1891), 83.

13 G.-F. Baillairgé, *Notices biographies no. 4*, 109–11. Théophile Baillairgé's plans and elevations for market halls are simple and rudimentary, indicating that he had not been trained professionally in architecture. Illustrations of his design for a market hall in Lower Town are shown in Luc Noppen and Marc Grignon, *L'art de l'architecte* (Quebec: Musée du Québec/Université Laval 1983), 208–9.

14 James Macpherson Lemoine, *Maple Leaves*, ser. 7 (Quebec: Frank Carrel 1906), 134.

15 ASQ, exercices publics: Séminaire de Québec, programs of studies, Quebec, 1830–42; Charles Baillairgé, *Bilan de M. Baillairgé, comme Architecte, Ingénieur, Arpenteur-Géomètre, durant les 21 ans, avant d'entrer au service de la Cité, ès-qualité d'Ingénieur des Ponts et Chaussées, ou de 1845 a 1866. Puis – entre heures – de 1866 à 1899, mais non compris les Travaux Civiques relatés dans un rapport supplémentaire* [cited hereafter as *Bilan de 1845 à 1866*] ([Quebec]: n.p. [1899]), iii.

16 "Éloge du cours donné au Séminaire," *Le Canadien*, 14 Aug. 1839, cited in Honorius Provost, *Le Séminaire de Québec: documents et biographies* (Quebec: Archives du Séminaire de Québec 1964), 319–22.

17 Charles Baillairgé, *Divers, ou les enseignements de la vie* [cited hereafter as *Divers*] (Quebec: C. Darveau 1898), 33.

18 NA, RG 11, vol. 19, no. 19,850, letter from Charles Baillairgé to Hon. Jean Chabot stating his capacity as an architect and engineer, Quebec, 7 Jan. 1853: "J'ai reçu mon éducation au Séminaire de Québec dont je suis sorti en Rhétorique. J'avais trop le désir de m'avancer dans les connaissances philosophiques & mathématiques pour pouvoir suivre avec patience le progrès tardif de l'institution dont je viens de parler. Aussi me suis-je mis à l'étudier jour et nuit pour apprendre en un an, ce qu'au Séminaire je n'aurais appris que dans trois ans."

19 Charles Baillairgé, *A Summary of Papers read at Different Times before the Royal Society of Canada, the Canadian Association of Civil Engineers and Architects, and Literary, and Scientific Societies, or which have appeared occasionally in scientific and other publications* [cited hereafter as *A Summary of Papers*] (Quebec: H. Chassé Printing [1903], 71–4.

20 AVQ, fonds Charles Baillairgé, nos. 6–49 and 6–50, plans, elevation, and sections for Saint Paul Market, Quebec, July 1843.

21 NA, RG 11, vol. 19, no. 19,850, letter from Baillairgé to Chabot, Quebec, 7 Jan. 1853; the drawings may be found in AVQ, fonds Charles Baillairgé, nos. 6-45 to 6-47.

22 NA, RG 11, vol. 19, no. 19,850, letter from Baillairgé to Chabot, Quebec, 7 Jan. 1853.

23 NA, RG 4 B 28, vol. 134, no. 1216, bond of Charles Baillairgé to Her Majesty, Quebec, 14 July 1848.

24 NA, RG 11, vol. 19, no. 19,850, letter from Baillairgé to Chabot, 7 Jan. 1853. *Le Journal de Québec*, 13 March 1849, 3: "Le soussigné est maintenant prêt à recevoir un nombre limité d'élèves à être instruits dans les diverses branches de l'Architecture, de l'Arpentage, et du Génie Civil, conjointement ou séparément, au gré de l'élève. Le soussigné aussi, mésurement de toute espèce, géométrie, mathématiques, mécanique etc. Chas. Baillairgé."

25 NA, RG 11, vol. 19, no. 19,850, letter from Baillairgé to Chabot, Quebec, 7 Jan. 1853: "Je suis aussi parfaitement Ingénieur Civil qu'il est possible de l'être par l'Etude, c'est-à-dire que je suis dans le cas de celui qui aurait fait une cléricature entière."

26 A list of François Baillairgé's books is included in the inventory made after the death of his wife, in ANQ, gr. Roger Lelièvre, no. 3803, inventaire, Quebec, 30 May 1808. A partial transcription may be found in David Karel et al., *François Baillairgé*, 9. Judging from the inscription of Thomas Baillairgé's copy as listed in the architectural library of Charles Baillairgé, the volume by James Gibbs was obviously purchased by Thomas Baillairgé after the death of Quebec architect John Cannon in 1833. For other books from Cannon's library see Christina Cameron, "John Cannon," *Dictionary of Canadian Biography*, vol. VI (Toronto: University of Toronto Press 1987), 119–21.

27 ANQ, P 0092/2, fonds Jean-Jacques Girouard, letter from Thomas Baillairgé to Madame Girouard, Quebec, 11 April 1853; ASQ, polygraphie 19, no. 59, testament of Thomas Baillairgé, passed before Mtre Charles M. DeFoy, no. 5567, Quebec, 5 Aug. 1848. Among the clauses one finds:

5⁰ Je donne & lègue à Charles Baillairgé, Architect, mon petit cousin, mes livres suivants concernant ma profession, savoir Blondel, description de Versailles, Édifices de Paris, Antiquités

Romaines, en quatre volumes folio, Philibert de Lorme, livre d'Architecture de James Gibb *in folio*, et le grand Vignole, aussi *in folio*, & plus tous mes ustencils à dessiner.

6⁰ Je donne & lègue à Raphael Giroux, sculpteur, tous mes cahiers de desseins, modèles & autres livres d'architecture ainsi que tous mes outils de menuiserie, sculpture & peinture.

28 NA, RG II, vol. 19, no. 19,850, letter from Baillairgé to Chabot, Quebec, 7 Jan. 1853: "J'ai fait venir d'Europe et des Etats-Unis à grands frais pour mes faibles moyens tous les meilleurs traités sur l'Arpentage, l'Architecture & le Génie Civil & une grande quantité de volumes sur les arts, les sciences et les manufactures. J'ai lu & relu et étudié à maintes reprises ces volumes, et je connais non seulement tous les ouvrages de quelqu'importance qui ont existé & existent encore en Europe & dans les autres parties du monde, mais je suis aussi au fait de tous les moyens dont on s'est servi dans la construction de ces ouvrages. Je souscris à des publications qui me mettent au fait de tout ce qui se passe dans le monde scientifique."

29 See Appendix 3, Bibliography, Architectural Library of Charles Baillairgé.

30 G.-F. Baillairgé, *Notices biographiques no. 3*, 81–3.

31 NA, RG II, vol. 15, no. 12,239, letter from Charles Baillairgé to Thomas Begley, Quebec, 26 Aug. 1850; vol. 19, no. 19,850, letter from Baillairgé to Chabot, Quebec, 7 Jan. 1853: "J'ai visité toutes les principales villes des États-Unis et ai resté des journées entières aux endroits où je voyais un pont, une écluse, en construction pour considérer tous les moyens pratiques à employer dans la confection de ces ouvrages."

32 A.J.H. Richardson, "Guide to Buildings in the Old City of Quebec," *APT Bulletin* 2, nos. 3–4 (1970): 36–51.

33 Noppen, "Le renouveau architectural," 374, 409.

34 Ibid., 549–51; Pierre-Georges Roy, "Notes sur les premières années de la paroisse de Saint-Roch-de-Québec," *BRH* 33 (1927): 76.

35 QMM, Blackader, WF/II G352, James Gibbs, *A Book of Architecture, containing Designs of Buildings and Ornaments*, 2nd ed. (London: W. Innys and R. Manby, J. and P. Knapton and C. Hitch 1739), 3.

36 Since the 1845 proposal has no precise title, it has been identified as the plan for the 1857 Jacques Carter Market Hall by Luc Noppen, Claude Paulette, and Michel Tremblay, *Québec: trois siècles d'architecture* (Quebec: Libre expression 1979), 317. This attribution is based on the fact that a two-storey market hall was erected at the Jacques-Cartier Market, that the corner visible in a later photograph appears similar to this design (insofar as one can see it), and that one of the drawings has written on the backing "set of plans market hall Jac Cart C. Baillargé [sic] before 1866," *not* in Baillairgé's handwriting. What the authors failed to see was the inscription "C. Baillairgé studens" on the front of each sheet of the plans. Charles Baillairgé's son, Charles, was only five years old in 1857, so he could not be the "studens" in question. Moreover, in a contemporary newspaper report about the new Jacques Cartier Market Hall, it is stated that "le plan est de M. Théophile Baillairgé, inspecteur des chemins" (*Le Canadien*, 23 July 1857, 4). In support of the 1845 date is the close stylistic similarity to the episcopal palace of the same period and the survival of an isolated foundation drawing clearly identified for the Saint Paul Market and signed "1845 Invt. Delt. C. Baillairgé." AVQ, fonds Charles Baillairgé, no. 6–48.

37 Geneviève G. Bastien, Doris D. Dubé, and Christina [Cameron] Southam, *Inventaire des marchés de construction des archives civiles de Québec 1800–1870* in *History and Archaeology/Histoire et archéologie*, IA (Ottawa: Parks Canada 1975), 238; Antonio Drolet, *La ville de Québec, histoire municipale III, de l'incorporation à la Confédération (1833–1867)* in Cahiers d'histoire, 19 (Quebec: Société historique de Québec 1967), 80.

38 AVQ, conseil et comités, halles (marché) 2, report of market committee, Quebec, 5 Oct. 1843; Bastien et al., *Inventaire des marchés*, 230; Théophile Baillairgé's Upper Town Market Hall is illustrated in Noppen et al., *Québec: trois siècles*, 321. Théophile Baillairgé's specifications are simpler and less professional than those written by his son Charles.

39 Jean-Claude Marsan, *Montréal en évolution* (Montreal: Fidès 1974), 210–11; Luc d'Iberville–Moreau, *Lost Montreal* (Toronto: Oxford University Press 1975), 154–5; J. Douglas Stewart and Ian E. Wilson, *Heritage Kingston* (Kingston: Agnes Etherington Art Gallery and Queen's University 1973), 134–44.

40 G.-F. Baillairgé, *Notices biographiques no. 3*, 72.

41 Charles Baillairgé, "The Prevention of Steam Boiler Explosions," *CE* 3 (May 1895): 5–6.

42 G.-F. Baillairgé, *Notices biographiques no. 4*, 116–17.

43 NA, RG II, vol. 19, no. 19,850, letter from Baillairgé to Chabot, Quebec, 7 Jan. 1853.

CHAPTER 2

1 John Soane, *Plans, Elevations and Sections of Buildings erected in the counties of Norfolk, Suffolk, Yorkshire, Staffordshire, Warwickshire, Hertfordshire, etcaetera [sic]* (London: Messrs Taylor at the Architectural Library, Holborn 1788), 3.

2 Ibid. 7.

3 ASQ, Université 36, no. 66b, letter from Charles Baillairgé to Procurer of Seminary, Quebec, 23 Aug. 1858.

4 These observations are based on perusal of most of Baillairgé's specifications and many other architects' contracts, as part of the work involved in preparation of Geneviève G. Bastien, Doris D. Dubé, and Christina [Cameron] Southam, *Inventaire des marchés de construction des archives civiles de Québec 1800–1870* in *History and Archaeology/Histoire et archéologie*, IA-B-C (Ottawa: Parks Canada 1975).

5 ASQ, Université 36, no. 66b, letter from Baillairgé to Procurer, Quebec, 23 Aug. 1858.

6 ASQ, Université 36, no. 66a, account of Charles Baillairgé, Seminary of Quebec, Quebec, 23 Aug. 1858; AVQ, fonds Charles Baillairgé, nos. 2–1 to 2–41, plans, elevations, sections, and details for Laval University, Quebec (1854–7).

7 Charles Baillairgé, *A Summary of Papers, Read at Different Times before The Royal Society of Canada, the Canadian Association of Civil Engineers and Architects, and Literary, and Scientific Societies, or Which Have Appeared Occasionally in Scientific and Other Publications* (Quebec: H. Chassé Printing [1903]), 58.

8 Charles Baillairgé, "A Plea for a Canadian School of Architecture," *CAB* 6 (1893): 106.

9 Charles Baillairgé, *On the Necessity of a School of Arts for the Dominion: A Paper Read Before the Canadian Society of Civil Engineers at their Meeting of the 26th May 1887* (Quebec: n.p. 1887), 2.

10 ASQ, Université 36, no. 50, estimates for cut stone for pensionnat, Quebec, 6 Sept. 1855.

11 ASQ, Université 36, no. 40, plan for iron door, Quebec, n.d.

12 ASQ, Université 36, no. 59, letter from Charles Baillairgé to Abbé Casault, Quebec, 15 Dec. 1857.

13 ASQ, Université 36, no. 59, account of Baillairgé to Laval, Quebec, 21 Jan. 1856.

14 ANQ, gr. Edouard Lemoine, nos. 347–8, protest and reply, Seminary of Quebec to Pierre Châteauvert, Quebec, 15 May 1855. Châteauvert defended the fact that some stone did not conform to the specifications by explaining that a boat had sunk in the Saint Lawrence River en route from Deschambault to Quebec.

15 Le Canadien, 16 May 1856, 3.

16 An examination of the role of architects from the seventeenth to the nineteenth centuries in Quebec, including that of Thomas Baillairgé, is found in Ramsay Traquair, The Old Architecture of Quebec (Toronto: Macmillan Company of Canada 1947), 93–4. In his Maîtres artisans de chez nous (Montreal: Les éditions du Zodiaque 1942), 55, Marius Barbeau places the decline of skilled craftsmanship in Quebec at about 1840.

17 Baillairgé had at least three apprentices in his office in 1849, as these legal contracts prove: ANQ, gr. Edward Cannon, no. 379, indentures, Charles Larue–Charles Baillairgé, Quebec, 21 March 1849; no. 408, indentures, Laughlin Smith–Charles Baillairgé, 24 April 1849; no. 525, indentures, Eugène Larue–Charles Baillairgé, Quebec, 21 Nov. 1849. The apprentices paid £20 or £25 and pledged to act "in a decent and becoming manner as an apprentice to any liberal profession ought to do"; Baillairgé undertook to instruct them and issued certificates at the end of their training. It was Eugène Larue who drew the plan for Bilodeau's store. AVQ, fonds Charles Baillairgé, no. 1–12, plan for Bilodeau store, Quebec, Nov. 1849.

18 NA, RG II, vol. 19, no. 19,850, letter from Baillairgé to Chabot, Quebec, 7 Jan. 1853. Among these apprentices were three in surveying, namely Frédéric Bélanger, Etienne Grondin, and George Le Bouthillier. ANQ, gr. Thomas Gauvin, no. 107, brevet de cléricature, Frédéric Bélanger to Charles

Baillairgé, Quebec, 17 Jan. 1850; no. 134, brevet de cléricature, George Le Bouthillier to Charles Baillairgé, Quebec, 12 May 1850; no. 140, brevet de cléricature, Etienne Grondin to Charles Baillairgé, Quebec, 2 July 1850. Baillairgé signed as a guarantor for their Lower Canada Land Surveyors' Bonds. NA, RG 4 B 28, vol. 135, no. 2298, Bond of Frédéric Bélanger, Quebec, 8, Feb. 1853; no. 1723, Bond of George Le Bouthillier, Quebec, 11 Jan. 1854.

19 ANQ, gr. Alexandre-Benjamin Sirois, no. 10,363, brevet de cléricature, Charles-Édouard Gauvin to Charles Baillairgé, Quebec, 14 April 1871.

20 Including the apprenticeships mentioned in notes 17 and 18, the following list constitutes Baillairgé's known apprentices and the year in which they were bound by indentures: Charles Larue (1849), Eugène Larue (1849), Laughlin Smith (1849), Frédéric Bélanger (1850), Etienne Grondin (1850), George Le Bouthillier (1850), Elzéar Lavergne (1855), Charles-Edouard Michaud (1859), Samuel O'Brien (1859), Ovide Paris (1859), Eugène-Etienne Taché (1860), René Steckel (1862), Jules-Emile Taché (1870), Charles-Edouard Gauvin (1871), Pierre-Marie-Alphonse Genest (1873) and Charles-Auguste Parent (1874). ANQ, gr. Charles Cinq-Mars, no. 1062, brevet, Elzéar Lavergne to Charles Baillairgé, Quebec, 4 Sept. 1855; no. 1497, brevet, Charles-Edouard Michaud to Charles Baillairgé, Quebec, 17 Oct. 1859; gr. Philippe Huot, no. 2492, indenture [architecture], Samuel O'Brien to Charles Baillairgé, Quebec, 14 Sept. 1859; no. 2771, indenture [surveying] Samuel O'Brien to Charles Baillairgé, Quebec, 8 May 1860; gr. Charles Cinq-Mars, no. 1480, brevet, Ovide Paris to Charles Baillairgé, Quebec, 4 July 1859; no. 1530, brevet, Ovide Paris to Charles Baillairgé, Quebec, 13 April 1860; gr. Philippe Huot, no. 2622, brevet, Eugène-Etienne Taché to Charles Baillairgé, Quebec, 18 Jan. 1860; gr. Charles Cinq-Mars, no. 1639, brevet d'arpentage, René Steckel to Charles Baillairgé, Quebec, 17 July 1862; gr. Jean-Alfred Charlebois, no. 283, brevet de cléricature, Jules-Emile Taché to Charles Baillairgé, Quebec, 7 Oct. 1870; gr. Georges-Théophile Tremblay, no. 1992, brevet de cléricature, Pierre-Marie-Alphonse Genest to Charles Baillairgé, Quebec, 11 Jan. 1873; gr. Philippe Huot, no. 7022, brevet de cléricature, Charles-Auguste Parent to Charles Baillairgé,

Quebec, 21 Jan. 1874.

21 An announcement for the firm appears in Le Canadien, 12 Oct. 1853, 3.

22 NA, RG II, vol. 19, no. 19,850, letter from Baillairgé to Chabot, Quebec, 7 Jan. 1853: "J'ai bien pris soin d'apprendre tout ce que l'on a coutume de négliger & non seulement je suis capable des opérations ordinaires de l'Arpenteur, telles que la division ou le bornage d'un terrain; mais aussi des opérations géodésiques les plus étendues & les plus difficiles, telles que les relevés nécessaires pour une carte géographique, où il faut prendre en considération la courbature de la surface du globe."

23 NA, RG II, vol. 19, no. 19,850, letter from Baillairgé to Chabot, Quebec, 7 Jan. 1853.

24 Charles Baillairgé, Rapport de l'Ex-Ingénieur de la Cité, des travaux faits sous le Maire, Hon. S.N. Parent et le Conseil-de-Ville actuels et sous leurs prédécesseurs durant le dernier tiers de Siècle: 1866 à 1899 (Quebec: C. Darveau [1899]), 72–3. The watercolour survives at the municipal archives in Quebec City. [Charles Baillairgé], Exposition universelle à Paris, an 1900: exhibit de M.C. Baillairgé arcte. et ingr. de Québec, Canada: Système de fonder des piliers de ponts à eau profonde de 100 à 200 pieds ou plus (Quebec: n.p. 1899).

25 Baillairgé, Rapport de l'Ex-Ingénieur 1866–1899 73.

26 Le Canadien, 14 June 1852, 2; 28 July 1852, 2; 6 Oct. 1852, 2; 22 Oct. 1852, 2; 9 May 1853, 4; Charles Baillairgé, "Baillairgé's Marine Revolving Steam Express," CE 5 (1897–8): 166–7.

27 ANQ, P 0092/2, fonds Jean-Jacques Girouard, letter from Thomas Baillairgé to Madame Girouard, Quebec, 11 April 1853.

28 Le Journal de Québec, 10 Sept. 1853, 2.

29 Baillairgé, Description et plan d'un nouveau calorifer, 22.

30 Le Canadien, 19 Jan. 1853, 3; 2 Feb. 1853, 3; several letters of invitation from the secretaries of the Institut canadien and the Association de la chambre de lecture de Saint-Roch are conserved in MQ, cahier Charles Baillairgé, n.p.

31 "Lecture à St-Roch," Le Canadien, 21 Jan. 1853, 2.

32 Le Canadien, 4 Feb. 1853, 2.

CHAPTER 3

1 For the identification of buildings and their cost, see Appendix 1, summary catalogue of architectural works by Charles Baillairgé. Although the catalogue of architectural works is as complete a list as current research permits and provides a valid basis for the evaluation of his work, it should be kept in mind that the true extent of Charles Baillairgé's practice is revealed in his 1853 letter to Chabot in which he claims by that date to have designed and supervised over sixty houses, shops, warehouses, churches, and presbyteries. NA, RG 11, vol. 19, no. 19,850, letter from Charles Baillairgé to Hon. Jean Chabot, Quebec, 7 Jan. 1853.

2 These observations are based on general knowledge of building in Quebec City acquired through work as a team member for A.J.H. Richardson's work on Old Quebec for the Canadian Inventory of Historic Building from 1970 to 1975 and on a general impression acquired through reading Le Canadien from 1846 to 1860, inclusive.

3 Jean Hamelin and Yves Roby, Histoire économique du Québec 1851–1896 (Montreal: Fides 1971), 77–84; Albert Faucher, Québec en amérique au XIXᵉ siècle: essai sur les caractères économiques de la laurentie (Montreal: Fides 1973), 70–2; Narcisse Rosa, La construction des navires à Québec et ses environs, grèves et naufrages (Quebec: Imprimerie Léger Brousseau 1897), 14

4 The drawing, showing two sections for the church, is illustrated in C. Baillairgé arct. ing. dessins architecturaux (Quebec: Ministère des Affaires culturelles 1979) 19. The 1846 date seems to be erroneous since the drawing clearly belongs to a set dated 1847 and since the purchase of a site for the church did not occur until August 1846. Saint-Jean-Baptiste de Québec: album publié à l'occasion du 50ᵉ anniversaire de l'érection canonique de la paroisse et du jubilé d'or de Mgr J.-E. Laberge, curé Quebec: l'action catholique 1936, 49.

5 Luc Noppen, "Le renouveau architectural proposé par Thomas Baillairgé au Québec, de 1820 à 1850," doctoral thesis, Université Toulouse-Le Mirail, 1976, 377.

6 Ibid., 379.

7 M.-A. Laugier, Essai sur l'architecture, reprint of 1755 ed. (Farnsborough, Hants: Gregg Press 1966), 10–11.

8 See Appendix 3, Bibliography, Architectural Library of Charles Baillairgé, under Durand and Rondelet; Henry-Russell Hitchcock, "The Doctrine of J.-N.-L. Durand and its Application in Northern Europe," Architecture Nineteenth and Twentieth Centuries, 3rd ed. (Harmondsworth, Middlesex: Penguin 1968), 20–3.

9 Laugier, Essai, 178–9.

10 James Macpherson Lemoine, Quebec Past and Present (Quebec: Augustin Côté 1876), 398.

11 Le Journal de Québec, 6 Sept. 1849, 2; James Macpherson Lemoine, Queen's Birthday, 1880: Quebec, Its Gates and Environs (Quebec: Morning Chronicle 1880), 83; Lemoine, Quebec Past and Present, 398.

12 Louise Voyer, Églises disparues (Quebec: Libre expression 1981), 50, 52.

13 Alan Gowans, "Notre-Dame de Montréal," JSAH 11 (March 1952): 20–6; Franklin Toker, The Church of Notre-Dame in Montreal: An Architectural History (Montreal and London: McGill-Queen's University Press 1970), 77–8; Noppen, "Le renouveau architectural," 254–60, 515–20.

14 CMC, CCFCS, Barbeau colection, sculpture, Baillairgé 1 (30), transcription by Marius Barbeau of letter located in archives of parish of Notre-Dame de Montréal, from Thomas Baillairgé to parish priest, Quebec, 26 Feb. 1824.

15 Jacques-François Blondel, Cours d'architecture, ou traité de la décoration, distribution et construction des bâtiments (Paris: Desaint 1771–7), vol. 1, 81–4; ASQ, manuscrit M–129, tablette 4, Jérôme Demers, Précis d'architecture pour servir de suite au traité élémentaire de physique à l'usage du Séminaire de Québec, Quebec, 1828, articles 11 and 12. Blondel wrote that "l'architecture gothique … était massive et pesante; la moderne dont nous parlons, fut peut-être trop légère, trop délicate & trop chargée & de mauvais goût." Blondel, Cours, vol. 1, 82–3.

16 Wesleyan church, 42, rue Saint-Stanislas, Quebec (1848–50), is documented by A.J.H. Richardson, "Guide to Buildings in the Old City of Quebec," APT, 2, nos. 3–4 (1970): 64, and illustrated in Luc Noppen, Claude Paulette, and Michel Tremblay, Québec: trois siècles d'architecture (Quebec: Libre expression 1979), 170.

17 AAQ, 61 CD, Sainte-Marguerite, 1–149, letter from Charles Baillairgé to Monseigneur Baillargeon, Quebec, 16 June 1860.

18 Mathilde Brosseau, Gothic Revival in Canadian Architecture in Canadian Historic Sites: Occasional Papers in Archaeology and History, 25 (Ottawa: Parks Canada, Environment Canada 1980), 9.

19 Charles Baillairgé,, "A Plea for a Canadian School of Architecture," CAB 6 (1893): 107.

20 Soeurs de la Charité de Québec, Mère Mallet 1805–1871 et l'Institut des Soeurs de la charité de Québec(Quebec and Montreal: Maison-mère des Soeurs de la Charité 1939), 145–6.

21 Robert Caron, Un couvent du XIXᵉ siècle: la maison des Soeurs de la Charité de Québec (Quebec: Libre expression 1980), 16–8.

22 Ibid., 30–1.

23 NA, RG 11, vol. 89, n.n., report of Messrs Browne, Baillairgé, et al., on the Hospice de la Charité fire, Quebec, 21 June 1854.

24 AAQ, 81 CD, ss Charité de Q., 1–35, letter from Charles Baillairgé to Monseigneur, Quebec, July 1853.

25 Another pupil of Thomas Baillairgé, architect Raphaël Giroux, used double galleries at the same time for the interior of the parish church at Saint-Roch (1848–51), illustrated in Noppen et al., Québec: trois siècles, 187. Charles Baillairgé, however, was the first to use triple galleries, as shown in cross-sections of the chapel of the Soeurs de la Charité dated 1854 in Caron, Un couvent du XIXᵉ siècle, 70.

26 Le Journal de Québec, 13 Sept. 1856, 2. This letter refers to the chapel as rebuilt after the 1854 fire, using Baillairgé's original designs.

27 AAQ, 81 CD, ss Charité de Q., 1–30, letter from Charles Baillairgé to Monseigneur, Quebec, 9 Oct. 1852.

28 "Améliorations locales," Le Journal de Québec, 24 Oct. 1850, 2.

29 The building is located at 1146, rue Saint-Jean. The owners were lawyer François Evanturel and master Joiner Isaac Dorion. The stonework was carried out by master mason George Blaiklock and the plasterwork by associated master masons François Baillairgé and Miles Cavanagh. Bastien et al., Inventaire des marchés, 645.

30 For Henry S. Scott's store, the master mason was again George Blaiklock and the

master joiner Isaac Dorion. Ibid., 295; *Le Journal de Québec*, 11 May 1850, 2. This move towards taller cut-stone commercial blocks also occurred in Kingston, Ontario, in the early 1840s, particularly in the work of architect George Browne (whose connections with Quebec City are well established). Mowat's round-cornered building at Princess and Bagot streets is a close parallel to Patry's building in Quebec City.

31 *Le Journal de Québec*, 11 May 1850, 2.

32 Bilodeau's advertisement first appeared in *Le Canadien*, 29 Sept. 1851, 3.

33 "La Fabrique de Notre-Dame de Québec contre Louis Bilodeau, marchand," *Le Canadien*, 24 Feb. 1854, 2; "M. le rédacteur," *Le Canadien*, 27 Feb. 1854, 2.

34 "Améliorations locales," *Le Journal de Québec*, 24 Oct. 1850, 2: "Combien, en voyant monter lentement ces longues colonnes de pierre, sur lesquelles on plaça une maçonne massive et haute, n'ont-ils pas dit: 'M. Bilodeau n'achèvera jamais cette maison; c'est une entreprise folle, au-dessus de ses forces.' Et si le mauvais temps arrêtait un instant les ouvriers au milieu de leur travail, il y avait bien des voix qui répétaient à l'unisson: 'L'ouvrage est arrêté!'"

35 Tout autour et à peu près à mi-hauteur, entre les deux planchers, circule une vaste galerie supportée par dix colonnes, élégamment ornées, du genre égyptien; on y monte par un vaste escalier situé au fond du magasin et divergeant à droit et à gauche. Dix colonnes, semblables aux premières, supportent le plafond qui est tout en tables renforcées, richement ornementées. La corniche de la galerie est massive et fortement accentuée; une légère et délicate balustrade la couronne dans toute son étendue.

Une magnifique lampe descend du plafond pour éclairer le centre de l'édifice et 66 autres becs de gaze [sic] jettent une clarté inconcevable sur tous les points de ce vaste bâtiment. Ibid.

36 NA, RG, 11, vol. 26, no. 29,692, letter from Charles Baillairgé to François Lemieux, Quebec, 3 May 1856.

37 Many row houses inspired by British prototypes still survive in Old Quebec, including 41–3, rue Saint-Louis (1832–3), 49–51, rue Saint-Louis (1833–4), 48–50, rue Saint-Louis (1830–2), 56, rue Saint-Louis (1830–1), 60–6, rue Saint-Louis (1828–30), 65–7, rue Saint-Louis (1844–5), 9, rue Haldimand (1831–2), 16–18, rue Garneau (1829), 20, rue Garneau (1829), 11–19, rue Sainte-

Angèle (1833–4), and 77–83, rue d'Auteuil (1845). They share common characteristics including three-and-one-half-storey height, off-centre door, side stair hall, second-storey parlour, and smaller third-storey windows. For further details see Richardson, "Guide," 41–54, Christina Cameron and Monique Trépanier, *Vieux-Québec: son Architecture intérieure* (Ottawa: National Museum of Man 1986), and Canadian Inventory of Historic Building.

38 Town houses with recessed arcading which survive in Quebec include 73, rue Sainte-Ursule (1830), 9, rue Haldimand (1831–2), 56, rue Saint-Louis (1832–4), and 29, rue Desjardins (1841–2). Richardson, "Guide," 39–40, 42, 44–5, 47–8.

39 "Des arches seront faites dans la front de la maison sur 2ième étage si le propriétaire le juge à propos et les ravalements seront faits jusqu'à telle hauteur que l'architecte jugera convenable pour la meilleure apparence de la maison." ANQ, gr. Joseph Petitclerc, no. 5612, article 17, marché, François-Xavier Méthot–Isaac Dorion, Quebec, 27 Feb. 1850. The model for this idea is a four-storey brick house with rows of recessed arcading situated at 72, rue Sainte-Ursule (1844–5). Richardson, "Guide," 53–4.

40 The moulding type itself, symmetrical with centre bead, had scarcely changed from work being done by joiners in Quebec fifteen years earlier. Christina Cameron, "Selecting an Appropriate Vernacular Moulding," *APT* 10, no. 4 (1978): 80–7.

41 Minard Lafever, *The Modern Builder's Guide* (New York: Henry C. Sleight 1833), plates 60, 66–70, 75, 77, 80–2. The first person to point our Charles Baillairgé's adoption of Lafever's Greek detail was Richardson in "Guide," 60.

42 Louis Bilodeau had chosen the same motif for the iron railing of his store's balcony. Elzéar Bédard, well-known for his nationalist sympathies, had the scroll newel for his house at 18, rue Mont-Carmel, Quebec, carved with maple leaves and beavers. The latter is illustrated in Richardson, "Guide," 117.

43 James Macpherson Lemoine, *Maple Leaves: Canadien History and Quebec Scenery*, ser. 3 (Quebec: Hunter, Rose 1865), 92, 94; Lemoine, *Monographies et esquisses* (Quebec: n.p. 1885), 204–6, 215–19.

44 France Gagnon-Pratte, *L'Architecture et la nature à Québec au dix-neuvième siècle: les villas* (Quebec: Musée du Québec, Ministère des Affaires culturelles 1980), 70–1.

45 NA, RG, 11, vol. 14, no. 10,388, letter from Charles Baillairgé to Thomas Begley requesting information on proposed Montreal Court House, Quebec, 12 Dec. 1849.

CHAPTER 4

1 The plans and elevations survive in AVQ, fonds Charles Baillairgé, nos. 6A–58 to 6A–66, and are signed and dated by the architect. In Luc Noppen, Claude Paulette, and Michel Tremblay, *Québec, trois siècles d'architecture* (Quebec: Libre expression 1979), 281, the authors incorrectly attribute Baillairgé's 1850 elevation to his 1885 proposal for City Hall.

2 There are many plates which contain similar detail in Lafever's work, see in particular Minard Lafever, *The Beauties of Modern Architecture* (New York: D. Appleton 1835), plates 1, 2, and 25.

3 The evolution of their titles can be traced in individual entries in Geneviève G. Bastien, Doris D. Dubé, and Christina [Cameron] Southam, *Inventaire des marchés de construction des archives civiles de Québec 1800–1870*, in *History and Archaeology/Histoire et archéologie*, 1A–B–C (Ottawa: Parks Canada 1975). Baillairgé's disdain is recorded in ASQ, Université 36, no. 59, letter from Charles Baillairgé to Seminary, Quebec, 15 Dec. 1857, where he writes: "Pour ce qui est de Gauvreau, Patry ou Larue, j'ai honte de dire pour la profession que s'ils savent multiplier les pieds par les picds, ils ignorent la manière d'en faire autant pour les pouces et les ligues."

4 Howard Colvin, "Christopher Staveley," *A Biographical Dictionary of British Architects 1600–1840* (London: John Murray 1978), 777.

5 *Le Canadien*, 16 Oct. 1846, 3.

6 For a synopsis of the careers of George Browne and Goodlatte Richardson Browne see A.J.H. Richardson, "Guide to the Architecturally and Historically Most Significant Buildings in the Old City of Quebec," *APT* 2, nos. 3–4 (1970): 76–7, and A.J.H. Richardson, Geneviève Bastien, Doris Dubé, and Marthe Lacombe, *Quebec City: Architects, Artisans and Builders* (Ottawa: National Museum of Man 1984), 117–21; for a closer examination of George

Browne's work in Kingston see J. Douglas Stewart, "Architecture for a Boom Town: The Primitive and the Neo-baroque in George Browne's Kingston Buildings," *To Preserve & Defend: Essays on Kingston in the Nineteenth Century*, ed. Gerald Tulchinsky (Montreal and London: McGill–Queen's University Press 1976), 37–61.

7   *Le Canadien*, 12 Jan. 1849, 3; Bastien et al., *Inventaire*, IA, 110.

8   "La nouvelle salle de musique de la rue St-Louis," *Le Canadien*, 10 Jan. 1853, 3; *Le Canadien*, 13 Oct. 1851, 2; "Association de la salle de musique de Québec," *Le Canadien*, 18 May 1853, 2.

9   Thomas Baillairgé built the organ for Notre-Dame de Québec as well as a smaller one for his own house, from lead pipes that he imported from France. He used to take George-Frédéric – and probably Charles – with him on his Saturday excursions to tune the cathedral organ. G.-F. Baillairgé, *Notices biographiques. Fascicule no. 3: Thomas Baillairgé … et François-X. Baillairgé* (Joliette: Bureaux de l'étudiant, du couvent et de la famille 1891), 80–1. In June 1851 Baillairgé is listed as secretary in *Le Canadien*, 23 June 1851, 3, but six months later C.R. O'Connor appears as secretary in *Le Canadien*, 29 Dec. 1851, 3.

10   "Association de la salle de musique de Québec," *Le Canadien*, 18 May 1853, 2: "Dans le cas de ce monsieur [Frédéric Mimée, fils, responsible for scenery designs] (de même que dans celui de C. Baillargé [sic], écuyer, l'architecte de l'édifice), le comité se loue d'avoir convenablement encouragé les talents indigènes méritants."

11   Ibid., 12 May 1851, 2; 23 June 1851, 3; 29 Dec. 1851, 3; 26 Jan. 1852, 3.

12   ANQ, gr. Amable Bélanger, no. 1902, agreement, Quebec Music Hall Association–Antoine Pampalon, Quebec, 11 Nov. 1851; AVQ, fonds Charles Baillairgé, no. 6–15, plan and details for concert hall seats, Quebec, n.d.

13   ANQ, gr. Amable Bélanger, no. 1902, agreement, Quebec Music Hall Association–Antoine Pampalon, Quebec, 11 Nov. 1851.

14   Books include the following as listed in the bibliography of Baillairgé's architectural library: Benjamin, Foulston, Gwilt, Hope, Jackson, Knight, Lafever, Nicholson, Normand, and Soane.

15   *The Modern Practice of Staircase and Hand-rail Construction* (1838) was highly specialized, and *The Architectural Instructor* (1856), published posthumously, drops the Greek Revival in favour of later revival styles.

16   Minard Lafever's *The Modern Builder's Guide* (New York: William D. Smith 1841), was one of the books listed in the 1878 inventory of Baillairgé's property. An 1835 copy of *The Beauties of Modern Architecture*, now located in the rare books library of Université Laval, does not bear Baillairgé's signature, although it belonged to the fonds Dussault before being acquired by Laval. Given the fact that another Baillairgé book (Pugin and Willson) came to the same library from the fonds Dussault, it is possible that this copy of Lafever did once belong to Charles Baillairgé.

17   Lafever, *Modern Builder's Guide*, 3–4.

18   Minard Lafever, *The Beauties of Modern Architecture*, intro. Denys Peter Myers (New York: Da Capo Press 1968), vi.

19   Minard Lafever, *The General Instructor* (Newark, NJ: W. Tuttle 1829), 29, plate 10; other illustrations of the temple of Minerva were found in Lafever, *Beauties*, plate 41; *Modern Builder's Guide*, plates 45, 52, 53.

20   James Stuart and Nicholas Revett, *The Antiquities of Athens*, vol. 2 (London: Priestley and Weale 1835), plate IX.

21   Lafever, *Beauties*, plates 1–2; *Modern Builder's Guide*, plates 80, 89.

22   Lafever, *Beauties*, plates 1, 6, 14, 19, 46.

23   "The New Music Hall," *Quebec Mercury*, 20 Jan. 1853, 2.

24   AVQ, fonds Charles Baillairgé, no. 6–12, elevation of door for concert hall, Quebec, n.d.; NA, RG 11, vol. 91, no. 175351, letter from Thomas Begley to D.W. Macdonald about damage done to Music Hall during tenancy of Legislative Assembly, Quebec, 4 May 1855.

25   Charles Baillairgé, *Les progrès du XIXe siècle* ([Québec]: n.p. 1901), 10; NA, RG 11, vol. 91, no. 175351, letter Begley-Macdonald, Quebec, 4 May 1855.

26   NA, RG 11, vol. 21, no. 23418, report from Charles Baillairgé, Thomas Andrews, and Pierre Gauvreau to commissioners of public works on heating system at Music Hall, Quebec, 25 Aug. 1854.

27   Charles Baillairgé, *Description et plan d'un nouveau calorifer [sic] à air chaud, sur le système tubulaire, pour chauffer les édifices privés et publics* (Quebec: Bureau et Marcotte 1853).

28   Charles Baillairgé, *Report of the City Surveyor and Water-Works Engineer for the year 1872–73* (Quebec: C. Darveau 1873), 40–1.

29   Charles Baillairgé, "The Chicago Theatre Fire," *CAB* 17 (1904): 57.

30   *Le Journal de Québec*, 8 Feb. 1853, 2.

31   *Le Canadien*, 7 Feb. 1853, 2.

32   "Inauguration du salon de musique de Québec," *Le Canadien*, 9 Feb. 1853, 2–3: "L'apparence de la salle est vraiment magnifique, les ornements en sont classiques et d'un goût choisi: ses proportions telles qu'on peut tout voir et entendre d'aucune partie de l'appartement."

33   "Music Hall," *Quebec Mercury* [1853], clipping in MQ, cahier Charles Baillairgé, n.p.

34   "Bal de M. Jackson et M. Betts," *Le Canadien*, 26 Oct. 1853, 2.

35   The play was performed on 30 June 1873 in the Salle Jacques Cartier and 4–5 September 1873 at the Music Hall. *L'Événement*, 26 June 1873, 2; MQ, cahier Charles Baillairgé, poster; *L'Événement*, 2 July 1873, 2. The play was apparently never published. "La pièce du feu M. Charles Baillairgé, *Le diable devenu cuisinier* … a-t-elle été publiée?" *BRH*, 31 (1925): 512.

36   Richardson, "Guide," 67; CIHB, group D, 81, rue Dalhousie, Quebec, Quebec, compiled 1970–4.

37   "Maison Têtu," *Le Canadien*, 20 Feb. 1854, 2.

38   AVQ, fonds Charles Baillairgé, nos. 1–25, 1–29, 1–30, details from iron shutters for Têtu store, Quebec, n.d.

39   ANQ, gr. Joseph Petitclerc, no. 7141, marché, Laurent Têtu and Cirice Têtu – Isaac Dorion, Quebec, 12 April 1853.

40   "Maison Têtu," *Le Canadien*, 20 Feb. 1854, 2. "Les MM Têtu sont maintenant engagés exclusivement dans le commerce en gros, et pour faire face à l'extension croissante de leurs affaires, qui est devenue nécessaire, ils ont construit un magnifique magasin surpassant de beaucoup en solidité, en capacité et en commodité tout ce que nous avons dans ce genre en cette ville, et égal à aucun magasin existant dans la prov-

ince ou aux États-Unis."

41 The house, situated at 16, rue Saint-Denis, was erected for merchant Hammond Gowen by contractor Joseph Archer in 1850–1. ANQ, gr. Edward George Cannon, no. 612, contract, Hammond Gowen-Joseph Archer, Quebec, 13 March 1850.

42 Detailed information about these buildings comes from the building contracts, catalogue of architectural works by Charles Baillairgé, residential, in Christina Cameron, "Charles Baillairgé, Architecte," doctoral thesis, Laval University, 1982, Appendix II.

43 AVQ, fonds Charles Baillairgé, nos. 1–78 to 1–82, plans, elevations, and sections for T.J. Murphy house, Quebec, n.d. [1861].

44 ANQ, gr. Joseph Petitclerc, no. 7032, marché, Charles Drolet – Jean Vézina, Quebec, 21 Feb. 1853. Gutta percha was a tough flexible substance, greyish black in colour, that came from the condensed juice of various Malayan trees.

45 Lafever, Young Builder's Instructor, 43, plate 4.

46 ANQ, gr. Joseph Petitclerc, no. 6891, marché, Cirice Têtu-Isaac Dorion, Quebec, 16 Nov. 1852.

47 The earliest use of the flanked window is in the house located at 43, rue d'Auteuil, Quebec, designed in 1834 by British architect Frederick Hacker. The window, used in conjunction with the Doric attached columns of the doorway, is consciously Greek Revival. It is a single decorative window, used as the central focus of the design; Baillairgé enlarges on this idea to use the window type for all the windows of the Têtu house. Richardson, "Guide," 38–9; Bastien et al., Inventaire, IB, 808.

48 Lafever, Beauties, plates I, II, 13, 14, 25.

49 One of the plasterers for the Têtu house, Thomas Murphy, also owned a copy of George Jackson and Sons, Part of the Collection of Relievo Decorations as Executed in Papier Maché & Carton Pierre (London: George Jackson and Sons n.d. [185?]). His well-thumbed copy, signed "T.J. Murphy," then "J.F. Peachy, Quebec, 1857," now belongs to the library of Laval University, NK/8555/J12/1856/Ex.A.

50 NA, RG II, vol. 314, no. 45724, letter from Cirice Têtu to Hon. John Rose offering his house, Quebec, 7 March 1860.

51 R.H. Hubbard, Antoine Plamondon 1802–1895: Théophile Hamel 1817–1870: Two Painters of Quebec (Ottawa: National Gallery of Canada 1970), 104–5, 164–5.

52 Charles Baillairgé, Divers, ou les enseignements de la vie (Quebec: Darveau 1898), 47, 152–3.

53 AVQ, fonds Charles Baillairgé, no. 1–55, elevation for Bilodeau house, Quebec, 1853.

54 ANQ, gr. John Greaves Clapham, no. 3220, contract, Joseph W. Leaycraft-William MacKay and John Walker, Quebec, 3 July 1857.

55 France Gagnon-Pratte, L'architecture et la nature à Québec au dix-neuvième siècle: les villas (Quebec: Musée du Québec, Ministère des Affaires culturelles 1980), 78, 195.

56 ANQ, gr. Joseph Petitclerc, no. 7244, marché, Eugène Chinic-Isaac Dorion, Quebec, 13 June 1853.

57 Henri Têtu, Histoire des familles Têtu, Bonenfant, Dionne et Perreault [Quebec: Dussault, Proulx 1898], 553; Pierre-Georges Roy, Old Manors, Old Houses (Quebec: Ls.-A. Proulx 1927), 219; Raymonde Gauthier, Les manoirs du Québec (Quebec: Fidès 1976), 162–3; Roland Martin, Saint-Roch-des-Aulnaies in Cahier d'histoire 10 (La Pocatière: Société historique de la côte-du-sud 1975), 82–3. Apparently basing her hypothesis on the fact that Pascal-Amable Dionne's father, Amable Dionne, purchased the property in 1833, Raymonde Gauthier conjectures that the manor house was built in the 1830s and modified by Charles Baillairgé in the 1850s. What she fails to take into account is the fact that Amable Dionne owned two seigniories, and that he lived and died in his manor house at Sainte-Anne-de-la-Pocatière. In 1851 he deeded the property at Saint-Roch-des-Aulnaies to his wife and his son Pascal-Amable, then completing his law studies at Quebec City. When the father died in 1852, the son inherited half the seigniory and probably had the manor house erected soon after.

58 Têtu, Histoire des familles, 230, 552.

59 Jean-Claude Marsan, Montréal en évolution (Montréal: Fidès 1974), 127–8; Roy, Old Manors, 211–15.

60 Louis-Marie Normand, Paris moderne, ou choix de maisons construites dans les nouveaux quartiers de la capitale et dans ses environs, vol. 2 (Paris: l'auteur, Bance fils and Carilian-Goeury 1843), plate 12.

61 Têtu, Histoire des familles, 554.

62 NA, RG II, vol. 19, no. 19,850, letter from Baillairgé to Chabot, Quebec, 7 Jan. 1853: "Je n'ai jamais encore eu à faire, une bâtisse où il m'ait fallu déployer plus qu'une petite partie de ma capacité; mais, qu'on me dise, qu'il y a tel édifice à construire, & que dans cet édifice, il faut tant d'appartements d'à-peu-près telles dimensions & devant servir à tels usages, & je saurai bien tout construire, distribuer & décorer à propos; car il ne faut pas croire que pour être architecte, l'on doive nécessairement connaître les besoins de tout le monde; mais seulement connaissant les exigences, il faut savoir y pourvoir, ce dont je me sens surtout capable. En un mot je puis dire avec assurance que je me sens au fait de tout ce que l'on pourrait attendre d'un bon architecte."

63 Le Canadien, 21 Jan. 1853, 2.

CHAPTER 5

1 L'Université Laval 1852–1952 (Quebec: Les Presses universitaires Laval 1952), 9–12.

2 "L'Université Laval," Le Journal de Québec, 7 Aug. 1856, 1.

3 James Macpherson Lemoine, Quebec Past and Present (Quebec: Augustin Côté & Co. 1876), 361.

4 Le Canadien, 22 Sept. 1854, 2; ASQ, SME, adoption of plans for pensionnat, Quebec, 16 April 1855.

5 "L'Université Laval," Le Journal de Québec, 7 Aug. 1856, 1; Le Canadien, 9 Sept. 1857, 4; ASQ, Université 36, no. 66, account from Charles Baillairgé to Seminary, Quebec, 23 Aug. 1858; SME, payment for Charles Baillairgé, Québec, 6 Sept. 1858.

6 ASQ, Université 36, no. 56, comparative cost estimate for sloped roof of School of Medicine and platform roof by Charles Baillairgé, Quebec, 25 June 1856; Université 36, no. 63, letter from Charles Baillairgé to abbé Casault, Quebec, 13 June 1857; Université 36, no. 47, letter from Charles Baillairgé to abbé Casault, Québec, n.d. [1856].

7 ASQ, Université 36, no. 63, letter from Baillairgé to Casault, Quebec, 13 June 1857; ASQ, Journal du Séminaire, vol. 2, new French roof for central pavilion, Quebec, 31 May 1875.

8 Lemoine, Quebec Past and Present, 362.

9 ANQ, gr. Edouard Lemoine, no. 379, marché, Seminary of Quebec-Phillip

Whitty, Quebec, 27 Nov. 1855; ASQ, Université 36, no. 58, account of Charles Baillairgé to Laval University, Quebec, 21 Jan. 1856.

10 "The Laval University," *Morning Chronicle*, 28 June 1856, 2.

11 ASQ, Université 36, no. 38, specifications for pensionnat by Charles Baillairgé, Quebec, 13 March 1855; "L'Université Laval," *Le Journal de Québec*, 7 Aug. 1856, 1–2.

12 Carl W. Condit, *American Building: Materials and Techniques from the First Colonial Settlements to the Present* (Chicago and London: University of Chicago Press 1968), 81.

13 Ibid. Although American builders had occasionally used cast iron for structural supports since the 1820s, more regular use of cast iron in construction dates from the 1850s, when James Bogardus, the technological innovator, and Daniel Badger, the marketing specialist, created an important industry of cast-iron architectural components, facades, and even entire buildings. Bogardus produced the first complete cast-iron building in 1850, thereby paving the way for the development of the steel frame structures of the 1890s.

14 Ibid., 76–84; Margot Gayle, David W. Look, and John G. Waite, *Metals in America's Historic Buildings* (Washington: Technical Preservation Services Division, Heritage Conservation and Recreation Service, U.S. Department of the Interior 1980), 42–50. Cast iron was used as early as the thirteenth century in England but, since it could only be produced in small quantities, it was never used for large building components. With the development of new smelting techniques during the Industrial Revolution, greater quantities of cast iron could be produced at reasonable cost, thereby increasing the use of the metal in construction. Though reputedly fireproof, cast iron had a tendency to collapse under intense heat.

15 The earliest known example of a full cast-iron façade in Canada is the Coombs building, 1883–5 Granville Street, Halifax, built in 1860. C. Anne Hale and Janet Wright, "Old Coombs English Shoe Store, Halifax," Agenda paper, Historic Sites and Monuments Board of Canada, June 1980 135–52.

16 ASQ, Université 36, no. 57, letter from Phillip Whitty to Rev. Farques concerning cast iron columns, Quebec, 6 May 1856.

17 Charles Baillairgé, *Rapport de l'Ex-Ingénieur de la Cité, des travaux faits sous le Maire, Hon. S.N. Parent et le Conseil-de-Ville actuels et sous leurs prédécesseurs durant le dernier tiers de Siècle: 1866 à 1899* (Quebec: C. Darveau [1899]), 53: "Au corps central de la grande batisse ... il n'y a pas eu un quart de pouce de refoulement dans une hauteur de 80 pieds, en y plaçant les colonnes, fer sur fer sans discontinuité du bas en haut de l'édifice."

18 "L'Université Laval," *Le Journal de Québec*, 7 Aug. 1856, 2.

19 AVQ, fonds Charles Baillairgé, no. 2–39, detail of balustrade of Laval University, Quebec, n.d. The drawing is reproduced in the exhibition catalogue *C. Baillairgé Arct. Ing. dessins architecturaux* (Quebec: Ministère des Affaires culturelles 1979), 10.

20 ASQ, Université 36, no. 44, estimate of cost by Charles Baillairgé for iron balustrade for large ceremonial hall, Quebec, n.d.

21 The drawing is apparently the work of Abbé Charles-Auguste Laverdière, based on a Livernois photograph of 1860, MAC, IBC, fonds Morisset, vol. 1/13887–957 (1), dossier Québec, Québec, Université Laval. The photograph has not been located. The drawing belongs to the collection of the archives du Séminaire de Québec. A curious composite photograph, based on the drawing, exists in copy negative form only at the National Archives of Canada (c-9233) and was published (in truncated form) in *L'Université Laval 1852–1952*, 13.

22 *Le Journal de Québec*, 25 Aug. 1860, 1: "La grande salle de l'Université Laval ... était simplement mais richement décorée. Un trône avait été érigé pour le Prince, en arrière duquel était une tenture magnifique, surmontée de la couronne du prince de Galles. Partout régnait l'élégance et cette sévérité classique qui disait à tous les yeux qu'on était dans le temple saint de la science."

23 "Laval University," *Morning Chronicle*, 28 June 1856, 2.

24 H.-J.-J.-B. Chouinard, *Fête nationale des canadiens-français célébrée à Québec en 1880* (Quebec: A Coté et Cie 1881), 72–5.

25 Pierre-Georges Roy, *Toutes petites choses du régime anglais*, vol. 2 (Quebec: Edition Garneau 1946), 98–9.

26 Chouinard, *Fête nationale*, 73.

27 Pierre-Georges Roy, *Les monuments commémoratifs de la province de Québec*, vol. 1 (Quebec: Ls-A. Proulx 1923), 13–14, 17, 161–5.

28 Lemoine, *Quebec Past and Present*, 297.

29 Chouinard, *Fête nationale*, 80; "Monument at St. Foye, near Quebec," *London Illustrated News*, 2 Jan. 1864, 13.

30 ANQ, gr. Joseph Petitclerc, no. 7610, marché, George Hall-Toussaint Vézina, Quebec, 6 Feb. 1854.

31 ANQ, gr. Alexandre Benjamin Sirois, no. 5582, marché, Caisse d'économie Notre-Dame de Québec–Phillip Whitty, Quebec, 6 May 1857.

32 "Construction nouvelle," *Le Journal de Québec*, 24 Dec. 1858, 2.

33 Preliminary plans for this building were drawn by Baillairgé in 1852 but were not carried out at that time. AVQ, fonds Charles Baillairgé, nos. 1–35 to 1–42, plans, elevations, and sections for Taché building, Quebec, 1852. Assessment rolls indicate that the new building appeared in 1859.

34 "Construction nouvelle," *Le Journal de Québec*, 24 Dec. 1858, 2.

CHAPTER 6

1 In the case of the church at l'Isle-Verte, the parish called in 1853 for tenders from contractors to complete the walls, gables, roof, and steeples of the church. The formulation of the announcement, "pour l'achèvement de la dite église," gives the impression that the church had already been started at some earlier date. There is no mention of an architect in the notice which simply states that "pour plans et devis, s'adresser au curé du lieu." Since Baillairgé lists the church at l'Isle-Verte as one of his accomplishments, one can assume that he merely sold the plans to the parish and had no further connection with the construction. *Le Journal de Québec*, 17 Nov. 1853, 3; *Le Canadien*, 18 Nov. 1853, 3; Charles Baillairgé, *Bilan de M. Baillairgé, comme Architecte, Ingénieur, Arpenteur-Géomètre, durant les 21 ans, avant d'entrer au service de la Cité, ès-qualité d'Ingénieur des Ponts et Chaussées, ou de 1845 à 1866. Puis – entre heures – de 1866 à 1899, mais non compris les Travaux Civiques relatés dans un rapport supplémentaire* (Quebec): n.p. [1899], v.

2 ANQ, gr. Edward George Cannon, no. 3177, contract, Ursuline Sisters–Edouard Gaboury, Quebec, 23 April 1853.

3 AAQ, 61 CD, Ste-Marguerite, 1–149, letter from Charles Baillairgé to Monseigneur Baillargeon, Quebec, 16 June 1860.

4 Honorius Provost, *Sainte-Marie de la Nouvelle-Beauce: histoire religieuse*, vol. 1 (Quebec: la Société historique de la Chaudière 1967), 97–8.

5 Ibid., 143–9.

6 For Chalmers Free Presbyterian church see Geneviève G. Bastien, Doris D. Dubé, and Christina [Cameron] Southam, *Inventaire des marchés de construction des archives civiles de Québec 1800–1870* in *History and Archaeology/Histoire et archéologie*, 1A (Ottawa: Parks Canada 1975), 151–2, and Mathilde Brosseau, *Gothic Revival in Canadian Architecture* in *Canadian Historic Sites: Occasional Papers in Archaeology and History*, 25 (Ottawa: Parks Canada, Environment Canada 1980), 38–9. For Saint-Colomb de Sillery see Bastien et al., *Inventaire des marchés*, 1C, 1144–5, and A.J.H. Richardson, Geneviève Bastien, Doris Dubé, and Marthe Lacombe, *Quebec City: Architects, Artisans and Builders* (Ottawa: National Museum of Man 1984), 121.

7 Phoebe Stanton, *Pugin* (New York: Viking Press 1971), 84–5.

8 John Henry Parker, *A Glossary of Terms Used in Grecian, Roman, Italian and Gothic Architecture*, 5th ed., vol. 1 (Oxford: David Bogue 1851), 508.

9 Provost, *Sainte-Marie*, 146, 148–9.

10 Charles Baillairgé, *A Summary of Papers, Read at Different Times before the Royal Society of Canada, the Canadian Association of Civil Engineers and Architects, and Literary and Scientific Societies, or Which Have Appeared Occasionally in Scientific and Other Publications* (Quebec: H. Chassé Printing [1903], 67.

11 *CAB*, 3 (1890), opp. 78; "Province of Quebec Association of Architects," *CAB*, 5 (1892): 96.

12 Ibid.; ANDQ, carton 24, nos. 173–4, letter from Charles Baillairgé to fabrique Notre-Dame de Québec, Quebec, 9 May 1858; nos. 175–81, tenders for chapel at cimetière Belmont addressed to Charles Baillairgé, Quebec, May–June 1858; "Le nouveau cimetière de Saint-Roch," *Le Canadien*, 1 June 1855, 2.

13 ANDQ, carton 8, nos. 78–9, marchés for presbytery of Saint-Jean-Baptiste, Quebec, 14 Oct. 1858; carton 8, no. 82, letter from Charles Baillairgé to Charles Cinq-Mars, Quebec, 9 Oct. 1858.

14 ANDQ, carton 8, no. 82, letter from Baillairgé to Cinq-Mars, Quebec, 9 Oct. 1858.

15 *Le Journal de Québec*, 7 Feb. 1860, 3.

16 AAQ, 61 CD, Ste-Marguerite, 1–148, certificate, Quebec, 31 May 1860. The architects and builders who signed the petition were Louis Larose, Thomas Fournier[?], Louis Amiot, Isaac Dorion, Joseph Breton & Frère, Chs. Baillairgé, F.X. Berlinguet, Edwd Staveley, F.X. Malouin, Joseph Archer, and S. & C. Peters.

17 AAQ, 61 CD, Ste-Marguerite, 1–149, letter from Charles Baillairgé to Monseigneur Baillairgeon, Quebec, 16 June 1860:

Je vous demande en grâce, ne forcez pas les paroissiens de Ste-Marguerite malgré leur volonté et surtout malgré le certificat de tous les meilleurs ouvriers de Québec à exécuter un plan qui devra leur coûter beaucoup d'argent tout en mettant leur vie en danger et en les obligeant de recommencer dans 20 ans une église qui … devrait durer au moins cent ans …

Vous les adressez tous chez Giroux ou à défaut de ce dernier chez Bernard. Monseigneur, je vous déclare devant Dieu que plusieurs curés (au moins 5 ou 6) se sont plaint à moi de l'obligation de votre part de faire faire des plans par Giroux ou d'autres …

Vous persistez à me répudier, quoique j'ai été employé pour tant d'années par Monseigneur l'Archevêque … Vous avez le malheur de vous fier trop à votre propre goût et jugement en affaire de plans d'Eglise. Ce n'est pas vous insulter que de vous dire qu'Excellent Evêque vous pouvez être très indifférent comme architecte. Chacun son métier … en tout ce qui concerne la Religion et l'Eglise je dois me soumettre à mon Evêque; mais en matière de construction je prétends m'y entendre; et j'empêcherai par tout moyen légal que l'on ne construise en ce pays d'après les plans tellement défectueux.

CHAPTER 7

1 Brian Hallett, *Public Records Division General Inventory Series: no. 8, Records of the Department of Public Works (RG 11)*, Peter Gillis and Glenn T. Wright, eds. (Ottawa: Public Archives Canada 1977), xi, 1; J.E. Hodgetts, *Pioneer Public Service: An Administrative History of the United Canadas, 1841–1867* (Toronto: University of Toronto Press 1955), 177, 190–2.

2 Hodgetts, *Pioneer Public Service*, 176. The portrait of Killaly was painted by the Reverend Agar Adamson in *Salmon-Fishing in Canada*, ed. Colonel J.E. Alexander (London 1860), and cited by Hodgetts.

3 The letter from John Langton, auditor of the Province of Canada and vice-chancellor of the University of Toronto, to his brother, dated 9 November 1856, is cited by Hodgetts, *Pioneer Public Service*.

4 Canada (Province), Statutes, 9 Vic., ch. 37, an Act to amend the law constituting the Board of Works, 1846.

5 Hodgetts, *Pioneer Public Service*, 193–4.

6 Douglas Owram, *Building for Canadians: A History of the Department of Public Works 1840–1960* (Ottawa: Public Works Canada 1979), 41.

7 Hodgetts, *Pioneer Public Service*, 4.

8 NA, RG 11, vol. 100, no. 10,086, letter from Charles Baillairgé to department asking for information so as to prepare plans for Montreal Court House, Quebec, 8 Nov. 1849.

9 George-Frédéric Baillairgé, civil engineer and surveyor, joined the Department of Public Works on 23 November 1844. He began as an assistant draughtsman, working principally on canal construction, though he apparently doubled as a translator. He eventually rose through the ranks to become deputy minister of the Department of Public Works in 1879. NA, RG 11, vol. 8, no. 859, letter from G.F. Baillairgé to Commissioner of Public Works, Montreal, 28 Feb. 1849; "Baillairgé, George Frederick," *A Cyclopaedia of Canadian Biography being Chiefly Men of the Time*, ed. Geo. Maclean Rose [Toronto: Rose Publishing Company 1888], 69–70.

10 "TRAVAUX PUBLICS – L'honorable M. Bourret, commissaire adjoint, est attendu à Québec ces jours-ci, avec pouvoir d'ordonner la démolition de la vieille aile du palais législatif … et de recevoir des soumissions pour compléter l'édifice … Ce sera, dit-on M. Baillairgé, du même département, qui surveillera ces travaux." *Le Canadien*, 23 Aug. 1850, 2.

11 NA, RG 11, vol. 15, no. 12,239, letter from Charles Baillairgé to Thomas Begley concerning Parliament wing, Quebec, 26 Aug. 1850. No drawings have ever been located for Baillairgé's proposal, suggesting his attempt was limited to correspondence

with the Department of Public Works.

12 NA, RG II, vol. 19, no. 20,000, letter from Charles Baillairgé to Hon. Jean Chabot stating rate at which he will superintend erection of a balustrade around Parliament Building, Quebec, 21 June 1853; vol. 125, no. 13,559, letter from Thomas Begley to Charles Baillairgé accepting proposition, Quebec, 22 June 1853.

13 NA, RG II, vol. 19, no. 19,850, letter from Baillairgé to Chabot, Quebec, 7 Jan. 1853.

14 NA, RG II, vol. 24, no. 27,339, letter from Charles Baillairgé to Hon. François Lemieux, sending account for professional services, Quebec, 18 Sept. 1855.

15 NA, RG II, vol. 23, no. 26,139, letter from Charles Baillairgé to Thomas Begley, secretary of public works, reporting on Marine Hospital railing, Quebec, 4 June 1855.

16 Ibid. The authority for transferring the works from the Parliament site to the Marine Hospital, with a new total cost of £1521 (being the difference between the sum total for the wall at Parliament and the sum claimed for indemnification), was an extract from a report of the Executive Council on matters of state found in NA, RG II, vol. 52, no. 1254, public building authorities, Quebec, 22 Feb. 1854.

17 NA, RG II, vol. 22, no. 25,153, progress report from Charles Baillairgé to Thomas Begley, Quebec, 7 March 1855.

18 NA, RG II, vol. 127, no. 16,594, letter from Thomas Begley to Charles Baillairgé concerning irregularity of Pye's certificate, Quebec, 5 Jan. 1855; vol. 22, no. 24,542, explanation from Charles Baillairgé concerning Pye's certificate, Quebec, 8 Jan. 1855; vol. 127, no. 17,203, letter from Thomas Begley to Charles Baillairgé concerning irregularities in McDonald's account, Quebec, 27 March 1855; vol. 22, no. 25,411, explanation from Charles Baillairgé concerning McDonald's certificate, Quebec, 29 March 1855; vol. 127, no. 17,726, letter from C.D. Shanly to Charles Baillairgé concerning irregularities in Whitty's account, Quebec, 1 June 1855; vol. 23, no. 26,145, explanation from Charles Baillairgé concerning Whitty's account, Quebec, 4 June 1855; vol. 127, no. 17,816, letter from Thomas Begley to Charles Baillairgé concerning irregularities in Châteauvert's account, Quebec, 30 June 1855.

19 NA, RG II, vol. 24, no. 27,339, letter from Baillairgé to Lemieux, Quebec, 18 Sept. 1855.

20 Robert Caron, *Un couvent du XIXᵉ siècle* (Quebec: Libre expression 1980), 62–72.

21 NA, RG II, vol. 35, no. 40,031, letter from Charles Baillairgé to Hon. John Rose, Quebec, 15 Feb. 1859.

22 Ibid.; vol. 91, no. 1502, letter from Charles Baillairgé to Hon. L.V. Sicotte, Quebec, 6 Sept. 1858.

23 NA, RG II, vol. 20, no. 22,100, estimation from Charles Baillairgé for cost of constructing new Custom House, Quebec, 15 March 1854.

24 MQ, cahier Charles Baillairgé, n.p., transcript of letter from O.L. Robitaille to mayors of Boston, New York, and Portland, Quebec, 23 Jan. 1856:

Je prends la liberté de vous adresser Charles Baillargé [sic], écuyer, architecte de cette ville, qui doit se rendre prochainement à Boston, New-York & Portland, chargé d'un mission spéciale de la part du Gouvernement Canadien.

Ce Gouvernement ayant décidé de faire construire en cette ville un édifice destiné à servir de Douane envoie Mr. Baillargé visiter ceux qui ont la même destination aux États-Unis et dans lesquels où l'on a porté très loin les perfectionnements dans la distribution intérieure surtout.

La ville de Québec regardera comme faits à elle-mème les services que vous pourrez rendre à Mr. Baillargé touchant l'objet de sa Mission.

25 NA, RG II, vol. 26, no. 29,844, letter from Charles Baillairgé to to Thomas Begley asking return of his plans, Quebec, 16 May 1856.

26 NA, RG II, vol. 26, no. 29,692, letter from Charles Baillairgé to Hon. François Lemieux, Quebec, 3 May 1856.

27 Ibid.: "Sans doute, si j'avais voulu faire un dôme pour paraître à l'extérieur et être vu du même coup d'oeil que le reste de l'édifice, sans doute, j'aurais très mal réussi; mais ... je n'ai jamais eu de semblable idée.... Il suffit de poser une règle touchant le dessus de mon abat-jour et le rebord de la corniche ou couverture de la bâtisse et l'on verra de combien il faudra prolonger cette ligne pour lui faire atteindre un point au-dessus du niveau du sol égal à la hauteur de l'oeil ... il faudrait être éloigné de l'édifice pour pouvoir même apercevoir la partie supérieure de l'abat-jour."

28 NA, RG II, vol. 27, no. 32,175, explanation from Charles Baillairgé to chief commissioner of public works on his supervision of works at the Marine Hospital, Quebec, 22 Dec. 1856: "Lorsque j'ai fait mes premiers plans de Douane ... l'on était entiché de moi; l'on parlait de m'envoyer en Angleterre aux frais du Gouvernement – M. Chabot pourrait vous en dire quelque chose – le Gouverneur et M. Hincks avaient admiré mon plan et ont dit à cette époque qu'ils ne savaient pas que dans ce pays il fut possible de faire si bon."

29 Ibid.: "Comme certaines personnes mal informées, ou pour me nuire, se plaisent à répéter que j'en ai fait coûter £2500 au Gouvernement pour les *Water Closets* dernièrement faits à l'hôpital de la Marine, et que c'est pour cette raison que j'ai perdue la confiance du Gouvernement et qu'on ne me donne plus rien à faire, je dois, en justice pour moi-même réfuter de toutes mes forces de telles assertions."

30 Ibid.

31 NA, RG II, vol. II, vol. 22, no. 25,163, report from Charles Baillairgé, Pierre Gauvreau, Adolphe Larue, and G.R. Browne recommending purchase of Jones property as site for new Custom House, Quebec, 8 March 1855; vol. 91, no. 1502, letter from Baillairgé to Sicotte, Quebec, 6 Sept. 1858.

32 NA, RG II, vol. 27, no. 32,175, explanation from Baillairgé, Quebec, 22 Dec. 1856: "Regardez donc, me dit-il, cet avertissement où M. Gauvreau signe son nom comme architecte du Bureau; je suis contre cela M. Baillairgé entièrement, M. Gauvreau n'est pas un homme de l'éducation et de la capacité requises pour cette place; c'est vous M. Baillairgé qui devriez être l'architecte du Gouvernement. J'en ai déjà parlé deux ou trois fois à M. Chabot et je lui en parlerai encore."

33 *Le Canadien*, 5 May 1856, 3.

34 NA, RG II, vol. 27, no. 32,175, explanation from Baillairgé, Quebec, 22 Dec. 1856.

CHAPTER 8

1 NA, RG II, vol. 27, no. 32,175, explanation from Charles Baillairgé to chief commissioner, Quebec, 22 Dec. 1856.

2 NA, RG II, vol. 91, no. 1531, letter from Charles Baillairgé to H.H. Killaly to superintend new jails and court houses, Quebec, 6 Sept. 1858.

3 NA, RG II, vol. 91, no. 1502, letter from Charles Baillairgé to Hon. L.V. Sicotte asking to be appointed to superintend the construction of jails and court houses in Lower Canada, Quebec, 6 Sept. 1858.

4 J.E. Hodgetts, *Pioneer Public Service: An Administrative History of the United Canadas, 1846–1867* (Toronto: University of Toronto Press 1955), 194–5; 22 Vic., ch. 3, an Act to amend and consolidate the several acts respecting the public works: organization of the department of public works, 1859.

5 Hodgetts, *Pioneer Public Service*, 195.

6 Geneviève G. Bastien, Doris D. Dubé, and Christina [Cameron] Southam, *Inventaire des marchés de construction des archives civiles de Québec 1800–1870* in History and Archaeology/Histoire et archéologie, IC (Ottawa: Parks Canada 1975), 1055.

7 NA, RG II, vol. 399, no. 56,992, letter from Thomas Begley to F.P. Rubidge asking for preliminary estimates for Legislative Buildings, Toronto, 28 March 1856. For a thorough and well-documented analysis of this question see David B. Knight, *Choosing Canada's Capital: Jealousy and Friction in the 19th Century* (Toronto: McClelland and Stewart 1977), 90–127.

8 "Siège du gouvernement," *Le Canadien*, 2 March 1857, 2; 3 June 1857, 4; 9 June 1857, 4; 11 Aug. 1856, 2; 1 Sept. 1857, 4; "Québec la Capitale!" *Le Canadien*, 16 July 1857, 4.

9 NA, RG II, vol. 139, no. 1817, letter from Hon. John Rose to Right Hon. Sir Edmund Walker Head, Toronto, 25 Feb. 1839; Knight, *Choosing Canada's Capital*, 182.

10 Charles Baillairgé, *Bilan de M. Baillairgé, comme Architecte, Ingénieur, Arpenteur-Géomètre, durant les 21 ans, avant d'entrer au service de la Cité, ès-qualité d'Ingénieur des Ponts et Chaussées on de 1845 à 1866; Puis-entre heures – de 1866 à 1899, mais non compris les Travaux Civiques relatés dans un rapport supplémentaire* (Quebec: n.p. 1899), iv; AVQ, fonds Charles Baillairgé, no. 6A–116, plan of improvements in Palace Ward, Quebec, n.d.

11 NA, RG II, vol. 91, no. 1502, letter from Baillairgé to Sicotte, Quebec, 6 Sept. 1858: "Je suis considéré homme de talent et de génie en Architecture, en Arpentage et en Génie Civil. J'espère avoir bientôt l'occasion de présenter à votre Département un plan pour les édifices parlementaires du Canada et en cette occasion je saurai me montrer je crois l'égal de, si non supérieur,

à qui ce soit dans la même ligne sur ce Continent."

12 NA, RG II, vol. 36, no. 40,506, letter from Charles Baillairgé to Hon. John Rose offering plans for Parliament Buildings, Quebec, 28 March 1859.

13 Charles Baillairgé, *Les édifices publics pour la province de Québec* [Quebec]: n.p. [1875], [1–3]. Baillairgé wrote a long commentary on his Parliament House proposal in 1875 when he presented the same plan to the province for its proposed Legislative Assembly. That it is the same building is proven by the attached photograph by Livernois of the façade elevation. Copies of this pamphlet with photograph are located in ASQ and NA, RG II, vol. 550, no. 48,881.

14 NA, RG II, vol. 36, no. 40,506, letter from Baillairgé to Rose, Quebec, 28 March 1859.

15 Baillairgé, *Les édifices publics*, [1]. When Baillairgé entered this proposal in the Province of Quebec Association of Architects' exhibition in 1904, a reviewer noted that the "great Corinthian colonnaded façade [was] reminiscent of the Louvre." "P.Q.A.A. Exhibition," *CAB*, 17 (1904): 44.

16 J. Mordaunt Crook, *The Greek Revival: Neo-Classical Attitudes in British Architecture 1760–1870* (London: John Murray 1972), 128.

17 Baillairgé, *Les édifices publics*, [3]: "Veut-on savoir encore l'effet que produit une architecture grandiose et monumentale … c'est comme l'impression que nous laisse la chute de Niagara dont au premier abord on ne saisit pas les grands traits. L'homme a besoin d'être préparé pour ce chef d'oeuvre de la nature. Oui, il lui faut voir et revoir ces chutes éternelles pour en comprendre toute la grandeur, et plus il les revoit, plus il les admire, plus il est impressionné et stupéfait. Il les reverra mille fois et le charme en sera toujours nouveau, toujours inexplicable."

18 NA, RG II, vol. 131, no. 27,693, letter from J.W. Harper to Charles Baillairgé, Toronto, 1 April 1859.

19 NA, RG II, vol. 842, exhibit 1, notice to architects by John Rose, Toronto, 7 May 1859.

20 NA, RG II, vol. 637, no. 45,070, Charles Baillairgé acknowledges receipt of set of plans "Stadacona" and states there is another set still to be returned to him, Quebec, 30 Jan. 1860.

21 NA, RG II, vol. 842, exhibit 2, scale of comparison for designs for Parliamentary Buildings and scale of comparison for designs for Departmental Buildings, Toronto, 20 Aug. 1859.

22 NA, RG II, vol. 769, nos. 30,629 and 30,728, letters from Toussaint Trudeau to Charles Baillairgé, Quebec, 28 Jan. and 3 Feb. 1860.

23 *Le Canadien*, 5 Sept. 1855, 2.

24 Ibid., 11 Jan. 1856, 3; *Le Journal de Quebec*, 10 Jan. 1856, 3; *Le Canadien*, 2 April 1856, 1.

25 IBC, vol. 3/20–144/12.96/1–3/dossier la prison de Québec by le groupe de recherche en art du Québec, Quebec, Feb. 1975, 46–53; Monique La Grenade-Meunier, *La prison des plaines d'Abraham* in Collection des retrouvailles, 2 (Quebec: Ministère des Affaires culturelles 1977), 5.

26 NA, RG II, vol. 27, no. 27, 32,175, letter from Charles Baillairgé to Hon. François Lemieux, Quebec, 22 Dec. 1856.

27 NA, RG II, vol. 26, no. 29,692, letter from Charles Baillairgé to Hon. François Lemieux concerning Quebec Custom House competition, Quebec, 3 May 1856.

28 Canada (Province), Statutes, 20 Vic., ch. 28, an Act for establishing Prisons for young offenders for the better government of Public Asylums, Hospitals and Prisons, and for the better construction of common gaols, 10 June 1857.

29 NA, RG II, vol. 276, no. 47,129, letter from E.A. Meredith, secretary of Board of Prison Inspectors to chief commissioner of public works transmitting J.C. Taché's memorandum on new jail, Quebec, 21 May 1860. The board considered that the Quebec Jail gave the inspectors their first opportunity to apply the principles of prison reform to an actual building in Canada. Canada (Province), House of Assembly, "Report of the Board of Inspectors of Asylums, Prisons, etc." *Sessional Papers 1861* (Quebec: Hunter, Rose 1862), n.p.

30 NA, RG II, vol. 770, no. 31,641, letter from Toussaint Trudeau to Charles Baillairgé, Quebec, 16 April 1860.

31 NA, RG II, vol. 274, no. 47,361, order in council for New Jail Quebec, Quebec, 4 June 1860.

32 NA, RG II, vol. 274, no. 49,506, letter from Charles Baillairgé to Toussaint

Trudeau, concerning the new jail at Quebec, Quebec, 5 Oct. 1860.

33 NA, RG II, vol. 276, no. 47,129, letter from Meredith to chief commissioner, Quebec, 21 May 1860.

34 Ibid.

35 NA, RG II, vol. 274, no. 49,506, letter from Baillairgé to Trudeau, Quebec, 5 Oct. 1860.

36 Nikolaus Pevsner, *A History of Building Types* (Princeton: Princeton University Press 1976), 159, 166, 168; C. James Taylor, "The Kingston Ontario Penitentiary and Moral Architecture," *Social History* 12, no. 24 (1979): 395–7.

37 NA, RG II, vol. 26, no. 29,692, letter from Baillairgé to Lemieux, Quebec, 3 May 1856: "Quant à la prison, je ne pourrais envoyer mes plans pour le temps voulu, et j'en suis fâché, car après avoir vu et visité toutes les prisons et penitentières de Québec à Washington et m'être entretenu avec les surintendants de tous ces édifices sur les bons et mauvais points de chaque et sur les améliorations à faire et après avoir remporté avec moi ma valise à demi pleine de descriptions de toutes ces bâtisses – et l'on sait que sur ce sujet les États-Unis sont supérieurs à l'Europe – (puisque les meilleures prisons d'Angleterre ont été imitées des modèles trouvés à Philadelphie etc.) je pense à bon droit pouvoir faire un plan de prison supérieur – au moins sous tous les rapports de discipline, de classification des prisonniers et d'arrangement intérieur à tout ce que j'ai vu."

One of the books that Baillairgé brought home with him in his "suitcase half full of reports and pamphlets" was William Parker Foulke's *Remarks on the Penal System of Pennsylvania* (1855), praised by contemporary reformers because "it exhibits in the clearest manner the defects of our present system ... and furnishes a vast amount of practical information touching the plans, construction, and expense of such a prison as every county should possess." ("Remarks on the Penal System of Pennsylvania," *Pennsylvania Prison Society Journal*, 10, no. 2 (1855): 232.

38 Canada (Province), House of Assembly, "Report of the Board of Inspectors," *Sessional Papers 1861*, n.p.

39 "Prison de Québec," *Le Journal de Québec*, 10 Jan. 1861, 2.

40 NA, RG II, vol. 700, no. 32,430, letter from Toussaint Trudeau, secretary, to Charles Baillairgé awarding him Quebec Jail, Quebec, 11 June 1860.

41 NA, RG II, vol. 274, no. 49,506, letter from Baillairgé to Trudeau, Quebec, 5 Oct. 1860.

42 Ibid.

43 Bastien et al., *Inventaire des marchés*, IC, 835, 1059, 1123. Murphy seems to have been involved, possibly as a builder, in the construction of the jail at Saint-Germain de Rimouski in 1860 (1055).

44 NA, RG II, vol. 712, nos. 51,952, 52,353, 52,936, 53,010, 53,417, progress reports by Charles Baillairgé on new jail, Quebec, March–June 1861; vol. 713, nos. 53,899, 54,384, 54,829, 55,365, 56,293, 56,294, progress reports, Quebec, July–Dec. 1861. In a letter to the contractors on 23 Oct. 1861, Baillairgé congratulated them on their "very satisfactory progress," cited in printed document in NA, RG II, vol. 435, no. 31,159, *The New Jail, Quebec*, Ottawa, 3 April 1865, 15.

45 NA, RG II, vol. 714, no. 59,731, progress report from Charles Baillairgé showing balance overpaid to contractors at new jail in Quebec, Quebec, 11 July 1862.

46 Baillairgé, *The New Jail, Quebec*, 2–3, 7–8. The newspaper attacks were led by the *Daily News* and the *Vindicator*.

47 NA, RG II, vol. 715, no. 60,781, progress report from Charles Baillairgé stating that works are completely stopped at new jail in Quebec, Quebec, 19 Sept. 1862; vol. 638, no. 64,044, letter from Charles Baillairgé to department, calling attention to complete state of abandonment of works at new jail, Quebec, 20 April 1863.

48 NA, RG II, vol. 274, no. 64,070, letter from Charles Baillairgé to Toussaint Trudeau, resigning as architect of new jail in Quebec, Quebec, 22 April 1863.

49 NA, RG II, vol. 639, no. 45,148, letter to Joseph Ferdinand Peachy appointing him architect at new jail in Quebec, Quebec, 24 April 1863; no. 46,485, letter from Toussaint Trudeau to Joseph Ferdinand Peachy dispensing with his services, Quebec, 21 Aug. 1863; vol. 796, no. 73,244, order in council concerning expenditures at new jail in Quebec, Quebec, 16 Jan. 1865.

50 NA, RG II, vol. 774, no. 41,138, letter from Toussaint Trudeau to Charles Baillairgé enclosing communication from Murphy and Quigley, Quebec, 27 May 1862; vol. 274, no. 60,300, letter from Murphy and Quigley to Hon. U.J. Tessier, chief commissioner, asking for an inquiry into new jail in Quebec, Quebec, 14 Aug. 1862.

51 Baillairgé, *The New Jail, Quebec*, 3–4, 9, 19–20.

52 NA, RG II, vol. 774, no. 42,095, letter from Toussaint Trudeau to Charles Baillairgé authorizing fourth storey of new jail, Quebec, 15 Aug. 1862.

53 Baillairgé, *The New Jail, Quebec*, 9.

54 *Le Journal de Québec*, 27 May 1865, 3.

55 NA, RG II, vol. 91, no. 34,741, letter from Toussaint Trudeau to Thomas Murphy and Thomas Quigley, Quebec, 23 Nov. 1860.

CHAPTER 9

1 The Parliament and Departmental Buildings have been discussed by several authors: Courtney C.J. Bond, *City on the Ottawa* (Ottawa: Queen's Printer 1961), 122–5; Mathilde Brosseau, *Gothic Revival in Canadian Architecture* in *Canadian Historic Sites: Occasional Papers in Archaeology and History*, 25 (Ottawa: Parks Canada, Environment Canada 1980), 20–1, 120–5; Christina Cameron and Janet Wright, *Second Empire Style in Canadian Architecture* in *Canadian Historic Sites: Occasional Papers in Archaeology and History*, 24 (Ottawa: Parks Canada, Environment Canada 1980), 12–3, 42–5; Canada, National Film Board, *Stones of History: Canada's Houses of Parliament* (Ottawa: Queen's Printer 1967), n.p.; J.E. Hodgetts, "Constructing the Ottawa Buildings: A Case Study," *Pioneer Public Service: An Administrative History of the United Canadas, 1841–1867* (Toronto: University of Toronto 1955), 198–204; J. Daniel Livermore, *Departmental Buildings, Eastern Block, Parliament Hill, Ottawa* (Ottawa: Public Works Canada 1974), 1–236; Douglas Owram, *Building for Canadians: A History of the Department of Public Works 1840–1960* (Ottawa: Public Works Canada 1979), 83–7; John Page, "Report on the Public Buildings at Ottawa," *General Report of the Commissioner of Public Works for the Year Ending 30th June, 1867*, app. 21 (Ottawa: Hunter, Rose 1868), 201–48; Robert A.J. Phillips, *East Block of the Parliament Buildings of Canada* (Ottawa: Queen's Printer 1967), 1–68; Douglas Richardson, "The Spirit of the Place," *Canadian Antiques*

Collector 10, no. 5 (1975): 27–9; Shirley E. Woods, *Ottawa, The Capital of Canada*, (Toronto: Doubleday Canada 1980), 120–7.

2 Hodgetts, *Pioneer Public Service*, 198–204.

3 NA, RG II, vol. 842, exhibit 1, printed notice to architects from Hon. John Rose, Toronto, 7 May 1859.

4 Hodgetts, *Pioneer Public Service*, 199–200.

5 Ibid., 200; NA, RG II, vol. 796, no. 71,787, dismissal of Samuel Keefer as deputy commissioner of public works and inspector of railways, Quebec, 17 March 1864.

6 Hodgetts, *Pioneer Public Service*, 202; *Report of the Commission Appointed to Inquire into Matters Connected with the Public Buildings at Ottawa*, (Quebec: Blackburn 1863), n.p. [28].

7 *Report of the Commission*, n.p., testimony of John Rose on 9 Sept. 1862.

8 Ibid., n.p. [28], exhibits 70–84; NA, RG II, vol. 841, items 72–81, Joseph Cauchon's certificates in favour of Thomas McGreevy and Jones, Haycock & Company, Quebec, 1 Aug.–20 Nov. 1861.

9 Hodgetts, *Pioneer Public Service*, 202.

10 *Report of the Commission*, n.p. [43–4]; Page, "Report on the Public Buildings," 202.

11 *Report of the Commission*, n.p. [1, 43–4].

12 NA, RG II, vol. 776, no. 44,964, letter from Toussaint Trudeau to Charles Baillairgé appointing him associate architect of Parliament and Departmental Buildings, Quebec, 11 April 1863.

13 NA, RG II, vol. 322, no. 2870, petition of Thomas Fuller for compensation for services as architect of Parliament Buildings and on account of his abrupt dismissal, n.p., 11 March 1868.

14 NA, RG II, vol. 415, no. 83,116, copy of contract between Thomas McGreevy and Her Majesty, Ottawa, 18 April 1863.

15 NA, RG II, vol. 401, no. 63,746, order in council on Parliament Buildings, Quebec, 2 April 1863.

16 NA, RG II, vol. 412, no. 54,501, letter from Charles Baillairgé to Toussaint Trudeau offering his views on systems of measurement, Quebec, 10 Aug. 1861; vol. 412, no. 54,755, letter from Pierre Gauvreau to Toussaint Trudeau offering his views on system of measurement, Quebec, 29 Aug. 1861.

17 NA, RG II, vol. 401, no. 63,746, order in council, Quebec, 2 April 1863.

18 NA, RG II, vol. 401, no. 63,991, letter of acceptance from Charles Baillairgé to Toussaint Trudeau, Quebec, 16 April 1863; *Mitchell & Co's County of Carleton and Ottawa City Directory for 1864–5* (Toronto: W.C. Chewett 1864), 30.

19 NA, RG II, vol. 413, no. 66,502, copy of letter from Baillairgé, Fuller, and Rubidge to Jones, Haycock & Co. concerning ornamental slate, Ottawa, 24 Sept. 1863.

20 NA, RG II, vol. 422, no. 64,860, letter from Baillairgé and Fuller to Rubidge dated 9 June 1863 enclosed in letter from F.P. Rubidge to Toussaint Trudeau, Ottawa, 11 June 1863; vol. 422, no. 68,145, letter from Baillairgé to Rubidge concerning alterations and additions to Departmental Buildings, Ottawa, 26 Jan. 1864; vol. 423, no. 72,934, letter from Baillairgé to J.C. Taché concerning proposed room for models of agricultural department in the attic of the Eastern Block, Ottawa, 9 Dec. 1864.

21 NA, RG II, vol. 422, no. 67,677, letter from F.P. Rubidge to Toussaint Trudeau concerning Stent & Laver, Ottawa, 28 Dec. 1863; vol. 422, no. 68,986, letter from Stent & Laver to Toussaint Trudeau, Ottawa, 10 Nov. 1863.

22 NA, RG II, vol. 422, no. 67,538, quoted in letter from Stent & Laver to Toussaint Trudeau, Ottawa, 18 Dec. 1863.

23 NA, RG II, vol. 422, no. 67,677, letter from Rubidge to Trudeau, Ottawa, 28 Dec. 1863.

24 "The Ottawa Buildings," *Montreal Gazette*, 19 Dec. 1863, 2.

25 Charles Baillairgé, *The Public Buildings* ([Ottawa]: n.p. 1864), 2; NA, RG II, vol. 637, no. 68,427, printed reply to Stent's letter submitted by Charles Baillairgé, Ottawa, 28 Feb. 1864.

26 Baillairgé, *The Public Buildings*, 3.

27 For particular details on the scope of the French approach see the introduction in the *Précis* of Durand in Baillairgé's architectural library. Jean Nicolas Louis Durand, *Précis des leçons d'architecture données à l'Ecole royale polytechnique* (Liège: D. Avanzo & Cie 1840).

28 Baillairgé, *The Public Buildings*, 3.

29 Ibid.

30 NA, RG II, vol. 413, no. 65,629, letter from F.P. Rubidge, Charles Baillairgé, and Thomas Fuller which transmits complaint from contractors Thomas and Robert McGreevy against June estimates and John Bowes's report, Ottawa, 11 Aug. 1863.

31 NA, RG II, vol. 417, no. 10,788, copies of detailed instructions and drawings from superintendent and associate architects of the Parliament and Departmental Buildings written in June–July 1863 transmitted by John Bowes to department, Ottawa, 5 April 1870.

32 NA, RG II, vol. 413, no. 65,629, letter from Rubidge et al. transmitting complaint, Ottawa, 11 Aug. 1863.

33 Ibid., letter from John Bowes responding to contractors' complaints, Ottawa, 29 July 1863.

34 NA, RG II, vol. 422, no. 66,621, order in council, Quebec, 17 Oct. 1863.

35 NA, RG II, vol. 413, no. 66,502, synopsis of letter from Rubidge, Baillairgé, and Fuller to Thomas McGreevy, Ottawa, 30 Sept. 1863; no. 69,087, letter from F.P. Rubidge to secretary enclosing printed broadside on stone cutters' strike, Ottawa, 9 April 1864; vol. 423, no. 68,739, synopsis of letter from F.P. Rubidge to Jones, Haycock & Co., Ottawa, 10 March 1864; vol. 413, no. 68,192, letter from F.P. Rubidge to secretary enclosing letter from Robert McGreevy, Ottawa, 1 Feb. 1864.

36 NA, RG II, vol. 423, no. 69,164, letter from Jones, Haycock & Co. to secretary of public works, Ottawa, 18 April 1864.

37 NA, RG II, vol. 401, no. 69,115, letter from Charles Baillairgé to F.P. Rubidge with suggestions for the conduct of works at Parliament Buildings, Ottawa, 11 April 1864.

38 Ibid.

39 Ibid.

40 NA, RG II, vol. 423, no. 70,876, order in council, Quebec, 10 Aug. 1864.

41 NA, RG II, vol. 414, no. 71,984, order in council sending claims of contractors to arbitration, Quebec, 17 Oct. 1864.

42 NA, RG II, vol. 423, no. 71,815, letter from Jones, Haycock & Co. to commissioner of public works, Quebec, 10 Oct. 1864; no. 73,247, order in council, Quebec, 16 Jan. 1865; vol. 414, no. 73,264, order in council, Quebec, 16 Jan. 1865; vol. 414, no.

73,264, order in council, Quebec, 17 Jan. 1865.

43 NA, RG 11, vol. 414, no. 72,888, letter from John Page to F. Braun, secretary of public works, Ottawa, 16 Dec. 1864.

44 NA, RG 11, vol. 423, no. 72,774, telegram from John Page to F. Braun, Montreal, 13 Dec. 1864.

45 NA, RG 11, vol. 414, no. 73,636, order in council appointing John Bowes to assist F.P. Rubidge, Quebec, 10 Feb. 1865.

46 NA, RG 11, vol. 414, no. 73,670, letter from F.P. Rubidge to F. Braun, secretary of public works, Ottawa, 10 Feb. 1865.

47 NA, RG 11, vol. 780, no. 53,154, letter from F. Braun, secretary of public works, to Charles Baillairgé, Quebec, 17 Feb. 1865.

48 NA, RG 11, vol. 375, no. 38,197, account from Charles Baillairgé to Department of Public Works for extra time while employed as associate architect of Parliament and Departmental Buildings, Quebec, 29 Dec. 1873.

49 NA, RG 11, vol. 598, n.n., letter from Charles Baillairgé to Hon. J.C. Chapais, Ottawa, 3 April 1865.

50 Ibid.

On me dit que Murphy et Quigley sont encore à l'oeuvre, avec fortes menaces. C'est le fils de Mr Gauvreau qui travaille pour eux et le père sans doute s'applaudissant de tout ce qui pourrait me nuire et me noircir et satisfaire sa jalousie et son inimitié aurait été vous trouver et, d'un air de protection, vous aurait [sic] dit que ce pauvre Mr. Baillairgé se serait gravement compromis et vous de répondre à cela "qu'il était malheureux que les Canadiens savaient si peu faire les choses; qu'ils se mettaient toujours dans l'alternative de forcer le Bureau à les décharger pour sauver les apparences." "Un anglais," auriez vous ajouté, "peut voler tant qu'il veut et chacun de le respecter, tant il sait s'y prendre"; et Gauvreau d'approuver à ce que la moralité soit strictement observée.

Voilà qui est des plus grave, Monsieur, mais la franchise et la vérité, comme vous le verrez sous peu de jours dans une communication que je vous adresserai à ce sujet, n'auront aucune difficulté à triompher des mensonges et des apparences spécieuses.

51 NA, RG 11, vol. 780, no. 53,888, memorandum from Hon. J.C. Chapais to Governor General, Quebec, 28 April 1865.

52 Ibid., no. 53,918, letter from F. Braun,

secretary of public works, to Charles Baillairgé, Quebec, 1 May 1865.

53 NA, RG 11, vol. 758, p. 147, register for governor general and secretary, n.p., 1864–6.

54 Baillairgé, The New Jail, Quebec, 1–23; Le Journal de Québec, 11 May 1865, 2, 18 May 1865, 2; Le Canadien, 24 May 1865, 2; Le Journal de Québec, 27 May 1865, 3.

55 AVQ, fonds Charles Baillairgé, nos. 1–78 to 1–82, plans, elevations, and sections for T.J. Murphy house, Quebec, n.d.

56 Le Journal de Québec, 18 May 1865, 2.

57 Charles Baillairgé, Honble H.L. Langevin G.B. Ministre des Travaux Public (Quebec: n.p. 1873), 2; Murphy and Quigley's case was settled in 1867 at $17,000 in extras. Lemoine estimated the final cost of the Quebec Jail at $137,932.12. James Macpherson Lemoine, Quebec Past and Present (Quebec: Augustin Côté & Co. 1876), 427.

58 John Charles Dent, "The Hon. Joseph Edouard Cauchon," Canadian Portrait Gallery (Toronto: John B. Magurn 1881), 141.

59 NA, RG 11, vol. 414, no. 72,675, telegram from John Page to Hon. J.C. Chapais, Ottawa, 3 Dec. 1864.

60 NA, RG 11, vol. 637, no. 74,731, solicitor-general east transmits report to council concerning Baillairgé, Quebec, 1 May 1865; vol. 639, no. 75,558, letter from governor general's secretary, Quebec, 23 June 1865.

61 NA, RG 11, vol. 418, no. 14,180, letter from Sir John A. Macdonald to Hon. Hector L. Langevin, Ottawa, 14 Jan. 1871; no. 14,761, order in council concerning McGreevy's claim, Ottawa, 21 Feb. 1871; no. 16,317, letter from John Page to secretary of public works, Ottawa, 27 May 1871.

62 How an editorial in the Canadian Architect and Builder concerning the imprisonment of McGreevy must have delighted Baillairgé: "it is high time that a check was put on crooked practices in connection with the awarding of public contracts. The system of securing contracts by means of bribery is practiced to such an extent that it has become impossible for firms who are unwilling to resort to this method to obtain any business in certain quarters ... It leads to a great waste of public money, as contracts which are thus purchased are given at figures greatly above what would be obtained if honest competition prevailed."

CAB, 6 (1893): 122. For analyses of the McGreevy-Langevin scandal see Laurier L. LaPierre, "Joseph Israel Tarte and the McGreevy-Langevin Scandal," Canadian Historical Association Report (1961): 47–57, and Andrée Desilets, Hector-Louis Langevin: un père de la confédération canadienne (1826–1906) (Quebec: les Presses de l'Université Laval 1969), 390–6.

63 "La démission de M. Baillairgé," Le Canadien, 31 May 1865, 2.

64 Ibid.

65 Baillairgé, Honble H.L. Langevin, 1: "Il y a bientôt huit ans que l'on a sacrifié aux exigences impitoyables de la politique, à la cabale la plus éhontée et aux clameurs mensongères de journaux soudoyés par de riches et puissants contracteurs, l'homme le plus irréprochable ... que jamais un Gouvernement ait eu à son service." Baillairgé accused other politicians of having benefited from the corruption at the Parliament Buildings at Ottawa in an unsigned letter of about 1875 addressed to his friend, the editor of L'Événement. It is a malicious letter which begins by calling Cauchon or "le cochon" "Hypocrite, Tartufe 2d," "Rubrique en diable," and "Cynique"; it continues: "Si les héritiers de feu

Fr. Baby
McGreevy (Honble!
Alleyn (do !!
Killaly (do !!!
and   Le Cochon (do !!!!

sont riches, c'est dans le mesurage, ou plutôt, toisé de ces bâtisses que les cinq fripons ci-dessus nommés ont gagné $890,000. A. McGreevy $222,500; Baby $222,500; Killaly $200,000; Alleyn $122,500; Le Cochon $122,500." ASQ, polygraphie 20, no. 32v.

66 Page, "Report on the Public Buildings," 203–4; "Canadian Parliament Buildings, Ottawa," CAB 10 (1897): 6.

67 NA, RG 11, vol. 423, no. 84,956, letter from John Page to secretary of public works, Ottawa, 29 March 1867; vol. 415, no. 79,890, order in council, Ottawa, 12 April 1866.

68 NA, RG 11, vol. 415, no. 83,116, order in council transferring contract to Robert McGreevy, Ottawa, 6 Nov. 1866; vol. 417, no. 9861, order in council settling McGreevy's claim for cancellation of contract, Ottawa, 8 March 1870; vol. 418, no. 20,590, letter from John Page to secretary

of public works, Ottawa, 23 Jan. 1872.

69 Page, "Report on the Public Buildings," 239.

70 NA, RG II, vol. 434, no. 78,315, letter from Charles Baillairgé to commissioner of public works, Quebec, 3 Jan. 1866; vol. 275, no. 79,115, letter from Charles Baillairgé to Hon. F. Blair, president of executive council, Quebec, 1 Feb. 1866; vol. 723, no. 9023, letter from Charles Baillairgé to Hector L. Langevin, Quebec, 7 Dec. 1869; vol. 375, no. 38,197, letter from Charles Baillairgé to Hector L. Langevin, Quebec, 29, Dec. 1873; vol. 375, no. 42,335, letter from Charles Baillairgé to minister of public works, Quebec, 26 June 1874; vol. 532, no. 47,537, order in council awarding Charles Baillairgé $650 for extra professional services, Ottawa, 15 Jan. 1875.

71 ANQ, gr. Louis Panet, no. 14,739, Lease, Charles Baillairgé to widow Benjamin Torrance, Quebec, 11 Feb. 1864. One of the conditions of the lease stipulated that "it is understood and agreed that the said lessee will not allow dancing in the said house on account of the ceiling in plaster." The change of address can be traced through Quebec street directories from 1863 to 1866.

72 This unsigned text on the interior of Saint-Laurent church is presumed to be written by Gérard Morisset, probably in the 1950s when his son Jean-Paul undertook a photographic record of the church. MAC, IBC, fonds Morisset, I/7563–7611, dossier Saint-Laurent, Ile d'Orléans, 582.

73 ANQ, gr. Jean-Baptiste Pruneau, no. 5445, marché, William Venner–Isidore Morissette and Ambroise Bélanger, Quebec, 21 Nov. 1861.

74 Père Alexis, Histoire de la province ecclésiastique d'Ottawa et de la colonisation dans la vallée de l'Ottawa, vol. 1 (Ottawa: la Cie d'Imprimerie d'Ottawa 1897), 569; ASCO, letter from Mère Elisabeth Bruyère to Sr Phelan, Ottawa, 19 July 1866. I am grateful to archivist Soeur Huguette Bordeleau, SCO, for having drawn these letters to my attention and for having transcribed the pertinent sections.

75 ANQ, gr. Samuel-Isidore Glackemeyer, no. 3511, marché William Petry–Isaac Dorion, Quebec, 18 Aug. 1863; gr. John Greaves Clapham, no. 4016, contract, Joseph Knight Boswell–Simon Peters and Charles Peters, Quebec, 2 June 1863.

76 NA, RG II, vol. 375, no. 38,197, letter from Charles Baillairgé to Hector Langevin, commissioner of public works, Quebec, 29 Dec. 1873.

CHAPTER 10

1 NA, RG II, vol. 375, no. 38,197, letter from Charles Baillairgé to commissioner of public works, Quebec, 29 Dec. 1873.

2 Charles Baillairgé, Report of the Superintendent of Works of the Corporation of Quebec for the Year 1868 (Quebec: C. Darveau 1869), 63; Luc Noppen, Claude Paulette, and Michel Tremblay, Quebec: trois siècles d'architecture (Quebec: Libre expression 1979), 142.

3 MAC, IBC, fonds Morisset, vol. 1/13336–147, dossier Québec, Québec, portes, transcriptions of series of exchanges concerning Saint John Gate from Le Journal de Québec, Oct. 1865.

4 Charles Baillairgé, Bilan de M. Baillairgé, comme Architecte, Ingénieur, Arpenteur-Géomètre, durant les 21 ans, avant d'entrer au service de la Cité ès-qualité d'Ingénieur des Ponts et Chaussées, ou de 1845 à 1866. Puis – entre heures – de 1866 à 1899, mais non compris les Travaux Civiques relatés dans un rapport supplémentaire ([Quebec]: n.p. [1899]), v–vi.

5 Baillairgé, Report of the Superintendent 1868, 61–2.

6 Charles Baillairgé, Report of the City Surveyor and Water-works Engineer for the year 1872–1873 (Quebec: C. Darveau 1873), 18; Charles Baillairgé, Rapport de l'Ex-Ingénieur 1866 à 1899, 33.

7 Baillairgé, Report of the Superintendent 1868, 83.

8 Baillairgé, Report of the City Surveyor 1872–1873, 18; ANQ, gr. Joseph Allaire, no. 7683, marché, City of Quebec–William Joseph Peters, Quebec, 19 July 1897; Charles Baillairgé, Quebec, passé, présent, futur (Quebec: Jos.-A. Gingras & Cie. 1885), 4; Baillairgé, Rapport de l'Ex-Ingénieur 1866 à 1899, 34; Noppen et al., Québec: trois siècles, 143.

9 Baillairgé, Report of the Superintendent 1868, 31; AVQ, conseil et comités, employés (2), application to City of Quebec by Charles Baillairgé for post of superintendent of works, Quebec, 19 Sept. 1866. In his application, Baillairgé stated that he was vice-president of the Association of Provincial Land Surveyors and the Institute of Civil Engineers and Architects of Canada,

surveyor for Quebec Harbour Commission, engineer of the Quebec Turnpike Trust, designer of numerous public and private buildings, and inventor of machinery and other patented devices.

10 George-Frédéric Baillairgé, Notices biographiques. Fascicule no. 4: Théophile Baillairgé ... et Charlotte-Janvrin Horsley (Joliette: Bureaux de l'étudiant, du couvent, et de la famille 1891), 118–19.

11 Charles Baillairgé, The Municipal Situation (Quebec: P.G. Delisle 1878), 9; AVQ, conseil et comités, employés (2), report of finance committee, Quebec, 4 Oct. 1866.

12 Baillairgé, Report of the Superintendent 1868, 74.

13 Charles Baillairgé, Rapport de l'Ingénieur de la Cité pour 1890–91 ([Quebec]: n.p. [1891]), 21; Baillairgé, Report of the Superintendent 1868, 16–17, 61–3, 74; AVQ, conseil et comités, employés (2), report of finance committee, Quebec, 4 Oct. 1866.

14 Baillairgé, Report of City Surveyor 1872–73, 107–9.

15 Baillairgé, Report of the Superintendent 1868, 55, 60.

16 Ibid., 59.

17 Ibid., 31–3; Albert Jobin, Histoire de Québec (Quebec: n.p. 1947), 46–7; James Macpherson Lemoine, Quebec Past and Present (Quebec: Augustin Côté & Co. 1876), 303. The formation of a permanent brigade was accompanied by the installation of a fire alarm system from the United States. ANQ, gr. Alexandre Benjamin Sirois, no. 8917, marché, City of Quebec–John Fogg Kennard, Quebec, 15 Nov. 1866.

18 Baillairgé, Municipal Situation, 10.

19 Baillairgé, Report of the Superintendent 1868, 80–1.

20 Baillairgé, Report of City Surveyor 1872–1873, xi.

21 ANQ, gr. Alexandre Benjamin Sirois, no. 10603, marché, City of Quebec–Joseph Hudon, Quebec, 12 Aug. 1871; Baillairgé, Report of City Surveyor 1872–1873, 9, 28–9; AVQ, conseil et comités, marché Montcalm (2), plan, elevation, and specifications for Montcalm Market Hall by Charles Baillairgé, Quebec, 15 Jan. 1875; halles (marché) (3) report of market committee, Quebec, 30 Aug. 1876; fonds Charles Baillairgé, no. 6A–99, elevation of Montcalm Market Hall

by Paul Cousin, architect, with reworking by Charles Baillairgé, Quebec, 1875. Baillairgé's support of the new mansard roof instead of "the old quaint style" is made clear in his comments on the work of Peachy, Lepage, Peters, Staveley, and Dérôme.

22 Lemoine, *Quebec Past and Present*, 307–8.

23 Copies of the pamphlet, entitled *Les édifices publics pour la province de Québec* (Quebec: n.p. [1875]), exist at ASQ, Université 84, no. 67, and NA, RG 11, vol. 550, no. 48,881. Acknowledgement of the receipt of Baillairgé's pamphlet is found in NA, RG 11, vol. 792, no. 29,403, letter from F. Braun to Charles Baillairgé, Ottawa, 27 March 1875. Baillairgé invited M. Joly, the mayor of Quebec, M. Langelier, the minister of public works, and Nazaire Levasseur, editor of *L'Événement*, to examine his plans at his office in February 1875. ASQ, manuscript 759, 93, letter from Charles Baillairgé to Nazaire Levasseur, Quebec, 13 Feb. 1875.

24 Baillairgé, *Report of City Surveyor 1872–1873*, 47–51; "Conseil de Ville," *Le Canadien*, 21 Nov. 1859, 4.

25 Charles Baillairgé, *Report of the City Engineer, Quebec on the Proposed Improvements in the Mouth of the River St. Charles* (Quebec: n.p. 1875), 1–10; Charles Baillairgé, *Report of the City Engineer, Quebec, on the Proposed Dry Dock in the Mouth of the River St. Charles* Quebec: [C. Darveau] 1876), 1–4.

26 Charles Baillairgé, *On the Necessity of a School of Arts for the Dominion: A paper read before the Canadian Society of Civil Engineers at their meeting of the 26th May 1887* (Quebec: n.p. 1887), 6.

27 Charles Baillairgé, *The Aqueduct, Quebec* (Quebec: [G. Vincent] 1885), 5; NA, RG 11, vol. 491, no. 67,351, order in council choosing Levis as site for graving dock, Ottawa, 26 May 1877.

28 Charles Baillairgé, *Honble H.L. Langevin G.B. Ministre des Travaux Publics* (Quebec: n.p. 1873), 4. A copy of this brochure is located in NA, RG 11, vol. 435, no. 31,159:

Il n'y a pas Monsieur tant de distance qui nous sépare. Nous étions jadis compagnons de classe. Vous êtes dans une sphère où vous faites valoir vos talents et vos connaissances; placez-moi là où je pourrais utiliser les miens. J'ai déjà gagné mes £1000 par année, non seulement à Ottawa mais avant d'y aller; je puis les gagner encore et avec

intérêt.

Je suis abrutis ici à l'emploi de la Corporation de Québec par la qualité et la quantité de l'ouvrage que j'y fais et par un salaire indigne d'une cité qui se respecte. Je ne regrette pas d'y avoir passé quelques années, en vue de la pratique et de l'expérience acquises comme ingénieur de travaux de toutes sortes et de l'aqueduc, mais je n'y ai maintenant plus rien à apprendre, et je me sens de beaucoup audessus de la position que j'occupe.

29 ASQ, Manuscript 759, 87, letter from Charles Baillairgé to Nazaire Levasseur, Quebec, 27 Aug. 1874.

30 Baillairgé, *Report of City Surveyor 1872–1873*, 1.

31 Ibid., 17–23; "Les démolitions à Québec," *L'Opinion publique*, 14 Sept. 1871, 450.

32 Baillairgé, *Report of City Surveyor 1872–1873*, 2–3, 17–18; "Call for tenders," *L'Événement*, 4 March 1873, 2; ANQ, gr. Alexandre Benjamin Sirois, no. 11,043, marché, City of Quebec–Nicolas Piton, Quebec, 18 April 1873.

33 Baillairgé, *Report of City Surveyor 1872–1873*, 2.

34 Baillairgé, *Report of the Superintendent 1868*, 22–3; Baillairgé, *Report of City Surveyor 1872–1873*, 22–3.

35 James Macpherson Lemoine, *Historical Notes on the Environs of Quebec* (Montreal: Burland-Desbarats Lith. Co. 1879), 4, 38; *Picturesque Quebec: A Sequel to Quebec Past and Present* (Montreal: Dawson Brothers 1882), 245; Baillairgé, *Report of City Surveyor 1872–1873*, 53.

36 Letter from Lord Dufferin to the Earl of Carnarvon, Ottawa, 21 Dec. 1874, cited in *Dufferin-Carnarvon Correspondence 1874–1878*, ed. C.W. de Kiewiet and F.H. Underhill (Toronto: Champlain Society 1955), 124–5.

37 Achille Murphy, "Les projets d'embellissements de la ville de Québec proposés par Lord Dufferin en 1875," *JCAH* 1, no. 2 (1974): 18–29; Christian Rioux, "Le départ de la garnison britannique de Québec en 1872 et le sort des fortifications de 1871 à 1884, vus à travers les journaux," *Travaux inédit numéro 168* (Ottawa: Parks Canada 1974), 45–51; Christina Cameron, "Lord Dufferin, contre les goths et les vandales," *Cap-aux-Diamants* 2, no. 2 (1986): 39–41.

38 NA, MG 26 A, vol. 79, 733, extract of a confidential memorandum from Lord Dufferin to the Marquis of Lorne [Ottawa 1878].

39 [James Macpherson Lemoine], "Quebec Improvements – Lord Dufferin Plans for the Preservation of its Historic Monuments," *Morning Chronicle*, 25 Dec. 1875, n.p.; Lemoine, *Quebec Past and Present*, 325–42.

40 Lemoine, *Quebec Past and Present*, 341.

41 AVQ, conseils et comités, terrasse Dufferin (Durham), letter from Charles Baillairgé to mayor of Quebec, Quebec, 31 Aug. 1895.

42 NA, RG 11, vol. 553, no. 79,445, letter from Charles Baillairgé to John A. Macdonald, Quebec, 20 Jan. 1879.

43 NA, MG 26 A, vol. 79, 732–3, extract of memorandum from Dufferin to Lorne [Ottawa 1878].

44 Lemoine, *Quebec Past and Present*, 337; AVQ, conseil et comités, porte Saint-Jean, copies of plans of Quebec gates by William Lynn, Quebec, Sept. 1875; NA, NMC, RG 11M, 77803/39, plans of Quebec gates by William Lynn, n.p., n.d. ANQ, cartothèque, true copies by Charles Baillairgé of William Lynn's drawings for Quebec gates, Quebec, 1878; NA, RG 11, vol. 734, no. 57,635, Charles Baillairgé transmits two copies of proposed Dufferin Improvements, Quebec, 4 March 1876; vol. 794, no. 34,537, letter from secretary of public works to Charles Braun acknowledging receipt of copies of plans and forwarding one copy to governor general, Ottawa, 22 March 1876.

45 Charles Baillairgé, "Design of Kiosks on Dufferin Terrace, Quebec," *CAB* 13 (1900): 40.

46 AVQ, cartothèque, A-352.11 – (1878), plans for aquarium and restaurant on Dufferin Terrace by Charles Baillairgé, Quebec [1878]; NA, RG 11, vol. 553, no. 79,445, newspaper report of Quebec City engineer contained in letter from Baillairgé to Macdonald, Quebec, 14 Feb. 1879; Charles Baillairgé, "A Proposed Aquarium under Dufferin Terrace, Quebec," *CAB* 13 (1900): 93; Charles Baillairgé, "Un projet inouï: pourquoi ne pas installer un aquarium sous la terrasse," *Le Soleil*, 26 April 1900, 5; Charles Baillairgé, *A Summary of Papers read at different times before the Royal Society of Canada, the Canadian Association of Civil Engineers and Architects, and Literary, and Scientific Societies,*

or which have appeared occasionally in scientific and other publications (Quebec: H. Chassé Printing [1903], 50–2.

47 ASQ, Université 49, no. 107, invitation for laying of foundation stone of Dufferin Terrace, Quebec, 18 Oct. 1878; Lady Dufferin, *My Canadian Journal 1872–1878*, ed. Gladys Chantler Walker (Don Mills: Longmans Canada 1969), 312–13; *Canadian Illustrated News*, 21 June 1879, 385; 28 June 1879, 401.

48 Charles Baillairgé, "Quebec in 1894," *CAB* 7 (1894): 16.

49 David Karel, Luc Noppen, and Claude Thibault, *François Baillairgé et son oeuvre (1759–1830)* (Quebec: le Groupe de recherche en art du Québec de l'Université Laval et le Musée du Québec 1975), 21–2, 25–6.

50 "Remarkable Occurrences – 1879," *The Dominion Annual Register and Review for the Thirteenth Year of the Canadian Union, 1879*, ed. Henry J. Morgan (Ottawa: Maclean, Roger and Co. 1880), 213; "The Viceregal Visit," *Morning Chronicle*, 12 June 1879, 3.

51 Lemoine, *Quebec Past and Present*, 340.

52 NA, RG 11, vol. 553, no. 79,445, letter from Baillairgé to Macdonald, Quebec, 20 Jan. 1879; no. 79,710, petition from city council of Quebec, Quebec, 18 Feb. 1879.

53 James Macpherson Lemoine, *Historical and Sporting Notes on Quebec and its Environs* (Quebec: L.-J. Demers & Frère 1889), 31–2.

54 NA, RG 11, vol. 737, no. 80,010, letter from Charles Baillairgé applying for position of chief architect of dominion when vacant, Quebec, 26 March 1879.

55 ANQ, gr. Joseph Allaire, no. 3843, marché, City of Quebec–Georges Hudon, Quebec, 11 Sept. 1888; no. 6221, marché, City of Quebec–Barthélémi Leclerc, Quebec, 1 June 1894; Baillairgé, *Rapport de l'Ex-Ingénieur 1866 à 1899*, 12. Baillairgé did not give up his grandiose schemes. For the international meeting of the *Société Saint-Jean-Baptiste* in 1880, he proposed an open air dinner on his beloved Dufferin Terrace for 10,000 persons. This banquet did not take place. H.-J.-J.-B. Chouinard, *Fête nationale des canadiens-français célébrée à Québec en 1880* (Quebec: A. Côté et Cie 1881), 136.

56 Baillairgé, *Rapport de l'ingénieur 1890–91*, 14–15.

57 Baillairgé, *Rapport de l'Ex-Ingénieur 1866*

à *1899*, 67; "Quebec," *CAB* 3 (1890): 30.

58 "The Quebec City Hall," *CAB* 3 (1890): 134.

59 Charles Baillairgé, *Instructions to Architects Submitting Competing Designs for the New City Hall Quebec* [Quebec: E. Vincent 1889]), 1–15; AVQ, conseil et comités, hôtel de ville (nouvel) (1), reports and estimates, Quebec, 1889–96.

60 *CAB* 3 (1890): 2.

61 Ibid. 14.

62 "Quebec," *CAB* 3 (1890): 21.

63 *CAB* 3 (1890): 15.

64 "Quebec City Hall Competition," *CAB* 3 (1890): 28.

65 AVQ, conseil et comités, hôtel de ville (nouvel) (4), report of judges, Quebec, 31 Oct. 1890; "The Quebec City Hall," *CAB* 3 (1890): 134.

66 Victor Roy, "Quebec City Hall Competition," *CAB* 4 (1891): 55.

67 "The Quebec City Hall," *CAB* 3 (1890): 134; Roy, "Quebec City Hall Competition," *CAB* 4 (1891): 55; Luc Noppen et al., *Québec: trois siècles*, 282.

68 *CAB* 4 (1891): 29.

69 The building contracts are found in the file of notary, Joseph Allaire, beginning in December 1894. Consult Danielle Blanchet and Sylvie Thivierge, *Inventaire des marchés de construction des actes notariés de la ville de Québec, 1871–1899* in History and Archaeology/Histoire et archéologie, 62 (Ottawa: Parks Canada 1983).

70 Baillairgé, *Rapport de l'Ex-Ingénieur 1866 à 1899*, 67.

71 AVQ, conseil et comités, escaliers (1), report of road committee, Quebec, 4 April 1883.

72 Baillairgé, *Québec, passé, présent, futur*, 6.

73 AVQ, conseil et comités, chemins de fer-Québec-Lac Saint-Jean (Quebec Lake St-John Ry), reports by Charles Baillairgé, Quebec, 1884–8.

74 Charles Baillairgé, *Rapport du Chevalier C. Baillairgé, Ingénieur de la Cité de Québec sur l'Amélioration de son Aqueduc* (Quebec: Elzéar Vincent 1881), 1–82; AVQ, conseil et comités, aqueduc (1884–6), letters from Charles Baillairgé to mayor of Quebec, Quebec, 2 June, 7 July 1883.

75 ANQ, gr. Adolphe Guillet dit Tourangeau, no. 2654, contract, City of Quebec–Horace Janson Beemer, Quebec, 10 July 1883.

76 Charles Baillairgé, *Lettre au maire de Québec* (Quebec: n.p. 1884), 2; AVQ, conseil et comités, employés (2), claim for extra payment for aqueduct work from Charles Baillairgé to mayor of Quebec, Quebec, 19 Nov. 1886; Baillairgé, *The Aqueduct*, 4; *Rapport de l'Ex-Ingénieur 1866 à 1899*, 78.

77 F[rançois] Langelier, *Lettres sur les affaires municipales de la Cité de Québec* (Quebec: Imprimerie de l'Événement 1868), 15.

78 AVQ, conseil et comités, employés (2), letter from Mayor François Langelier to Charles Baillairgé, Quebec, 8 June 1883:

Vous n'êtes pas assez poli pour les conseillers et pour le public. La politesse chez un officier public est une qualité qui fait passer d'immenses défauts, et que les plus solides qualités peuvent difficilement remplacer. Vous n'avez pas d'idée de l'impopularité que vous jetez sur la corporation par des brusqueries et des mauvais procédés qui, je le sais, ne viennent pas d'un mauvais coeur.

Un autre reproche que je vous ai souvent fait aussi, c'est que vous ne tenez pas assez de compte du conseil, qui est votre maître après tout. À plusieurs reprises vous avez suscité contre nous des mécontentements que j'ai eu toutes les peines du monde à calmer, parce que vous faisiez le contraire de ce qu'avait décidé le conseil ou quelques comités.

Voilà le mal que j'ai dit de vous, et que je vous répète franchement pour que vous en fassiez votre profit. Mais j'ai toujours rendu justice à vos grandes connaissances et à vos rares habitudes de travail.

79 AVQ, conseil et comités, aqueduc (1884–6), letters from Baillairgé to mayor, Quebec, 2 June, 7 July 1883.

80 Baillairgé, *The Aqueduct*, 2; Baillairgé, *Report on completion of Beemer Contract*, 16.

81 Lemoine, *Historical and Sporting Notes*, 71.

82 Baillairgé, *Rapport de l'Ex-Ingénieur 1866 à 1899*, 84.

83 "L'Exposition," *L'Opinion du Peuple*, 15 Sept. 1871, n.p.; *Canadian Patent Office Record* 17 (1889): 146, 170.

84 Baillairgé, *A Summary of Papers*, 33.

85 "Electro-Chromatic Revolving Foun-

tain," *CAB* 10 (1897): 72.

86 Baillairgé, *A Summary of Papers*, 33.

87 J.M. Richards, "A Tower for London," *Architectural Review* 88 (1940): 141–2.

88 Frank I. Jenkins, "Harbingers of Eiffel's Tower," *JSAH* 16, no. 4 (1957): 22.

89 Baillairgé, *A Summary of Papers*, 52. Baillairgé mentions his visit to Sydenham, the place where promoters reconstructed the dismantled Crystal Palace following the Great Exhibition of 1851. He had several volumes on the Great Exhibition in his personal library.

90 Charles Baillairgé, *Baillairgé's London Eiffel Tower* ([Quebec]: n.p. [1890]), 1–4. Estimated cost was $925,516 and weight 14,303 tons.

91 Jenkins, "Harbingers," 25.

92 Frederick Charles Lynde, ed., *Descriptive Illustrated Catalogue of the Sixty-eight Designs for the Great Tower for London*, compiled and edited by Fred. C. Lynde for the Tower Company, Limited (London: Industries 1890), 1–150.

93 Baillairgé, *A Summary of Papers*, 33–4.

94 "Proposed Victoria Jubilee Tower for Quebec," *CE* 5 (May 1897): 11.

95 ANQ, P 0210/1, minute books and miscellaneous clippings for Quebec winter carnival, Quebec, beginning Nov. 1893.

96 ASQ, Séminaire 38, no. 95, letter from Charles Baillairgé to Université Laval sending sketches for proposed snow sculptures, Quebec, 30 Nov. 1895.

97 ASQ, Séminaire 38, no. 95, letter from Baillairgé to Laval, Quebec, 30 Nov. 1895; "The Spiral Slide," *CE* 4 (May 1896): 15.

98 Baillairgé, *Rapport de l'Ex-Ingénieur 1866 à 1899*, 20; Baillairgé, *A Summary of Papers*, 67–8.

99 Baillairgé, *A Summary of Papers*, 53.

100 ASQ, Séminaire 9, no. 3ᵉ, letter from priest at French Seminary in Rome to Très Rev'd M.I.G. Légaré, Quebec, 21 Feb. 1887; Lafontaine collection, correspondence from Charles Baillairgé to Cardinal Taschereau, Quebec, 1886–7. The house was purchased in 1867. Lafontaine collection, copy of sale before notary B. Pouliot, Dominique Lemieux to Charles Baillairgé, Saint-Michel de Bellechasse, 23 March 1867.

101 ANQ, Louis-Philippe Sirois, no. 75940,

donation from Louis-de-Gonzague Baillairgé to Charles Baillairgé, Quebec, 10 May 1887.

102 Charlotte (Mrs Daniel) Macpherson, *Old Memories: Amusing and Historical* (Montreal: the author [1890]), 85. Charles Baillairgé formalized the demolition by printing up signed certificates of authenticity dated 24 June 1891: "I hereby certify that each of the pieces of wood bearing the following inscription, 'portion of roof timber of house built some 233 years ago (demolished and rebuilt in 1890) in which the body of Gen. Montgomery of the U.S. Army was laid out 31st Dec., 1775,' is a portion of the original roof timbers, of the house alluded to (Lafontaine collection)."

103 Baillairgé et al., "Canadian Building Stones," *CAB* 3 (1890): 138.

104 Baillairgé, "Some Novel Architectural Features," *CAB* 13 (1900): 40.

105 Charles Baillairgé, *Radeau de sauvetage Baillairgé-Hurly* ([Quebec: n.p. 1901]), 1–5; Charles Baillairgé, *The Baillairgé, Hurly Safety Raft* ([Quebec: n.p. 1901]), 1–5.

106 Charles Baillairgé, *A Paper read before the Royal Society of Canada and before the Can. Soc. of Civil Engineers on the Construction of an Indestructible Vessel for a Voyage to the North Pole and how to reach it* (Quebec: Imprimerie Darveau [1903]), 1–17; Charles Baillairgé, "A Vessel for North Polar Navigation and Discovery," *CE* 10 (1903): 40–1.

CHAPTER 11

1 "Bibliography of C. Baillairgé," *Proceedings and Transactions of the Royal Society of Canada for the year 1894*, 12 (1895): 6.

2 "Baillargé [sic], Chevalier Chas. P.F.," *A Cyclopaedia of Canadian Biography being Chiefly Men of the Time*, ed. Geo. Maclean Rose (Toronto: Rose Publishing Company 1888), 168.

3 NA, MG 24, B 2 (Papineau papers), vol. 4. 5881–2, printed letter from Charles Baillairgé to Louis-Joseph Papineau seeking subscription to new treatise on geometry and including an announcement from *Le Canadien*, 5 Dec. 1859, Quebec, 30 Jan. 1860.

4 Charles Baillairgé, *Nouveau traité de géométrie et de trigonométrie rectiligne et sphérique, suivi du toisé des surfaces et des volumes* (Quebec: C. Darveau 1866), title page and p. III.

5 Charles Baillairgé, *Papers Read Before the*

Royal Society of Canada, 1882 & 1883 (Quebec: C. Darveau 1884), 17, 20.

6 "Literature," *Quebec Mercury*, 7 Jan. 1867, 2; "Book Notice," *Ottawa Times*, 18 Jan. 1867, 2; "Traité de géométrie," *L'Echo du peuple*, 7 March 1868, 2; NA, RG 11, vol. 372, no. 84,234, letter from George-Frédéric Baillairgé to Frederick Braun, secretary of public works, recommending his brother's book on geometry and enclosing copies of favourable reviews, Ottawa, 31 Jan. 1867. This last appeal was successful, for the department purchased twenty copies of the treatise. NA, RG 11, vol. 720, no. 84,714, receipt, Quebec, 4 March 1867.

7 "Literature," *Quebec Mercury*, 7 Jan. 1867, 2. One hundred years later, scholars re-evaluated the utility of Baillairgé's geometry textbook. Without citing any proof, in an article in the *Bulletin des recherches historiques*, an unidentified author recognized that the book was the first of its kind produced in Canada but hypothesized that it was never used in the schools. "Le premier manuel de géométrie," *BHR*, 68 [1966]: 144.

8 "Mr. Baillairgé's Lecture," *Quebec Gazette*, 22 March 1872, 2.

9 [Charles Baillairgé], *Prospectus of the Baillairgé Stereometrical Tableau* ([Quebec: n.p. 1872]), 1.

10 Charles Baillairgé, "Geometry, Mensuration and the Steretometrical Tableau," *Transactions of the Literary and Historical Society of Quebec*, new series, no. 9 (1871–2): 73.

11 Ibid., 100.

12 Ibid., 100–1.

13 "À l'exposition," *L'Événement*, 14 Sept. 1871, 1. Baillairgé's invention was also noted in "Ouverture de l'exposition," *Le Canadien*, 13 Sept. 1871, 2.

14 NA, RG 11, vol. 373, no. 20,441, letter from Charles Baillairgé to Hector-L. Langevin, Quebec, 4 Dec. 1871.

15 ASQ, Université 27, no. 69a, letter from Mgr Jean Langevin to Mgr Thomas-Étienne Hamel, Rimouski, 15 Nov. 1871.

16 ASQ, Journal SEM, vol. 2, 466, visit to Stereometrical Tableau of Mr Baillairgé, Quebec, 27 Nov. 1871.

17 NA, RG 11, vol. 373, no, 20,441, letter from L.F. Napoléon Mainguy to Charles Baillairgé, Quebec, 25 Nov. 1871.

18 AAR, registres, no. 187, copy of letter from Mgr Jean Langevin to Charles Baillairgé, Rimouski, 3 Oct. 1872.

19 Charles Baillairgé, *Geometry, Mensuration and the Stereometrical Tableau, Lecture read before the Quebec Literary and Historical Society 20th March 1872* (Quebec: C. Darveau 1873), 29–44.

20 "Mr. Baillairgé's Lecture," *Quebec Gazette*, 22 March 1872, 2.

21 "Literary and Historical Society," *Quebec Daily Mercury*, 21 March 1872, 2.

22 "Mr. Baillairgé's Lecture, *Quebec Gazette*, 22 March 1872, 2.

23 "Baillairgé's Stereometrical Tableau," *Scientific American*, 1 June 1872, 359.

24 MQ, cahier Charles Baillairgé, brevet d'invention de Paris no. 94081 from Department of Agriculture and Commerce, Paris, 19 April 1872.

25 Letter from Auguste Humbert to Charles Baillairgé, Paris, 1 Aug. 1872, reprinted in Baillairgé, *Geometry, Mensuration and the Stereometrical Tableau*, 40; MQ, cahier Charles Baillairgé, letter from H. Arnoux to Charles Baillairgé naming him corresponding member of the *Société libre d'instruction et d'éducation populaire*, Paris, 3 Oct. 1873.

26 ASQ, Manuscrit 759, 46, letter from Charles Baillairgé to Nazaire Levasseur, Quebec, 4 Sept. 1872.

27 MQ, cahier Charles Baillairgé, diploma from *exposition universelle et internationale du Pavillon de l'Enfance*, Paris, 4 Jan. 1874; letter from Auguste Humbert to Charles Baillairgé, Paris, 6 Jan. 1874, reprinted in *L'Événement*, 24 Jan. 1874, 2.

28 Letters from Auguste Humbert to Charles Baillairgé, Paris, 6 Jan. 1874, reprinted in *L'Événement*, 24 Jan. 1874, 2.

29 AVQ, conseil et comités, employés (2), report of finance committee, Quebec, 12 Feb. 1874; "Honneur à qui de droit," *L'Événement*, 24 Jan. 1874, 2; "Faits divers; personnel," *L'Événement*, 21 Feb. 1874, 2.

30 Charles Baillairgé, "Un projet inoui," *Le Soleil*, 26 April 1900, 5; Charles Baillairgé, *To the Jurors of the Educational Department of the Colonial Exhibition of London* (Quebec: n.p. 1886), 1; Charles Baillairgé, *A Summary of Papers read at different times before the Royal Society of Canada, the Canadian Association of Civil Engineers and Architects, and Literary and Scientific Societies or which have appeared occasionally in scientific or other publications* (Quebec: H. Chassé Printing [1903]), 52.

31 "Nouveau dictionnaire français de rimes et homonymes de M. Baillargé [sic]," *Le Quotidien*, 3 Nov. 1888, n.p.

32 "M. Chs. Baillairgé à Paris," *L'Événement*, 10 April 1874, 2.

33 "Extract from a Paris Letter," *Quebec Daily Mercury*, 5 May 1874, 2.

34 Charles Baillairgé, *Divers, ou les enseignements de la vie* (Quebec: C. Darveau 1898), 536–7; Baillairgé, *A Summary of Papers*, 44; Charles Baillairgé, *M. Le Rédacteur du Journal "Paris Canada"* (Quebec: n.p. 1887), 1; David H. Pinkney, *Napoleon III and the Rebuilding of Paris* (Princeton, NJ: Princeton University Press 1958), 25–104.

35 Baillairgé, *A Summary of Papers*, 20; Charles Baillairgé, *The Free and Liberal Ventilation of Sewers in its Relation to the Sanitation of our Dwellings* (Quebec: C. Darveau 1892), 3.

36 Baillairgé, *Divers*, 63.

37 Alphonse Jules Baillairgé, *Album du château de Blois restauré et des châteaux de Chambord, Chenonceaux, Chaumont et Amboise* (Blois: A. Prévost 1851), 1–107.

38 The three engravings that Charles received from Alphonse Baillairgé, two being views of Tours, one being a plate of technical drawings by Alphonse of the funeral monument from the church of l'abbaye de Solesmes, have survived in his scrapbook. MQ, cahier Charles Baillairgé, n.d. Each has been inscribed by the executor of Alphonse Baillairgé's estate: "A monsieur Baillairgé architecte à Québec, Souvenir de son parent. A.J. Baillairgé décédé à Tours le 26 février 1882. G. Marquelez."

39 ASQ, Manuscrit 759, 86, letter from Charles Baillairgé to Nazaire Levasseur, Quebec, 8 Aug. 1874.

40 Charles Baillairgé, *20 ans après: Le Club des 21 en 1879* ([Quebec]: n.p. [1899]), 1–12.

41 [Charles Baillairgé], *London Colonial Exhibition 1886: Canadian Educational Exhibit. Solid Geometry Made Easy: The Baillairgé Stereometricon* ([Québec]: n.p. 1886), 1.

42 MQ, cahier Charles Baillairgé, letter from George D. Fuchs to Charles Baillairgé, Quebec, 13 May 1874.

43 Ibid., "Monsieur le Comte," n.p., n.d.

44 ANQ, P 1000/131, AP-P 81, diplomas of Charles Baillairgé, Bordeaux, Paris, Quebec, Marseille, 1872–7.

45 Ibid.; ASQ, Manuscrit 759, 127, letter from Charles Baillairgé to Nazaire Levasseur, Quebec, 1 May 1876.

46 MQ, cahier Charles Baillairgé, n.p., letter from J. Perrault to Charles Baillairgé, Philadelphia, 2 Aug. 1876.

47 ANQ, P, 1000/131, AP-P 81, diplomas of Charles Baillairgé, Bordeaux, Paris, Quebec, Marseille, 1872–7.

48 Ibid.; MQ, cahier Charles Baillairgé, "Monsieur le Comte," n.p., n.d.

49 ANQ, P 1000/131, AP-P 81, diplomas of Charles Baillairgé, Bordeaux, Paris, Quebec, Marseille, 1872–7.

50 MQ, cahier Charles Baillairgé, "Monsieur le Comte," n.p., n.d.

51 Thomas C. Keefer, *Paris Universal Exhibition, 1878*: Report for the Canadian Commission (Ottawa: Maclean, Roger & Co. 1881), 36.

52 MQ, cahier Charles Baillairgé, n.p.

53 Charles Baillairgé, *[Suggestion aux géomètres à propos d'une nouvelle édition d'Euclide], Mémoire lu par l'auteur, C. Baillairgé, devant la Société Royale du Canada, durant sa séance de mai 1888* ([Quebec]: n.p. [1888]), 7.

54 Charles Baillairgé, *Clef du tableau stéréométrique Baillairgé* (Quebec: C. Darveau 1874), IV, XXIII, XXVII; "Baillargé [sic], Chevalier Chas. P.F.," *A Cyclopaedia of Canadian Biography*, 168.

55 ASQ, Manuscrit 759, 151, letter from Charles Baillairgé to Nazaire Levasseur concerning lecture on geometry, Quebec, 28 Feb. 1877; Université 48, no. 61, letter from Charles Baillairgé to Louis Turcotte concerning lecture on geometry, Quebec, 2 Jan. 1878; Charles Baillairgé, *The Stereometricon-Originator: C. Baillairgé, [sic] M.S. ... Promoter: Thomas Whitty* (Montreal: John Lovell & Son 1880), 1–38; [Baillairgé], *London Colonial Exhibition 1886*, 1–12.

56 Charles Baillairgé, *To the Jurors of the Educational Department of the Colonial Exhibition of London* (Quebec: n.p. 1886), 1.

57 "Charles Baillairgé," *Rivista Universale*, 10 (Feb. 1878): n.p.; MQ, cahier Charles Baillairgé, "Monsieur le Comte," n.d., n.p.

58 "Charles Baillairgé," *L'Opinion publique*, 25 April 1878, 194:

Il a fait une découverte dans une science où il semble que le génie de l'homme ne pouvait pas aller plus loin: il a trouvé le secret de mesurer tous les corps par une seule et même formule.

Son tableau stéréométrique est un chef-d'oeuvre qui le place au premier rang parmi les savants du monde entier ... Il est assez curieux que les savants d'Europe soient devancés par un Canadien-français dans une science si peu cultivée parmi nous. C'est un honneur pour lui et pour son pays.

59 MQ, cahier Charles Baillairgé, diploma of Charles Baillairgé for the Canadian Academy of Arts, Toronto [1880]; NA, MG 28, I 126, vol. 12, catalogue of 1880 exhibition of Canadian Academy of Arts, n.p. 1880, no. 380.

60 NA, MG 28, I 126, vol. 1, minutes of the Canadian Academy of Arts, 1880–95, 118, meeting of council, Toronto, 15 May 1885. I am grateful to Evelyn McMann of Vancouver for information about the early years of the Royal Canadian Academy.

61 Baillairgé, *Papers Read Before the Royal Society*, 3–5; *Proceedings and Transactions of the Royal Society of Canada for the Year 1882*, vol. I (Montreal: Dawson Brothers 1883), XVIII–XIX

62 *Proceedings and Transactions of the Royal Society of Canada*, 1st ser., vols. 1–12 (Montreal: Dawson Brothers 1883–94); 2nd ser., vols. 1–12 (Ottawa: James Hope & Company 1895–1906). Baillairgé gave the following papers:

1882 meeting
"Utility of Geometry as applied to the Arts and Sciences"
1883 meeting
"Hints to Geometers for a New Edition of Euclid"
"Simplified Solutions of Two of the More Difficult Cases in the Parting-off or Dividing of Land; also a Case in Hydrographical Surveying"
"Le toisé des surfaces des triangles et polygones sphériques sous un rayon ou diamètre quelconque"
1884 meeting
"A Particular Case of Hydraulic-Ram or Water-Hammer"
"On the Form of the Contracted Liquid Vein affecting the Present Theory of the Science of Hydraulics" [by René Steckel, read by Baillairgé]

1885 meeting
"Concernant la théorie de M. Steckel sur la veine liquide contractée" [read in absentia]
1887 meeting
"A Practical Solution of the Great Social and Humanitarian Problem, Escape from Buildings in Case of Fire"
1888 meeting
"Éléments de géométrie"
1891 meeting
"An Attempt at Deducing the Pressure under which a Steam Boiler Explodes from the Dynamic Effects Produced by the Explosion"
"A Paper Relating to the Steam Boiler Explosion at Sillery, near Quebec"
1892 meeting
"The Free and Liberal Ventilation of Sewers in its Relation to the Sanitation of our Dwellings"
1894 meeting
"Technical Education of the People in Untechnical Language"
1897 meeting
'How Best to Learn to Speak or Teach a Language: Better because Easier – Easier for Being Quicker"
"The Abstract and Concrete in Education: The Word, the Image, the Reality"
1899 meeting
"La Société de Géographie de Québec"
"Le grec – le latin: Leur utilité pour apprécier la signification des mots actuels de la langue, et dans la composition de nouveaux mots"
"La vie, l'évolution, le matérialisme"
"L'antiquité de la terre et de l'homme"
1902 meeting
"An Introduction to the Author's Forthcoming Volume on the Origin, Signification, Translation, Classification and Etymology of Proper Names"
1903 meeting
"The North Pole of the Earth"

63 Charles Baillairgé, *Educational: Word Lessons* (Quebec: C. Darveau [1899]), 3, 4, 12, 15.

64 Charles Baillairgé, *Nouveau dictionnaire français: système "éducationnel", rimes, consonnances, homonymes, décomposition des mots, combinaisons variées de leurs éléments et équivalents, jeux de mots* (Quebec: C. Darveau 1888), XXX.

65 [Charles Baillairgé, ed.], *Dictionnaire des homonymes par Charles Baillairgé: appréciations* (Joliette: Imprimerie de l'étudiant et du

couvent 1889), 1–4.

CHAPTER 12

1 ANQ, P 1000/131, address of students from Quebec School of Arts and Trade to Charles Baillairgé, Quebec, 18 April 1872.

2 "Générosité," *Le Journal de Québec*, 17 Feb. 1880, 2: "Initié de bonne heure à l'étude des styles divers qui se partagent le domaine de l'ornementation, à la majestueuse simplicité de l'antique, aux légères et délicates arabesques du moyen-âge aux riches et élégantes décorations de la renaissance, il [the artisan] sait en faire de nombreuses applications ou en faire naître des combinaisons multiples, qui s'appuient constamment sur les principes reconnus par l'homme de l'art."

3 Charles Baillairgé, "Rapport sur l'état actuel de l'art de bâtir dans la Province de Québec et des moyens à prendre pour y remédier," in H.-J.-J.-B. Chouinard, *Fête nationale des canadiens-français célébrée à Québec en 1880* (Quebec: A. Côté et Cie 1881), 413, 429–36.

4 Charles Baillairgé, "On the Necessity of a School of Arts for the Dominion," *Transactions of the Canadian Society of Civil Engineers* 1, no. 2 (1887): 68–76.

5 Ibid., 69, 73.

6 NA, RG 4, B 28, vol. 134, no. 1216, bond of Charles Baillairgé to Her Majesty, Quebec, 14 July 1848. Although surveyors had worked in Quebec since the seventeenth century, known under a variety of titles including arpenteur, arpenteur-royal, arpenteur-juré, and arpenteur-provincial, the profession was reorganized under the Act of Union in 1841, at which time the title provincial land survey or PLS was created. AVQ, dossier exposition Charles Baillairgé, text entitled "au fils des ans" appended to a letter from J. Roland Pelletier, a.g., to Ginette Noël, Sainte-Foy, 14 Nov. 1979.

7 Charles Baillairgé, *Bilan de M. Baillairgé, comme Architecte, Ingénieur, Arpenteur – Géomètre, durant les 21 ans, avant d'entrer au service de la Cité – ès-qualité d'Ingénieur des Ponts et Chaussées, ou de 1845 à 1866. Puis – entre heures – de 1866 à 1899, mais non compris les Travaux Civiques relatés dans un rapport supplémentaire* ([Quebec]: n.p. [1899]), iii; "Ages and other Data Respecting Living Canadian Public Men," *The Dominion Annual Register and Review for the Eighteenth Year of the Canadian*

Union, 1884, ed. Henry J. Morgan (Toronto: Hunter, Rose and Company 1885), 382.

8 "Association of Architects, Civil Engineers and P.L. Surveyors of the Province of Canada," *Journal of the Board of Arts and Manufactures for Upper Canada* 1 (1861): 14.

9 Quebec (Province), Statuts, 45 Vic., ch. 16, Acte concernant les arpenteurs de la province de Québec et les arpentages, 27 May 1882; AVQ, dossier exposition Charles Baillairgé, "au fil des ans," Sainte-Foy, 14 Nov. 1979.

10 *Transactions of the Canadian Society of Civil Engineers*, 2 (1888): 14; 5 (1891): 27.

11 Charles Baillairgé, "The Boston Gas Works," *CE* 7 (April 1900): 313–14, 324; *Transactions of the Canadian Society of Civil Engineers* 15 (1901): n.p.; 21 (1907): 13. On his return to Quebec, Baillairgé collected five photographs of his architectural works, including the Quebec Music Hall, proposed Parliament Buildings, a kiosk and bandshell on Dufferin Terrace, and 3, ruelle des Ursulines, and sent them with his compliments and a few descriptive notes to the Boston Public Library. They are still in the library.

12 "Charles Baillairgé, C.P.E., M.A., F.R.S.C. etc.," *CE* 2 (May 1894): 16–17; *CE* 3 (May 1895): 11; "The Ball-Nozzle Fire Jet," *CE* 3 (Aug. 1895): 96–7; "The Ball Nozzle," *CE* 4 (May 1896): 20; "The Spiral Slide," *CE* 4 (May 1896): 15–16; "Proposed Victoria Jubilee Tower for Quebec," *CE* 5 (May 1897): 11–12.

13 *CAB* 2 (1889): 19–20; *CAB* 3 (1890): 112. The Ontario Association of Architects grew out of the Architectural Guild of Toronto. 1889.

14 "Organization of the Province of Quebec Association of Architects," *CAB* 3 (1890): 112.

15 "Province of Quebec Association of Architects," *CAB* 4 (1891): 24; "An Act to Incorporate the Province of Quebec Association of Architects," *CAB* 4 (1891): 35.

16 "Organizations of the Province of Quebec Association of Architects," *CAB* 3 (1890): 115–16.

17 Ibid., 114; *CAB* 6 (1893): 99; *CAB* 7 (1894): 121; *CAB* 8 (1895): 118–19; *CAB* 9 (1896): 1; *CAB* 10 (1897): 105; *CAB* 11 (1898): 1. There is a file of letters from the secretary of the Province of Quebec Association of Architects to Charles Baillairgé in the municipal archives. AVQ, conseil et comités, architectes [association des], Montreal, 1897.

18 *CAB* 4 (1891): 89; "Province of Quebec Association of Architects," *CAB* 5 (1892): 96; *CAB* 6 (1893): 104; *CAB* 8 (1895): 13, 145; *CAB* 9 (1896): 56, 196; *CAB* 10 (1897): 210; "Examination Papers, Ontario and Quebec Associations of Architects," *CAB* 4 (1891): 92.

19 "Province of Quebec Association of Architects," *CAB* 5 (1892): 97; Charles Baillairgé, "A Plea for a Canadian School of Architecture," *CAB* 6 (1893): 105–8; Charles Baillairgé, "Foundations in Deep and Unreliable Soils," *CAB* 7 (1894): 128–30; Charles Baillairgé, "A Quick and Easy Way of Getting at the Weight of Iron Scantlings, Girders, Columns, etc.," *CAB* 7 (1894): 154–5; Charles Baillairgé, "On the Bearing and Resisting Strength of Structures and that of their Component Parts and Materials," *CAB* 8 (1895): 122–4; *CAB* 8 (1895): 119.

20 "Province of Quebec Association of Architects," *CAB* 5 (1892): 96; *CAB* 17 (1904): 44.

21 "Province of Quebec Association of Architects," *CAB* 4 (1891): 91.

22 "Funérailles de M. Chs. Baillargé [sic]," *Le Soleil*, 12 May 1906, 16.

23 Outlooker, "Canadian Architects," *CAB* 1 (1888): 3.

24 *CAB* 3 (1890): opp. 78; "Canadian City Engineers: 11: Mr. Charles Baillairgé," *CAB* 4 (1891): 107; *CAB* 7 (1894): 123.

25 *CAB* 5 (1892): 56; 8 (1895): 43, 115; 10 (1897): 156; 12 (1899): 115; 16 (1903): 107.

26 "Personal," *CAB* 8 (1895): 81.

27 "The Necessity for Proper Fire Escapes for Public Buildings," *CAB* 14 (1901): 3–4; NA, MG 26 G, vol. 184, 52345–53, letter from Charles Baillairgé to Hon. Sir Wilfrid Laurier concerning legislation for fire safety and enclosing Baillairgé's printed pamphlet, Quebec, 10 Jan. 1901; "Electro-Chromatic Revolving Fountain," *CAB* 10 (1897): 72; "Exhibits for the Paris Exposition," *CAB* 12 (1899): 128. Baillairgé exhibited plans, models, and descriptions of some of his inventions in the Paris Exhibition of 1900, including his fire escape system, his Quebec bridge proposal, and diverse towers, fountains, slides, and monuments. The three posters or exhibits have survived in the municipal archives in Quebec.

29 The complete guest list was published in two local papers: "Architects at Dinner," *Chronicle*, 1 Jan. 1901, 5; "Dîner fin-de-siècle," *L'Événement*, 2 Jan. 1901, 2. It comprised Sir Wilfrid Laurier (prime minister of Canada), Sir Alphonse Pelletier, Sir Sandford Fleming (Ottawa engineer for CPR), T.C. Keefer (Ottawa engineer), Mgr J.C.K. Laflamme (Laval University mathematician), Hon. C. Fitzpatrick, Hon. Mr. Duffy, Hon. Mr. Turgeon, Hon. Israel Tarte (federal minister of public works responsible for exposing the Langevin–McGreevy scandal), Hon. Mr. Dechêne, Hon. Jules Tessier, T.C. Casgrain, Lt-Col. Oscar Pelletier, Lt-Col. E.F. Pinault, Lt-Col. Thos Roy, Lt-Col. Forrest, L.J. Cannon (assistant attorney general and relative), Capt. F. Pennée, Capt. Léonce Stein (relative), Georges Tanguay (Quebec member of parliament), Onéziphore Talbot (Quebec member of parliament), Albert Malouin (Quebec member of parliament), Amédée Robitaille (Quebec member of parliament), Rodolphe Roy (Quebec member of parliament), Joseph Archer (builder), Sir J.G. Bourinot (senator), C.E. Roy (alderman), Mr Evans (electrical engineer), E.A. Hoare (engineer of Quebec City bridge), Georges-Emile Tanguay (president of the Province of Quebec Association of Architects), Joseph-Ferdinand Peachy (architect and former partner), René-P. Lemay (architect), Dussault (architect), François-Xavier Berlinguet (architect), Eugène Talbot (architect), Raymond (architect), Buissière (architect), David Ouellette (architect), Eugène-Etienne Taché (architect), Joseph Ouellette (architect), Pageau (architect), Harry Staveley (architect), Resther (architect), Major Nazaire Levasseur (consul of Brazil, editor of *L'Événement*, and personal friend), Ovide Fréchette (consul of Spain), Mr. Hoecher (consul of Germany), J.A. Charlebois (contractor), M.P. Davis (contractor), H.J. Beemer (contractor who did Quebec aqueduct and Lake Saint John Railway), François Parent (contractor), J.U. Gregory (agent of marine and fisheries), Dr Edwin Turcot, Dr Ahern, Dr Marois, Dr Brousseau, Dr Hamel, Dr Grondin, Dr Beaupré, Dr Simard, Dr Dionne, Louis Fréchette (writer), Mr Préfontaine (mayor of Montreal), Dr Roy (MRSC), Ludovic Brunet, Hon. E.J. Flynn, Mr DeCazes, F. Legendre (MRSC), L.Z. Joncas, P.B. Dumoulin, Judge

Routhier, Judge Langelier, Judge Lemieux, Judge Chauveau, Hon. Chs. Langelier, and Judge C. Pelletier; the following were engineers, Cooper, Clea Walbank, Hobson (Victoria bridge), Félix Turcotte, Col. Anderson (Ottawa), Robert Surtees (Ottawa city engineer), Mountain (Ottawa), Steckel (Ottawa engineer and partner with Baillairgé in bid for heating contract for Ottawa buildings), Kennedy, Bovey, McLeod, Jennings, Keating, Henning, T. Berlinguet, Bignell, Boswell, Gauvin, Stein, Gallagher, Roy, Brown, Girard, Russell, Pigot, Gosselin, Oliver, L.A. Vallée, H. O'Sullivan, de Puyjalous; Senator P.B. Casgrain, Hon. M. Ouimet (former minister of public instruction who promoted the Stereometrical Tableau), Dr Arthur Simard, Rev. Abbé Mathieu, Filion, Dr Catellier, Dr Stewart, Hon. T. Chapais, J.C.L. Lafrance (city treasurer), Frank Carrel (publisher), L.-J. Demers (publisher), Chs. DeGuise, Ernest Pacaud, Cinq-Mars, E. Chouinard, T.W.S. Dunn, T. Levasseur, H. Chassé, Fergus Murphy (lawyer), J.I. Lavery (lawyer), Joseph Lemieux, Edward Archer (builder), Adolphe Stein (relative), S.H. Townsend (relative), G. DeLery, Joncas, Adolphe Tourangeau (notary), Dr L. Bacon, and Wilson Baillairgé (son).

30 "Dîner fin-de-siècle," *L'Événement*, 2 Jan. 1901, 2; "Welcoming the New Century," *CAB* 14 (1901): 5.

31 "Architects at Dinner," *Chronicle*, 1 Jan. 1901, 5.

32 "Dîner fin-de-siècle," *L'Événement*, 2 Jan. 1901, 2.

CONCLUSION

1 Charles Baillairgé, *Rapport de l'Ex-Ingénieur de la Cité des travaux faits sous le Maire, Hon. S.N. Parent et le Conseil-de-Ville actuels et sous leurs prédécesseurs durant le dernier tiers de Siècle: 1866 à 1899* (Quebec: C. Darveau [1899]), 50. "Votre ex-ingénieur croit ... qu'il a l'intuition de bonnes et belles choses; mais peut-être moins de talent de les concevoir lui-même que d'en juger lorsqu'elles sont projetées par d'autres."

2 "Mr. Charles P. Baillairgé," *CAB* 19 (1906): 66.

3 A.J.H. Richardson, Geneviève Bastien, Doris Dubé, and Marthe Lacombe, *Quebec City: Architects, Artisans and Builders* (Ottawa: National Museum of Man 1984), 517.

4 Ibid., 450–4.

5 Ibid., 525–6.

6 "Mort de M. Charles Baillargé [sic]," *L'Événement*, 11 May 1906, 5.

7 "Aged Citizen Dead: Mr. Charles Baillairgé, F.R.S.C., late City Engineer, Passes Away," *Quebec Chronicle*, 11 May 1906, 5; "Death of Chevalier Baillairgé," *Quebec Telegraph*, 11 May 1906; n.p.; "Deceased Members," *Proceedings and Transactions of the Royal Society of Canada* 12, 2nd ser. (1906): viii–ix; "Feu M.C. Baillairgé: l'ancien ingénieur de la cité meurt à l'âge avancé de quatre-vingts ans," *Le Soleil*, 11 May 1906, 1; "Funérailles de M. Chs. Baillargé [sic]," *Le Soleil*, 12 May 1906, 16; "Obituary of Charles P. Baillairgé," *Transactions of the Canadian Society of Civil Engineers* 21 (1907): 13; "Regret Expressed by Association of Architects at Death of Chevalier Baillairgé," *Quebec Chronicle*, 12 May 1906, 6; "The Late Chevalier," *Quebec Chronicle*, 14 May 1906, 6.

8 "Funérailles de M. Chs. Baillargé [sic]," *Le Soleil*, 12 May 1906, 16.

Index